THE ARCHAEOLOGY OF LAKE SETTLEMENT IN IRELAND

The Archaeology of Lake Settlement in Ireland

Aidan O'Sullivan

Discovery Programme Monograph No. 4

First published in 1998
by the Royal Irish Academy
19 Dawson St, Dublin 2.

ISBN 1-874045-62-3

British Library Cataloguing-in-Publication Data.
A catalogue record for this book is available from the British Library.

Editor: Emer Condit
Cover design: Geraldine Garland

Typeset in Ireland by Wordwell Ltd.
Origination by Wordwell Ltd, The Type Bureau and Lithographic Plate Plan.
Printed by Brookfield Printing Co. Ltd.

Cover image—Detail from Richard Bartlett's seventeenth-century depiction of an attack on a Gaelic Irish crannog (see Pl. 56).

An Chomhairle Oidhreachta
The Heritage Council

The Discovery Programme gratefully acknowledges the financial contribution of the Heritage Council towards the cost of publishing this book.

Discovery Programme/Royal Irish Academy, Dublin 1998

Contents

Acknowledgements

Many people, past and present, have contributed to the study of lake settlement in Ireland. In writing this book, I have been lucky to have been helped by many individuals who have given generously of their time and knowledge. I am very grateful to Amanda Kelly for her patient work in obtaining the photographic illustrations, for drawing the regional and site maps, for endless proof-reading and cleaning up of the text and references, and for her good sense of humour. I also thank Barry Masterson and Paul Synnott for their help with production of the maps and GIS images. I am also grateful to Nick Maxwell, Emer Condit and Ger Garland for their work on the production of this book. Mary Deevy also helped me greatly during the research, in particular conducting many of the journal searches. I am grateful to the (then) programme manager, Ronan O'Flaherty, who was always positive, supportive and encouraging through all stages of this work. The Discovery Programme subcommittee on the feasibility studies—Ronan O'Flaherty, Claire Foley, Terry Barry and John Bradley—were also very supportive throughout, providing both practical and academic advice at crucial stages. I would like to thank the directorate and council of the Discovery Programme for their support and comments. Kieran O'Conor provided much-needed discussion and advice through the six-month research period and in the later write-up stages.

I am particularly grateful to Professor Barry Raftery, who generously provided me with his father's illustrations and text of the Lough Gara excavations in advance of their forthcoming publication. We also spent an interesting and dusty morning looking at the Lough Gara finds. Victor Buckley allowed me to read some of the texts from the crannog conference proceedings in advance of his edited volume and offered many comments from his own experience in lake settlement archaeology. Victor also supplied many photographs from his own collection. I would also like to thank John Bradley for providing me with photographs and information from his excavations at Moynagh Lough crannog. Claire Foley provided me with much information on the Fermanagh crannog surveys and lent me photographs from her own collection. Eamonn P. Kelly also gave generously of his time and knowledge of Irish crannogs. Kevin Barton and Colin Brown kindly read my text on remote sensing and offered information that has greatly improved this section. I am also very grateful to Donal Boland and Colin Breen for our many conversations on underwater archaeology. John Coles offered much encouragement and advice from his wealth of experience in wetland archaeological projects, and I am very grateful to him for his comments.

Conor Newman, John Waddell and Etienne Rynne helped to obtain copies of Lough Gara photographs from the UCG Department of Archaeology's photographic collection, in particular those taken by Michael V. Duignan in the 1950s. I am grateful to Terence Reeves-Smyth, Claire Foley and Tony McNamara for their assistance in obtaining photographs from the Environment and Heritage Service, DOE(NI), Belfast. John Scarry, Tony Roche and Con Brogan helped in the provision of photographs from *Dúchas*—The Heritage Service, Department of Arts, Culture and the Gaeltacht, Dublin. Conor MacDermott, Jane Whittaker and Nora Bermingham provided me with photographs from the Irish Archaeological Wetland Unit's archive, and to them I offer my thanks. Michael Ryan generously provided texts and photographs of his excavations at Lough Boora, and Mary Cahill and Raghnall Ó Floinn helped with the National Museum of Ireland collection. Stefan Bergh provided me with a photograph of William Wood-Martin's portrait, and Rhoda Kavanagh gave me an illustration of William Wilde. The St Joseph photographs were generously provided by the Cambridge University Committee for Aerial Photography.

Several archaeologists and historians have read and commented upon sections of the text at various stages. Edel Bhreathnach and Raghnall Ó Floinn read an early draft of this text, offering many comments for its improvement. I am also grateful to Victor Buckley, Gabriel Cooney, Tom Condit, Eoin Grogan, Martin Doody, Eamonn P. Kelly, Colin Breen, Barry Masterson, Finola O'Carroll, Angele Smith, Niall Brady and Mary

Deevy for reading and offering critical comments on several sections of the book. I thank Eoghan Moore for his comments and advice. Many individuals have helped in obtaining articles and discussing aspects of lake settlement. I would like to thank Aoife Daly for advice and comments about palaeoenvironmental studies and the use of GIS in vegetation modelling in ancient landscapes. I also thank Richard Brunning, Bryony Coles, Claire Cotter, Sara Cross, Alan Lane, James Lyttleton, Michael Moore, Conor Newman, Richard Warner, Martin Timoney and Christina Fredengren. However, while their comments have frequently greatly improved this work, these individuals are not to be blamed for its shortcomings. I am grateful to the director and staff of the National Museum of Ireland, the Royal Society of Antiquaries of Ireland, the National Library of Ireland, the Royal Irish Academy, and the staff of *Dúchas*—The Heritage Service. I would also like to thank my colleagues and friends in the Discovery Programme for all their help.

Finally, and most of all, I thank Mary Deevy for all her support and encouragement during the writing of this book.

List of figures

List of plates

PREFACE

The nineteenth-century Irish antiquarian William G. Wood-Martin, in the preface to his book *The lake-dwellings of Ireland*, commented on the fact that during archaeological research we always have to stand on the shoulders of our predecessors. In other words, we work from a fund of knowledge built up by earlier scholars, to which we then add our own insights and discoveries. Wood-Martin pointed to the contribution to lake settlement studies made by his own contemporaries, such as William Wilde, George Kinahan, William Wakeman, Bishop Reeves and Bishop Graves. Since his words were written, there have been over a hundred years of lake settlement archaeological survey and excavation in Ireland. To the names of those nineteenth-century antiquarians should be added the names of more recent scholars, such as Hugh O'Neill Hencken, Oliver Davies, Pat Collins, Frank Mitchell and Joseph Raftery, amongst many others. The archaeology of lake settlement in Ireland is now rich, complex and intriguing, and has the potential to provide us with many insights into the development of the Irish landscape.

In 1997 the Discovery Programme decided to investigate the potential for a major programme of research on the archaeology of lake settlement in Ireland. It was agreed that a full feasibility study would first be carried out, so that decisions on such a programme could be based on a thorough understanding of the diverse and complex nature of the subject. To that end, Aidan O'Sullivan was commissioned to write this feasibility study, the most important component of which would be an authoritative and substantive review of the current state of knowledge. As Wood-Martin (1886a, vi) himself wrote, the intention was 'to collect carefully all the information hitherto furnished by the explorers of Irish lake-dwellings, and to present that information in an abridged form'. The author was also requested to present a history of lake settlement studies, to identify themes for study, to outline methodologies for future research, and to propose a series of projects operating at different scales and resources.

The chapter on the history of lake settlement studies clearly shows how the excavations carried out in the late nineteenth century and in the 1930s continue to dominate archaeological interpretations. The detailed review of the archaeology of lake settlement recovers large parts of the evidence which have been largely ignored, particularly the evidence for Mesolithic and Neolithic lakeshore occupations and the historical and archaeological evidence for medieval and post-medieval activities on crannogs. Bronze Age lake settlements and Early Historic and Viking Age crannogs can be seen to have been investigated in more detail, but much remains to be understood and investigated. Priorities for future research on the archaeology of lake settlement are outlined, focusing on the themes of settlement permanence and mobility, the role of lake settlements in the wider landscape, and the relationships between settlement and environmental change. It is argued that the archaeology of lake settlement now needs to be investigated by means of multiperiod, regional landscape studies integrating a wide range of archaeological, historical and palaeoenvironmental evidence.

This is neither the first nor the last word on the archaeology of lake settlement in Ireland. Its aim is to prepare a background for the next phase of research by the Discovery Programme, during which it is hoped that the archaeology of lake settlement in Ireland will be explored in a fruitful and exciting way. Indeed, this new phase of research can be seen to have already started with this publication.

George Eogan

Chairman
Discovery Programme

1. Introduction

Introduction

People have lived by lakes in Ireland since earliest times. Mesolithic hunter-gatherers exploited their rich wetland resources of fish and fowl from camps on the lakeshore, leaving behind them spreads of flint and chert blades and stone axes. Neolithic farmers and foragers are also known to have occupied lakeshores and islands, the archaeological evidence ranging from lakeside villages to small wooden structures and spreads of pottery and stone tools. Bronze Age farmers and metalworkers occasionally lived in enclosed lakeshore settlements, and their working areas, cooking sites, boats, tools, ornaments and weaponry have all been found around Ireland's lakes. While there is little archaeological evidence for Iron Age lake settlement in Ireland, the discovery of artefacts and metalwork hoards in lakes and ponds certainly hints at it. In the Early Historic period and the Viking Age there is abundant archaeological and historical evidence for entire settlement systems on lakes, with contemporary crannogs, island ringforts and cashels, promontory forts and monastic islands implying widespread lakeland activity. In the medieval period there is also good evidence for the occupation of crannogs, natural islands, castles and monastic settlements by both the Gaelic Irish and the Anglo-Normans. Historical, archaeological and cartographic evidence attests to post-medieval occupation and military activities on lake islands, crannogs and castles. The archaeology of lake settlement in Ireland is rich and complex. It can be defined as the study of the character and dispersal of past human settlement activities on lake islands, lakeshores and in lakeland landscapes.

Ireland is a damp country. Its temperate climate, high effective precipitation, topography, and extensive low-lying, waterlogged soils mean that its landscape abounds with wetlands, whether coastal (estuarine, lagoonal), freshwater aquatic (rivers, lakes, turloughs) or mires (fens, raised bogs and blanket bogs). Ireland's lakes, turloughs and ponds offer complex and varied aquatic habitats, ranging from static water in small lakes and ponds to constantly flowing water at river mouths. Many Irish lakes undergo significant seasonal changes in water-levels and vegetation, and they typically have extensive fringing reed beds, fens, marshes and carr woodlands. Lakes are most common in Ireland in the midlands, west and north-west, although smaller lakes are found throughout most of the country (Fig. 1). In some parts of the country, lakes are the dominant topographical feature of the physical landscape and there can be almost as much water as land. Hence there are some parts of the country where living by a lake was almost inevitable. But it is also true that people often deliberately chose to live by the lakeshore.

There are various reasons for living on a lakeshore. The abundant wetland resources of food, water and raw materials were probably often the main attraction for settlement. Duck, geese, fish, sedges, reeds and carr woodlands are all commonly found along lakeshores and would have been an important source of food and raw materials. Fuelwood, clay, water and ores were needed for various industrial activities. Cattle and other livestock could be grazed on the rich grasslands found on the slopes and marshes that surround lakes. However, politics, warfare and religion were as important to early societies as subsistence and industry. Not all lake settlements were constructed and occupied to enable their inhabitants to reap the rich wetland harvests. Isolation and safety must occasionally have been useful in troubled times, and lake islands could have been a useful neutral location between territories for gatherings or other social

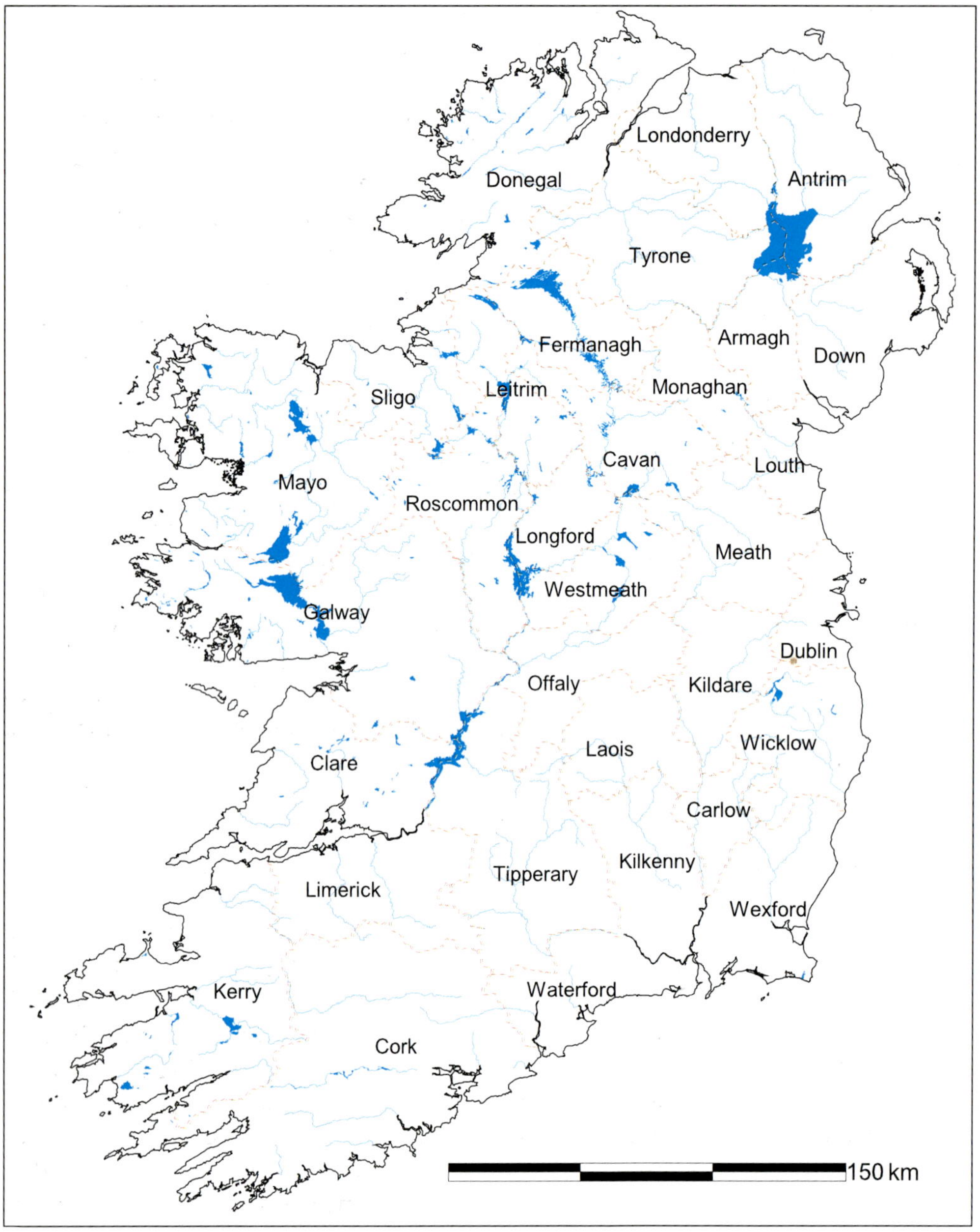

Fig. 1—*Map of Ireland, showing lakes and counties.*

occasions. On the other hand, living on an island or lakeshore would have been important for the powerful in society, who by living in highly visible crannogs or castles signalled to others their status and prestige. The impact of tradition and history can also be seen in the long-term continuities evident in some lake settlement archaeology. Lake settlements could have been important in terms of their siting on routeways. People do not live only in one place; they move continuously through the world around them—to work their farms, to meet with their neighbours, to fight battles with rivals, or to exchange goods and information. Lakes and rivers provided the fastest means of travel and communication in the early Irish landscape, and settlement may have been influenced by the speed and ease of boat travel. The sacred landscape or the ritual importance of lakes and ponds needs to be considered when we explore the reasons for a lakeside existence. Before the arrival of Christianity, these dark, deep waters may have been seen as places between worlds, where the spirits and gods could more easily be contacted. Even afterwards, monsters and fantastic creatures were probably still believed to exist below the water. Ordinary, everyday life is continuously informed by religious beliefs, so we should expect to find aspects of ritual beliefs in the settlement archaeological record too.

Historically, lake settlement is a subject at the heart of Irish archaeology, and can be linked with most of the important developments therein. The antiquarian origins of the discipline spring from the early discovery and description of numerous lake settlements. Irish archaeology witnessed the introduction of scientific excavation techniques during the Harvard expedition's campaigns of excavation on Bronze Age lake settlements and Early Historic and Viking Age crannogs. The cultural-historical study of artefact typologies has often depended on the range of finds from excavated lake settlements. Recently, there has been an explosion of interest in wetland and underwater archaeology, leading to multidisciplinary archaeological surveys and excavations, although lake settlements have still to be tackled. The fact that lake settlements typically have waterlogged, archaeologically rich deposits containing well-preserved structures, artefacts and palaeobotanical evidence has meant that they have often become important sources of information for Irish archaeology. Even a quick reading of the various Irish syntheses of prehistoric and historic archaeology reveals how much interpretation depends on the results of a few lake settlement excavations. Mesolithic occupation sites, Bronze Age lakeshore settlements, wooden platforms, post alignments, Iron Age finds and Early Historic crannogs in lakes have provided much of the material on which our knowledge of early settlement organisation, agriculture, industry, economy and crafts is based. The study of this archaeology is important because the material is interesting in itself. However, it is also useful, because its richness provides us with a means of looking at Irish landscape, settlement and environment since earliest times.

Aims and objectives

This study will outline the potential and priorities for archaeological research on lake settlement in Ireland. It will be shown that there is already a large database available in published surveys and excavations, artefactual and palaeoenvironmental studies, and the archives and collections held in museums. However, it will also be seen that there is great potential for asking new questions of this archaeology, making use of such innovative techniques as landscape archaeology, underwater geophysics, underwater survey and excavation, and the range of multidisciplinary investigations that are part of modern archaeological excavations. Lake settlement archaeology offers great potential for collaboration with early Irish and medieval historians, placename studies, historical geographers and other archaeological institutions and researchers. Furthermore, the landscape archaeological approach allows the study of lake settlements in their wider social, economic and ideological contexts.

This study aims to provide a detailed review of the known archaeological evidence for lake settlement in Ireland. This is an ambitious aim, as the subject is broad and has been studied for well over 100 years. It is therefore mostly based only on the published literature (books, articles, finds catalogues), as it would have been impossible to carry out original research or fieldwork in the time available. A large number of journals were consulted, including the *Proceedings of the Royal Irish Academy*, the *Journal of the Royal Society of Antiquaries of Ireland* and the *Ulster Journal of Archaeology,* as well as a number of international, regional and local journals. A brief period of research was spent on the published Sites and Monuments Record maps and files held in the National Monuments Service, *Dúchas*—The Heritage Service, and the files of the Environment and Heritage Service, Northern Ireland. A rapid review of some of the registers and archives of the National Museum of Ireland was carried out, and a number of archaeologists active in lake settlement research, survey and excavation were interviewed and consulted. However, this study cannot hope to reflect the experience and knowledge of the many Irish archaeologists who have worked in the field. It is only the work of one person. It should be emphasised that this work is a precursor to research, not an outcome of it. Without a doubt (in fact hopefully), much will need to be rewritten after more extensive archaeological research.

A historiographical and bibliographical review of Irish lake settlement studies is presented first, examining their history from the earliest antiquarian excavations to more recent developments in archaeological survey, excavation and underwater archaeology. The following chapter provides a detailed review of the current state of knowledge of lake settlement in Ireland, describing the results of site excavations, regional surveys and discoveries from Irish lakelands and how they have been interpreted by archaeologists. This is presented in chronological terms. Too little has been done or understood as yet to warrant the equally valid approaches of regional and thematic studies. The potential and priorities for future archaeological research on lake settlement are then outlined, leading to the presentation of a number of key questions. The methodological approaches that should be used in projects (e.g. theoretical approaches, geophysics, archaeological research, underwater survey and excavation, dendrochronological and radiocarbon dating, and palaeoenvironmental studies) are discussed. A number of research projects, at various scales of analysis, duration and funding, are proposed in an appendix. A comprehensive bibliography is also included.

Chronological periods

This study is organised according to traditional chronological periods, not because these are perfect or even appropriate but just because they are convenient. People living by lakeshores had little sense of living in the 'Neolithic' or the 'medieval' period, and probably carried on with their lives as they had done for generations, in tune with the rhythms of the seasons and the longer-term changes in landscape and environment. Hopefully, the results of future archaeological research will bear this out. But for the moment the chronological periods used in this study are defined as follows: Mesolithic (7000–4000 BC), Neolithic (4000–2500 BC), Bronze Age (2500–600 BC), Iron Age (600 BC–AD 400), Early Historic (AD 400–800), Viking Age (AD 800–1100), medieval (AD 1100–1350), late medieval (AD 1350–1534) and post-medieval (AD 1534–1700). There has been much debate in Irish archaeology about the use of these terms, and there is particular disagreement on the terminology relating to the earlier part of the historic period. Ironically, a study runs into most problems in terms of its terminology when it attempts to cross boundaries, from prehistory into history or from early history to the Middle Ages. Archaeologists concentrating solely on the historic period (whether Late Iron Age, Early Christian, Early Historic, Viking Age, early medieval or late medieval) tend to use their own preferred terms. The term 'Early Christian', with its outmoded implied emphasis on high crosses, manuscripts and clerics, is no longer widely used in settlement studies. The author proposes to use the terms Early Historic and Viking Age instead. The term 'early medieval' is admittedly useful, given that it allows for discussion across the period between AD 400 and AD 1150, where it can be difficult to distinguish between 'Early Historic' and 'Viking Age' settlements. However, there are some problems in the use of the term. It is obviously a problem when it is used in the same book as the term 'medieval'. So why not abandon the latter term? Unfortunately, the historical geographers' term, 'late medieval', has still not found favour amongst Irish archaeologists, and this is an archaeological work. It is also considered important not to conflict with the partner volume in this monograph series, Kieran O'Conor's (1998) monograph on medieval rural settlement. In conclusion, when the chronological terms listed above are used in this study, the author is thinking in terms of the time-spans as defined.

Terminology

There are also ongoing problems of terminology in Irish lake settlement studies. In particular, there has been some debate over the use of the term 'crannog'. Some archaeologists (e.g. Lynn 1983) have suggested that the term 'crannog' be reserved only for a certain type of Early Historic or Viking Age artificially constructed islet, surrounded by a wooden palisade. However, many Bronze Age lake settlement sites would fit these criteria, while ironically some Early Historic examples do not (e.g. Keane 1995). Some archaeologists have suggested that 'crannog' should be a neutral term, used in the interim for all lake settlement sites irrespective of form or date (Morrison 1985; Keane 1995). The term 'lake settlement' could be used to describe small stone platforms, wooden enclosures, the classic crannog (with its mound, palisade and structures), stone-built islets, and stone cashels and duns on natural islands. However, this classification does not even begin to deal with other lake settlements, such as castles and tower-houses and monastic sites in lakelands. Even the term 'settlement site' is open to criticism, as it necessarily precludes discussion of those off-site lake settlement activities that do not leave large, formal structures (e.g. cattle-grazing on meadows, hunting in woodlands, fishing from boats). In this study, the term 'crannog' is generally reserved for the classic type of Early Historic artificially constructed islet with defensive palisade, but its use is not intended to separate these sites from other lake settlement forms. The author proposes to spell it as the English word 'crannog' (plural crannogs), rather than the Gaelic word *crannóg*, which would require the use of the uncommonly used plural *crannóga*.

2. The history of lake settlement studies

Introduction

The subject of lake settlement studies is almost as old as the discipline of Irish archaeology itself, originating in the work of antiquaries of the early nineteenth century. However, although there was indeed an early phase of discoveries before 1850, the golden age of lake settlement research was undoubtedly the late nineteenth century. This was a time when Irish antiquarians, like their European colleagues, were diligently searching for stone and wooden structures and finds on drained lakebeds, and large numbers of artefacts found their way into early museum collections. Lake settlement research continued over the following decades, but in a less focused way. The third main phase occurred in the mid-twentieth century, when the American-sponsored Harvard Archaeological Expedition renewed Irish interest in Bronze Age lake settlements and Early Historic and Viking Age crannogs. In particular, there were two fascinating decades of work in the 1950s and 1960s, when astonishing discoveries were made on Lough Gara, Co. Sligo, and when several Bronze Age and Early Historic lake settlements were excavated in Northern Ireland. Since about 1980 the subject has been boosted again through the emerging results of archaeological surveys in the Republic and in Northern Ireland and through the discoveries of treasure-hunters in the midland lakes. Most recently, an explosion of interest in wetland archaeology worldwide has caused lake settlement to become a subject of renewed interest for Irish archaeologists.

Some recurrent patterns and themes are clearly evident in the history of lake settlement archaeology. Lake settlement studies in Ireland, like much of the rest of Irish archaeology, have tended to concentrate on site-specific approaches (i.e. individual site descriptions or excavations). While there are some exceptions, there have been very few regional studies or attempts to understand the role of lake settlements in their wider social, economic and ritual landscapes. There has been little attempt at the long-term, diachronic approach to a settlement record that effectively spans the period from the Mesolithic to the post-medieval. Indeed, lake settlement in Ireland has typically been identified in terms of the distribution and form of the classic Early Historic crannog. Ironically, the very richness of Early Historic crannog excavations, with their waterlogged deposits of metal, bone, wood, leather and plant remains, has tended, firstly, to suffocate the more synthetic study and, secondly, has caused archaeologists to be wary of large-scale lake settlement investigations. Indeed, in many ways, the archaeology of crannogs dominates this study too, although an attempt has been made to tease out the medieval and post-medieval use of these sites. However, it will be shown in this review that hidden in amongst the archaeology of Early Historic crannogs there is much of wider chronological and thematic interest. The impression remains of a dearth of inquiries amidst a wealth of archaeological riches.

The earliest discoveries, 1810–60

The first hints, 1810–37

It is generally believed that antiquarian interest in Irish lake settlements was first inspired by the lowering of lake levels in 1853–4 in Switzerland which revealed large Neolithic and Bronze Age lake villages, leading scholars around Europe to search for similar structures (Keller 1866; 1878; Harding 1980; B.J. Coles and Coles 1989; J.M. Coles and Coles 1996). In fact, Irish antiquarians were part of the earliest wave of lake settlement studies in Europe, a fact recognised by the Scottish antiquary Robert Munro in his *Ancient Scottish lake-dwellings or crannogs* (1882). The earliest known discovery of a lake settlement site in Ireland came about after lake drainage in 1810 at Lough Nahinch, near Roscrea, Co. Tipperary. The site was described by a Mr Trench, who stated that there was a large, circular, plank-built structure which resembled 'the top of an immense tub, about sixty feet in diameter'. This was almost certainly the wooden palisade of a prehistoric or historic crannog. Little more antiquarian investigation was done on the site (Wood-Martin 1886a, 213). Another possible crannog discovery was made in 1809, when a log-boat was found with four paddles on a 'stratum of burnt oak' at Ardbrin, Co. Down. This lake also produced an Iron Age bronze horn (B.J. Coles and Coles 1989, 13).

A peculiar wooden 'house', a rectangular box-like structure with two 'floors', was discovered in a bog at Drumkelin, Inver, Co. Donegal, in 1833 (Wood-Martin 1886a, 39, 140). The 'house' lay on a substructure of hazel branches and sand, and was surrounded by a staked enclosure with gates. There was a pathway leading to a 'hearth, with charcoal, ashes and turf'. A stone with a hollow was found in association with broken hazelnuts. A stone axe, a piece of a 'leather sandal', a flint arrowhead and a 'wooden sword' were found, and the investigators noted that the structural wood had been cut with stone tools, given the characteristic abraded and rough appearance of the toolmarks (Wood-Martin 1886a, 40; O'Sullivan 1996c). It has recently been suggested that the structure was a Neolithic mortuary house rather than a wetland settlement site (B.J. Coles and Coles 1989, 16–17).

Lewis's *Topographical dictionary* (1837) refers to a lake settlement in Lough Annagh, Co. Offaly, stating that 'in the middle of this lake, where it is most shallow, certain oak framing is yet visible and there is a traditional report that in the war of 1641 a party of insurgents had a wooden house erected on this platform, whence they went out at night in a boat and plundered the surrounding country' (Lewis 1837, 175). This interesting piece of local folklore was to be confirmed in 1868, when seventeenth-century armour, an iron halberd, iron swords, a matchlock and a gun-barrel of small calibre were some of the finds made on 'an island-like patch rising a little above the water level, of piles', with broken querns, burnt brick and stone in the vicinity (Dunne 1868–9; Stanley 1868–9; Wood-Martin 1886a, 209–11). The site appears to have been a post-medieval crannog.

Early discoveries at Lagore, Co. Meath, 1839–48

However, these discoveries were only the first hints of the coming wave of antiquarian work. Irish lake settlement studies really begin in 1839, when local labourers cutting drains through the peats of a dry lakebed uncovered huge amounts of bone in a large artificial mound at Lagore, near Dunshaughlin, Co. Meath. The site is now known to have been the seventh- to tenth-century 'royal' crannog of the Southern Uí Néill, and for many reasons is one of the most important archaeological sites in Ireland (Wilde 1840; Wood-Martin 1886a, 23–5; Macalister 1928, 301; Hencken 1950, 36; B.J. Coles and Coles 1989, 15). About 150 cartloads of bones had been removed and exported to Scotland for fertiliser by the time it came to the notice of antiquarians. A dealer, Mr Underwood, began bringing antiquities, said to be found near Dunshaughlin, for sale to the staff of the Topographical Department of the Ordnance Survey of Ireland (Wood-Martin 1886a, 24). George Petrie and William Wilde were intrigued and decid-

Pl. 1—*Lagore crannog, Co. Meath. This immensely rich Early Historic 'royal' crannog was first discovered in 1839 and excavated by the Harvard Archaeological Expedition in 1950 (from Hencken 1950).*

ed to visit the location; they found, thrown on the floor of a barn at Lagore House, a large collection of antiquities, including iron swords, daggers, spears, axes, saws, chains, shears, pins and brooches of bronze, and bone and wooden objects. In the absence of his master, Mr Barnewall, the local steward was unwilling to part with any of the items, and by the time Petrie returned the collection had been widely scattered, although a few objects made their way into the collection of the Royal Irish Academy (Wood-Martin 1886a, 23–5; Petrie 1850–3).

Petrie and Wilde apparently intended to publish an account of the bone and artefactual finds, but this came to nothing because of some now-forgotten quarrel (Macalister 1928, 301). Indeed, William Wakeman stated that the account would have been written but for 'the mutual jealousies of Petrie and Wilde' (de hÓir 1990, 112). Nevertheless, Wilde (1840) published the notes of his visit (in the first volume of the *Proceedings of the Royal Irish Academy*), describing the site, its environs and some of the exposed structures. He described the crannog as a circular mound 520 feet in diameter, slightly raised above the surrounding bog or marsh, with upright posts defining the circumference. James Talbot (1849) also published a brief account of some of the Lagore finds. The second main phase of activity at Lagore came several years later. Between 1846 and 1849, cleaning of the small river beside the site and turf-cutting on it led to the discovery of more quantities of bone, wooden palisades and wooden hut structures. The latter were described in 1882 by Wakeman, who visited the site almost daily over a month in the summer of 1848. He saw an apparent rectangular wooden substructure or house built of sill-beams, grooved uprights and plank cladding caulked with moss, and gathered a range of finds from the site himself (Wakeman 1879–82b, 325; Wood-Martin 1886a, 24; de hÓir 1990, 112–16). The crannog site at Lagore was excavated in the 1930s by the Harvard Expedition (Pl. 1), and the site director, Hugh O'Neill Hencken, reckoned that Wakeman's account of the rectangular structures was a mistaken description of part of the palisade (Hencken 1950, 46).

Other crannogs were noted around the same time. In about 1839 the artificial lowering of the water-levels at Roughan Lake, near Dungannon, Co. Tyrone, meant that 'an island artificially formed was exposed to view'. The island produced large amounts of pottery, bones, a bronze pin, a few bronze spearheads and a decorated upper stone of a rotary quern (Wood-Martin 1886a, 88). Interestingly, it is known historically that a Gaelic Irish crannog on Lough Roughan, near Dungannon, Co. Tyrone, was captured by the English general, Lord Mountjoy, on 1 July 1602. The English cartographer Richard Bartlett's well-known depiction of an attack on a Ulster crannog may actually be a representation of this incident (Hayes-McCoy 1964). Intriguingly, there are also historical references to one *Raghan Isle* being the last retreat of Sir Phelim O'Neill in 1641, the island holding out against English forces until boats were brought to the lake in 1653 by Lord Charlemont to aid in the attack (Wood-Martin 1886a, 88, 148). Obviously more historical and archaeological research is needed here, but it may be that a crannog at Roughan Lough, Co. Tyrone, was occupied in the later prehistoric period (as suggested by the presence of bronze spearheads) and the Early Historic period (represented by the decorated rotary quern), and was used as a fortified settlement by the O'Neills during the wars of the seventeenth century.

At about the same time (1839), a stone-built lake settlement was discovered at Lough Gur, Co. Limerick. The site was known to locals and antiquities were gathered from the site, with large amounts of bone being seen, but no palisade was recognised. This crannog had been attacked by English forces in 1599 (Wood-Martin 1886a, 25, 27). Lough Gur is also known to have been the findspot for several discoveries of Bronze Age metalwork, and the Knockadoon peninsula in the lake was extensively settled in the Neolithic and the Middle Bronze Age (Cooney and Grogan 1994).

The draining of Ballinderry Lough, near Moate, Co. Westmeath, in 1844 revealed the heavy oak posts of an Early Historic crannog (Ballinderry crannog no. 2). The site was dug over by locals, producing vast quantities of bones and a range of antiquities, including two dugout boats (Wilde 1857, 223; Graves 1883–4; Wood-Martin 1886a, 205; Ffrench 1902; Newman 1986; forthcoming). The site was initially recorded by a Mr Hayes, who sent William Wilde a description of the site along with a plan and a map of its location (Wilde 1857, 223; Wood-Martin 1886a, 205). A range of these finds ultimately made their way to the National Museum of Ireland, where they were later examined by Hugh O'Neill Hencken (Hencken 1942). Some antiquities from the environs of the site may have been erroneously assigned to the crannogs, but there was certainly much activity in this landscape in the Late Bronze Age, the Early Historic period and the Viking Age. Ballinderry crannog no. 1, Co. Westmeath, and Ballinderry crannog no. 2, Co. Offaly, were excavated in the 1930s by the Harvard expedition (Hencken 1936; 1942).

The Commission for Arterial Drainage and Inland Navigation, 1843–52

About 1843 the Board of Works, through the Commission for the Arterial Drainage and Inland Navigation of Ireland, began a programme of extensive drainage works in the Irish landscape. The Board's officers had rightly anticipated that 'the arterial drainage works would afford opportunities rarely possessed for obtaining antique remains from places under water, which remains, if faithfully described, would be useful adjuncts to our local history'. In 1852, after nine years of these works, these antiquities were gathered together and presented to the museum of the Royal Irish Academy, along with a detailed report prepared by W.T. Mulvany (Mulvany 1850–3). The Board of Works was determined to fully record antiquarian discoveries. Mulvany sent a circular letter to the local engineers, encouraging the close recording of the find contexts of the objects from lakes and rivers:

> 'An object of great importance is to have the antiquities identified with the locality where they were found, and we therefore wish to have

> attached to each thing found, a card, with a description on one side of the place where found, name of townland, parish, barony, and county . . . and on the other side of the card a description of the precise locality, the material in which imbedded, its depth, allusion to other antiquities found with it, and such other matters of interest as occur to you to record' (Mulvany 1850–3, xxxiii; J. Raftery 1966).

For its time, this was an extraordinarily sophisticated approach to recording antiquities, essentially adopting the stratigraphical and contextual recording system that was not to be paralleled until the development of modern excavation techniques. Between 1843 and 1852, 25 crannogs and 377 objects were discovered by the drainage schemes, mostly in Roscommon and Leitrim, with smaller numbers in Cavan, Monaghan, Limerick, Meath, Westmeath, Down, Offaly and Tyrone. These were also recorded in some detail, as Mulvany had also recommended that 'In cases where islands of artificial construction, raths, or other works, have been discovered or cut into, descriptive drawings and sections will be of the greatest importance and you are requested to forward them'. Interestingly, the phrase 'islands of artificial construction' was being used three years before the Swiss lake-dwellings came to public notice (Mulvany 1850–3; J. Raftery 1966).

The crannogs of Drumaleague, Co. Leitrim, and Cloonfree, Cloonfinlough and Ardakillen, near Strokestown, Co. Roscommon, were amongst those recorded by the Board of Works engineers in some detail; plans and cross-sections were prepared, indicating stone, clay and peat stratigraphy and vertical walls and timbers (Fig. 2). Large numbers of finds from the crannogs were presented to the museum of the Royal Irish Academy. At Cloonfinlough two crannogs were exposed; one was found to have palisades, a radial arrangement of timbers in the foundations, a wooden jetty or a pier, and layers of stone, black earth and animal bone. A human skull and two dugout boats were recovered from the periphery of the site, along with Early Historic and Viking Age bronze, iron and stone artefacts, and medieval and post-medieval coins (D.H. Kelly 1850; Wood-Martin 1886a, 233–9). One of the four crannogs at Ardakillen was also trenched by the engineers, revealing that it was constructed of lower layers of peat, clay and stones, intermingled with ash and bone. The islet was defined by a wooden palisade and an enclosing stone wall was constructed on the upper levels of the site.

The largest crannog at Ardakillen produced up to 50 tons of animal bone, much of which was removed for manure. Near this crannog was a large dugout canoe with a

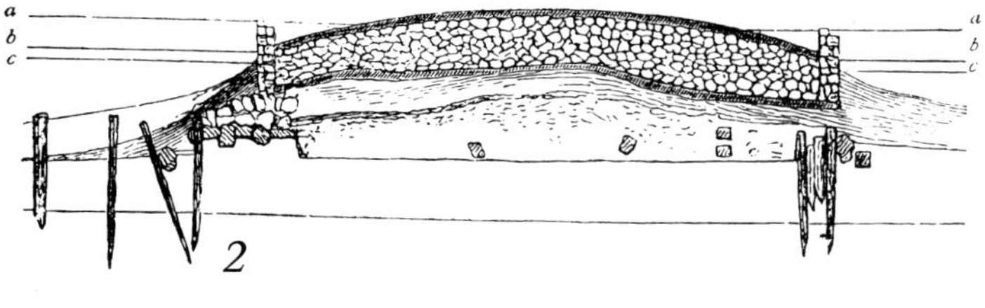

Fig. 2—*(1) Plan of Drumaleague crannog, Co. Leitrim, and (2) cross-section of Ardakillen, Co. Roscommon, illustrating the high quality of the records made by the Commission for Arterial Drainage in the 1840s (from Wood-Martin 1886a).*

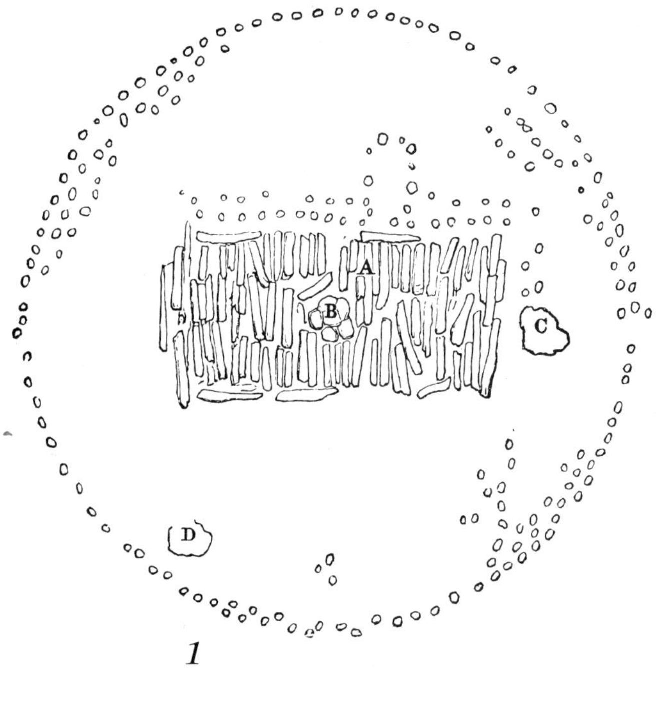

human skull, a bronze spearhead and a bronze pin; near this was a twenty-foot-long iron chain and collar (Wood-Martin 1886a, 236). These crannogs had added antiquarian interest because they were in the landscape of the 'royal residences of Connaught, and in the vicinity of Carn Free, the crowning places of its kings, and of Rathcroghan, the Tara of the west' (Wilde 1857, 26).

The impact of the Swiss lake village discoveries, 1853–7

In the winter of 1853–4, exceptionally low water-levels resulted in the exposure of piles and stone axes, bone points, pottery and wooden artefacts in the lake muds at Obermeilen, Lake Zürich. These discoveries were communicated by a local teacher to the Swiss antiquary Ferdinand Keller, president of the Antiquarian Society of Zürich, who proceeded to publish accounts of the site (B.J. Coles and Coles 1989; J.M. Coles and Coles 1996; Harding 1980; Keller 1866; 1878). These 'wonderful pfahlbauten' discoveries inspired several other Swiss antiquaries to collect antiquities in the pile dwellings, often from a boat using pincers and draw-shovel. One intrepid underwater explorer, Adolphe von Morlot, even donned lead boots, put a bucket on his head to which air was pumped, and walked 'amidst those ancient posts in the bluish twilight', gathering finds with a pick and butterfly net (Blot 1996; J.M. Coles and Coles 1996, 4). One particular site, Robenhausen, was more accessible as it was submerged in peat. It was excavated by Jacob Messikomer, who, uniquely for the time, realised and argued for the importance of 'stratigraphy, context, economy and environment' (B.J. Coles and Coles 1989, 26–31). A range of other discoveries were subsequently made around the Swiss lakes, and some sites—such as Cortaillod, Auvernier and Neuchatel—have become key sites in Swiss archaeological research (B.J. Coles and Coles 1989).

Inspired by these discoveries, antiquaries in Germany, France, Italy and Austria also began searching the Alpine lakeshores, dredging with steam-driven mud-engines, rakes and other tools, and recovering huge numbers of Neolithic and Bronze Age objects from amongst the piles (although the wooden structures were rarely recorded). Ferdinand Keller's publications were made available to English readers in 1866 through translations by John Edward Lee (Keller 1866). The preferred location for Swiss lake villages was a sunny, sheltered bay with a soft and gently-shelving bottom. Three types of lake-dwelling were proposed: pile dwellings, frame pile dwellings and fascine dwellings. The latter were 'formed by layers of fagots, alternating with brushwood, clay, gravel and stones, one over the other, till the top reached the required level above the surface of the water; piles were driven in around to bind the heap together, and the whole overlaid by a wooden floor, upon which the dwellings were erected' (Wood-Martin 1886a, 12).

Scottish lake settlement discoveries, 1857–70

Scottish lake settlement studies also have a long history, but work did not begin in earnest until after the Swiss discoveries. In 1857 Joseph Robertson presented a paper to the Society of Antiquaries of Scotland on the subject of Scottish crannogs. The first crannog excavation was carried out by John Grigor, who investigated two sites in the Loch of the Clans, Nairnshire, discovering oak timbers projecting from a cairn (Grigor 1863). In 1863, Lord Lovaine surveyed crannog sites on the Loch of Dowalton, Wigtownshire, and reported them to his colleague, John Stuart. In 1866 Stuart published articles on these crannogs and listed the other examples known from elsewhere in Scotland in the *Proceedings of the Society of Antiquaries of Scotland* (Stuart 1864–6). This can be considered the beginning of serious crannog studies in Scotland (Dixon 1991). Stuart also contributed a notice on Scottish crannogs to Keller's *Lake-dwellings* (Keller 1866, 389–92).

Robert Munro, a retired doctor from Ayrshire, was active in Scottish crannog studies from about 1879. His involvement began with the publication of crannog excavations at Lochlee, Buston and Lochspouts. His book *Ancient Scottish lake-dwellings or crannogs* was published in 1882, and in 1888 he gave the Rhind Lectures in Edinburgh on the subject of 'The lake-dwellings of Europe', based on the results of an extensive study trip through Europe (Dixon 1991). Munro was also to take an interest in Irish crannogs (Munro 1894; 1885–6) and was subsequently an adviser to Arthur Bulleid during his excavations of the English Iron Age lake village at Glastonbury, Somerset (J.M. Coles and Coles 1996, 5).

William Wilde's *Catalogue of antiquities* (1857)

In Ireland, in 1857, Sir William R. Wilde (Pl. 2) published the first volume of his *Descriptive catalogue of the antiquities in the museum of the Royal Irish Academy,* in which he stated that 46 crannogs were known (Wilde 1857). He noted that although they had been alluded to since the ninth century, it was remarkable that it was not until 1839 that a crannog was first examined by antiquarians. Wilde stated that the clusters of lakes in the areas of Strokestown, Co. Roscommon, Keshcarrigan, Co. Leitrim, and Castleblaney, Co. Monaghan, were districts where many crannogs were to be found. He described their typical form and made suggestions as to their defensive function:

Pl. 2—*William Wilde (by courtesy of Dr Rhoda Kavanagh, UCD).*

> 'They were not strictly speaking, artificial islands, but cluans, small islets or shallows of clay or marl, in these lakes, which were probably dry in summertime, but submerged in winter; these were enlarged and fortified by piles of oaken timber, and in some cases by stone-work. A few were approached by moles or causeways, but generally speaking they are completely insulated, and only accessible by boat; and it is notable that in almost every instance an ancient canoe was discovered in connexion with the crannoge. Being thus insulated, they afforded secure places of retreat from the attacks of enemies, or were the fastnesses of predatory chiefs or robbers, to which might be conveyed the booty of a marauding excursion, or the product of a cattle raid' (Wilde 1857, 221).

Wilde's (1857; 1857–61; 1861–4) accounts of Irish crannogs were also brought to a wider European audience through their publication as a chapter in *The lake-dwellings of Switzerland and other parts of Europe* by Ferdinand Keller (1866, 380–8). Wilde followed the *Catalogue* with a short article published in 1861, describing three 'crannoges', or stockaded islands, bringing the number of known Irish crannogs to 49 (Wilde 1857–61). The article included an account of a crannog (an islet with an artificial, built-up floor enclosed by very narrow wooden piles) at Lough Rinn, Co. Leitrim, and a crannog at Derryhollow, Co. Antrim, where there were piles, stone hearths, weapons, tools and iron implements, copper, bronze and wooden dishes and bronze pins, as well as a coin of Charles II. A crannog in the lake formed by the River Shannon at Castleforbes, Co. Longford, was also briefly mentioned. Wilde also complained of the poor preservation of dugout boat discoveries, noting that many had been broken up for firewood since their recovery. He concluded this article with an important and perhaps highly influential statement on the culture and chronology of Irish lake settlements, based on his comparisons with Scottish and Swiss lake-dwellings:

> 'I think, I am warranted in stating, that the remains of flint and stone weapons and tools, in the Swiss crannoges, show that they were constructed by a people in a less advanced state than those who made the Irish crannoges, and that they were chronologically much anterior. Certainly the evidences derived from the antiquities found in ours, and which are chiefly of iron, refer them to a much later period than the Swiss; while we do not find any flint arrows, or stone celts, and but very few bronze weapons in our crannoges. Moreover, we have positive documentary evidence of the occupation of many of these fortresses in the time of Elizabeth, and some even later' (Wilde 1857–61, 152).

Although stone tools and bronze weaponry finds *were* known from Irish lake settlements (and more would be found in the years ahead), the idea was definitely forming that Irish lake settlements were not to be dated to the Stone Age or Bronze Age. Indeed, Wood-Martin (1886a, 26) was later to claim that the Swiss lake village discoveries actually diverted Irish antiquarians from crannog research. In his opinion, William Wilde's statement that Irish crannogs never produced stone artefacts, and only occasionally bronze, promoting a date of between the ninth and the seventeenth centuries, was crucial, leading Irish antiquarians to believe that little of prehistoric interest could be found in Ireland's lake settlements.

Another antiquary active in lake settlement research at this time was Rev. Dr Reeves. In one paper he published several post-medieval historical references to crannogs (*insula fortificata*) in the Ulster Inquisitions of 1605. He stated that these sites were the 'headquarters of a little territorial chieftaincy' or 'little primitive capitals' of the neighbouring tuaths. Each placename reference was tentatively linked to known crannog sites (Reeves 1857–61a). In a second paper he provided genealogical notes on the inhabitants of a crannog at Inishrush, Co. Antrim (Reeves 1857–61b).

From the 'golden age' to a 'field untilled', 1860–1932

William Wakeman, George Kinahan and other antiquarians, 1860–86

The late nineteenth century saw the main bulk of crannog work, which was drawn together in William Wood-Martin's (1886a) synthesis *The lake-dwellings of Ireland*. It is important to remember that there were a number of scholars active in the field and articles were being published in various journals and newspapers. For example, a crannog discovered at Drumkeery Lough, Co. Cavan, was described along with its finds in a paper in the English journal *Archaeologia* (Harkness 1863). In 1867 George Morant excavated an unusual wooden floor and hearth in a bog at Cargaghoge, near Carrickmacross, Co. Monaghan. This was a platform (17ft 6in. across) of logs and planks laid closely together, with a hearth of 'blue clay' and stones at the centre. The platform was approached by a timber trackway. The only finds consisted of considerable quantities of broken hazelnut shells, 'very rude' pottery and some small worked flints (rounded at one end). There was also a stone which Morant took to be a 'small corn-crusher'. He was obviously aware of the importance of stratigraphy, as he closely examined the layers next to the floor in the hope of making finds, and also showed a modern wetlands archaeological concern for the preservation of the structure, directing it to be covered with sods during the warm summer weather. The site appears to have been a Neolithic or Bronze Age wetland occupation site (Morant 1868–9; Wood-Martin 1886a, 42).

Moving from the prehistoric to the post-medieval period, we must review the discoveries at Lough Annagh, Co. Offaly, in 1868. General Dunne and Thomas Stanley described the structures and finds from a crannog on that lake, most of which were clearly seventeenth-century in date. They also drew attention to historical references which indicated a battle between English and Irish forces on the neighbouring hill in 1691 (Dunne 1868–9). The publication in 1870 of a sixteenth-century description of an assault by English troops on a crannog near Omagh also confirmed this use of lake settlements in the post-medieval period (Caulfield 1870). An interesting debate was briefly published about this time in *The Irish Builder* concerning the etymology of the word 'crannog', with short notes on the subject by Rev. W. Kilbride (1869) and J. O'B. Crowes (1869). Crannogs had already been described in this journal in a paper by W. Hughes (1886).

After 1870, there were regular publications of notes and observations on lake settlement explorations. George Kinahan (1861–4; 1864–6; 1886a; 1886b; 1886c; 1897) of the Geological Survey of Ireland published a range of papers on crannogs and stone forts on islands in Donegal and Mayo. He also wrote an interesting review essentially

Pl. 3—*William F. Wakeman (from* JRSAI **30** *(1900), 381).*

arguing for research designs in future crannog excavations (Kinahan 1870–1). Based on his experience of excavating crannogs on Lough Rea, Ballinlough and Lough Naneevin, Co. Galway, and on Lough Nahinch, Co. Tipperary (Trench and Kinahan 1864–6), he proposed that excavators should aim to closely record a crannog's floor, its evidence for multiperiod occupation, the nature of its internal structures and the location of the hearth. He further suggested that future excavations should also aim to provide a site plan and an account of any secondary stone structures (*ibid.*). Kinahan was interested in whether houses were to be found at the centre of crannogs or around the edges. Indeed, in a reconstruction drawing (one of the first published of an Irish crannog) of Lough Naneevin, he proposed that an unusual circular structure occupied most of the island, with an open-roofed central courtyard (Kinahan 1866–9, 31).

But it is perhaps William Wakeman (Pl. 3) who emerges from these years as the most active and percipient antiquarian working on Irish lake settlements. If Wood-Martin had not published his synthesis *The lake-dwellings of Ireland* (often largely based on Wakeman's published notes), it would undoubtedly be Wakeman that we would

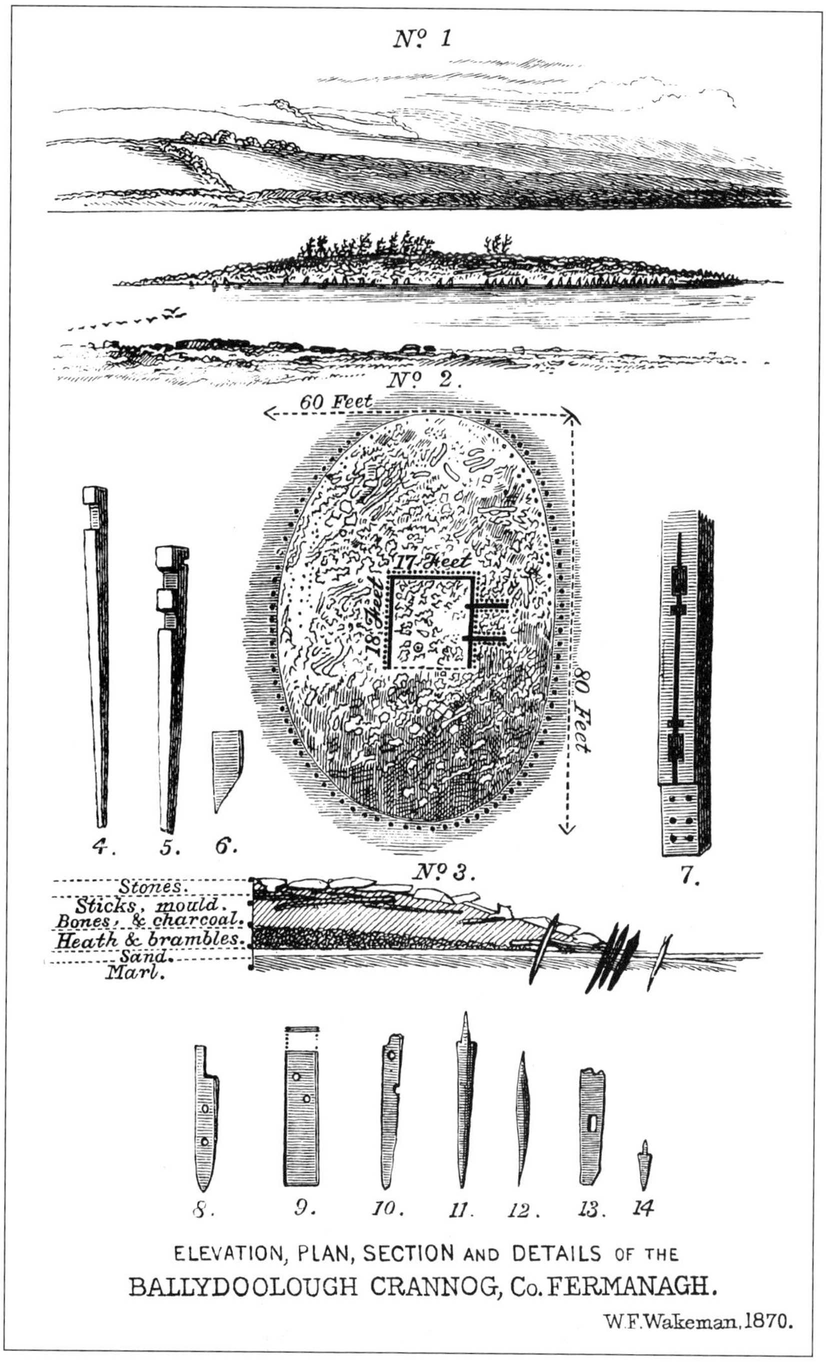

Fig. 3—*William Wakeman's landscape drawing, plan, section and details of Ballydoolough, Co. Fermanagh (from Wood-Martin 1886a).*

most associate today with Irish crannog archaeology because of his frequent notes on finds and structures (Wakeman 1861; 1879–82a; 1879–82b; 1885–6). Wakeman published accounts of crannogs at Ballydoolough, Co. Fermanagh (Wakeman 1870–1b), Drumgay Lake, near Enniskillen (Wakeman 1870–1a; 1870), Lough Eyes, Co. Fermanagh (Wakeman 1870–1d), and Cornagall, Co. Cavan (Wakeman 1870–1c). At Ballydoolough, Co. Fermanagh, either drainage or long-term drought revealed a submerged forest on the bed of a small lake, as well as a small island with medieval pottery, wooden artefacts and animal bone scattered around the surface (Fig. 3). An unusual rectangular wooden structure was also exposed at the centre of the island (Wakeman 1870–1b; Wood-Martin 1886a, 181). Several crannogs were exposed on Lough Eyes and appeared to be linked by peat and wooden causeways, leading Wakeman and Wood-Martin to conjecture that they were once the settlements of a lake village community (Wood-Martin 1902, 222–4).

In 1872 Wakeman published a major regional review of crannogs in Fermanagh, noting the existence of 29 in eighteen different places in the county. He considered them to be of great age on the basis of coarse pottery with comb and incised decoration (Wakeman 1872). Wood-Martin (1886a, 181–93), who later summarised many of these surveys and discoveries, was also aware of the importance of the lake islands in the wars of the sixteenth and seventeenth centuries and suggested medieval and post-medieval occupation phases for some of them. S.F. Milligan was also active in crannog surveys, describing the crannogs or lake-dwellings of Cavan in a paper presented to the Royal Historical and Archaeological Association of Ireland, which was also published in the *Irish Builder* (Milligan 1885; 1885–6). Another notable publication was an account of a crannog on the intertidal zone at Ardmore, Co. Waterford (Ussher and Kinahan 1879; Ussher 1903).

The Iron Age 'trouvaille' of Lisnacrogher

In 1882, workmen cutting turf on the bed of a drained lake at Lisnacrogher, Co. Antrim, uncovered a massive hoard of Iron Age artefacts. The finds, which included bronze scabbards, iron swords, bronze spearheads, spearbutts, bronze ornaments, iron tools, and a range of other high-status objects, were found somewhere in or on the border between Carcoagh and Lisnacrogher townlands, and have been the subject of several publications (e.g. B. Raftery 1983; 1984; 1994). However, one of the problems of Irish archaeology is understanding the relationship between the metalwork and a mysterious wooden structure seemingly exposed at the same time. Unfortunately, the site was mostly destroyed by the time Irish antiquarians realised its importance, and in any case it was jealously guarded by its owner. R.A.S. Macalister describes in bitter tones the destruction of the site:

> 'Every scholar must feel, when this place is mentioned, that a periodical act of humiliation should be performed in the shrine of Irish archaeology . . . Let it suffice to say that Lisnacrogher was the site of a lake-dwelling which had the misfortune to lie close at hand to the dwelling of a collector of whom it was said, among other virtues recorded in an obituary notice, that "he made it a rule never to leave his house without carrying back something to enrich his collection". The lake-dwelling of Lisnacrogher was for such a man a gold-mine, and he spent much of his spare time in looting it (to use the only adequate expression)' (Macalister 1928, 242).

William Wakeman (1883–4; 1889; 1890–1) visited the site and has provided the most complete contemporary accounts. He described it as being situated within the boundary of a formerly drained lough in the townland of Lisnacroghera. He recorded large quantities of timber, some with mortised ends, and encircling stakes, and also noted possible post-and-wattle. The Iron Age finds at Lisnacrogher may well have been associated with a wooden structure, similar to the wooden bridge or jetty at La Tène, Switzerland. However, it may only have been an Early Historic crannog coincidentally exposed at the time near the hoard site. Certainly this was the explanation proposed by the Scottish antiquary and expert in lake settlements, Robert Munro, on his visit in 1886 (B. Raftery 1994). In any case, it is highly likely that the Iron Age finds at Lisnacrogher were actually the result of a ritual wetland deposition, similar to such sites as Llyn Fawr and Llyn Cerrig Bach in Wales (R. Bradley 1990; J.M. Coles and Coles 1996, 66).

Lake settlements were being explored in these years throughout County Antrim. At Lough Ravel, Loughmagarry and Loughtarmin, crannogs had been known since earlier in the century, and numerous finds had been taken from Toome Bar on Lough Neagh (Wood-Martin 1886a, 163–5). At Lough Mourne, near Carrickfergus, temporary lowering of water-levels in 1882 in a lake near the sea exposed a group of four small stone cairns, a larger crannog and a wooden canoe. The cairns were built of mounds of stone laid over wooden foundations and piling. The larger crannog lay in deeper water and was built in a fashion reminiscent of Scottish types, with timbers radiating from the centre and mortised at their outer ends to vertical piles (Wood-Martin 1886a, 171–3; Gray 1883–4a; 1883–4b; Lockwood 1883–4; Munro 1885–6; Reilly 1902).

Pl. 4—*William G. Wood-Martin (by courtesy of Mr Richard Wood-Martin; photo: Stefan Bergh).*

Wood-Martin's *The lake-dwellings of Ireland* (1886)

By 1886 at least 220 crannogs were known in Ireland, and sufficient other evidence was available for the Sligo landlord William Gregory Wood-Martin (1886a) to write his book *The lake-dwellings of Ireland or ancient lacustrine habitations of Erin commonly called crannogs*. As has been pointed out, it 'must still be regarded as a seminal work. There has been little synthesis since' (Edwards 1990, 35). Indeed, it is difficult to assess the archaeology and history of Irish lake settlements without referring to this work, now over 100 years old. Aideen Ireland has written a brief biography of the antiquary (Ireland, forthcoming). William Wood-Martin (Pl. 4) was born in 1847 in Sligo, educated in Ireland, Switzerland and Belgium, and became an archivist in the Royal Military Academy in 1866. He was a prolific author and highly active in various Irish antiquarian associations. His other publications include *The rude stone monuments of Ireland* (1888), *History of Sligo, county and town* (1882–92), *Pagan Ireland* (1895) and *Traces of the elder faiths of Ireland* (1902). The latter included a section on lake-dwellings. However, he is best remembered for his classic work on Irish crannogs. *The lake-dwellings of Ireland* was largely based on a review of the many articles and notes by then published in Irish journals, and was clearly influenced by contemporary European work. Wood-Martin made particular use of his fellow antiquaries George Kinahan and William Wakeman. He was undoubtedly inspired, like many of his contemporaries, by Ferdinand Keller's *The lake-dwellings of Switzerland and other parts of Europe* (Keller 1866; 1878) and Robert Munro's (1882) *Ancient Scottish lake-dwellings or crannogs*.

The lake-dwellings of Ireland remains a major source of information on Irish crannogs. Indeed, it can make unnerving reading for the modern Irish archaeologist. There are questions asked in it which have never been answered, and many of the interpretations and ideas there have still to be revised. The book was divided into two parts. In Part I, Wood-Martin described thematically the many structures and finds known from Irish crannogs. In Part II, he provided a descriptive catalogue of crannogs, organised on a province and county basis. The book begins with an introductory chapter which attempts to describe the wooded and wild nature of ancient Ireland. The succeeding chapters describe the structure of wooden and stone crannogs, their siting, palisades, gangways and canoes. There are ten chapters on the finds from crannogs, including stone, bronze and iron finds, food and vegetable remains, objects of household economy, personal ornaments, musical instruments, gaming-pieces, ogham inscriptions, money, horse furniture and other miscellaneous articles. There is an extensive chapter on historical references to crannogs. The book was illustrated by William Wakeman, with 41 crannog reconstruction drawings (e.g. Fig. 4.1), site plans

IRISH LAKE DWELLING OF THE ISOLATED TYPE.
Ideally restored from inspection of numerous sites.

Fig. 4.1 —*William Wakeman's reconstruction drawing of an Irish crannog, an image which still shapes our perception of these sites (from Wood-Martin 1886a).*

Fig. 4.2 —*Wakeman's reconstruction drawing of a hypothetical lake village on Lough Eyes, Co. Fermanagh (from Wood-Martin 1902).*

Fig. 4.3 —*Wakeman's dramatic reconstruction drawing of a raid on an Irish lake-dwelling (from Wood-Martin 1902).*

and sections, and 197 drawings of artefacts. *The lake-dwellings of Ireland* became the standard reference work for all subsequent crannog research. It also directly led to the discovery of other sites. In particular, one reader, Owen Smith, contacted Wood-Martin with information about a crannog near Nobber, Co. Meath (Wood-Martin 1886b). In June 1887, Wood-Martin exhibited objects from the crannog at the museum of the Royal Society of Antiquaries; these were later sent to the Royal Irish Academy museum. Wood-Martin obtained a grant from the Royal Irish Academy to investigate the site further. He apparently completed a paper on these excavations, but inexplicably it was not to be published (John Bradley, pers. comm.).

George Buick, Rev. D'Arcy and others, 1890–1920

In 1890 W.B. Yeats published his *Lake Isle of Innisfree*, professing a romantic desire to retreat to a clay and wattle house on an isolated island home. Presumably he was romantically inspired by the continuing antiquarian interest in crannogs and other lake settlements that had continued unabated to the end of the nineteenth century. The most extensive crannog excavations in this period were those of George Buick over five summers between 1887 and 1893 on a crannog at Moylarg, near Cullybackey, Co. Antrim (Buick 1893; 1894). The excavations were exhaustive but the recording strategies employed were very poor, leaving little sense of the structure of the crannog. No site plan or sections were published. Nonetheless Buick was clearly conscientious about his work, claiming that every spadeful of material was closely examined for finds.

There certainly appears to have been a period of Late Neolithic or Early Bronze Age activity on the site. Finds from a spread of ash and bone at the centre of the site included a stone axe, pottery, flint scrapers and a hollow-based arrowhead, while a large number of flint cores, scrapers and flakes and two stone axe fragments were found elsewhere about the site (Buick 1893, 28–30). Unfortunately, the stratigraphy of this possible hearth is unclear, even contradictory. In other respects, Moylarg appears to have been a classic Early Historic crannog, even a high-status one, producing a decorated bronze ladle of eighth-century date (E.P. Kelly 1991b), a penannular brooch, a bronze ingot with its stone mould, a crucible fragment and stones for sharpening bronze pins, a barrel-padlock and spindle-whorls, glass beads and bracelets, leather objects and iron knives. The pottery appears to have been largely souterrain ware of Early Historic or Viking Age date, although some prehistoric pottery may also have been present. Interestingly, the pottery finds were illustrated by William Wakeman. It is difficult to assess the site in terms of its structures, but the published photographs indicate that the site was enclosed by a large timber palisade or ring of posts, and horizontal timber planks and beams were also noted in the internal areas (Buick 1894).

In 1894, the Scottish crannog expert Robert Munro wrote two papers in the *Journal of the Royal Society of Antiquaries of Ireland* on the subject of Swiss lake-dwellings, in particular describing their structural features (Munro 1894). Stone forts on islands were also a focus of attention in the late nineteenth century. A stone fort in Lough-na-Cranagh, Co. Antrim, on the coast at Fair Head had already been investigated in 1885 (M'Henry 1886). In 1897, E.L. Layard described 'fortified stone lake-dwellings' in Lough Skannive, Connemara (Layard 1897), and a stone fort on an island in Lough Cullen, Co. Mayo (Layard 1899). George Kinahan (1897) also referred to stone forts on Lough Bola, in Gorten Lough, Co. Donegal, and to forts on islands in Lough Mask, Lough Corrib and Lough Cong. W.J. Knowles (1897) described a number of finds from Carcoagh crannog, Co. Antrim, adjacent to the Lisnacrogher Iron Age hoard. In 1898, the Rev. William Falkiner described a crannog with bronze and bone artefacts, timbers and animal bone at Loughatrim, Co. Westmeath (Falkiner 1898–1900). An unusual find was made at Coolnasluasty Lough, Co. Clare, where workmen exposed a wooden platform with human skulls and bone, buried at depth in peats under a former lake. Numerous mounds of burnt clay and bone were noted around the margins of the lake (Westropp 1895).

Rev. S.A. D'Arcy was active in lake settlement archaeology in the vicinity of Clones at this time. He published the results of his crannog excavations in Killyvilla Lake, Co. Monaghan (D'Arcy 1897), followed by an account of his excavations of two lake-dwellings at Drumacrittin, Co. Fermanagh (D'Arcy 1900). Prehistoric material was found in both these sites, including flints, a stone axe and a saddle quern stratified at depth in crannog 1, and a barbed and tanged arrowhead in crannog 2. P. Bardan (1898a; 1898b) described crannogs at Lough-a-Trim and White Lough, Co. Westmeath. George Coffey and W.J. Knowles carried out excavations in 1901 at Craigywarren crannog, Co. Antrim, where incidentally they were assisted by the Rev. George Buick (Coffey 1906). Another crannog (or possible *fulacht fiadh*) at Loughgall, Co. Armagh, was noted by R.G. Berry (1906). Knowles described several crannog sites in Ulster, including that of Inishrush, Co. Antrim (Knowles 1903; 1904). Crannogs were found at Mountcashel (Westropp 1901), Drumcliff and Clareen, Co. Clare (Parkinson 1905). Lett (1905) described a crannog on Loughbrickland, Co. Down, where a palisaded island produced charcoal and ash, coarse pottery and iron slag. T. Hall (1907; 1910) carried out work on some of the crannogs in Cavan, particularly in the vicinity of Belturbet. Knox (1908) described worked stone on one crannog. R.A.S. Macalister, George Armstrong and Robert Lloyd Praeger excavated a medieval 'crannog' or marshland settlement at Loch Pairc, Co. Galway. Indeed, this was the first Irish archaeological excavation on which it could be said that palaeoenvironmental studies played an active role in the interpretation (Macalister *et al.* 1914). Irish lake settlement studies of the period may have been influenced by the excavations of Arthur Bulleid on the Iron Age lake village at Glastonbury, Somerset (Bulleid and Gray 1911; 1917; J.M. Coles *et al.* 1992; J.M. Coles and Minnitt 1995).

Lake settlement research fell into abeyance in the following twenty years. In his book *The archaeology of Ireland* (1928), R.A.S. Macalister commented on crannog studies: 'A field untilled, almost fallow, awaits the systematic student of this later lake-dwelling civilisation, the available literature of which is painfully amateurish and unsystematic'. The situation was to change dramatically in the 1930s, mainly through the work of the Harvard Archaeological Expedition to Ireland.

The impact of the Harvard Archaeological Expedition, 1932–80

The Harvard Archaeological Expedition to Ireland in the 1930s and 1940s

The Harvard Archaeological Expedition to Ireland was carried out as part of the Harvard Irish Survey, directed by Professor E.A. Hooton of Harvard, which aimed to combine physical and social anthropology and archaeological research to explore the origins of the Irish. The physical anthropological studies included such work as the measurement of volunteers' skulls across the country. The archaeological aspects of the Harvard mission, led by the American archaeologists Hugh O'Neill Hencken and Harold Movius, are well known. A five-year programme of research was laid out, mostly based on large-scale excavations of prehistoric and historic sites (including Mesolithic coastal and riverine occupations, Neolithic megalithic tombs and cairns, and Bronze Age, Early Historic and Viking Age settlement sites). The Harvard Archaeological Expedition began its fieldwork in 1932 and it is fairly clear that a 'Celtic origins' ethos lay behind the studies, as might be expected in the Ireland of those years. There was little or no attempt to explore any archaeological topics dating from after the Viking Age.

Major programmes of archaeological excavation were carried out on three crannogs (Pl. 5)—the neighbouring sites of Ballinderry crannog no. 1, Co. Westmeath (Hencken 1936), and Ballinderry crannog no. 2, Co. Offaly (Hencken 1942), and Lagore, Co. Meath (Hencken 1950). The expedition was clearly welcomed by the archaeological community and the National Museum: for example, Adolf Mahr recommended that the expedition investigate Ballinderry crannog no. 1, and even sent

Pl. 5—*The Early Historic crannog of Ballinderry no. 2, Co. Offaly. A large dugout boat lies in the foreground, a wooden floor lies behind, and the enclosing palisade curves around at the right (from Hencken 1942).*

Hencken a barrel of wood preservative from the Museum. Contemporary newspapers and official accounts of the excavations were highly supportive. *The Irish Times* carried several articles about the work, noting the high quality of the finds and what it perceived as the highly scientific approach. Ballinderry crannog no. 1 was visited by its reporter on 16 June 1932, when the young American could be seen supervising six local men, with the crannog divided into four sections, the first section already half done. 'On the side of the drain, opposite the workmen were seated three young ladies, quietly looking on. Over all presided the majesty of the law in the person of a civic guard.'

The Harvard expedition had a major impact on Irish archaeology (Cooney 1995). Firstly, the excavation reports were fully published in the *Proceedings of the Royal Irish Academy* and in the *Journal of the Royal Society of Antiquaries of Ireland*, usually in great detail, making the results available to other scholars. Secondly, it is often thought that the expedition introduced systematic excavation techniques to Irish archaeology (although contemporary lake settlement excavations in Europe were certainly of a higher standard). Thirdly, the Ballinderry and Lagore excavations produced huge artefactual assemblages, which were to become the mainstay of many subsequent typological and artefactual studies. The crannog excavations carried out by the Harvard Archaeological Expedition have come to dominate the interpretation of Bronze Age and historic period lake settlement archaeology in Ireland.

The Harvard expedition inspired much interest and confidence amongst Irish archaeologists. Adolf Mahr and Harold Leask used its impetus to persuade Irish politicians to establish funding for other large-scale excavations, partly as a solution to the chronic unemployment situation (J. Raftery 1988, 23–4). Joseph Raftery obviously gained much experience through being a supervisor on the Ballinderry excavations, as he directed his own excavations in 1937 at a Bronze Age lake settlement at Knocknalappa, Co. Clare (J. Raftery 1942), and subsequently the major multiperiod crannog excavations at Rathtinaun, Co. Sligo (J. Raftery 1957). Archaeological excavations were also carried out about this time of a Late Neolithic lake settlement at Rathjordan, Co. Limerick (Ó Ríordáin and Lucas 1946–7). The impact of the Harvard expedition and the continuing interest in crannogs can also be seen in the chapter devoted to them in Seán P. Ó Ríordáin's (1942a) *Antiquities of the Irish countryside*.

Little attempt was made to tap the rich potential of the waterlogged settlement deposits for in-depth palaeoenvironmental investigations. Knud Jessen and Frank

Mitchell did carry out some pollen analysis at Ballinderry crannog no. 2 and there was a brief experiment with tree-ring studies at Ballinderry crannog no. 1, abandoned owing to a lack of success. It could be argued that the intimidating scale of the results from the excavations stifled the subsequent development of wetland archaeology in Ireland (John Coles, pers. comm.). Indeed, these excavations may well have contributed to the overarching interest of Irish archaeologists in typological, art and ornament studies between 1930 and 1960. During this period Irish archaeology was formed around empirical approaches and cultural-historical interpretations, at a time when archaeologists in other countries were making ventures into settlement studies, palaeoenvironmental research and even theoretical archaeology.

Oliver Davies and lake settlement excavations in Ireland, 1940–50

From about 1940, archaeologists in Northern Ireland became active in lake settlement research. Oliver Davies, an archaeologist in the Classics Department, Queen's University, Belfast, made a particularly important contribution. He carried out both archaeological survey and excavation of a large number of crannogs and islands across Ulster (e.g. Davies 1940). In 1940 he began four seasons of excavations at the complex multiperiod crannog at Island MacHugh, Co. Tyrone. This was subsequently published under the auspices of the Belfast Natural History Society (Davies 1950).

Davies carried out extensive archaeological survey during the war years along and across the border with the Republic. After fieldwork for the Irish Tourist Association in the summer of 1941 in Cavan, Leitrim, western Monaghan and south Donegal, he wrote a major regional review of crannogs in south Ulster (Davies 1942). This article is interesting for the number of issues that it raised. He noted that the distribution of crannogs was not necessarily complementary to that of lakes (the Donegal lakes have relatively few) and that crannogs and monastic islands were mutually exclusive in their distribution. Medieval churches were typically found on larger, natural islands that could have supported cattle herds. In terms of chronology, Davies reviewed the Mesolithic and Neolithic finds from crannogs, the occasional Bronze Age artefacts from lake islands, and the frequency of medieval castles and tower-houses on rocky lake islands.

Like his contemporaries Adolf Mahr and Joseph Raftery, Oliver Davies was interested in the formal similarities to Swiss lake settlements. He discussed the various types of lake settlement site, such as crannog-cairns (circular piles of stone retained by a palisade), clay mounds, log-platforms (timber beams laid radially in the manner of Scottish crannogs), and the *Packwerk*-crannog, built of layers of branches, twigs and sand and pegged by piles, but having little other formal structure. The article also reviewed his excavations of a crannog at Hackelty, Co. Cavan (Davies 1942). It contained notes on a Bann flake from Mahanagh, Lough Allen, Co. Leitrim, as well as accounts of unpublished crannog excavations from County Cavan, such as Corraneary Lough, Rivory Island, Aghavoher, Killywilly and Deredis Upper. Davies also excavated a settlement on a natural island in Lough Eske, Co. Donegal.

At Deredis Upper, Co. Cavan, he investigated a number of lake settlements on Lough Inchin and Farnham Lough (Davies 1946a). On Farnham Lough he discovered three crannogs, one of which produced a sixteenth/seventeenth-century Bellarmine jar, a clay pipe and a rotary quern fragment (*ibid.*, 19). A crannog at the narrow north end of Lough Inchin produced only scanty habitation remains, which he compared to the 'small Neolithic crannogs on which Bann flakes may be found; of these several have been identified in the Monaghan–Cavan area' (*ibid.*, 19). A larger multiperiod crannog at the south-west corner of Lough Inchin was excavated in 1942. The earlier phase produced wooden beams, wattlework, flint, chert, animal bone and some fragments of iron. This may have been an Early Historic lake settlement. The later occupation was on a platform of stone, wood and clay. The associated finds included eighteenth-century pottery, iron objects and bird and animal bone. This was taken to be the scanty remains of a post-medieval settlement site (*ibid.*).

The County Down Archaeological Survey and Northern Ireland, 1950–66

The emphasis shifted to County Down in the early 1950s, when several Early Historic crannogs, amongst other sites, were excavated in the barony of Lecale by the Archaeological Survey of Northern Ireland. These excavations were mostly focused on sampling in an attempt to gain insights from a wide range of settlements. In 1951 and 1952, Pat Collins excavated an Early Historic crannog at Lough Faughan (Collins 1955). Pat Collins and Bruce Proudfoot carried out trial excavations in June 1956 on a crannog at Clea Lakes, Co. Down (Collins and Proudfoot 1959). These excavations were mostly carried out by means of test-trenches or small sample areas, and thereby differed from the more extensive Harvard excavations of the 1930s. Nevertheless, much interesting material was produced, and these studies were the first to be carried out within a broader research design—in this case the investigation of historic settlement in south Down (Ryan 1997). The continuing impact of modern drainage works and agricultural developments also led to other lake settlement investigations in the 1950s. In 1952 Pat Collins and William Seaby investigated an unusual Bronze Age lakeshore settlement complex at Lough Eskragh, Co. Tyrone (Collins and Seaby 1960). Later in the decade, in the dry summer of 1956, W.H. Hodges also excavated a small lake settlement at Cullyhanna Lough, Co. Armagh (Pl. 6). Pat Collins was also involved in these investigations. The Cullyhanna Lough lakeshore settlement was subsequently dated to the Middle Bronze Age (Hillam 1976; Mallory and McNeill 1991).

Pl. 6—*Middle Bronze Age lakeshore settlement at Cullyhanna Lough, Co. Armagh, excavated in June 1956 (photo: Pat Collins).*

Discoveries at Lough Gara in the 1950s and 1960s

Arterial drainage was to have a major impact in the Republic over the next two decades. In 1952 a local drainage scheme at Lough Gara on the Sligo/Roscommon border lowered lake levels by over 2m. An astonishing wealth of archaeology lay exposed on the lake foreshore (J. Raftery 1957; forthcoming a; forthcoming b; Anon. 1952; Cross 1953; Fredengren 1998a; 1998b). Initially, two archaeological surveys were carried out, the first by R.E. Cross, chief engineer of Public Works, who published his map of identified 'crannogs' (Cross 1953). This was followed by a more detailed survey by P. Ó hEailidhe around the mouth of the Boyle River, in Tivannagh, Derrymaquirk and Coolnagranshy townlands especially. There were also large concentrations of sites on the eastern shore of the lake, at Emlagh, Derrymore Island and Ross townlands. Paddy Healey recorded hundreds of the River Boyle sites and they were systematically annotated on a 25-inch Ordnance Survey map (Barry Raftery, pers. comm.). The Lough Gara archaeology was astonishing in its chronology and range; in many ways these years were an Irish version of the Swiss lake discoveries of the mid-nineteenth century. Joseph Raftery (1957) claimed that there were at least 360 individual spreads of stone, large stone cairns, crannogs and wooden post alignments, but it is likely that a more sustained survey would have revealed even larger numbers (Pl. 7). Recent archaeological surveys on Lough Gara by the Swedish Crannog Research Programme have confirmed that sites can also be located elsewhere around the lake (Christina Fredengren, pers. comm.; Fredengren 1998a; 1998b).

Pl. 7—*Archaeologists inspecting a crannog 'cairn' of stone and timber exposed on the Lough Gara foreshore in 1952 (photo: Dept of Archaeology, UCG).*

Most of the 'crannog' sites were small, low, flat spreads of stone, occasionally retained by small vertical piles, often reached by narrow causeways. These sites (typically termed 'metalling sites' because they were made of spreads of small stones) were mostly found on the reedy flats of lower Lough Gara. Cross (1953, 94) stated that in every instance these smaller sites produced 'pre-Bronze Age material', such as Bann flakes, as well as animal bone and charred wood. The larger 'crannog' sites consisted of large cairns of stones with horizontal timbers and encircling palisades, also often reached by zigzag causeways. These larger sites often produced Bronze Age artefacts, and also common were Bann flakes, cores, hammerstones, stone axes and saddle querns. Forty dugout boats were exposed on the Lough Gara foreshore, and local people and archaeologists gathered large assemblages of Mesolithic and Neolithic chert flakes, stone axes and other implements, Bronze Age tools, weaponry and ornaments, Iron Age swords, spearheads and spearbutts, Early Historic iron axes and high-status metalwork, such as copper-alloy finger-rings, belt-buckles and penannular brooches, as well as Viking Age ringed pins and axes (Pl. 8).

At Coolnagranshy, Co. Roscommon (on the Boyle River), probable Late Mesolithic Bann flakes, stone axes and hammerstones were taken from an exposed cairn or mound retained by vertical birch piles. At Ross, Co. Sligo (at the south-east corner of the large lake), Late Bronze Age metalwork was gathered from one probable lake settlement site. A fifth- to sixth-century copper-alloy finger-ring was picked up on 'Crannog 88' at Derrycoagh, Co. Roscommon. Two crannogs were excavated in Lough Gara by Joseph Raftery. Crannog no. 124 at Tivannagh, Co. Roscommon, located at the

Pl. 8—*A range of Neolithic, Bronze Age, Early Historic and medieval artefacts found on the Lough Gara foreshore in the 1950s (photo: David Jennings, Dept of Archaeology, UCD).*

mouth of the River Boyle, produced archaeological evidence for both prehistoric and Early Historic occupation. Crannog 61 at Rathtinaun, Co. Sligo, was totally excavated between 1952 and 1955, revealing a complex multiperiod site dating from the Late Bronze Age to the Viking Age (J. Raftery 1957; forthcoming b). Until recently, it was thought that Crannog 61 had an Iron Age phase, but recent radiocarbon dating indicates that this is probably not the case (Evans 1966, 191–2; B. Raftery 1994; Barry Raftery, pers. comm.). These were exciting years for Irish archaeology. Although the Lough Gara discoveries were not published in detail like the Harvard investigations, they quickly entered the Irish archaeological consciousness.

Frank Mitchell embarked on a programme of fieldwork around the exposed lakeshore at Lough Gara in the hope of finding an 'Irish Star Carr' (i.e. a Mesolithic occupation site with well-preserved organics) (Mitchell 1990, 205). He had been inspired to this work by contemporary discoveries in England (between 1949 and 1954), where the Cambridge archaeologist Grahame Clark (1954) had carried out excavations on the famous Mesolithic site of Star Carr in the Vale of Pickering, Yorkshire. The fact that Harry Godwin and Donald Walker had joined Clark's team to investigate the environmental setting of the site meant that the full potential of that wetland's archaeological potential was being exploited. No intact occupation site was found on Lough Gara, although much material of Mesolithic, Bronze Age, Iron Age and medieval date was recovered. Away from Lough Gara, a small-scale investigation of a lake settlement was carried out by David Liversage on Garret Island, Lough Gur, Co. Limerick. These excavations were inconclusive and the results are difficult to interpret, but it seems that this was some form of Neolithic lake activity site (Liversage 1958).

Mesolithic lithic scatters and medieval monastic islands

Frank Mitchell was to continue his search for a Mesolithic lakeshore occupation site in the midlands. Drainage of the River Inny system in the late 1960s, lowering lake levels in Cavan, Longford and Westmeath, led to a series of interesting Late Mesolithic discoveries in the late 1960s. This phase of work started in 1969, when Joseph Raftery of the National Museum of Ireland recorded a dugout boat exposed on the foreshore at Lough Derravarragh, Co. Westmeath, and noted the presence of lithic scatters on the exposed foreshore at Derrya and Clonava, at the north-west end of the lake. Frank Mitchell started fieldwork along the foreshore, noting the presence of crannogs, wooden structures and other features. Lithic scatters, both water-rolled on the lake foreshore and embedded in peats, seemed to indicate a good potential for wetland preservation of a 'Larnian' occupation site. Mitchell carried out excavations on several of these sites in Clonava townland (Mitchell 1972). Similar drainage projects around the north-west led to other prehistoric and historic stray finds being gathered from lakeshores in the

Pl. 9—*The monastic island of Inis Cealtra, Lough Derg, excavated by Liam de Paor in the 1970s (photo: Dúchas—The Heritage Service).*

region. The River Inny drainage had also lowered lake levels at Lough Kinale, Co. Longford, and a local amateur archaeologist had found lithic scatters on the shore of a large dryland island on the south-east shore. In 1969 Barry Raftery and Nuala Sproule carried out several days of fieldwork on the lakeshore at Derragh townland, recovering literally hundreds of Mesolithic flints and chert from three separate sites (Mitchell 1970). A sample of these was gathered from the foreshore and presented to the National Museum, but the sites were not cleared or investigated in detail.

There is a long tradition of archaeological research on monastic lake islands, particularly on those of Lough Ree and Lough Erne (e.g. Wakeman 1879; Davies 1938; Lowry-Corry 1933; 1959; Ralegh Radford 1970), but elsewhere too (e.g. Fennell 1904). Until the 1970s, most of this work was concentrated on the description of church architecture and stone sculpture, and rather less on the settlement and economy of these island monasteries. This was partly changed in the early 1970s, when Early Historic, Viking Age and medieval occupation evidence was excavated on two monastic islands. Liam de Paor's extensive excavations on the monastic island of Inis Cealtra, Lough Derg, Co. Clare (Pl. 9), produced a range of architectural and industrial evidence, including a copper-working area, a furnace and a motif-piece, indicating on-site metalworking (de Paor 1972; 1974; 1975; Harbison 1991; Ryan 1988). Dudley Waterman's (1979) brief excavations at the monastic site at Devenish, Lough Erne, Co. Fermanagh, produced finds of imported pottery, indicating the importance of the island as a hostel for medieval pilgrims.

The Fermanagh crannogs and dendrochronology in the 1970s

In 1973, artificially reduced water-levels at Lough Eskragh, Co. Tyrone, exposed the foreshore peats and clays. Fissuring of the lakebed peats threatened the Bronze Age sites recorded there in 1952 (Collins and Seaby 1960), so these were reinvestigated by a team led by Brian Williams through the wet and windy months of November and December (Williams 1978). In 1977 Claire Foley carried out an extensive crannog survey in the lakelands of Fermanagh, as part of the ongoing county archaeological survey being carried out by the Department of the Environment, Northern Ireland. The summers of 1976–7 in Ireland were amongst the hottest and driest in living memory, and lake levels were considerably lower than usual. Many previously identified crannogs became visible after years of submergence, including some of the sites (e.g. Ballydoolough) originally described by William Wakeman. An intensive phase of cartographic research led to the preliminary identification of islands and likely

Pl. 10—*Medieval Gaelic Irish crannog and seventeenth-century Scottish planter castle at Monea, Co. Fermanagh. The crannogs of the county were the subject of detailed survey in 1977 (photo: Environment and Heritage Service, DOE(NI)).*

crannogs, which were marked up on maps before fieldwork. Claire Foley and an assistant, using a small rubber dinghy and oars, visited at least 120 sites through the long, hot summer of 1977. Although there was no attempt at underwater survey, it was possible to float gently around sites and to identify piles and wooden structures lying in the shallow water. The crannogs were found to be mostly in the small lakes in the vicinity of Upper and Lower Lough Erne and in the drumlin lakes to the south of the county (Claire Foley, pers. comm.) (Pl. 10).

At the same time, Michael Baillie at the Palaeoecology Centre at Queen's University, Belfast, was taking dendrochronological samples from oak timbers from numerous archaeological structures and bog oaks, in an attempt to establish a long oak chronology for Ireland (Baillie 1979; 1982; 1995a). Assisted by Victor Buckley and others, Baillie visited a large number of Fermanagh crannogs and took samples from exposed palisades. A destroyed crannog at Teeshan, Co. Antrim, proved to be a vital link in the dendrochronological programme (Baillie 1979). The importance of this work was that several northern crannogs proved to have construction dates between the late sixth and early seventh centuries AD, suggesting that this was the origin of Early Historic crannogs in Ireland, a model which has yet to be altered. A second important discovery was the number of Fermanagh crannogs which produced firm dating evidence from the fifteenth and sixteenth centuries AD (Baillie 1982). Other dendrochronological work from lake settlements included the absolute dating of timbers from the Cullyhanna Lough lake settlement to the Middle Bronze Age (Hillam 1976).

Archaeological investigations were also carried out on an Early Mesolithic lake settlement in the Republic. In 1978 Michael Ryan carried out excavations for the National Museum of Ireland on an Early Mesolithic site in Broughal townland at Lough Boora, Co. Offaly. These excavations significantly extended the distribution of Early Mesolithic settlement in Ireland and produced much evidence for the activities of early Irish hunter-gatherers in a lakeland environment (Ryan 1980).

Renewed interest, survey and excavation, 1983–98

A wave of new interest

The early 1980s saw a revival of interest in lake settlement archaeology in Ireland, leading to survey and excavation projects, a number of important publications and a crannog conference in Dublin. In 1983 Beaver Press and Dublin University Press printed a facsimile of Wood-Martin's *The lake-dwellings of Ireland*, making this seminal text available to more than just bibliophiles and university students. A number of important papers were also published in the *Journal of Irish Archaeology*. Chris Lynn (1983) produced a highly influential critique of the early dating of Irish crannogs, separating Bronze Age and suspected Iron Age lake settlements from the classic Early Historic or Viking Age crannog. Lagore crannog became the focus of interest after a seminar on the site was chaired by Frank Mitchell in the Royal Society of Antiquaries of Ireland in December 1984. Two papers emerged from that seminar. Chris Lynn (1985–6) reinterpreted the structure and stratigraphy of Lagore and Ballinderry 1 crannogs, while Richard Warner (1985–6) reassessed the dating of Lagore. A number of survey and excavation projects started in the early 1980s, including Victor Buckley's surveys of the crannogs of Westmeath, Cavan, Louth and Monaghan, John Bradley's excavations at Moynagh Lough, Co. Meath (J. Bradley 1991), Cormac Bourke's (1986; 1987; forthcoming) excavations at Newtownlow, Co. Westmeath, and the work of the Crannog Archaeological Project on Lough Ennell. The crannog of Island MacHugh was re-excavated by Richard Ivens and Derek Simpson in 1985 and 1986 (Ivens *et al.* 1986).

The Wood-Martin crannog conference, 1986

This renewed archaeological interest, combined with the example of an Edinburgh conference commemorating Robert Munro's publication of *Ancient Scottish lake-dwellings or crannogs,* set the stage for an Irish crannog conference commemorating the centenary of the publication of William Wood-Martin's *The lake-dwellings of Ireland.* The conference, organised by Victor Buckley, was held in December 1986 in Trinity College, Dublin. It was the first time that the results of modern archaeological surveys, excavations, finds studies, scientific dating techniques and historical studies were brought together through the presentation of eighteen papers in one forum. The conference was subsequently reviewed by John Bradley (1987) and is worth examining in detail.

Victor Buckley presented a history of crannog research since Wood-Martin's work in 1886. Aideen Ireland gave a biography of William Wood-Martin's life and work, the crannog work being examined in the context of his other antiquarian research. Séamus Caulfield reviewed the impact of the Harvard Archaeological Expedition on Irish archaeology, in particular illustrating the circular arguments in the dating of Ballinderry crannog no. 1, Ballinderry crannog no. 2 and Lagore, and asserted that the historical documentation could no longer be considered a reliable source. Joseph Raftery reviewed his work at Lough Gara and confirmed the unsuitability of the term 'crannog' in the light of the range of sites uncovered there. Brian Williams outlined the results of the Fermanagh crannog survey, which had revealed a distribution with a preference for small lakes often drained by small, navigable streams. Only six lakes contained more than one crannog. In contrast, Michael Gibbons, then of the Sites and Monuments Record office, presented new evidence from Connemara, not for wooden palisaded crannogs but for stone duns and 'watercashels'. Excavation summaries were provided from the tenth- to thirteenth-century AD crannog at Newtownlow, Co. Westmeath (by Cormac Bourke), the sixth- to ninth-century AD crannog at Moynagh Lough, Co. Meath (by John Bradley), and the Island MacHugh crannog excavations, where ninth-century BC and seventh-century AD evidence was revealed (by Richard Ivens and Derek Simpson). Ian Morrison reviewed Scottish crannog research.

Richard Warner examined the complexity of the relationships between royalty and crannogs in early Ireland. Raymond Gillespie reviewed the historical evidence for the use of crannogs in the sixteenth and seventeenth centuries AD. He suggested that crannogs were mainly places of defence, but that they were occasionally stores for munitions, prisons, storehouses for wealth, places of refuge and hospitals. Michael Baillie reviewed the evidence of dendrochronology, which suggested that the construction of crannogs took place mainly in the late sixth and early seventh centuries AD. The animal bone evidence from Moynagh Lough was discussed by Finbar McCormick. Raghnall Ó Floinn suggested that the poor-quality crannog ware was a response to thirteenth-century market forces. There were two further papers on the interaction of archaeology with the public. Etienne Rynne described the construction of the replica crannog at Craggaunowen and Robert Farrell spoke about the importance of involving sports divers in crannog investigations.

John Bradley (1987, 24) suggested that four main points emerged from the conference. Firstly, there was the necessity of refining the term 'crannog'. Secondly, there was a need to compile an inventory of different crannog types. Thirdly, it was now thought necessary to excavate crannogs of all periods, but particularly prehistoric and later medieval sites. Finally, the importance was stressed of work in western Ireland, where crannog features differ greatly from those in the midlands and east. Other issues, such as the need for multidisciplinary and landscape studies, appear not to have emerged with such clarity.

Treasure-hunters and the State, 1980–7

In years to come, archaeologists may well view the early years of the 1980s as the period of most intense activity on Irish lake settlements since the late nineteenth century. At this time treasure-hunters, using metal-detectors, removed thousands of artefacts from archaeological sites throughout the Irish landscape (E.P. Kelly 1993a; 1993b; 1993c; 1994). Metal-detectors had been in use in Ireland since the 1970s, but the discovery of a hoard of Viking Age metalwork at Derrynaflan, Co. Tipperary, led to a surge in their popularity after 1980. By the early 1980s, crannogs were being regularly searched by divers and other interested parties using metal-detectors. Intriguingly, the experience enabled many divers and treasure-hunters to recognise significant patterns in the settlement landscape, so that only the richest sites (not all of them obvious) were being chosen by them for investigation. If nothing else, this phenomenon clearly indicates that it is possible for experienced fieldworkers to trace settlement hierachies and site functions in the Irish landscape. There were a range of spectacular archaeological discoveries (such as an Early Historic book-shrine at Lough Kinale, Co. Longford, and a processional cross at Tully Lough, Co. Roscommon), but it is apparent that many other objects were lost to the country through illegal exporting and an illicit antiquities trade. Early Historic decorated stones and cross-slabs were another target, examples being removed from the monastic islands of Iniscealtra, Co. Clare, and Inchcleraun, Co. Longford (E.P. Kelly 1993a, 378–80). In summer 1986 several fragments of a large eighth-century AD book-shrine were picked up in 2m of water by an underwater diver near a crannog in Lough Kinale, Co. Longford (E.P. Kelly 1993b). A three-week season of survey was carried out by the National Museum of Ireland on this crannog in 1987 (Farrell *et al.* 1989).

In July 1987, the enactment of the National Monuments (Amendment) Act made it illegal to search for archaeological objects, using metal-detectors, magnetometers or other electronic detecting devices, without a licence. Police powers were included in the act which would enable police to conduct searches, under warrant, for looted antiquities. Since then the main phase of the metal-detecting era seems to have ended, although it is undoubtedly still going on (E.P. Kelly 1993a, 381). It is worth pointing out that not all treasure-hunters were motivated solely by the prospect of monetary reward; for many it had as much to do with obtaining and owning objects from the distant past. However, it would be difficult to overemphasise the harm that was done to the archaeological heritage in these years. Metal-detector surveys were carried out on literally hundreds, and more probably thousands, of Irish archaeological sites. It is clear

Pl. 11—*Crannogs and islands on the western shore of Lough Ennell, Co. Westmeath. Cró-Inis is the island in the bottom right corner; Dún na Sgiath ringfort is the tree-covered mound on the drylands (CUCAP AVH 20; reproduced with the permission of the Cambridge Committee for Aerial Photography).*

that lake settlements bore the brunt of the attack, and many must have been damaged by illegal digging and the removal of important artefactual or environmental evidence. Although many individuals cooperated with the National Museum authorities, it is also clear that large personal collections of finds were amassed, from crannogs in particular (*ibid.*, 378). The National Museum has now taken thousands of these archaeological objects into the care of the State, and many collectors have provided vital information on the provenances of these artefacts. It is intended that a series of catalogues accounting for these finds will be published (Eamonn Kelly, pers. comm.).

The Crannog Archaeological Project, 1983–93

The first underwater archaeological surveys in Ireland started in the midland lakes in 1983. They were carried out by a team of American archaeologists, led by Robert Farrell from Cornell University, Michael Ryan from the National Museum of Ireland and Victor Buckley from the Archaeological Survey of Ireland (Farrell 1990a; 1990b). In 1987 the Crannog Archaeological Project was formed, with the broad aim of encouraging amateur divers to become involved in systematic, professional archaeological projects. It began with a brief survey of sites in Lough Ennell and Lough Analla, Co. Westmeath. Wooden structures were located underwater at the crannog of Cró-Inis (Farrell and Buckley 1984). The survey continued in Lough Oughter, Co. Cavan, Lough Kinale, Co. Longford, and Lough Ennell and Lough Lene, Co. Westmeath, with the help of Eamonn Kelly and Nessa O'Connor from the National Museum of Ireland. Underwater survey in Lough Lene led to the discovery of wooden structures at Nun's Island and Castle Island (Farrell 1989). A previously known Iron Age boat plank from the eastern part of the lake was also re-recorded (Brindley and Lanting 1990; Ó hEailidhe 1992; B. Raftery 1994). Lough Ennell, Co. Westmeath (Pl. 11), gradually became the focus of all the surveys, which continued around the eastern part of the lake in later years, at Carrick Bay and Cherry Island. Large numbers of features, including crannogs, stone platforms, underwater jetties and breakwaters, were discovered (Farrell 1991; Karkov and Ruffing 1990–1; 1992–3).

The Crannog Archaeological Project was important in that it effectively introduced systematic underwater surveys to Irish archaeology. As the project was primarily focused on survey, only two small-scale excavations were carried out, one of them a stone cairn on the lake foreshore at Robinstown (Brady 1994b). Hence the chronology and function of most of the lake sites remain poorly understood. It is important to note that the Crannog Archaeological Project was carried out by student volunteers over a few short summer weeks, so it would be wrong to expect it to match the results of a long-term study. There have been more recent attempts to link the lake settlements with the Early Historic and Viking Age political landscape that surrounds Lough Ennell (Karkov and Ruffing 1997), confirming that lake settlement research needs to be carried out within a regional landscape context. Indeed, the Lough Ennell discoveries hint at the great potential of lake settlement archaeology in Ireland.

The Archaeological Survey of Ireland, 1980–98

The Office of Public Works began archaeological surveys of sites and monuments in the 1960s, but in these early stages crannogs were not included. In 1980 an archaeologist, Victor Buckley, was employed to remedy this situation. A boat and lifejackets were obtained and a team of four archaeologists and surveyors started to record the crannogs of Westmeath, Louth, Meath, and Monaghan (Pl. 12). The results of these surveys subsequently appeared as numerous site descriptions in the county inventories for Cavan (O'Donovan 1995), Meath (Moore 1987), Monaghan (Brindley 1986) and the county survey of Louth (Buckley and Sweetman 1991). The Sites and Monuments Record under the direction of Michael Gibbons and Geraldine Stout carried out 'paper surveys' for other counties. These have been amongst the most influential pieces of work carried out and have transformed our knowledge of the archaeology of Ireland. The paper surveys included archival and journal reviews, artefact research, detailed cartographic research and a programme of air photograph analysis. The sites recorded from these sources included large numbers of potential lake settlement sites (including crannogs, monastic islands, island cashels, castles, tower-houses and lake promontory forts).

Pl. 12—*Lake settlement site or crannog at Annaghmoose, Co. Monaghan (photo: Dúchas—The Heritage Service).*

The records of the National Monuments Service and the Environment and Heritage Service now indicate that there are at least 1045 known 'crannogs' in the Republic and several hundred in the North (Buckley 1996). There is little or no evidence for the date of the vast majority of these sites. Indeed, as this figure is based on paper surveys, not all of them are confirmed archaeological monuments; many may be natural islands. They are mainly distributed in the midlands and the north and west of the country. Particular concentrations are found in the lakes of the upper River Shannon drainage, Upper and Lower Lough Erne, Co. Fermanagh, and on Lough Corrib, Co. Galway. The smaller lakes of the drumlin belt across Cavan and Monaghan also have high numbers of crannogs. Lake settlements are also known in west Galway and Donegal, where they have been found to be constructed mainly of stone.

Recent developments in lake settlement archaeology

Recent developments in Irish lake settlement research

Interest in lake settlement archaeology has abated somewhat since the late 1980s. One positive outcome of the treasure-hunting era was the establishment in 1990 of the Irish Underwater Archaeological Research Team (IUART), whereby several divers who had formerly been active in metal-detecting came on-side with the archaeological community and carried out archaeological surveys on coastal wrecks and riverine fords (Boland 1990; O'Connor 1989; E.P. Kelly 1993c). However, there have also been a few underwater surveys of crannogs, such as those on Lough Arrow and Lough O'Flynn, Co. Roscommon (E.P. Kelly 1995, 47). Underwater surveys on Lough Carra, Co. Mayo, led to the discovery of an unusual, if as yet incompletely understood, Bronze Age post alignment crossing the lake (Lavelle 1992). More recently, one of the founding members of IUART, Donal Boland, has established an underwater archaeological diving company (Management for Archaeology Underwater) which has been active in archaeological underwater survey in advance of river dredging schemes and other commercial developments.

Moynagh Lough crannog, Co. Meath, continues to be the subject of sustained archaeological excavations (J. Bradley 1991). The site has produced material dating from the Late Mesolithic, Neolithic, Early, Middle and Late Bronze Age and Early Historic periods. In this latter period it appears to have been a high-status settlement, possibly mainly focused on industrial production, especially metal- and glass-working (J. Bradley 1993). A Late Bronze Age lake settlement at Clonfinlough was excavated by the Irish Archaeological Wetland Unit between 1991 and 1993 (Moloney *et al.* 1993) (Pl. 13). The Wetland Unit has also inspected a Viking Age metalworking site on the lakeshore at Bofeenaun, Co. Mayo (Keane 1995), and a lakeside settlement at Ardreagh Lough (Bermingham 1996). There have also been some significant recent papers on Early Historic and Viking Age crannogs, notably those of Eamonn Kelly on the midlands crannogs (1991a; 1991b) and Richard Warner's (1994) paper on the relationship between Early Historic crannogs and kings. The prehistoric and historic lake settlements of Lough Gara, Co. Sligo, are now being reinvestigated through the research of the Swedish Lough Gara Project directed by Christina Fredengren (1998a; 1998b).

The Discovery Programme's North Munster Project has shown the usefulness of the landscape approach to lake settlement through its exploration of later prehistoric settlement in the lakelands of south-east Clare. The Late Bronze Age lake settlement of Knocknalappa can now be assessed as an element in wider social and economic landscapes (Grogan *et al.* 1995). Underwater diving surveys were briefly carried out by the present author at Knocknalappa, leading to the discovery of several other lake settlements and other archaeological features in the waters of Rosroe Lough (O'Sullivan 1997a). Recent underwater archaeological excavations on an early ninth-century wooden bridge at Clonmacnoise, Co. Offaly, will undoubtedly set the standard for underwater archaeology over the next few years (Boland and O'Sullivan 1997).

Pl. 13—*Late Bronze Age lake settlement at Clonfinlough, Co. Offaly, under archaeological excavation (photo: Irish Archaeological Wetland Unit).*

Recent developments in European lake settlement archaeology

Lake settlements and other forms of wetland archaeology have also become a subject of wide and intense interest in world archaeology in recent years (B.J. Coles and Coles 1989; J.M. Coles and Coles 1996; J.M. Coles and Lawson 1987; B.J. Coles 1992; J.M. Coles 1984; 1991). Lake settlements are a common feature of European archaeology and have been the focus of many large-scale projects which have confirmed the variation in lake settlement organisation across Europe. Although these sites are often very different from Irish lake settlements, there are instructive lessons in the range of approaches taken and the integration of multidisciplinary techniques which indicate the potential of wetland archaeology.

Mesolithic wet site excavations have recently been carried out at Friesack, Poland (Gramsch 1992), and Noyen-sur-Seine, France (Mordant and Mordant 1992), while the lakeland site of Star Carr, Yorkshire, has continued to be of importance in Mesolithic studies in Britain. Neolithic and Bronze Age pile dwellings have been excavated in recent years in the Alpine lakes and outwash valleys of central and southern Europe (B.J. Coles and Coles 1989; J.M. Coles and Coles 1996). In Switzerland, both underwater excavations and large-scale open-air excavations have been carried out on such lake settlements as Cortaillod-Est (Arnold 1986; 1990), Auvernier-Nord (Arnold 1982) and Hauterive-Champréveyres (Benkert 1993), as well as other sites on Lake Neuchâtel and its neighbour, Lake Morat. Similarly, there have been lake village excavations in southern Germany (Schlichterle 1997). Neolithic lake settlements have also been investigated in the lakes of the French Jura mountains at Clairvaux-les-lacs and Chalain (Petrequin 1989; 1997a; 1997b), and at Charavines-'Les Baigneurs' on Lac de Paladru (Bocquet 1987; Bocquet *et al.* 1986), at Fiavé in northern Italy (Perini 1984), and at Lake Sennica, Russia (Miklyaev 1990). A Neolithic pile dwelling is known from lakelands at Alvastra, Sweden (Malmer 1991). The influence of these excavations on national and regional archaeologies has been immense, in effect helping to rewrite the prehistory of the Neolithic and Bronze Age of Europe (J.M. Coles and Lawson 1987).

The Iron Age and Early Historic lake fortresses of central and eastern Europe have also long been a focus of attention and are witnessing a current revival of interest. These are large, complex, proto-urban sites with rectangular blockhouses, streets, houses, enclosures and industrial working areas (B.J. Coles and Coles 1989; J.M. Coles and Coles 1996). Recent projects on lake settlements in eastern Europe include the archaeological excavations of a ninth- to tenth-century lake fortress at Araisi, Latvia (J.M. Coles 1995), underwater investigations of a seventh-century settlement in Lake Valgjärv, Estonia (Selirand 1988), and on a medieval lake settlement on Lake Skarlin, Poland (Grazawski and Niegowski 1998). There has also been renewed interest in the Iron Age lake fortress at Biskupin, Poland (Niewiarowski *et al.* 1992; Piotrowski and Zajaczkowski 1993; Wazny 1993; Rajewski 1980). A massive Late Viking Age lake island fortress has been investigated at Bulverket on Lake Tingstäde, Gotland, Sweden (Rönnby 1990). Closer to home are the Iron Age lake villages of Glastonbury and Meare East, Somerset, which have recently been the subject of detailed reinterpretations (J.M. Coles and Minnitt 1995).

Smaller lake settlements similar to Irish crannogs are also known in Europe. At Charavines-Colletière, in Lac de Paladru in southern France, underwater excavations by Eric Verdel and Michel Collardelle have revealed a spectacularly well-preserved eleventh-century AD fortified lake-dwelling (Collardelle and Verdel 1993). However, Scottish archaeologists have led the field in crannog investigations. Later prehistoric and Early Historic Scottish crannogs that have been excavated in recent times include Milton Loch, Dumfriesshire (Piggott 1953), Loch Glashan, Argyllshire (J.G. Scott 1960), Loch Arthur, Dumfriesshire (J. Williams 1971), and Buiston, Ayrshire (Barber and Crone 1993). Scottish archaeologists have also been highly active in underwater archaeological survey of lochs (Morrison 1985; Henderson, forthcoming a; forthcoming b). Underwater excavations have been carried out on a Neolithic site in the Outer Hebrides (Armit 1986; 1987; 1988; 1989) and at Oakbank, Loch Tay (Dixon 1984). Many recent projects in Scotland have emphasised the importance of the landscape approach in lake settlement archaeology, integrating the results of wider geographical studies with the results of detailed archaeological survey and excavation and historical research (Barber and Crone 1993; Morrison 1985). Recently, an open-air reconstruction of the Iron Age crannog at Oakbank, Loch Tay, has enabled a new understanding of the constructional methods used in the original settlement (Andrian 1995).

The interpretation of lake settlement archaeology in Ireland

What has been the impact of the history outlined above on the patterns of research and interpretation of lake settlement archaeology? It is obvious that the history of the subject is dominated by Early Historic crannog excavations. Indeed, Early Historic and Viking Age crannogs have usually been seen as a valuable source of artefacts for typological or chronological studies rather than as a means of obtaining wider insights into the settlement organisation, economy and beliefs of past societies. Ironically, it would seem to be a common perception that there have been a large number of crannog excavations, yet there have actually been quite few, the vast majority carried out long before the advent of modern scientific investigation techniques. Recent crannog excavations (with the exception of Moynagh Lough) have tended to be short-term projects operating with limited resources, leading to relatively little sustained archaeological investigation, little sense of a wider settlement context and virtually no palaeoenvironmental studies. Most investigations have concentrated on the structure, form and date of the individual site. Only rarely have archaeologists widened the scope of their enquiries to explore the relationship between lake settlements and other sites on neighbouring drylands, one exception being the recent interest in the relationship between Early Historic crannogs and ringforts (Karkov and Ruffing 1997; Warner 1994).

One way to explore the history of the interpretation of lake settlements is to examine their portrayal in reconstruction drawings, as these give us some impression of the thoughts of past researchers. Such drawings are usually seen as a useful, perhaps even highly important, means of conveying to others a general sense of the past, although in most people's opinion they should not be treated as seriously as the site plan or description. However, these drawings often have a more lasting impact, as they condition subsequent researchers to certain fixed images. The crannog is usually depicted as an object in an otherwise empty landscape, with few signs of life elsewhere or of people moving about (indeed, it is striking how few people are found in any archaeological reconstruction drawings). The view of crannogs is always from the outside and there is always a sense of slight paranoia or defensive isolation. It is surprising how little has changed since Wakeman's original frontispiece (Wood-Martin 1886a). His view was from the shore, looking towards a large island with an enclosing defensive palisade and three large rectangular houses. A dugout boat lies on the foreshore while a second approaches the island, and some people are grouped around an open-air fire (Fig. 4.1). In contrast to this is Wakeman's dramatic reconstruction drawing of a hypothetical lake village on Lough Eyes, published in Wood-Martin's (1902, 223–4) *Traces of the elder faiths of Ireland*, which shows several palisaded lake settlements in one lake, all linked together by wooden causeways (Fig. 4.2). There is a great sense of community, activity and the wider settlement landscape. Another drawing in that volume (Wood-Martin 1902, fig. 72) shows the impact of raiders on a lake settlement, with the attackers moving away in their war canoe from a burning wooden platform (Fig. 4.3). These dynamic images failed to take hold and were never to be repeated.

The reconstructions built in the 1970s at the open-air heritage park at Craggaunowen, Co. Clare (Rynne and MacEoin 1978), and more recently at Ferrycarrig, Co. Wexford (based on Moynagh Lough), are more or less the same as Wakeman's original drawing (*ibid.*). They have a single enclosing palisade with wattles, circular or rectangular houses and a defended entrance. For practical reasons, there is only a limited portrayal in the heritage parks of the debris of daily life; craft areas, abandoned structures or middens of animal bone, waste and household rubbish are all missing. This image of crannog life has become fixed in Irish archaeological interpretations (in contrast to the history of more varying representations of Scottish and Swiss lake-dwellings). More recently, Warner (1994, fig. 2) has challenged the conventional image of an Irish crannog. He depicts a huge wooden thatched house encompassing the entire crannog of Island MacHugh. A ringfort can be seen on the distant drylands. Indeed, this is one of the few drawings which link lake settlements with their wider settlement landscapes.

Interestingly, the few published reconstruction drawings of prehistoric lake settlements (e.g. Cullyhanna Lough, Clonfinlough) are very similar to the typical Early Historic crannog reconstruction drawings, with their circular houses with conical thatched roofs and the sites surrounded by high palisades. Here again there is little sense of community life or any links with settlements elsewhere. This point is not meant as a criticism of the artists or the archaeologists; it is just an indication of how we let a natural caution in drawing the past convey a static image of settlements as merely wooden structures on islands. These images then make us even more cautious in our subsequent interpretations. To continue the exploration, we can see that there are few, if any, drawings of Mesolithic hunter-gatherers on lakeshores or of the activities of Neolithic or Bronze Age farmers herding their cattle down to lakeshores or foraging along the foreshore. Ironically, the only illustrations of Irish crannogs which place them in their wider settlement landscapes, with nearby houses, fields and roadways, are those of the seventeenth-century English cartographer Richard Bartlett. It is time to widen our view of lake settlement life.

3. LAKE SETTLEMENT ARCHAEOLOGY IN IRELAND

Introduction

The archaeology of lake settlement in Ireland ranges widely in time and space—much more widely than the common perception would have it, as will be shown below. Although the archaeology of Early Historic lake crannogs is indeed a rich and complex field of enquiry, it will be demonstrated that there is much else of prehistoric and historic settlement interest to be investigated in Ireland's lakelands. Because this is a vast archaeological record, this review will be presented in a structured and consistent way. The archaeological and historical evidence for all settlement in each period will be summarised first, thus providing the context for the following detailed discussion of lake settlement. A series of thematic questions are then raised, querying the role of lake settlements in society, warfare, communications, agriculture, crafts and production, and religious beliefs. As will be seen, although some of these questions can be answered directly, most will require the initiation of a programme of research before we can achieve understanding.

Lakes, turloughs and river systems in Ireland

Introduction

The character and location of Ireland's lakes will be briefly described, mainly on a regional basis with reference to the main river drainage systems. Ireland's high rainfall, poor transpiration rates and extensive low-lying soils mean that it abounds in wetlands, whether these be lakes, ponds, rivers, bogs or coastal. However, Ireland's freshwater wetlands form some of its most distinctive and hidden landscapes. Although lakes are found all over Ireland, as a dominant feature of the landscape they are typically found in the northern half of the country, with the midlands, west and northwest especially rich in lakes (Fig. 1). It is worth remembering that Ireland was even more covered with lakes in the early post-glacial period; many of these areas are now under raised bogs.

Irish lakes vary in origin, although most are remnant features of the last glaciation. These include the small corrie lakes found in most Irish uplands, the small bogland lakes typically found in Connemara, and the numerous seasonal turloughs found in limestone areas mostly in south Mayo, east Galway and north Clare. Turloughs, although obviously part of Ireland's lakelands, have played a lesser role in prehistoric and historic settlement landscapes by reason of their isolation and seasonality. Consequently they will be described in less detail here.

The River Shannon lakelands

Lough Derg

The River Shannon, Ireland's largest river, has numerous lakes along its length and along its major tributaries, such as the River Brosna, the River Inny, the River Suck and the River Boyle. It also has some large lakes on its own length—Lough Derg, Lough Ree and Lough Allen (Fig. 5). The southernmost example, Lough Derg, is the largest lake

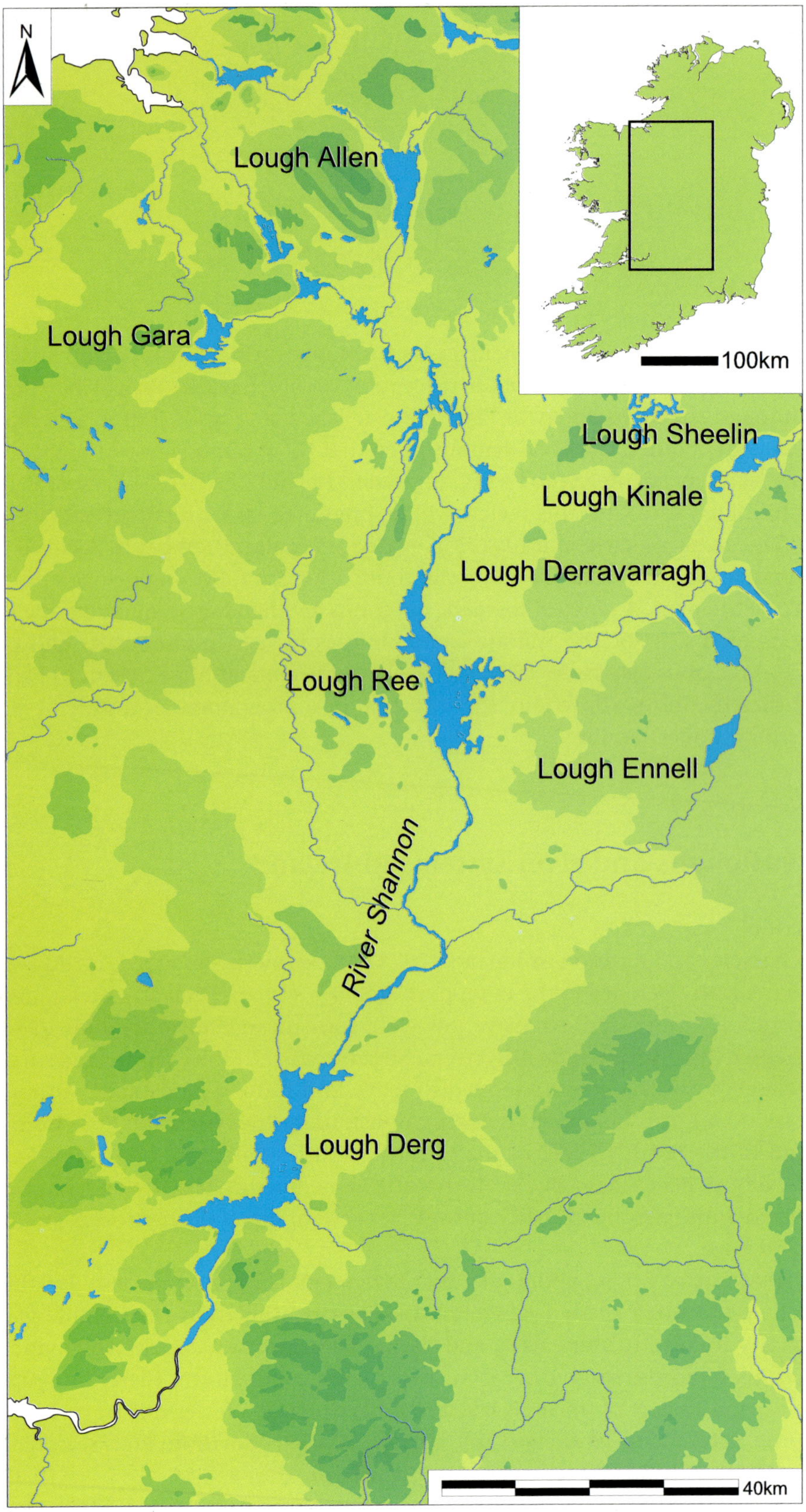

Fig. 5—*The lakes of the River Shannon system: Lough Allen to Lough Derg and the midland lakes.*

on the lower River Shannon drainage, measuring 38km from Portumna to Killaloe. It is at its widest between Dromineer and Mountshannon, with bays reaching into Tipperary and Clare. The lake is fairly shallow to the north, with numerous islands. To the south it lies between the Arra mountains and the Slieve Bernagh, and reaches depths of up to 30m.

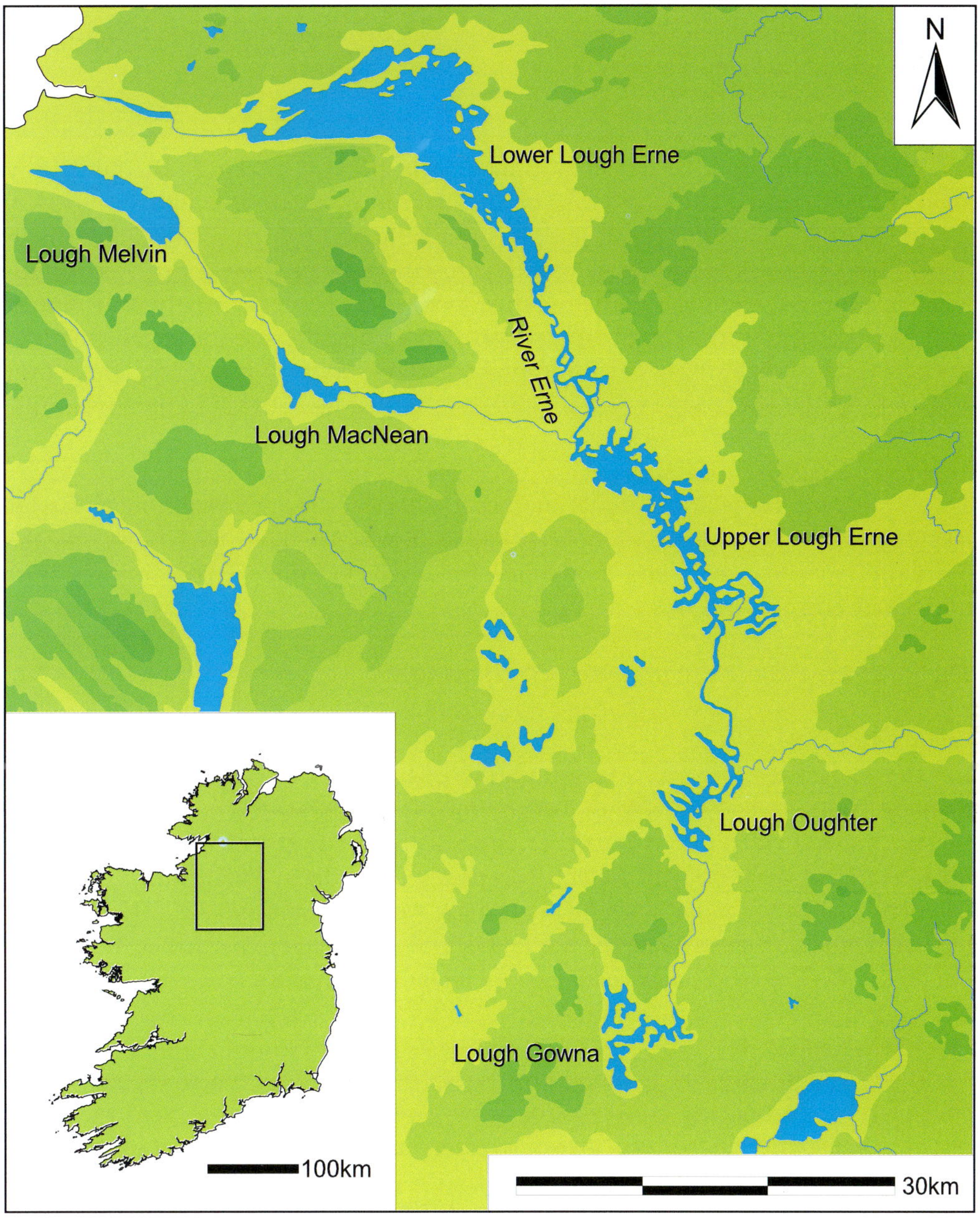

Fig. 6—*The lakes of the River Erne system: Lough Gowna, Co. Cavan, to Lower Lough Erne, Co. Fermanagh.*

Lough Ree

Lough Ree, on the middle to upper length of the River Shannon, runs for 23km from Lanesborough in the north to Athlone in the south. It has a large bay extending to the east towards the outlet of the River Inny. The lake is typically shallow, but reaches depths of 35m in parts.

Lough Allen

Lough Allen is the third-largest of the main River Shannon lakes, lying close to the source of the river in County Leitrim. Unlike the other two lakes, it is fringed by high mountains and has few islands on its waters. The River Shannon also forms smaller lakes along its length at various locations, such as at Lough Forbes, Lough Bofin and Lough Boderg.

River Boyle lakes

The River Shannon has a series of large tributaries on its uppermost length. The largest is the River Boyle, which flows out of Lough Gara. This lake is itself fed by the River Lung, which rises in the lakelands of west Roscommon (from such lakes as Urlaur

Lough, Cloonagh Lough and Cloonacolly Lough). The River Boyle flows through Lough Key, a shallow lake with numerous large, wooded islands, and into Drumharlow before joining the River Shannon above Carrick-on-Shannon.

River Inny lakes

The River Shannon has two main tributaries in the east midlands, the River Inny and the River Brosna. The largest lake on the River Inny system is Lough Sheelin, Co. Cavan. The river flows out of this lake, westwards through Lough Kinale and Derragh Lough, before flowing down to the south into Lough Derravarragh, Co. Westmeath. Lough Derravarragh has an unusually varied topography along its length. At its north-west end the land is low-lying with extensive raised bogs; to the south-east, the lake lies between two high ridges. The River Inny then flows westwards through Lough Iron and on to Lough Ree. Lough Owel also drains into the lower stretch of the River Inny.

River Brosna and River Suck lakes

To the south is the River Brosna, another tributary of the River Shannon. Its largest lake is Lough Ennel, situated to the south of Mullingar. The River Suck flows into the Shannon from the Galway side. It originates in Lough O'Flynn, Co. Roscommon, at its north-west end.

The River Erne lakes and drumlin belt lakelands

Lower Lough Erne

The River Erne also has a wide expanse of lakelands on its upper and middle drainage (Smith *et al.* 1991) (Fig. 6). Lough Erne extends across the northern quarter of Ireland and is divided into two parts at Enniskillen. The northern lake, Lower Lough Erne, is a great open body of water, occasionally quite deep, which runs north-west from Enniskillen for about 20km before turning westwards towards Belleek. There are a number of large islands along the northern shore, Boa Island in particular. The southern part is shallow with many small islands, including Devenish and White Island.

Upper Lough Erne

Upper Lough Erne begins about 10km south of Enniskillen, where the River Erne widens into a particularly broad area of water. The river upstream of here widens in places, so that the landscape is a confusion of many lakes, islands, headlands and peninsulas, dominated by numerous drumlins. If a line had to be drawn, Lower Lough Erne could be said to stop about 4km north of Belturbet. Lough Gowna is the largest lake on the uppermost stretches of the River Erne.

The lakes of the drumlin belt

The landscape of north Cavan and west and north Monaghan is dominated by numerous small drumlin lakes, comprising small boggy lakes separated by low, steep-sided hills. This is a complex mosaic of water, bogs and poorly drained land, mostly centring around Lough Oughter. To the west of Belturbet are the lakes of Derrycassna Lough, Garadice Lough and Lough Scur. Lough Ramor is the largest lake in south-east Cavan. In Monaghan, drumlin lakes are also common, especially in the west of the county.

Donegal lakes and other lakelands in the north-west

There are a number of lakes in the north-west. Lough Arrow and Lough Gill drain into Sligo Bay, while Lough MacNean Upper and Lower and Lough Melvin drain into Donegal Bay. Donegal has numerous small lakes, including Lough Derg, Lough Eske, Lough Gartan and Lough Glenveagh. On the western coast are the numerous small lakes of The Rosses, with Lough Nacung and Altan Lough to the north.

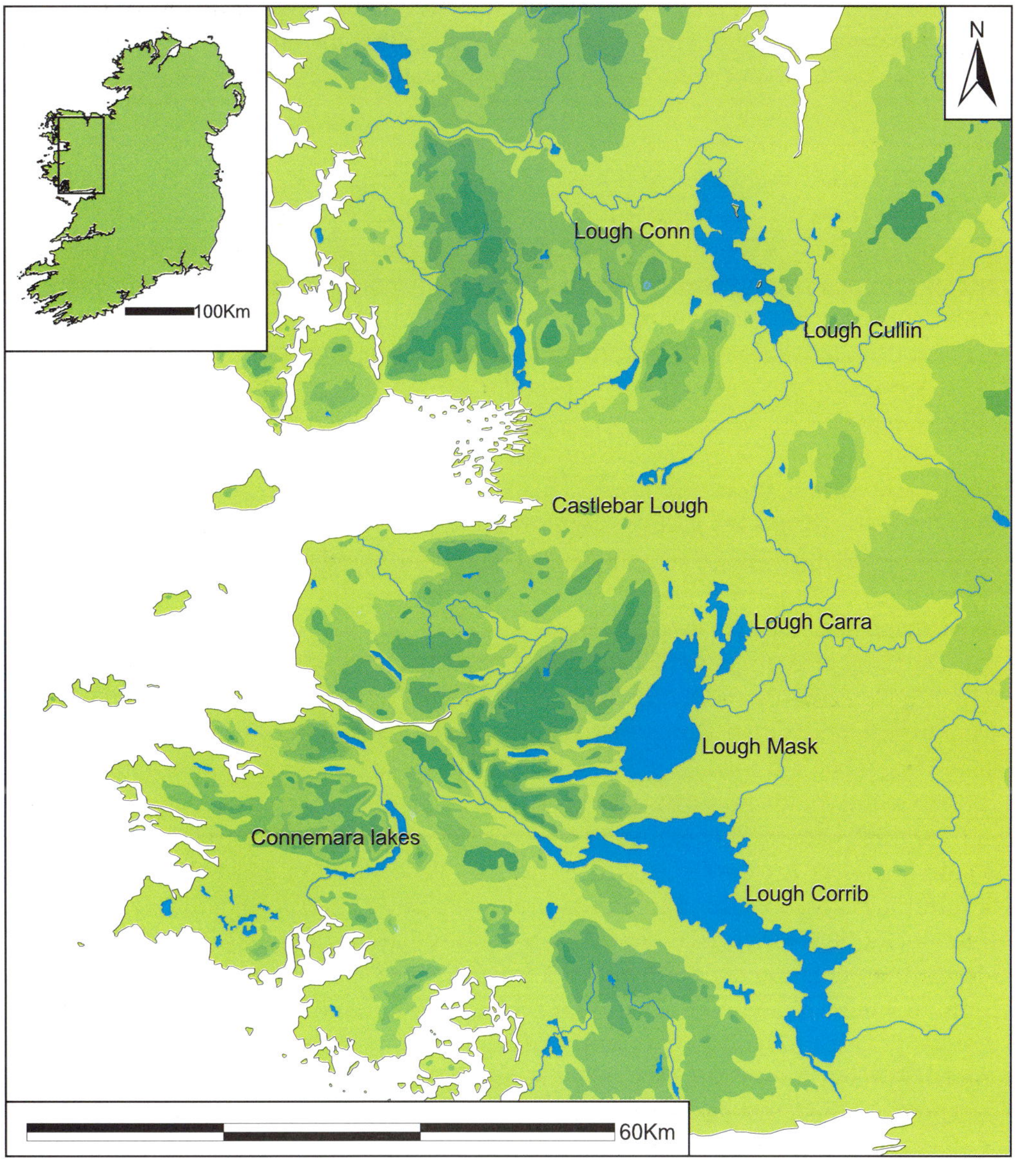

Fig. 7—*The lakes of Connacht: Lough Corrib, Co. Galway, to Lough Conn, Co. Mayo.*

Lough Neagh, Down and Antrim lakes

Lough Neagh in north-east Ireland is the largest lake in the British Isles, covering an area of 373km^2. Despite its expanse the lake is relatively shallow, typically not exceeding 15m in depth. The lakesides are marshy with gradually sloping shorelines, especially on the south-west where the water is shallow for a considerable distance offshore. It is drained by the River Bann, with Lough Beg situated just to the north of this outlet. Lough Neagh is highly important in terms of the fishing industry, with the largest eel fishery in western Europe. There are also a number of small lakes in mid-Down, such as Clea Lakes and Lough Faughan. Antrim has a few lakes, many of which were drained in the last century or had formed bogs over the centuries. Much of archaeological interest was recovered from these lakes in the late nineteenth century.

The western lakes

Lough Corrib

Lough Corrib is the second-largest lake in Ireland, defining the boundary between Connemara and the plains of east Galway (Fig. 7). It is divided into two parts—a south basin which runs from Annaghdown to just north of Galway, and a north basin stretching westwards. The south basin is typically shallow (1m in parts), with dense reed beds along its edges. The north basin is quite different. Its shore is steep and the water reaches depths of 46m. It has numerous islands, many of which are small and flat, merely showing above the surface.

Lough Mask and Lough Carra

Lough Mask lies to the north and is mainly joined to Lough Corrib by underground streams. It is 58m in maximum depth. The Partry Mountains stand on the western side of the lough. Its eastern shore is level, with a maze of rocky bays and outcrops with numerous islands. Lough Carra lies to the north-east of Lough Mask. The lake water is unusually clear, with a scatter of islands and headlands.

Lough Conn

Lough Conn is the largest lake in north Mayo. It is drained from the south by the River Moy, which flows out into Killala Bay. Lough Cullin lies to the south, with Derryhick Lough and Levallinree Lough to the south-west. There are a range of lakes in west Mayo, such as Lough Feeagh, Beltra Lough and Islandeady Lough.

Connemara lakes and the western turloughs

The Connemara region has a range of small bogland and rockland lakes, some of which have certainly produced archaeological sites. These lakes are too numerous to list, but run more or less along the coast from Spiddle to Clifden. There are also a number of larger lakes in the region's mountain valleys, such as Inagh Lough and the lakes in the vicinity of Maam Cross.

Turloughs are most common in the limestone areas of the central lowlands, west of the Shannon (in Galway, Clare, Mayo and Roscommon). Most flood during the autumn, usually in October, and then dry up again between April and July. A few are tidal, including Caherglassan Lough near Galway Bay. Turloughs vary in size and are typically about 2m in depth. However, a few near Gort, Co. Galway, are about 5m deep in midwinter. Turloughs are notable for their vegetation, mostly springy, short-cropped grasses, sedges and herbs. Many Irish turloughs have been drained out of existence in modern times, despite the fact that the annual deposition of lime-rich silts creates excellent summer grazing.

Lakes in south-west Ireland

Lakelands in Clare

Clare, both in the Burren region, east Clare, and the south-east part of the county around Kilkishen, has large numbers of small, shallow lakes, typically over limestone and therefore greatly affected by seasonal changes in water-levels. Turloughs are also commonly found in the Burren region.

Lakes in Kerry and Cork

The lakes of Killarney are amongst the most famous in Ireland, scenically set in the Reeks Mountains of County Kerry. There are three major lakes, Lough Leane (the lower lake), Muckross Lake and the Upper Lake. Lough Leane is bounded by mountains to the west and by hilly ground to the east. Lough Leane is 67m deep and 8km long, and is fed by the River Fleask. All the Killarney lakes empty into the sea by means of the River Laune. The Iveragh Peninsula also has a number of coastal and upland lakes, such as Lough Currane and Lough Caragh. Small mountain lakes are also found in Cork (near Inchageelagh).

Mesolithic lake settlement

Introduction

The evidence for Mesolithic settlement in Ireland derives principally from a small number of site excavations and the character and distribution of worked stone recovered from ploughed fields, riverine deposits, raised beach deposits and coastal midden sites (Cooney and Grogan 1994; Harbison 1988; Mallory and Hartwell 1997; O'Kelly 1989; Woodman 1978; 1985; Woodman and Anderson 1990). Mesolithic hunter-gatherers were clearly present throughout the island from earliest times, operating either from seasonal base-camps or moving continuously through a largely wooded landscape, with natural clearances along rivers and the coast (Mitchell and Ryan 1997). Most Mesolithic sites are found in low-lying areas close to water, along the island's coastline, rivers and lakes. Mesolithic subsistence strategies in Ireland were influenced by the island's limited fauna and flora in the early post-glacial period, and were based primarily on fishing, plant food gathering, and the hunting of small mammals such as hare and wild pig (Cooney, forthcoming; Cooney and Grogan 1994; Woodman 1978).

The Irish Mesolithic has been divided into Early and Late periods, largely on the basis of marked changes in lithic typologies. The Early Mesolithic (7500–6500 BC) has been characterised by a microlithic flint industry with flake and core axes, similar to toolkits in contemporary north-west Europe (Anderson and Johnson 1995; Woodman 1978). Early Mesolithic microliths were probably used in composite tools, such as harpoons and fishing spears, but may also have been used in plant-processing (Nyree Finlay, pers. comm.; Woodman 1978). The Late Mesolithic (5500–3800 BC) period has, in contrast, a uniquely Irish lithic industry dominated by heavy flint and chert flakes produced by a hard hammer percussion technique. The two most diagnostic artefact types are the single-platformed, uniplane flint cores and the retouched/butt-trimmed forms that are described under the broad term 'Bann flakes', named after the River Bann valley where they were first recorded in numbers. Bann flakes and Larnian cores only occur together on sites dated to the final phases of the Irish Mesolithic (Anderson and Johnson 1995; Woodman 1978). Ground stone axes and a limited range of scrapers, picks and burins are also common (Woodman and Anderson 1990). It has been proposed that this insular Late Mesolithic lithic industry represents a new population influx, although the lack of British or European parallels makes this most unlikely. It is more probable that the Late Mesolithic in Ireland represents an insular, indigenous development, with little evidence for outside contacts (Mallory and Hartwell 1997, 3; Mitchell 1987).

Early Mesolithic settlements that have been the subject of archaeological excavations include Mount Sandel, Co. Derry (Woodman 1985), and Lough Boora, Co. Offaly (Ryan 1980). At Mount Sandel, several circular hut sites, hearths and pits were found on bluffs overlooking the River Bann. The site's lithic technology was dominated by small blades or microliths, including scalene triangles, rods, needles and obliquely blunted points. The core types used were single- and dual-platformed cores worked in a circular fashion. The presence of such food debris as hazelnuts, wild pig bone, salmon and eel bone and water-lily seeds suggested the year-round exploitation of seasonal resources. Mount Sandel has been interpreted as a base-camp which could have been occupied for much of the year, only the late winter being a period of potential food scarcity (Woodman 1985). The Early Mesolithic lake settlement of Lough Boora will be discussed below. Late Mesolithic sites have most commonly been investigated in coastal locations, such as at Bay Farm, Co. Antrim (Woodman and Johnson 1996), Dalkey Island, Co. Dublin (Liversage 1968), Sutton, Co. Dublin (Mitchell 1972), and Ferriter's Cove, Co. Kerry (Woodman and O'Brien 1993). There have also been some Mesolithic discoveries in river valleys, such as at Newferry, Co. Antrim, on the lower River Bann (Woodman 1977), at Kilcummer on the River Blackwater valley, Co. Cork (Anderson 1993), and along the River Barrow valley (Zvelebil *et al.* 1996).

However, very few Mesolithic occupation sites in Ireland have produced domestic structures, palaeobotanical evidence or good organic preservation. In contrast, several European Mesolithic occupation sites in Denmark (e.g. Ertebolle, Tybrind Vig), The Netherlands (e.g. Hazendonk), France (e.g. Noyen-sur-Seine) and Poland (e.g. Friesack) have been excavated under waterlogged conditions, leading to the recognition there of the potential complexity of Mesolithic material culture. Mesolithic wetland sites have produced such finds as finely made dugout canoes, ornate decorated paddles, complex fishing equipment and wooden implements (B.J. Coles and Coles 1989; J.M. Coles and Coles 1996). In the absence of an excavated waterlogged settlement site in Ireland (Mitchell and Ryan 1997), Mesolithic studies concentrate on typological developments in lithic technologies and on the procurement strategies (mostly) for flint and chert. The understanding of subsistence strategies is based on a few excavated faunal and palaeobotanical assemblages, suggesting the hunting of wild pig, hare and red deer, salmon-, trout- and eel-fishing, fowling and the gathering of such plant foods as hazelnuts, crab-apples and water-lilies. Red deer were not present in large numbers and appear to have played little or no role in the Irish Mesolithic diet (van Wijngaarden-Bakker 1989).

There have been some recent attempts to interpret the Mesolithic in terms of both social organisation, settlement and subsistence strategies. Traditionally, the interpretation of Mesolithic settlement in Ireland envisaged a shift from a stable, semi-sedentary pattern in the Early Mesolithic period to a highly mobile one in the Late Mesolithic (Mallory and Hartwell 1997; Woodman 1978). In the Early Mesolithic, this model envisaged that families and bands moved seasonally from coastal sites in the spring to inland lakes and rivers for the summer and autumn runs of salmon and eel, to upland hunting of wild pig for the winter. Certain favourable locations, such as Mount Sandel, could have attracted longer-term settlement in the form of base-camps. In the Late Mesolithic, because most known settlement sites seem to be only short-stay/specialised function camps and there appears to have been a shift in lithic procurement strategies, it is believed that there was a change to a highly mobile, low-density economy (Woodman 1986). It is possible that this technological shift may have made residential camps much more difficult to identify (Woodman and Anderson 1990, 381, 386). In terms of lithic production, the transition is often seen as a change from an efficient, complex use of resources with a scheduled procurement strategy in the Early Mesolithic to an inefficient, expedient use of resources in an embedded procurement scheme in the Late Mesolithic (Cross 1996; Mallory and McNeill 1991, 25; Woodman 1978, 146, 188).

Mesolithic settlement and subsistence strategies in Ireland have recently been the subject of a radical reinterpretation, envisaging a model of increasing sedentariness from the Early Mesolithic to the Late Mesolithic. This interpretation runs parallel with much interpretation for north-west Europe, although it has to be admitted that present Irish archaeological evidence cannot sustain this model. However, it could also be pointed out that previous interpretations are largely based on a single Early Mesolithic base-camp, Mount Sandel, Co. Derry. The reinterpretation additionally implies a role for Late Mesolithic societies in the introduction of farming and their own transformation to an Early Neolithic society. There has also been debate about the degree of overlap between the Mesolithic and the Neolithic and the role of hunter-gatherers in the introduction of farming (Cooney and Grogan 1994; Cross 1996). It is possible that there was some continuity of Mesolithic forager-fisher groups and their mobile subsistence economy well into the Neolithic period (e.g. O'Sullivan 1997b).

Mesolithic lake settlement in Ireland

In the early post-glacial period the Irish midlands would have been substantially more waterlogged than today, with open bodies of water where there are now bogs, and lakes that were much larger in extent (Mitchell 1972; Mitchell and Ryan 1997). The landscape went through important changes, with the development of oak, elm and pine woodlands towards the end of the period. There are various reasons why we might expect Mesolithic settlement activities along Irish lakes. The resources of Irish freshwater wetlands are well known, from the fish (salmon, eel, trout, charr, pollan, perch and tench), waterfowl and plants to the animal life of fen, carr woodlands and hazel woods that fringe lakes and rivers. The hypothetical importance of plant foods in the Mesolithic diet has been discussed, but too few studies of waterlogged palaeobotanical material have been carried out to clinch the argument. We might also expect Mesolithic settlement in these locations for the practical reasons of travel and communications, as lakes and rivers were the most open parts of a heavily wooded landscape, the waterways providing a means of movement through the landscape. The gradual filling in of these lake basins by fen peat and later by raised bogs and rising lake levels means that much of the Mesolithic settlement zone is probably covered (Cooney 1987, 59). This has led to some pessimism about the chances of uncovering Mesolithic settlement sites in the absence of large-scale, modern landscape change (i.e. peat-cutting or drainage works).

However, there have been significant lakeshore discoveries from the period, with individual site excavations at the Early Mesolithic site at Lough Boora, Co. Offaly (Ryan 1980), and at Late Mesolithic sites at Clonava, Lough Derravarragh, Co. Westmeath (Mitchell 1972), and at Moynagh Lough, Co. Meath (J. Bradley 1991). There is extensive archaeological evidence for Mesolithic activities around the shores of Lough Neagh, as well as downstream from the lake on the lower River Bann, at Newferry (Woodman 1978). Late Mesolithic lithic scatter assemblages have also been gathered from lakeshores at Derragh, Lough Kinale, Co. Longford (Mitchell 1972), Cullenhugh, Lough Iron, Co. Westmeath (Mitchell 1972), at various locations on Lough Gara, Co. Sligo, and at Cormonaghan and Drummans Lower, on Lough Allen, Co. Leitrim (NMI files; Condit and Gibbons 1989; Mitchell 1972), as well as several other lakes elsewhere in the midlands and north-west (Woodman 1978). Although undated, the frequent presence of diagnostic forms (butt-trimmed Bann flakes, bar forms, uniplanar cores, core picks) confirms a Late Mesolithic date for most of these lithic scatters (Woodman 1978). They appear on occasion to have been associated with stone platforms or mounds, suggesting that it may be possible to associate the lithic scatters with actual domestic structures.

This lakeshore archaeology has generally been neglected in Mesolithic studies and surprisingly little has been done to examine the individual sites in detail. There has been no attempt either to systematically sample these lithic scatters or to excavate for subsoil or organic structures or artefacts. No underwater surveys or excavations have been carried out in the shallow lake waters in the vicinity of known lithic scatters. There has been little or no attempt to search the wider landscape for Mesolithic evidence. If these lakeshore sites were occupied as part of a seasonal circuit, then other short-stay/specialised sites and base-camps must be located on the lakeshores, islands, neighbouring hillslopes and upland ridges of the midlands. It must also be presumed that early post-glacial lake marls and lakeshores are by now exposed at many different locations in the Irish midland bogs, but Irish archaeology has taken little cognisance of this fact. It is therefore highly probable that lakeshore sites under bogland, such as that found at Lough Boora, remain to be discovered and investigated using multidisciplinary archaeological techniques. The evidence for Mesolithic lake settlement archaeology will now be reviewed in detail.

Early Mesolithic settlement

Lough Boora, Co. Offaly

The Early Mesolithic lake settlement at Lough Boora, Co. Offaly, is a vitally important site in Irish prehistory, indicating a human presence in the Irish midlands by at least 7000 BC (Ryan 1978; 1980; 1984). Boora bog, near Kilcormac, Co. Offaly, was once one of the largest raised bogs in the Irish midlands. In the 1940s, a small peat-floored lake in the middle of the bog was drained by Bord na Móna (Pl. 14). In 1976,

Pl. 14—*Aerial photograph of Lough Boora, Co. Offaly, taken in the 1950s, showing the modern lake in the peat basin, with the post-glacial shoreline emerging from the peats. A hunter-gatherer community living on the original lakeshore caught fish, wildfowl and wild pig in the wetlands (photo: National Museum of Ireland).*

peat-harvesting within the lake basin exposed what appeared to be a causeway and a crannog. The National Museum staff recognised that these were natural geomorphological features, the 'causeway' being the eastern storm beach of an early post-glacial lake (which was probably originally about 320ha in area) and the knoll being a natural peninsula in the lake (Ryan 1984, 407; Feehan and O'Donovan 1996, 449). However, the site produced evidence of human occupation and was excavated in 1977 (Ryan 1978; 1980; 1984), combined with a pollen-sampling and stratigraphical coring programme by Michael O'Connell (1980). A detailed study of molluscs and ostracods was carried out near the site in 1989 (Griffiths 1985, 196–215), upon much of which the following landscape reconstruction is based.

The early post-glacial lake of Lough Boora would originally have been connected to the River Shannon by the River Boora and the Silver River. This connection was lost and the lake obliterated by later fen peat formation, while much later again the modern lake formed in the basin. It is likely that the former hydrology was very different to that of today. The mollusc and ostracod studies indicate a cool, temperate, shallow-water lake (depth 3–8m), calcareous, nutrient-rich and biologically productive. The edges of the lake were swampy, with abundant amounts of marsh fern indicating a fen environment, merging towards the drylands with alder carr woodland. The lake changed little during the early post-glacial; occasionally wetter conditions caused the waters to deepen and the littoral areas became more swampy (Griffiths 1985, 212–14). There was evidently some dryland woodland in the vicinity, as pine, oak and elm pollen was recorded (Ryan 1980). However, there was little palaeoenvironmental indication of any human impact on the woodlands (O'Connell 1980). The presence of red deer and wild pig suggests that at least some of the landscape was fairly open, with patches of grassland and herbs amongst the woods.

The Early Mesolithic occupation layer was situated on a relatively dry peninsula jutting out into the lake. It was spread over a large area (over $2000m^2$) and rested on a thin, uneven deposit of silty clay. The occupation was composed of a series of hearths,

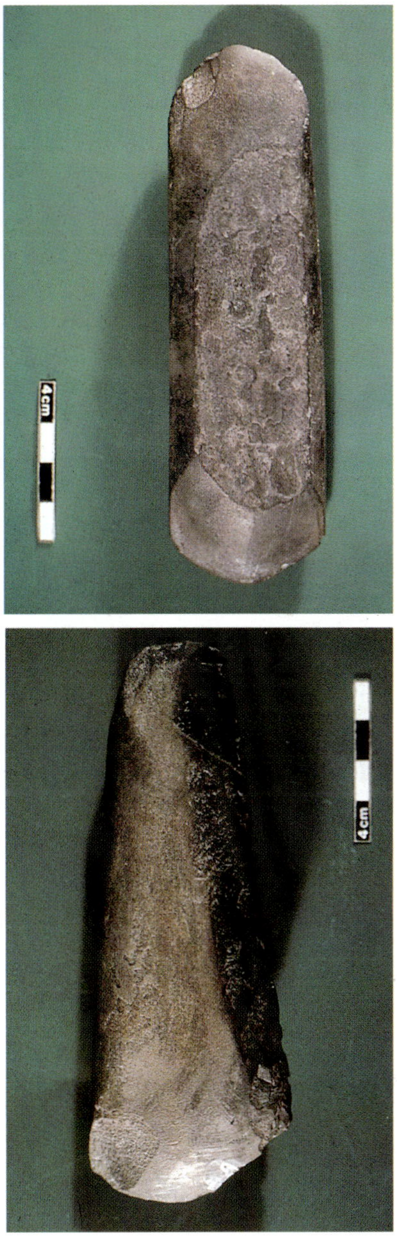

Pl. 15—*Early Mesolithic axes (right), chert cores (above), and flint and chert blades (top) from Lough Boora (photo: National Museum of Ireland).*

a stone-working area with spreads of charcoal, charred food remains, stone tools, cores and flakes (Ryan 1984). At least fourteen principal hearths were recorded. Charcoal from the hearths containing microliths provided radiocarbon dates of 8475 ± 75 BP (6525 BC; UB-2199), 8350 ± 70 BP (6400 BC; UB-2200), 8450 ± 70 BP (6500 BC; UB-2267), and 8980 ± 360 BP (7030 BC; UB-2268). A large number of artefacts were recovered, including over 200 microliths (including mostly rod forms, with needle points and scalene triangles), 424 chert and 90 flint blades, 20 chert scrapers, several ground stone axes and chert debitage, including some 200 cores (Pl. 15). The chert could have been locally gathered, although it was of a poor quality. Shales and limestones were used for the stone axes. Although there was no palaeoenvironmental or sieving programme, much was recovered about the site economy. The large faunal assemblage, much of it charred and calcined, included red deer, wild pig (mostly from immature animals), hares, birds and fish. The bones of Giant Irish Deer were also found, but clearly stratified in earlier layers pre-dating the archaeological horizons. Eel and trout were probably caught by the Lough Boora inhabitants in large numbers (van Wijngaarden-Bakker 1989). Hazelnut shells were abundant. Ryan (1980; 1984, 409) has pointed out the importance of the site for the interpretation of the Irish Mesolithic and has stated that it is unlikely to have been unique in the midlands despite the impression created by the lack of antiquarian activity in the region and the growth of peat.

Lough Boora appears to have been the wetland settlement site of a band of Early Mesolithic hunter-gatherers. Hunting wild pig and duck, fishing for eel and trout, and the gathering of plant foods were all important activities. The extent of the population of the site is difficult to determine; repeated visits by a small group might leave the same archaeological traces as one or two visits by a large group. Although structures were not apparently found, light huts, tents or wind-breaks might not have left much trace. Some shelter might have been provided by trees and bushes growing along the lake margins. It is clear that the lake would have been quite large, with a substantial wind-fetch producing strong waves and a storm beach. This was a large body of open water, but it was probably backed by extensive woodlands, marshes and fens. If the Early Mesolithic base-camp and extraction camp model of subsistence is accepted, then Lough Boora may have been an extraction or hunting camp occupied through the summer and early autumn by a community inhabiting the esker hills to the south. Alternatively, we may be looking at the activities of a much more widely ranging group, who travelled to this location from the coast.

Late Mesolithic settlement

Lough Derravarragh, Co. Westmeath

Late Mesolithic hunter-gatherers are known to have been present on a lakeshore at Clonava, at the north-west end of Lough Derravarragh, Co. Westmeath (Pl. 16). The archaeological evidence for their activities consists of lithic assemblages excavated *in situ* in fen peats exposed on the foreshore (Cooney 1987, 61–4; Mitchell 1972). The same drainage works on the River Inny which exposed Mesolithic material here also revealed sites on Lough Kinale and Lough Iron. Clonava was formerly a large island of

Pl. 16—*Aerial photograph taken in 1963, looking across Lough Derravarragh towards Clonava, Co. Westmeath. Frank Mitchell's excavations on the shore of this wetland 'island' produced a range of Late Mesolithic occupation evidence (photo: CUCAP AHH 43; reproduced with the permission of the Cambridge Committee for Aerial Photography).*

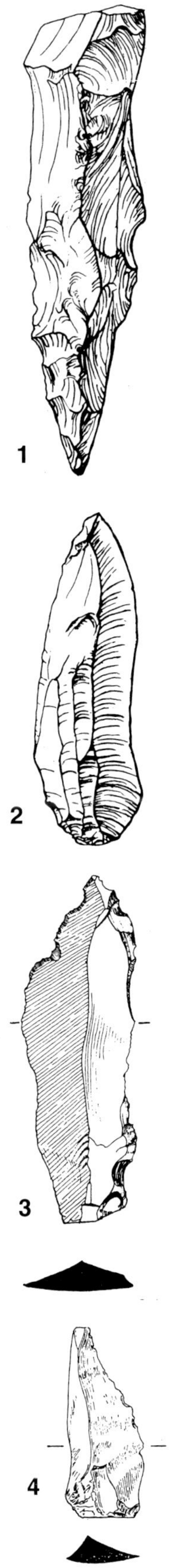

glacial till and bedrock, with chert outcrops in the limestone bedrock exposed along the foreshore situated in a vast area of wetlands. The Mesolithic scatters at Clonava were first noted as stray finds on the exposed foreshore between the inlet and the outlet of the River Inny, but these appeared mostly to be water-rolled and scattered about through riverine erosion. Frank Mitchell's excavations revealed small areas of *in situ* material, buried under small knolls of uneroded peat. He discovered that one of the uneroded knolls (Clonava Site 1) contained worked stone and charcoal in context in the peats over an area of $4m^2$. Woodman (1978, 321) re-inspected the site and recovered a polished stone axe, a pointed pick and a distally trimmed Bann flake from the foreshore. Cooney (1987, 62–4) also recovered struck chert flakes at Clonkeen, Co. Westmeath, just to the south-west of Clonava 1, further downstream on the course of the River Inny.

Clonava Site 1 was located to the north of Clonava island on the south bank of the River Inny. This was a small area of undisturbed material on a knoll of fen peat where a scatter of charcoal and struck chert could be traced in the fen peat and raised bog section by the riverbank. A small cutting ($4m^2$) was excavated in Site 1. Fen peat separated a lower, middle and top layer of chert waste. The basal layer was the main deposit. Two scatters of debitage were also found on the top and sides of the peat knoll. The main occupation layer, the lowest, was composed of charcoal, wood, hazelnuts, chert implements and debitage, and angular fragments of burnt sandstone. Charcoal provided a radiocarbon date of 3410 ± 110 uncal. BC (5360 ± 110 BP; I-4234). At the centre of this layer was a thicker mass of debitage, suggesting that this was the site of chert-knapping. Three implements were recovered during the excavations, along with 100 pieces of chert debitage (Fig. 8).

The Clonava Site 1 excavation was also significant in that an attempt was made to establish, through macrofossil studies, the original environmental conditions and economic activities on the site. Plants identified included water sedge, hazelnuts, yellow water-lily, buttercup, marsh woundwort and guelder rose. Charred hazelnuts and seeds of yellow water-lily (*Nuphar luteum*) were also found. The seeds and rhizomes of this plant are both edible. The seeds were randomly distributed through the samples, suggesting that they had not naturally fallen from the flower-head. Mitchell (1972, 165) interpreted this as evidence for food preparation by the Mesolithic inhabitants. He reconstructed the original environment of the sites through palaeobotanical studies in the fen peats. The landscape was a stretch of fen beside the lake, which had been dissected by numerous channels as the River Inny entered Lough Derravarragh. Mitchell suggested that the worked stone was the result of Mesolithic wildfowlers or fishers procuring and preparing chert implements while waiting by the lakeshore. The numerous mounds of stone and charcoal were therefore regarded as the result of 'casual

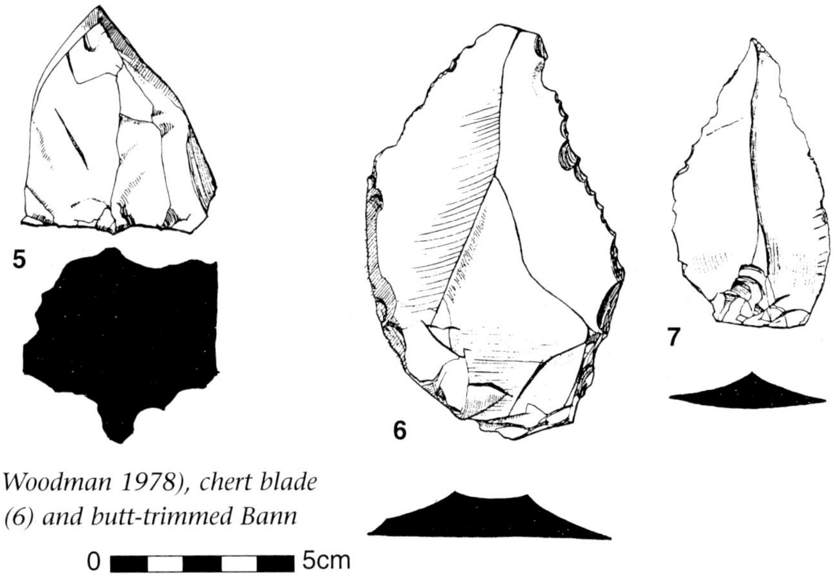

Fig. 8—*Late Mesolithic flint and chert artefacts from Clonava Site 1, Co. Westmeath. They include a pointed pick (1), a distally trimmed Bann flake (2) (after Woodman 1978), chert blade (3), flint point (4), chert core (5), chert flake (6) and butt-trimmed Bann flake (7) (after Mitchell 1972).*

visits' rather than long-term occupation. However, it is also possible that the island itself could have been the focus of longer-term occupation (Cooney 1987, 63).

Cooney (1987, 61–4) has reconstructed the landscape of the original Clonava site and its surrounding catchment on the basis of soils, drainage and topography. The early post-glacial landscape would have been drastically different to that of today. Clonava would have been an island of glacial till, some 2km in total length and 850m wide, set in a waterlogged landscape of lake, fen and marshy ground with the River Inny flowing through it. The chert outcrops were undoubtedly an attraction for Mesolithic hunter-gatherers, but the abundant wetland resources would also have been a factor in local settlement patterns. Lough Derravarragh today has large seasonal populations of mallard, coot, pochard and tufted duck. Brown trout are common in the lake, while eel and arctic charr may also have been present at the time. Clonava would have been well placed to catch eels moving down the River Inny on their autumn migration. The wetlands would have been fringed by willow, birch, pine and alder, and the drylands and island would have had a mantle of elm, oak and hazel woodlands. Presumably wild pig, hare and wildfowl would have been present in these woods. These wetlands and woodlands would have been high in food resources, not only in summer and autumn but throughout much of the year.

Lough Kinale, Co. Longford

Several Late Mesolithic lithic scatters were also found on the southern shore of Lough Kinale, at Derragh townland, Co. Longford. Lough Kinale is a small lake, partly enclosed by raised bog and drained by the River Inny, which flows into the lake from Lough Sheelin to the west. The drainage operations on the River Inny in the late 1960s which had exposed the Clonava material had also caused a large area of lake foreshore to be exposed, with extensive lithic scatters revealed on the lake muds. Three individ-

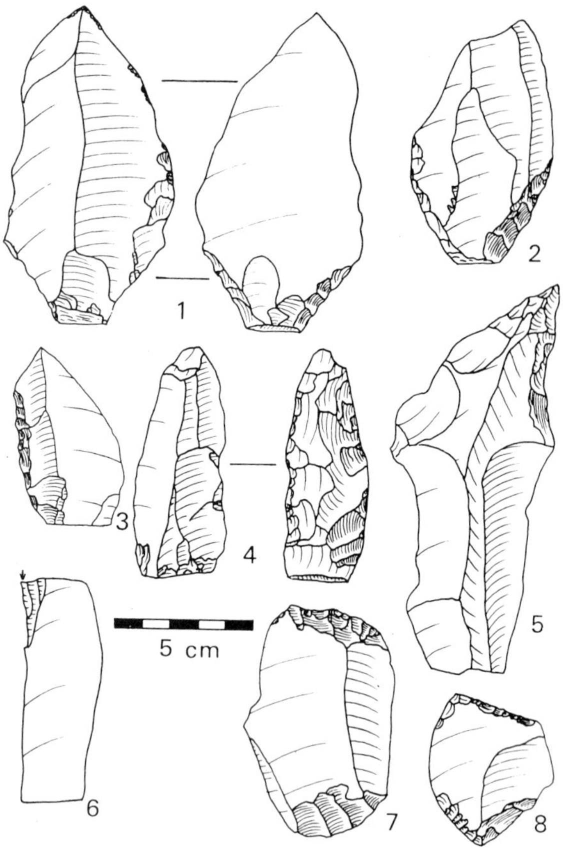

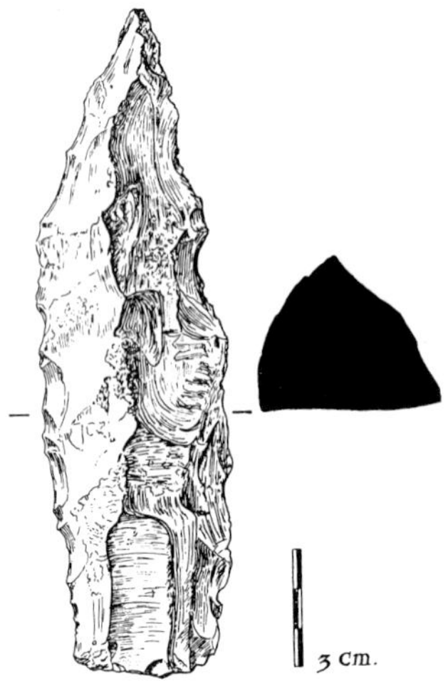

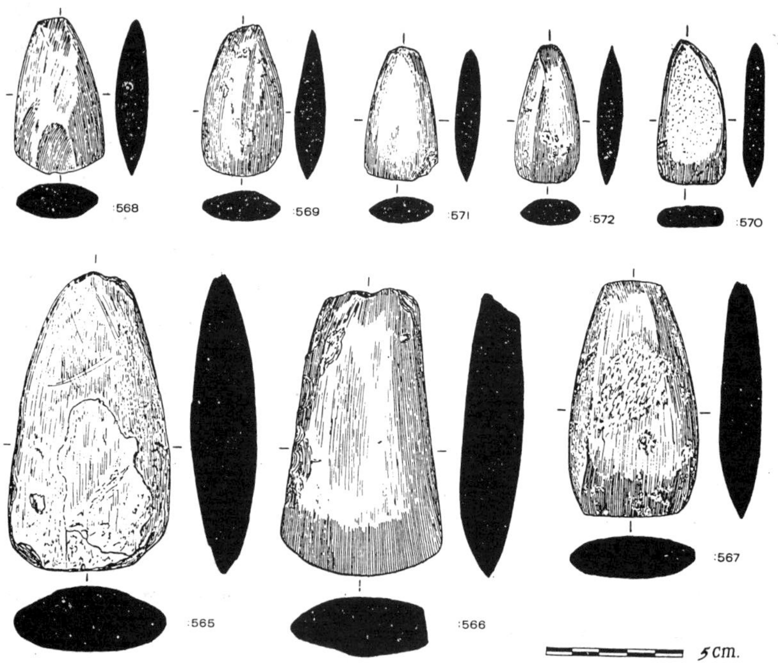

Fig. 9—*Late Mesolithic chert artefacts from a lakeshore occupation at Derragh, Co. Longford, on the southern shore of Lough Kinale. They include butt-trimmed Bann flakes, backed knives, bar forms, points, burins, scrapers and arrowheads (top) (after Woodman 1978), as well as a chert pick (above) and numerous stone axes (left) (after J. Raftery 1972).*

ual sites or scatters were recorded by field-walking and random collection (Cooney 1987, 64–6, figs 44–6; Mitchell 1970; J. Raftery 1972, 183, 187–90; 1973, 178–9, 181–2; Woodman 1978, 317). Butt-trimmed Bann flakes were found to the east, on the north bank of the River Inny, in Kilgolagh, Co. Cavan. Mitchell (1970, 7) also recorded lithic finds on the abandoned banks of the River Inny and at its new outlet from the southern shore of Derragh Lough. A large butt-trimmed Bann flake was found more recently in a bog at Derrysheridan, on the southern shore of Lough Sheelin, 4.5km to the east (Cooney 1987, vol. 2, 5).

Derragh Site 1 seems to have been the most productive site. It was located to the west of the original outlet of the River Inny, on an exposed peaty foreshore. The sites had been covered in peat which is now washed away (Cooney 1987, 65). There was a slightly rounded mound, *c.* 50cm in height and 15m in diameter. There were horizontal timbers, but it is unclear whether or not these were worked. The mound may have been a natural knoll rising slightly above the surrounding ground. A spread of loosely scattered flakes, axeheads and hammerstones occurred in the central area of the mound. A random collection of about 579 separate objects was deposited in the National Museum of Ireland. The finds (Fig. 9) included sixteen stone axes which varied in size, some being as short as 4.3cm. There were 81 Bann flakes of flint or chert, chert picks, a trapezoidal chert core, nine waste flakes and three hammerstones on the surface (Lucas 1989). Woodman's (1978) lithic analyses identified Mesolithic burins, scrapers and other implements in the Lough Kinale assemblage. Mitchell (1970, 7) also mentions finding a 'slug-knife and a fish-tail scraper', reputedly of Neolithic date. A Late Neolithic macehead is known from Finnea, on the River Inny. It is possible that this was actually found at Lough Kinale (Simpson 1990). Derragh Site 2 was located immediately to the west on the shore of the glacial till island. On the foreshore of this rise many finds were recovered, including 57 chert flakes, a small polished stone axe and a possible hammerstone. Derragh Site 3 was situated further westwards again along the peaty foreshore material, in amongst reeds. It produced 24 chert flakes, five stone axes and a hammerstone.

The Lough Kinale assemblage is, at first glance, an intimidatingly large assemblage of seemingly contextless material. It appears to be a discrete collection of artefacts, potentially from actual lakeshore occupation sites, probably short-stay or specialised function camps. This may have been a site for lithic production. Experimental flint-working indicates that large amounts of waste can build up on a knapping site over a surprisingly short period of time (i.e. hours), and it is evident that much of the Lough Kinale material comprises heavy primary struck flakes on which there was little evidence for secondary retouch. However, implements and blades are also present, butt-trimmed Bann flakes and stone axes are common, while burins, scrapers, points, bar forms, picks, core borers, backed knives, distally trimmed flakes and an arrowhead were also found (Woodman 1978, 316–17; Woodman and Anderson 1990, fig. 7). The presence of such a high number of stone axes is intriguing; indeed, the occupants of the site may have been involved in the production of stone axes. Cooney (1987) examined the stone axes from Lough Kinale and noted their generally small size. Petrological analysis was carried out on five stone axes from Lough Kinale, indicating that they were of greywacke and mudstone. These rocks would have been easily obtainable in the midland landscape (Woodman and Johnson 1991–2). Local river pebbles could have been quickly ground to axe shapes.

Cooney (1987, 64–7) has traced the original landscape setting of the Lough Kinale lithic scatters. The archaeological sites are now situated on the northern shore of an island of glacial till, with extensive raised bogs and a lake (Derragh Lough) to the south. In the Late Mesolithic, it is likely that Derragh was an island in a vast area of wetlands, stretching from Lough Sheelin to Lough Derravarragh. Limestone ridges were found to the west and small lakes amidst drumlin hills were located to the north. Oak woodlands would have dominated these drylands, but the lakes, fens and rivers would have provided an easier means of travel. The Lough Kinale sites, well located on an island

Pl. 17—*Aerial photograph of Moynagh Lough, Co. Westmeath. John Bradley's recent excavations on this multiperiod crannog have revealed that Late Mesolithic hunter-gatherers occupied two clay knolls on the shores of the original lake. The site was subsequently reoccupied through the Neolithic, Bronze Age and Early Historic periods (photo: Con Brogan).*

surrounded by wetlands, could have exploited waterfowl, while the siting by the River Inny flowing out of Lough Sheelin would have been well placed for catching salmon and eel.

Lough Iron, Co. Westmeath

Late Mesolithic lithic assemblages were also gathered from the north-east shore of Lough Iron, Co. Westmeath, a smaller lake to the south-west of Lough Derravarragh, 6km downstream on the River Inny. Drainage works led to deep excavation at the mouth of the River Inny. Mitchell (1970) mentions finding a flint core axe and various flakes in a thin, black shore sand at the mouth of the river on the eastern shore of the lough. Further to the south, in Cullenhugh townland, local landowners discovered in 1969 two crannogs, a dugout canoe, stone axes, Bann flakes and other artefacts. The site was visited by Joseph Raftery. Forty-one Bann flakes, several cores and waste flakes and two ground stone axes of limestone and mudstone were picked up on the foreshore. A crannog or low stone mound, 11m in diameter and 25cm in height, was also noted, from the surface of which a medieval bronze buckle was recovered. The Mesolithic finds were made on the neighbouring muddy foreshore.

Moynagh Lough, Co. Meath

At Moynagh Lough, Co. Meath, a Late Mesolithic hunter-gatherer group is known to have occupied two low clay knolls (measuring 10.5m and 9m across) that formed dry patches in a former lake on the River Dee (J. Bradley 1982–3, 12–19; 1984, 86; 1991) (Pl. 17). The clay knolls had relatively steep sides and had been deliberately enhanced by spreading lake mud and stones across them, with a layer of brushwood and twigs thrown down at the water's edge. This was identified as hazel (*Corylus* sp.) and bramble (*Rubus*), with various wetland margin plants (including *Alisma*, *Plantago lanceolata*, *Ranunculus* and *Carex*). Worked stone included a range of chert and flint objects, chert being much more common; 160 pieces of chert and flint were recovered from a layer of charcoal-flecked mud, including two cores, 49 implements, 33 flakes and 83 chert chips. The implements included leaf-shaped, pointed and parallel butt-trimmed flakes. The chert, outcrops of which occur within a few miles of the site, was of variable quality. Fifty-three pieces of flint were recovered, including one core, but the group was mostly comprised of tiny flint chips. A radiocarbon date of 4313–3980 BC (5270 ± 60 BP; GrN-11443) was obtained from a charcoal sample (J. Bradley 1984, 86). John Bradley (1991) suggested that the site may indicate that Late Mesolithic communities were penetrating the landscape by moving up along the River Dee, but pointed out that Earlier Mesolithic activity is also known in the region. This Late Mesolithic phase of occupation will be the subject of the final season's excavation at Moynagh Lough (John Bradley, pers. comm.).

The Late Mesolithic site at Moynagh Lough (which was also occupied in the Bronze Age and the Early Historic period, see below) lay at the southern margins of a medium-sized lake, in a location sheltered by a steep upland ridge to the south and west. The surrounding topography is primarily one of rolling hills dissected by relatively narrow river valleys. There are only a few small lakes within a 10km radius, such as at Whitewood Lake to the north-west. The River Dee catchment lies beside that of the Moynalty River, which is a tributary of the River Blackwater. It would have been easy for Mesolithic hunter-gatherers to reach the Irish Sea coast by dugout boat. The original landscape would not have been as wet and waterlogged as that of Lough Kinale or Lough Derravarragh; deciduous woodlands would probably have been the dominant ecosystem. These woodlands, of oak, elm and hazel, would have been dissected by rivers, with some lakes and marshes which in turn were fringed by alder and willow carrs. Moynagh Lough could have been the sheltered short-stay procurement camp of a hunter-gatherer community moving through this landscape, perhaps coming from, or going to, the coastline. Activities on the site included some working of chert and flint, but few traces of food remains have yet emerged. It is also worth noting that Late Mesolithic Bann flakes are known from elsewhere in this region (J. Bradley 1991; Cooney 1987, 68; Woodman 1978).

Pl. 18—*Archaeologists inspecting a spread of stones exposed on the foreshore of Lough Gara in 1952. Joseph Raftery commented that these small stone cairns typically produced Late Mesolithic Bann flakes, stone axes and animal bone (photo: Dept of Archaeology, UCG).*

Lough Gara, Co. Sligo

There is also abundant, yet largely unexplored, archaeological evidence for Late Mesolithic lakeshore occupations at Lough Gara, Co. Sligo. This includes a range of lithic scatters recovered from the foreshore after drainage operations, some of which may have been associated with stone and wooden structures. Late Mesolithic, Neolithic and Bronze Age chert and flint artefacts were recovered in abundance on the Lough Gara foreshore by Joseph Raftery and Frank Mitchell in the 1950s. Prehistoric and historic cairns, mounds and crannogs were also exposed at the same time on this foreshore. Raftery (1957, 7) classified these mounds into three different types. Type 1 were small circular crannogs or flat mounds of small, occasionally fire-cracked, stones. Timber, brushwood and vertical posts were occasionally found on the surface of the mounds. They were typically on a thin layer of dark mud, indicating that they had been built on a reedy, shallow-water environment. The mounds varied in shape, being oval or circular, ranging in diameter from 4m to 15m overall, but typically in the region of 10m. They were rarely higher than 45cm (Pl. 18). In several cases the mounds were grouped in lines along the foreshore. They occasionally had stone (and sometimes wooden) causeways leading towards them. The finds from these Type 1 mounds included charcoal, animal bone, polished stone axes, pounding or hammerstones and 'hundreds of implements made of flakes of a great variety of stones—flint, chert, limestone, sandstone etc. Many of these are waste flakes but many are finished artefacts of an interesting and important group to which the name "Bann flake" has been given' (J. Raftery 1957). Raftery noted their similarity to the Bann flakes from the River Bann in north-east Ireland, and stated that one Type 1 mound appeared to be a workshop site, as it produced 'all the items which went to the production of Bann flakes'.

'Crannog' no. 7 at Coolnagranshy, Co. Roscommon, produced Bann flakes, large waste flakes, cores and hammerstones and a number of polished stone axeheads. The finds came from a mound measuring 15m in length by 6.5m in width, 'held in position by birch piles'. Frank Mitchell's analysis of peat in the mound indicated a Late Mesolithic date for the occupation (J. Raftery, forthcoming b). At Tawnymucklagh, two polished axeheads, a portion of a stone chisel, oval hammerstones and a chert pick were recovered, along with arrowheads and scrapers on the north crannog. In Emlagh townland there were four mounds, 3–7m apart. On the southern shore of Inch Island several small sites were grouped together to form a continuous layer stretching over 30m. The metalling sites occasionally produced later material, such as a Late Bronze Age sunflower pin, but Raftery considered these to be later deposits.

Raftery counted as many as 300 'metalling' sites on the shores of Lough Gara. He pointed out that several other lakes in the region had such metalling sites. He recorded five on Lough Scur, Co. Leitrim, five on Cavetown Lough, and several on Clooncally Lake, on Croghan Lake and at Kilronan. In a rapid superficial survey, twenty examples were noted on Lough Allen. All these mounds had several things in common—a thin metalling layer, some wooden piles, small amounts of animal bone, charcoal, stone axes and Bann flakes. Raftery interpreted these sites as possible foundations for wooden huts or tents. He noted their clustering and proposed that they represented contemporary lake habitations.

What was the chronology and function of these mounds? The presence of large chert blades and flakes and stone axes does not preclude a later date. Bann flakes and stone axes were found on the Early Historic layers at Crannog 61, Rathtinaun, Co. Sligo. The flakes may have been produced on-site for use as tools, while the stone axes may have been used as linen smoothers (J. Raftery, forthcoming b). However, it is also possible that the inhabitants of the Early Historic crannog were simply gathering prehistoric artefacts from the lake foreshore, much as the archaeologists of the 1950s themselves had done at Lough Gara. Some symbolic or magical values may have been attached to these objects. It is also possible, given the abundance of the lithic assemblages at Lough Gara, that the Early Historic crannog-builders had simply accidentally incorporated them into the structural and habitation layers of the crannog. In any case,

Woodman's (1978) analysis of the Lough Gara lithic assemblages confirms that they are indeed primarily Late Mesolithic in date, while more recently it has been suggested that Early Mesolithic worked stone was also present at Lough Gara (Nyree Finlay, pers. comm.). What was the association between these Mesolithic assemblages and the stone and wooden structures? A definite link between the 'metalling' sites and the Mesolithic artefacts has never been clearly established. The worked stone may actually have been eroded out of the peats on the foreshore (although this would still indicate lakeshore occupation). The stone mounds may well be much later in date; they could have been Bronze Age lake settlements or small stone structures associated with Early Historic crannogs. Indeed, Christina Fredengren has recently excavated a small stone mound at Tivannagh as part of the Lough Gara Crannog Project. These excavations indicate several phases of occupation, few finds and some animal bone, but the site appears to be post-medieval in origin (Fredengren 1988a; 1998b).

But Joseph Raftery's contemporary accounts unambiguously state that the finds from these metalling sites exclusively comprised Bann flakes, polished stone axeheads and hammerstones. If his accounts are to be accepted, and he was the man on the spot, then it seems likely that the lakeshores of Lough Gara, Co. Sligo, had exposed in the 1950s a series of potential Late Mesolithic occupation sites with tools, debitage, animal bone and organic features. The interpretation of these sites is obviously difficult, given that none were excavated or even recorded in detail, but presumably they were short-stay camps associated with hunting, fishing and lithic production on the lakeshore and in the vicinity of the River Boyle.

Lough Allen, Co. Leitrim

Late Mesolithic assemblages are also known from the shores of Lough Allen, Co. Leitrim. Late Mesolithic assemblages have been found at Drummans Lower, Co. Leitrim, on the north-west shore of the lough. In 1968 a dry summer led to falling water-levels, and Frank Mitchell and Patrick Healy collected 'Bann flakes, plunging flakes, concave step-flakes, a small core, flakes and general debris' (Mitchell 1970). At Cormonaghan, on the south-east corner of the lough, local amateur archaeologists recovered more finds from the lakeshore in the early autumn of 1977 (a particularly dry summer) on a foreshore which was found to 'be littered with innumerable worked stones of all shapes and sizes' (NMI files). Five Bann flakes, one large broken flake, one flake axe, two cores and one waste flake, all of chert, were recovered. The records of the Irish Tourist Association from the 1940s also refer to unusual lake-dwellings at the southern extreme of Lough Allen (Condit and Gibbons 1989, 8). At least ten 'crannogs' emerged when water-levels dropped. These were circular platforms, 4–5m in diameter, arranged in a straight line parallel with the lakeshore. They may be similar to the features described from Lough Gara and elsewhere, although obviously they could be of later date.

The same local informants had earlier reported the discovery of a stone axe, Bann flakes and other chert flakes at Tully, Kiltoghert, Co. Leitrim, on the west bank of the River Shannon. This site was inspected by Joseph Raftery in 1974, who interestingly compared the site to many of 'the lakeshore sites with stone axeheads and "Bann" flakes found around Lough Allen, Lough Scur, Lough Gara, Croghan lake (near Boyle) and so on' (NMI topographical files).

Other Mesolithic lake archaeology

Mesolithic material is known from several other lakeshore locations in Ireland. There is extensive evidence for Mesolithic activity around Lough Neagh, Northern Ireland. A long tradition of archaeological investigation has been focused on the north end of this vast lake, particularly at Toome, Lough Beg and on the River Bann. Mesolithic worked stone has been gathered on the foreshore (mostly washed out of beach deposits) and in diatomite deposits in the valleys (Knowles 1912; Mitchell 1955; Woodman 1978). At Cushrush Island in Lough MacNean Lower, Co. Fermanagh, seven mudstone axes, a double-pointed pick and two possible rolled Bann flakes were picked up on the shore (Woodman 1978, 306). Mesolithic assemblages have been recovered from the northern drumlin lakelands, including Bann flakes from Annagh-ma-Kerrig lake, Lough Fea and Ballyhoe Lake, Co. Monaghan (Woodman 1978, 306). Bann flakes, both leaf-shaped and narrow types, were recovered on the east shore of Lough Eskragh, Co. Tyrone, during investigations of Bronze Age wooden platforms and post alignments (Collins and Seaby 1960). Two Bann flakes were found on an Early Historic crannog at Lough Ravel, Derryhollagh, Co. Antrim, and Bann flakes were found in Drumdarragh crannog, Co. Fermanagh. Further to the west of Ireland, a Bann flake was found on a crannog in Mahanagh townland, in a bay on Lough Allen, Co. Leitrim (Davies 1942, 25). A distally trimmed Bann flake was recovered as a stray find from the western shore of Lough Corrib, Co. Galway (Woodman 1978). A chert flake was found in peat in a raised bog at Carrickmaquirt, Co. Longford, and pollen analysis suggested a Late Mesolithic date (Cooney 1987). On Valentia Island, Co. Kerry, an area of raised bog in an upland basin has produced a timber and stone platform which has been radiocarbon-dated to the Late Mesolithic (Mitchell 1989). At Mitchelstowndown, Co. Limerick, excavations in advance of the gas pipeline development led to the recovery of worked stone and wood on a possible wooden and earthen platform. This has also been dated to the Late Mesolithic (E. Grogan, pers. comm.).

Chronology and culture

Do these lithic assemblages and possible stone and wooden features provide definite archaeological proof of Mesolithic lakeshore occupation? The evidence suggests that these sites are indeed an indication of Mesolithic hunter-gatherer activities on lakeshores and islands in the midlands and the north-west lakelands. This evidence occurs in various forms—as single lithic finds, as lithic scatters on lakeshores, and as substantial lithic spreads potentially associated with stone cairns or low earthen knolls with occasional wooden features. In terms of chronology, it is certain that most of this material is Late Mesolithic, with occasionally strong possibilities of a transitional phase with the Early Neolithic. However, it is also clear that Early Mesolithic settlement evidence can be expected in the heart of the Irish midlands. It is surprising that so little effort has been paid to investigating this material further, although it is true that only a few Irish archaeologists have paid any attention to this period generally.

There is a wide range of outstanding questions to be asked of this Mesolithic lake settlement archaeology. The Late Mesolithic assemblages from Lough Derravarragh, Lough Gara, Lough Kinale and Lough Allen have yet to be the subject of any in-depth lithic analysis or synthesis. Woodman's (1978) review of the Irish Mesolithic could only sketch the main features. It is therefore difficult to know much about their relative chronology, production, technology or typology. The few available radiocarbon dates suggest activity in both the Early Mesolithic and the Late Mesolithic and the lithic technology strongly suggests a final Late Mesolithic origin (Cooney 1987; Woodman 1978; Woodman and Anderson 1990; Woodman and Johnson 1996). However, it may well be possible to trace the presence of Neolithic objects amongst these assemblages and thereby explore the Mesolithic/Neolithic transition in Ireland. Is there any evidence that these lithic scatters are the product of succeeding Mesolithic and Neolithic occupations? Is there any other evidence of contacts here between Mesolithic foragers and Neolithic farmers? These questions make clear that it is vital that the cultural and chronological character of these lithic assemblages be investigated.

Structures and occupation

If these are short-stay camps or temporary occupation sites, is there any evidence for house structures, tents, platforms, pits, hearths or other features at these lake sites? Unfortunately, these lakeshore lithic scatters are one of the most ignored features of Irish archaeology and only two excavations have been carried out. At Moynagh Lough the knolls were almost certainly deliberately enhanced by laying down brushwood and branches. The Lough Gara scatters of Bann flakes, stone axes and hammerstones may have been associated with stone mounds, and Lough Kinale Site 1 may have been a constructed mound of clay and wood.

It is clear that in the 1940s, 1950s and 1960s a small group of researchers, such as Oliver Davies, Frank Mitchell, Joseph Raftery and others, were very familiar with these mound sites. They circulated their ideas and discoveries among themselves, comparing and occasionally contrasting them in private correspondence (NMI files). They regarded them as 'Larnian' hunting camps, dating from the Early Neolithic (Neolithic A). Modern archaeologists have accepted that such Larnian material is to be dated to the final phase of the Irish Mesolithic. Thus we have Joseph Raftery's comment referring to 'the lakeshore sites with stone axeheads and "Bann" flakes found around Lough Allen, Lough Scur, Lough Gara, Croghan lake (near Boyle) and so on' (NMI files). We also have Oliver Davies's (1946a) description from Lough Inchin of a crannog with scanty habitation remains, which he compared to the 'small Neolithic crannogs on which Bann flakes may be found; of these several have been identified in the Monaghan–Cavan area'. However, apart from Frank Mitchell's two publications, Mesolithic lakeshore archaeology has received relatively little attention.

If these mounds are accepted as deliberately constructed features, it may be that a stony layer served as a hut floor, raising the occupation surface above the waterlogged soils found on lakeshores and in the marshy ground adjacent to lakes. However, it is also important to point out that lakeshore activities may not have been of the duration or type to require formal structures. Simple wind-breaks woven of stray branches may have provided good shelter during the summer months. There is another important alternative. At Star Carr, in England, it has been suggested that the Mesolithic wooden platform and finds represent only the lake-edge element of a much larger Mesolithic dryland settlement (Clark 1954; Schadla-Hall 1989). It is possible that more permanent occupation structures are to be found at the Irish lakeshore sites, but situated slightly higher up the shore. Derragh, Clonava and Moynagh Lough are all within reach of dry, sheltered ground where shelters and huts could have been constructed.

Lithic production

What was the range of activities carried out on these lakeshore sites? Were they primarily lithic production and procurement sites or were they hunting camps associated with lakeshore hunting, fishing and fowling? Were they both? The random or unsystematic collection techniques used in the 1960s mean that there is little or no information on lithic density, spatial distribution or site extent. In contrast, a modern study of these lithic scatters would attempt to closely record the differential location of flakes, blades, cores and tools across the site. This would enable analysis of the lithic scatters in terms of knapping techniques, on-site activities and duration of occupation.

Clonava, Co. Westmeath, and Moynagh Lough, Co. Meath, produced relatively small lithic assemblages, suggesting the repair or preparation of tools rather than any large-scale production. However, Clonava is also situated near outcrops of chert, which might suggest that it was primarily a raw material procurement site. Derragh, Co. Longford, produced a wide range of chert waste and tools, as well as ground stone axes. Incidentally, the presence of stone axes at Derragh does not necessarily indicate a major investment of time and energy. Experiments have shown that mudstones and shales can be ground to an axe in only one or two hours. Is the lithic production part of a Late Mesolithic embedded procurement strategy, whereby chert was worked during visits to the lakeshore for hunting and fishing? It has been pointed out that such Late Mesolithic caches of blades and stone axes could be classic indicators of both curated and scheduled procurement strategies (Cross 1996), which have generally been taken to be the strategies of the Early Mesolithic only (Woodman and Anderson 1990, 383). If this is solely industrial production, why is there occasionally such a range of both lithic debitage and retouched implements (blades, picks, stone axes, cores)? Obviously these sites could have been occupied for a range of other reasons, apart from lithic production and food procurement, and perhaps social groupings may have congregated at these locations.

It difficult to say whether these lithic scatters are the product of one or more episodic visits, short-stay occupations or semi-permanent seasonal occupations. Were the sites revisited on several occasions? Certainly this could be suggested for Derragh, where it would seem unusual that so many stone axes were left lying around. Were the sites abandoned, with a view to returning there later in the year or perhaps in the following year? Such a locally mobile settlement and subsistence strategy might explain the large numbers of stone axes left on the sites. Mesolithic hunter-gatherers would have known that such caches of tools and raw materials would have been available to them at recognised locations. Alternatively, was there a base-camp in the immediate vicinity of these lakeshore occupations, perhaps on the islands behind them?

Seasonality and resource exploitation

How should these sites be interpreted in terms of economy, seasonality and resource exploitation in the landscape? Unfortunately, we lack the full range of settlement sites (base-camps, transitory sites, etc.), there have been few published palaeoenvironmental investigations in these landscapes, and we could certainly wish for more long-term excavations of waterlogged organic deposits with well-preserved evidence for diet and economy. However, it seems likely that there was some element of seasonality and movement through the landscape, certainly primarily focused on wetland exploitation, but with other social and ideological factors influencing settlement. Fish, wildfowl, nuts, berries and other plant foods would have been gathered on different parts of the lakeshore through the seasons of the year (Clarke 1976). Did Mesolithic communities move to a much wider extent? It has been suggested that both the Mesolithic east coast middens and the midland lake assemblages are the product of hunter-gatherer communities ranging widely over a very large territory (Woodman 1978, 187). Are there any lakeshore occupations that can be linked to coastal territories? The Lough Gara and Cormonaghan (Lough Allen) sites were certainly situated relatively close to the sea, with the abundant coastal resources of Sligo Bay not far away. Perhaps some coastal shells or other maritime materials might yet turn up in archaeological excavation of a midland lake settlement site.

Is it possible to construct alternative models of Late Mesolithic hunter-gatherers moving through an entirely lakeland landscape? The Late Mesolithic assemblage from Cormonaghan on the east shore of Lough Allen was located on a lakeshore at the base of steep slopes rising to high mountains to the east. It is possible that some form of cyclical, seasonal movement between such uplands and the low-lying wetlands could be reconstructed here. Are the Lough Boora, Lough Derravarragh, Lough Kinale and Lough Iron sites the settlements of hunter-gatherer groups who rarely, if ever, moved to the coast? Certainly, at Lough Derravarragh, Lough Boora and Moynagh Lough, the presence of hazelnuts and water-lily seeds suggests the gathering of local plant foods, possibly in association with fishing and fowling and hunting of wild pig. The sites are located by river mouths, well placed for catching fish during their seasonal movements. The Lough Gara mounds might have been hunting and fishing platforms, occupied in summer and autumn, constructed to provide shelter and dry ground above the lake marshes. Even if the Lough Gara material is not to be associated with these mounds, it could have been eroded out from peat along the lake edge. Could well-preserved occupation sites survive *in situ* in these peats?

The Lough Derravarragh, Lough Kinale and Moynagh Lough sites are located on large former islands or beside upland ridges, so base-camps could theoretically be situated relatively close by. It would be necessary to carry out archaeological prospection elsewhere around these lakes, particularly around the island margins in the nearby bogs and in areas of ploughsoil. Did Mesolithic hunter-gatherer communities manage the natural landscape by woodland clearance, burning and selective woodland management? It is thought that the absence of red deer from the Irish fauna of the period means that woodland clearance would have been pointless. Might it be done for other reasons, such as increased crops of hazelnuts? Detailed pollen and molluscan studies would be necessary to uncover such potential evidence. Apart from Clonava and Lough Boora, no Mesolithic lakeshore occupation has yet been the subject of detailed palaeoenvironmental investigations, despite their proximity to wetlands. Indeed, we know little about the organic material culture of these Mesolithic lakeshore sites. A wetlands archaeological excavation of a well-preserved Mesolithic occupation site would be of major importance in Irish archaeology, producing valuable information on diet, craft and economy and allowing us to view a wider range of artefactual evidence.

Hunter-gatherer societies and settlement organisation

Can we move towards a social interpretation of the activities of Mesolithic hunter-gatherers in these lakelands? What was the population density, social organisation and territory size of the hunter-gatherer communities that moved through this landscape? These might seem impossible questions to answer, but reconstructing the location of these sites in their original environment makes some suggestions possible. It has been suggested that the primary factors involved in the siting of hunter-gatherer base-camps were proximity to resources, shelter and protection from the weather, and a view for observation of game and strangers (Cooney 1987, 72). The Derragh and Clonava sites were located on islands formerly highly isolated in very extensive wetlands. In the Late Mesolithic, Clonava would have been a dryland island (about 2km in length) surrounded by open water, fens and reed-swamps. Otherwise, the surrounding landscape is generally one of low-lying ridges to the west, with quite prominent hills visible on the horizon further to the east. Similarly, the Derragh sites were on the north edge of an island surrounded by a hinterland of lakes and fens. Were the sites located on islands to provide extensive views over local wetland territories? Were the Mesolithic occupations situated on islands for isolation from competing groups? Were islands seen as 'central places' from which territories could be controlled, with pathways and boat routes leading out from them?

It has also been pointed out that the Mesolithic assemblages are often sited near the mouths of rivers flowing into or out of the lakes, such as at Lough Boora (Boora River), Derragh, Clonava, Cullenhugh (River Inny), Moynagh Lough (River Dee) and Lough Gara (River Boyle). Is this an indication of Mesolithic hunter-gatherers moving widely through the landscape by dugout canoes along rivers? Consequently, is it the case that these river-mouth locations, while effective in providing fish, also facilitated access to major routeways? Were these lakeshore sites visited by large groups on occasion, with different communities congregating from the neighbouring region at recognised islands or river mouths, to trade items, to exchange sexual partners or to swap information? It is difficult to move beyond such hypotheses, because these lakeshore sites undoubtedly represent only one element in the settlement patterns of Mesolithic groups. It will be necessary to investigate both the individual sites and the wider landscape for many of these answers. Nevertheless, there should be at least some attempt to interpret these lakeshore sites in terms of Mesolithic social organisation.

Neolithic lake settlement

Introduction

Farming, including arable agriculture and cattle-herding, was introduced into Ireland sometime shortly before 4200 BC. Large-scale woodland clearance and cereal pollen appear in these centuries in the pollen record (Molloy and O'Connell 1988; Monk 1993). There is also some pollen and cereal evidence that farming may have been introduced by as early as 4500 BC (Edwards and Hirons 1984; Lynch 1981), but this has failed to gain widespread acceptance (Cooney and Grogan 1994; O'Connell 1987). Neolithic settlements, with large rectangular houses and an economy based on cattle-herding, arable farming and some foraged resources, were certainly in place by *c.* 3700 BC (Cooney and Grogan 1994; Grogan 1996a; Harbison 1988; O'Kelly 1989). It is not known what role indigenous Mesolithic hunter-gatherers played in this transition to farming, but there are certainly some sites which indicate that they had contacts with the first farmers (O'Sullivan 1997b; Woodman and O'Brien 1993). It is generally believed that some measure of migration of Neolithic peoples occurred, because such animals as domesticated cattle, pig and sheep/goat and plants such as emmer and einkorn wheat had to be introduced onto an island (Cooney and Grogan 1994; Mallory and McNeill 1991). Neolithic farmers rendered major transformations in the Irish landscape—clearing woodlands, building permanent houses and creating extensive field systems—and also introduced the practice of burying their dead in large megalithic tombs and cairns. However, the beginning of the Neolithic in Ireland can also be viewed as a social transformation, in that it was social relations and the perception of the landscape that most changed. Evidence for Neolithic lake settlement in Ireland will be shown to be relatively scarce, suggesting new social and economic practices in these lakeland landscapes. However, there may also have been certain elements of continuity with the Late Mesolithic, as lakeshores may have been primarily used for hunting, wildfowling and foraging in the Neolithic.

Neolithic settlement in Ireland has traditionally been assessed on the basis of Neolithic house excavations, national and regional distributions of Neolithic megalithic tombs, and the distribution of diagnostic material culture, such as stone axes, worked stone and pottery (e.g. Harbison 1988; Herity and Eogan 1977; O'Kelly 1989). Passage tombs, court tombs and individual burials have also usefully been seen as indirect indicators of settlement activities (e.g. Cooney 1979; 1983). Neolithic settlement evidence has also occasionally been found under excavated megalithic tombs, such as at Knowth, Co. Meath (Eogan 1984), Ballyglass, Co. Mayo (Ó Nualláin 1972), and Newgrange, Co. Meath (O'Kelly 1983; 1989). Neolithic houses were excavated at Ballynagilly, Co. Tyrone (ApSimon 1969), and at Lough Gur, Co. Limerick (Ó Ríordáin 1954). In recent years, Neolithic houses have been excavated at Tankardstown, Co. Limerick (Gowen 1988), Ballygalley, Co. Antrim (Simpson 1995), and Newtown, Co. Meath (Gowen and Halpin 1992). These large rectangular and circular houses appear to be the permanent residences of families (Grogan 1996a, 54), and can occur singly, in small groups (e.g. Tankardstown) and in large-scale agglomerated settlements, such as at Lough Gur, Co. Limerick, and the possible Neolithic settlement at Mullaghfarna, Co. Sligo (Grogan 1996a). The social importance of the house can also be seen in its variable size and divisions, while Late Neolithic houses at Lough Gur were enclosed, possibly indicating an emerging social ranking (Grogan 1996a). Houses and settlement enclosures would have been set in a wider landscape. In the Céide field systems in north Mayo, domestic settlements and megalithic tombs are found amongst fields. The scale and layout of these fields are evidence both for an egalitarian society and for cattle-grazing on a grand scale (Caulfield 1978; 1983; 1988).

It is also possible to identify other, more transitory, seasonal or specialised Neolithic occupation structures, associated either with hunting or fishing or with flint-working, such as at Knocknarea, Co. Sligo (Bengsston and Bergh 1984; Grogan 1996a). Coastal foraging sites may have been identified on Dalkey Island, Co. Dublin (Liversage 1968), and at Carrigdirty Rock, Co. Limerick, on the Shannon estuary (O'Sullivan 1997b). Neolithic occupation material has also been found on sites in the absence of house structures. Neolithic stone axes are widespread in Ireland, indicating that few parts of the country did not witness early prehistoric settlement (Cooney and Mandal 1998). Flint scatters have been recorded in abundance in the ploughzone, heightening expectations of a wider settlement landscape outside the domestic sphere, which in turn emphasises the need to appreciate hidden archaeological evidence. The large-scale exploitation and management of the landscape can also be seen in many documented woodland clearances and in the extensive field systems identified at several different locations. Wooden trackways crossing boglands have also been excavated in regions that are otherwise sparsely represented by Neolithic megalithic tombs, artefacts or settlement evidence, such as at Corlea, Co. Longford (B. Raftery 1996).

The recent interpretation of Neolithic settlement evidence in Ireland has been at variance with models adopted in Britain. Many British archaeologists have interpreted Early Neolithic settlement in terms of continued mobile foraging economies, with occasional farmed clearances in an otherwise densely wooded landscape. It is believed that it was not until the Late Neolithic that permanent settlements developed (Thomas 1991; Whittle 1996). In contrast, there is abundant archaeological evidence in Ireland for permanent settlement, large domestic houses (e.g. Grogan 1996a), extensive field systems (Caulfield 1978; 1983; O'Sullivan and Sheehan 1997), and a sedentary economic strategy from the Early Neolithic (Cooney and Grogan 1994; Mallory and McNeill 1991; Cooney 1997). However, it can be recognised that there may also have been some settlement mobility, seasonal or otherwise, and a combination of a mixed arable, pastoral and foraged economy in the Irish Neolithic. It is also important to state that regional variations may exist. In terms of economy, and despite the relative lack of excavated faunal assemblages from domestic contexts, it is assumed that cattle were the most important domesticated animal, followed by pig and sheep. The main cultivated cereals were emmer wheat and barley. The subsistence strategy is difficult to assess, but it seems likely that cereal-growing was at least as important as stock-raising (Cooney and Grogan 1994, 37). There appears to have been at least some exploitation of wild resources. At Tankardstown, Co. Limerick, hazelnuts and crab-apples were found with emmer wheat grain inside the rectangular house (Gowen 1988).

Neolithic lake settlement

Lake settlement does not appear to be as significant a feature of the Irish archaeological record in the Neolithic as it is in other periods. Is this impression accurate? Could it just be a result of the history of Irish archaeological research and problems of archaeological visibility? If lake levels were generally higher in the Neolithic period,

Pl. 19—*A hoard of Neolithic flint flakes, blades and hollow scraper tightly packed into a shallow pit in early prehistoric open-water muds at Moynagh Lough, Co. Meath. Early Historic crannogs have often produced Neolithic flint blades, scrapers and arrowheads at lower levels. These largely ignored discoveries may represent Neolithic lakeshore occupation or the symbolic importance of these objects in later periods (photo: John Bradley).*

then Neolithic lake occupations should now be isolated up on, and buried under, dry land. But if that is the case, why have Mesolithic lithic assemblages been found from modern lakeshores? Is it possible that Neolithic lithic scatters have actually been misinterpreted as Mesolithic lithic scatters? It will be pointed out below that there is as much Neolithic as Mesolithic lake settlement evidence. It seems likely that lakes continued to be important features of the settlement landscape. It has been pointed out (Grogan 1996a, 57) that many Irish Neolithic houses are located on sheltered, south-facing slopes overlooking large lakes (e.g. Ballynagilly, Lough Gur) or rivers (Knowth, Newgrange, Tankardstown and Townleyhall). Is this because of the importance of pastoral farming and the need for water to be available to cattle herds? Were lakes of continued importance in terms of their wetland resources?

Many crannog excavations have produced possible early prehistoric flints at lower levels, but these are usually dismissed because of their irrelevance to the Early Historic occupation phases. Flint was certainly used in the Early Historic period, for strike-a-lights or blades, and it is probable that some crude thumb scrapers and hollow scrapers were made on crannogs at this time. It is also possible that prehistoric worked stone was taken onto crannogs in the Early Historic period for some symbolic reason, while some stone axes may have been used as linen smoothers. Prehistoric stone axes and flints may have been percieved as magical items. However, it could be that the basal deposits of many Early Historic crannog sites provide an insight into the true extent of Neolithic lakeside settlement. Wood-Martin (1886a, 58–9, 40, 45) records a range of lithic finds from several crannogs. A wooden floor at Cargaghoge, Co. Monaghan, may have been a Neolithic or Bronze Age wetland occupation (Morant 1868–9), while a wooden structure at Inver, Co. Donegal, may have been a Neolithic funerary house in a bog (Wood-Martin 1886a, 39).

Shirley (1846, 46) stated that the 'objects of greatest antiquity' from crannogs and islands in Monalty Lake and Lough na Glack, Co. Monaghan, were 'stone celts of the common type'. George Buick's (1893) excavations at Moylarg crannog led to the discovery of 250 flint objects, including five cores, nine scrapers, four hollow scrapers and fifteen flakes. While some of the assemblage could be Early Historic in date, the hollow scrapers at least are probably Neolithic. Furthermore, there was also bone, pottery, a flint arrowhead and three stone axes in an ash spread in the crannog. D'Arcy's (1900) excavations of two lake-dwellings at Drumacrittin, Co. Fermanagh, produced Neolithic material, including flints, a stone axe and a saddle quern stratified at depth in crannog 1 and a barbed and tanged arrowhead in crannog 2. Craigywarren crannog, Co. Antrim, produced flint flakes, scrapers and an arrowhead, three polishing stones, spindle-whorls and a stone axe fragment. The excavators decided that the flints were not strike-a-lights. However, because there were no cores to indicate on-site flint-working, they felt that the flints were introduced on to the site with stone and gravel during its construction (Coffey 1906). Oliver Davies's (1946b) excavations at Moylederg Island, Lough Eske, Co. Donegal, produced worked stone on a natural island which was later occupied as a crannog in the late medieval period. At Crannogeboy, Co. Donegal, a stone mound measuring 18m in length in marshy ground produced several stone axes and three saddle querns (Lacy 1983, 104). Lagore crannog produced a polished stone axe, Neolithic pottery, two flint knives, flint scrapers, a hollow-based arrowhead, a tanged arrowhead and flint debitage (Hencken 1950, 125, 177–8). A large number of stone axes are known from the lakeshore of Lough Inchiquin, Co. Clare, and wooden structures have also been noted from this lake (MacNamara 1901, 349). The ritual deposition of artefacts in watery places (lakes, rivers and bogs) had its origins in the Neolithic: for example, maceheads and stone axes are commonly found in watery contexts (Cooney and Grogan 1994, 82). Most recently, archaeological excavations at Moynagh Lough, Co. Meath, have produced a Neolithic hoard of flint blades and flakes, obviously deliberately laid as a formal deposit in a pit by the lakeshore (John Bradley, pers. comm.) (Pl. 19).

However, in the absence of wooden structures, other Neolithic lakeshore lithic scatters have been the subject of little archaeological attention. But there are at least three individual sites that appear to be actual Neolithic lake settlements or occupation sites—Rathjordan, Co. Limerick (Ó Ríordáin and Lucas 1946–7), Island MacHugh, Co. Tyrone (Davies 1950; Ivens *et al.* 1986), and Lough Enagh, Co. Derry (Davies 1941)—while at Tivannagh, Co. Sligo, a Viking Age lake settlement excavation may also have revealed a Neolithic horizon (Evans 1966; J. Raftery 1957). Lough Gur should also be considered as a lake settlement where an extensive complex of houses and enclosures was situated on Knockadoon hill. In early prehistory this would probably have been mostly enclosed by water (Grogan 1989; Grogan and Eogan 1987; Ó Ríordáin 1954). Garret Island, also on Lough Gur, was also the location of some form of Neolithic habitation (Liversage 1958).

Island MacHugh, Co. Tyrone

The crannog of Island MacHugh, at the south-west end of Lough Catherine, Co. Tyrone, was excavated in the 1930s and 1940s by Oliver Davies (1950), and subsequently re-excavated by Richard Ivens and Derek Simpson (Ivens *et al.* 1986; Ivens and Simpson, forthcoming). Although the site was primarily occupied in the Early Historic period, both excavations identified a Neolithic occupation level on the island. Indeed, the site first came to notice in 1909 when Neolithic flints and pottery were gathered from the adjacent lakeshore. At its earliest phase of Neolithic occupation the location was a small island of muds over gravels, with pond weeds, grasses, peat and trees rooted on the spot. Charcoal, broken hazelnuts, twigs, quartz chips, pottery sherds, flint and pine cones were found amongst these deposits (Davies 1950, 12). Brushwood mats were laid down along the shore and Neolithic occupation debris was found to be spread lightly over the island, mostly in the south-west. A single possible Neolithic structure was uncovered in the excavations. This was a stone bank resting on the peat surface, although there was little other clear stratigraphical or dating evidence (Ivens *et al.* 1986, 100). There is little further evidence for Neolithic activities on the site, although it should be pointed out that Oliver Davies's excavations did not go deeper than the upper peat surfaces.

Large quantities of Neolithic broad-rimmed pottery were recovered in the earlier excavations (Davies 1950; Herity and Eogan 1977; Ivens *et al.* 1986). Neolithic flint objects from Island MacHugh included over 100 hollow scrapers (Mallory and McNeill 1991, 50), and smaller numbers of round scrapers, end scrapers, arrowheads, two knives and a single Bann flake. There were also two stone axes and a fragment of porcellanite (Davies 1950; Ivens *et al.* 1986; Ivens and Simpson, forthcoming). The high percentage of finished flint implements may suggest some degree of on-site specialist production, but most of the implements had been brought onto the island, perhaps for working wood or cutting reeds. While the nature of the Neolithic occupation at Island MacHugh is uncertain, the quantity of material suggests that the site was more than simply a short-stay hunting or fishing camp. The range of evidence—pottery, scrapers, knives, stone axes and wooden structures—suggests that this was a long-term occupation site. It could have had a specialist function, with its residents engaged in crafts and trade.

Lough Enagh, Co. Derry

Rough Island, on Lough Enagh, Co. Derry, is also known to have produced Neolithic broad-rimmed pottery and hollow scrapers. These were uncovered during Oliver Davies's (1941) trial excavations on this small natural island, which revealed a succession of prehistoric and historic occupation layers. The excavations were carried out by means of a single trench, so that little information is available on structures. In the lowest occupation layer were sherds of Neolithic broad-rimmed ware, apparently associated with a few Bann flakes and hollow scrapers. The second layer produced more elaborate cord-ornamented broad-rimmed pottery, nineteen hollow scrapers, flint knives, round scrapers and other flint debitage. Rough Island also produced Late

Bronze Age finds and Early Historic pottery and appears to be somewhat similar to Island MacHugh in its occupation history. The presence of pottery, tools and flint waste seems to suggest a lake settlement of a small group of people, possibly staying for some extended period. The wetland resources of the lakeshore may well have been an attraction, but long-term occupation on the site may have been focused on specialist production of wooden objects, pottery or other artefacts. It is possible for a settlement site to be occupied over a long period without leaving much structural evidence, especially if people were living in light, stake-built structures.

Lough Gara and Tivannagh (Crannog 124), Co. Roscommon

Mesolithic, Neolithic and Early Bronze Age lithic scatters were recognised in large numbers on the foreshore of Lough Gara, Co. Sligo, during drainage operations in the 1950s. On occasion spreads of lithics could be associated with occupation deposits. At Tawnymucklagh, the south crannog produced Neolithic leaf-shaped arrowheads, lozenge-shaped arrowheads and a hollow scraper of chert. At Tivannagh, Co. Roscommon, Joseph Raftery excavated a multiperiod lake settlement (Evans 1966; J. Raftery 1957). The earliest occupations appear to date from the early prehistoric period, possibly the Early Neolithic. The site was located on a narrow spit of land, composed of grey boulder clay and peat, at the mouth of the River Boyle. The earliest settlement was on a circular platform of large horizontal timbers with a few vertical posts. A large, crudely made dugout canoe with a possible transom board, animal bone, charcoal and 'two Bann flakes of a rudimentary type' were found, the latter beside a wooden shaft. Pollen analysis indicated that the occupation pre-dated 3000 BC. The site was interpreted as a seasonal fishing habitation or a mooring-place for boats. It was abandoned and peat growth covered the timbers. A second occupation, dating in Raftery's (1957, 9) opinion to about 2500 BC, resulted in the laying of an extensive floor of well-woven brushwood, defined on the landward side by a small semicircle of wooden posts. This occupation was short-lived; during subsequent marshy conditions a considerable depth of *Phragmites* peat was laid over the platform.

The chronology of this site remains unclear, but there may have been a Neolithic occupation site on the lakeshore at the mouth of the River Boyle. If this were the case, then we are looking at similar siting patterns to the Mesolithic sites at Clonava, Lough Derravarragh and Derragh, Lough Kinale, which have been interpreted as sites placed to catch salmon and eels moving along the river. The Neolithic archaeology of Lough Gara needs to be explored in more detail. Lough Gara can also be linked to important Late Neolithic ritual monuments on the drylands, such as the henges of Knockadoobrusna, Co. Sligo (Condit 1993).

Rathjordan, Co. Limerick

A single Late Neolithic lake settlement has been excavated at Rathjordan, Co. Limerick (Ó Ríordáin and Lucas 1946–7). The site was first brought to attention about 1918, when the field was ploughed for tillage. Large numbers of stone axes were picked up from the ploughsoil over a four-year period, amounting to 'almost a ton of axes' from the land. The site was excavated in the 1940s, contemporaneously with the nearby Lough Gur excavations, while a number of barrows were investigated in the same townland. The site was a low, circular mound in a field. It had formerly stood in a lake marsh with open pools of water. Reeds and other organic material were preserved in the compacted lake muds under the site. The site was constructed by laying bundles of brushwood across each other and pegging them in place with sharpened stakes. A discontinuous layer of timbers was laid across this brushwood, creating a layer 11m in diameter. A mound of stones, 8m in diameter, was built up over the wooden substructure. Finds from this layer included stone axes, animal bone, wood, flint chips and large amounts of charcoal. The stones bore evidence of burning. The perimeter of the mound seems then to have become covered by natural peat growth, prior to the next phase of activity on the site. In this peat and on the edge of the stone mound two

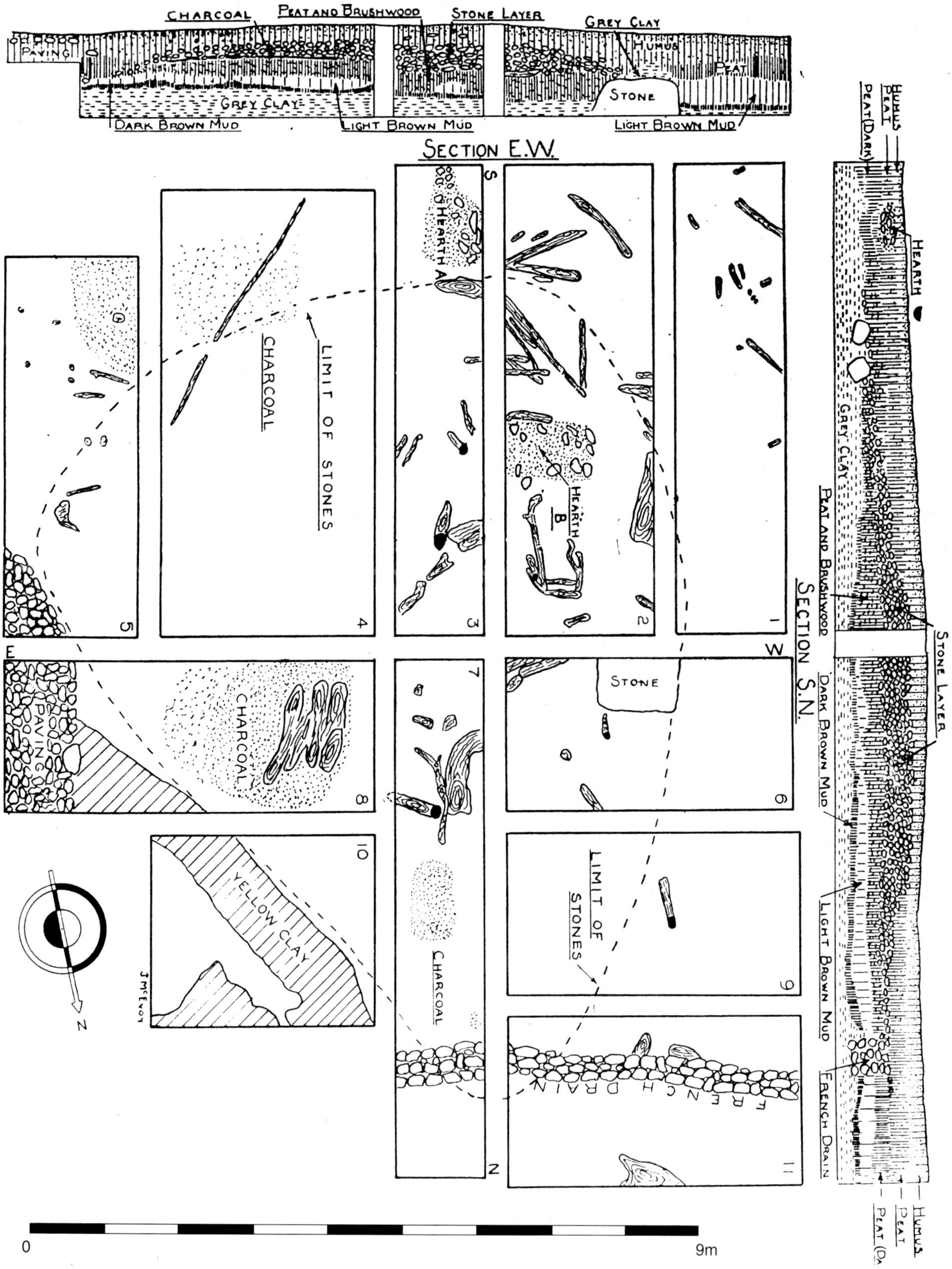

Fig. 10—*Late Neolithic lake or marshland settlement at Rathjordan, Co. Limerick: plan and cross-sections (after Ó Ríordáin and Lucas 1946–7).*

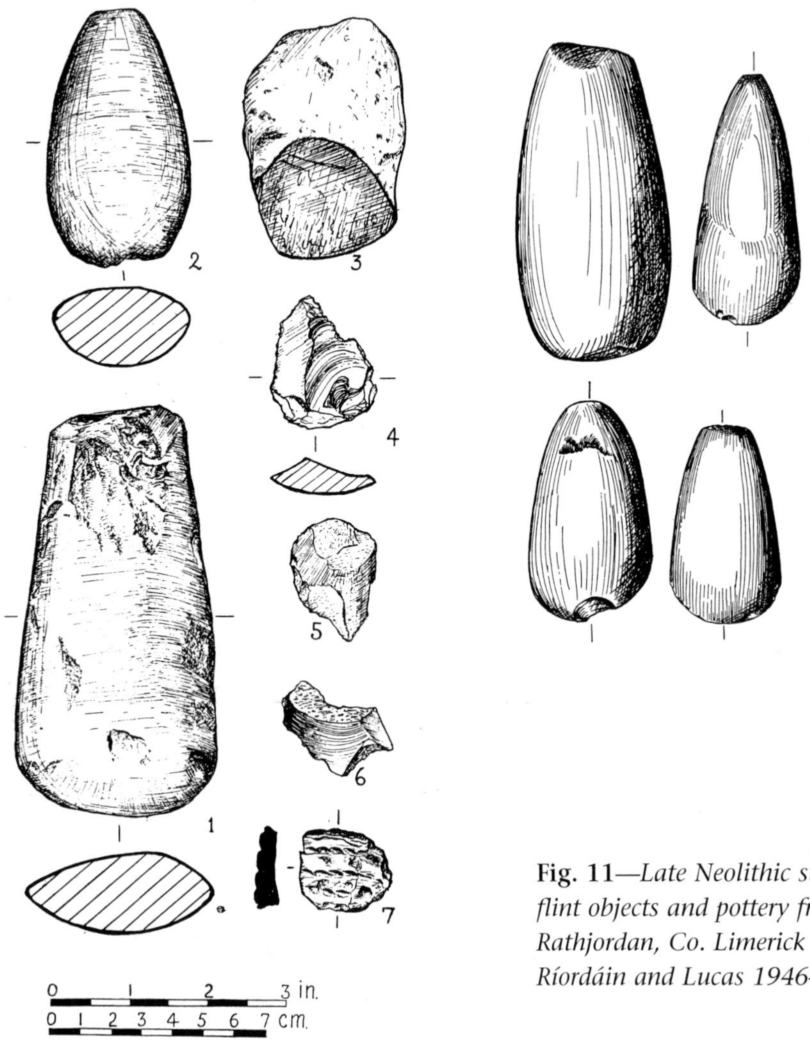

Fig. 11—*Late Neolithic stone axes, flint objects and pottery from Rathjordan, Co. Limerick (after Ó Ríordáin and Lucas 1946–7).*

hearths were constructed. A yellowish clay with charcoal underneath the hearth produced a single sherd of cord-ornamented pottery, identified by the excavators as Bronze Age in type but now known to be Late Neolithic Beaker pottery (Eoin Grogan, pers. comm.). It is likely, given the intermediate buildup of peat, that the earlier occupation was Middle Neolithic to Late Neolithic in date. The function of the site is unclear. However, it was obviously a significant wetland site, with a laid stone floor, wooden structures, hearths, pottery, stone axes, flint artefacts and wooden objects. It may have been a domestic settlement, although the reputedly large number of stone axes is intriguing, suggesting a specialist production site (Figs 10 and 11).

There is extensive evidence for Late Neolithic settlement in this immediate region, from the Neolithic settlements on Knockadoon, Lough Gur (Grogan and Eogan 1987), to the small Early Bronze Age wetland occupation at Rockbarton Bog (Mitchell and Ó Ríordáin 1942). A subrectangular enclosure defined by a ditch and low external bank was excavated elsewhere in the townland of Rathjordan (Ó Ríordáin 1948, 22–8). The site was also situated in the marshy ground that was on the lakeshore in prehistory. It produced a Late Neolithic assemblage, including Beaker pottery. Although interpreted by the excavator as a barrow, it is more likely that this was a settlement site (Eoin Grogan, pers. comm.). Further sites were also examined in the area, yielding Late Neolithic material (Ó Ríordáin 1949; MacDermott 1949). Given the wealth of evidence for the Late Neolithic in the area, we can assume that the Rathjordan sites must be assessed in relation to each other as they were not isolated features within a landscape.

Pl. 20—*Aerial photograph of Lough Gur, Co. Limerick. The Knockadoon peninsula was a long-term focus of settlement in the Neolithic and Bronze Age. Garret Island has also produced Neolithic finds (photo: Dúchas—The Heritage Service).*

Pl. 21—*A Late Neolithic settlement enclosure at Circle K, Knockadoon, Lough Gur, Co. Limerick (photo: Eoin Grogan).*

Knockadoon, Lough Gur, Co. Limerick

The Knockadoon peninsula in Lough Gur, Co. Limerick, has extensive and well-known archaeological evidence for settlement from the Middle Neolithic to the Late Bronze Age (Grogan and Eogan 1987; Grogan 1989; Cleary 1995). In early prehistory it is likely that the Knockadoon peninsula was a large island in the lake, the eastern side cut off by open water. A long-term programme of archaeological excavations in the 1940s on the hillslopes and subsequent fieldwork by various archaeologists in the environs of Lough Gur have revealed that Knockadoon was the focus for farming settlements over a long period of time. There are at least twelve habitation sites on the hill, ten of which have produced house structures. The earliest settlements, at Circle L and Site C, produced western Neolithic pottery and may be dated to as early as 3400 BC. There is also evidence that settlement continued on the site to the Late Neolithic, although several sites may in fact date from the Late Bronze Age. There are also some Late Neolithic burials (Pls 20 and 21).

The Neolithic occupation at Knockadoon formed an agglomerated settlement, with several houses existing contemporaneously, while many were reconstructed or replaced over generations. These Neolithic circular and rectangular wooden and stone houses, some of them enclosed within low walls, were the domestic settlements of communities who primarily herded cattle and raised some pigs and sheep/goat. There is some evidence for arable farming, including some possible garden plots, stone grain-rubbers and the presence of cultivation weeds and cereal pollen in pollen cores from the lake. Some wild animals (red deer, fox, cat, hare) and waterfowl (greylag goose, cormorant and duck) may have been hunted, and fish and freshwater oysters were probably caught in the lake. Therefore, while cattle-herding on the rich grasslands of the lakeshore and its hinterland was the main source of food, the inhabitants of Knockadoon practised some crop cultivation and the lake's resources of fish and fowl were tapped.

There is also some evidence for Neolithic lakeshore occupation on Garret Island, a small wooded islet in the lake just off Knockadoon. The site was discovered when flints were noticed in peats on the north-west side of the island. It was suspected that Mesolithic occupation material could be present, and a two-week excavation was carried out in August 1956 by G.F. Mitchell and David Liversage (Liversage 1958). The excavations comprised two trenches, several test-pits and a number of stratigraphical borings. The excavation recorded a possible clay floor, cobbling, pot-boilers and pottery, including Grooved Ware (Helen Roche, pers. comm.). The site was subsequently built over, possibly in the historic period. The Neolithic settlements on Knockadoon are only one aspect of the archaeology of the Lough Gur region. There are also several ritual monuments in the vicinity, such as a wedge tomb, an embanked stone circle at Grange, and several barrows and stone circles.

Neolithic hunter-gatherers on lakeshores

It has been shown that there is some, although admittedly not very much, evidence for Neolithic lake settlement activities in Ireland. The Middle and Late Neolithic settlements at Knockadoon, on the shore of Lough Gur, were evidently for long-term, permanent habitation by successive generations of farmers. The character of the lakeshore or marshland sites at Rathjordan, Island MacHugh and Lough Enagh is less clear, but the presence of structures, pottery, stone axes, flint scrapers, knives and arrowheads suggests that these were also significant lakeshore settlements. Other Neolithic lake occupation sites, surviving only as lithic scatters at the base of Early Historic crannogs, may only have been occupied by people engaged in fishing or wildfowling over several weeks or months. Indeed, it may be difficult to distinguish between Late Mesolithic and Early Neolithic lakeshore occupations. Woodman and Anderson (1990, 378) suggest that some Later Mesolithic and Neolithic lithic industries may be quite similar and difficult to distinguish from each other. Certainly, mudstone axes (a common find on lakeshore sites) were used in both the Mesolithic and Neolithic (Cooney 1989). The Ballylough project has suggested considerable continuity between the Late Mesolithic and Early Neolithic in lithic industries and settlement activities on Waterford Harbour (Cooney and Grogan 1994; Green and Zvelebil 1990, 83–4). This poses an interesting question. Is it possible to use the lakeshore sites to explore the evidence for continuities between the Mesolithic and Neolithic in Ireland? What are the implications of such continuities for the transition between hunter-gatherer and farming societies? Was there social interaction and trading contacts between these groups? Might it otherwise be suggested that Mesolithic groups themselves took up Neolithic social organisation and economic strategies? Alternatively, are we just recognising that certain locations in the landscape were similarly attractive to Mesolithic hunter-gatherers and Neolithic farmers, widely separated by time?

Neolithic farmers and lake settlements

What was the role of lakes in Neolithic settlement in Ireland? There is certainly little evidence in Ireland for the types of Neolithic lake villages known from throughout central Europe. It is possible that more substantial Neolithic lake settlement sites may yet be forthcoming in Ireland, similar, perhaps, to the Neolithic island settlement at Eilean Domhnuill, Loch Olabhat, on North Uist in Scotland (Armit 1986; 1987; 1988; 1989; Ashmore 1996, 58). However, there may already be archaeological evidence for both permanent Neolithic lakeshore settlements and seasonal foraging and hunting camps, which were being used at the one time by the same farming communities. The Garrett Island lakeshore site on Lough Gur (Liversage 1958) may be a fowling platform used by the farmers of the Neolithic settlement on the peninsula of Knockadoon (Grogan 1996a; Grogan and Eogan 1987). Neolithic settlement and economy in Ireland from an early stage seem to have been largely based on small dispersed farmsteads and the management of arable crops and cattle herds (Cooney 1987; Cooney and Grogan 1994). Neolithic houses are often sited on sheltered, south-facing slopes which overlook water, such as lakes (e.g. Ballynagilly, Lough Gur) or rivers (Knowth, Newgrange, Tankardstown and Townleyhall) (Grogan 1996a, 57). Grazing cattle would need access to water, whether stream, river or lake. Most importantly, Neolithic farmers needed access to good-quality, well-drained soils (brown earths, grey-brown podzolics) that could be cleared of woodland and ploughed for arable farming. Therefore, in the vicinity of lakes, optimum locations for Neolithic settlement can probably be picked out on the neighbouring upland ridges and on thin-soiled rocklands. It may be that Neolithic lake settlement needs to be viewed (like all other periods, in fact) in much broader terms (the wider social and economic landscape).

Neolithic societies and settlement in lakelands

It is clear that the archaeology of Neolithic lake settlement in Ireland takes a particular form, largely being one of small-scale sites on lakeshores, of people involved in farming, foraging and hunting. The distribution and character of Neolithic settlements, artefacts and megalithic tombs in lakelands should be integrated with palaeoenvironmental investigation and landscape reconstruction (Cooney and Grogan 1994; Harbison 1988; Herity and Eogan 1977; O'Kelly 1989). Neolithic artefactual evidence is certainly known from the midland lake region (e.g. Cooney 1987), while megalithic tombs are commonly found in the northern drumlin lakelands (Cooney 1979) and in the vicinity of the lakes of the west and Connemara (e.g. Gosling 1993). There are also many individual examples of Neolithic megalithic tombs actually on lakes (e.g. Creggandeveskey court tomb). The possibility of Neolithic ritual activities on lakeshores should be explored. The role of these lakeshore sites in the broader patterns of Neolithic settlement can only be investigated by looking at the wider landscape.

Bronze Age lake settlement

Introduction

The Bronze Age in Ireland has traditionally been studied in terms of its burial practices, its ritual monuments and its range of metal artefacts and pottery (Cooney and Grogan 1994; Harbison 1988; Herity and Eogan 1977; Mallory and McNeill 1991; O'Kelly 1989). Although there is good artefactual and burial evidence for the distribution of communities in the Early Bronze Age (2500–1700 BC), settlement evidence of this period remains relatively scarce. However, the archaeological evidence for settlement and economy in the Middle Bronze Age (1700–1200 BC) and the Late Bronze Age (1200–600 BC) has been greatly enhanced in recent years. Late Bronze Age hillforts have been identified at several locations. Archaeological excavations at Haughey's Fort, Co. Armagh (Mallory 1995), at Mooghaun, Co. Clare (Grogan 1996b; Grogan and Condit 1994b), at the cliff fort at Dun Aonghusa (Cotter 1996) and at Rathgall, Co. Wicklow (B. Raftery 1976), indicate that they were predominantly constructed in the

Middle to Late Bronze Age. The evidence for actual settlement on these sites varies; some, such as Dun Aonghusa, were certainly the location for some occupation and various craft and economic activities (Cotter 1996). Others seem not to have been the focus for permanent settlement and may have been regional centres or temporary defensive structures at times of political and social unrest. Coastal promontory forts may have been constructed in the Bronze Age; one site, at Dunbeg, Co. Kerry, has produced tentative dating evidence from the period (Barry 1981). Some promontory forts can also be associated with possible Bronze Age ring-barrows, as at Kilkee, Co. Clare (Condit 1997). The origins and function of such promontory forts, like those of many hillforts, remain unclear. These hillforts may well be high-status centres of some form, representing the upper level in a complex settlement hierachy constructed to mirror social organisation. It seems likely that later Bronze Age communities in Ireland witnessed several important changes in the social landscape, particularly the emergence of a stratified, hierarchical society increasingly focused on warfare and tribal identities towards the end of the period. Burial practices certainly seem to indicate social ranking, based on kin-group, age, gender and, latterly, prowess in combat. A theoretical settlement model which reflects this societal change has been proposed in relation to settlement archaeology in south-east Clare (Grogan *et al.* 1995; 1996), but its elements (hillforts, hilltop enclosures and smaller domestic enclosures) are beginning to be seen elsewhere in the country (Tom Condit, pers. comm.).

Smaller Middle and Late Bronze Age enclosed settlements are also known. These may have been farmsteads and are occasionally associated with field systems, *fulachta fiadh* and ritual monuments. They are typically situated on well-drained thin soils, well suited to arable agriculture, and can be enclosed by stone walls as at Carrigillihy, Co. Cork (O'Kelly 1951), and Aughinish, Co. Limerick (E.P. Kelly 1974), by a ditch as at Ballyveelish, by a wooden palisade as at Curraghatoor, Co. Tipperary (Doody 1997), or by a combination of earthen ditches and palisades as at Emain Macha, Co. Armagh (Mallory and McNeill 1991; Waterman 1997), and Chancellorsland, Co. Tipperary (Doody 1997). The enclosures typically contained one or more circular houses (more than one house existed at Clonfinlough, Co. Offaly, and Curraghatoor, Co. Tipperary). Other, unenclosed settlements are also known, such as a Late Bronze Age house at Lough Gur, Co. Limerick (Cleary 1995), and a Middle Bronze Age roundhouse with field systems at Belderg, Co. Mayo (Caulfield 1988). The inhabitants of these farmsteads were probably engaged in intensive mixed farming on light, well-drained soils, with cattle herds being moved around the landscape and arable crops being cultivated in small garden fields.

It is becoming clear that Bronze Age settlement landscapes were organised so as to facilitate the exploitation of various industrial and food resources. Early Bronze Age activity sites associated with the extraction of copper ores have been identified at Mount Gabriel, Co. Cork, and Ross Island, Co. Kerry. These sites were also undoubtedly the locations for specialist or metalworkers' occupations (O'Brien 1995). Coastal wetland occupations have also been found, such as the Middle Bronze Age houses, pits and features at Meadowlands, Co. Down (Pollack and Waterman 1964), and the Middle Bronze Age wooden hut structure associated with cattle bone at Carrigdirty Rock, Co. Limerick. These coastal sites may have been associated with seasonal cattle-grazing on the summer marshes (O'Sullivan 1995a; 1996a). Bronze Age coastal shell middens have also been recorded in sand-dunes at False Bay, Co. Galway. It seems likely that occasional use was being made of such littoral resources as shellfish and cattle-grazing on the thin machair grasslands (McCormick 1995). Early, Middle and Late Bronze Age trackways have been found in large numbers in the midland raised bogs, particularly at Corlea and Derryoghil, Co. Longford. These were constructed of planks, brushwood and hurdles, and frequently indicate long continuities of repair and replacement, suggesting settlement in the region (B. Raftery 1996). Bronze Age trackways have also been recorded on the Fergus estuary mudflats, Co. Clare, indicating an interest in communications across saltmarshes to isolated islands (O'Sullivan 1995a; 1996a). It is possible that in the Middle and Late Bronze Age a combination of high population pressure, social instability, increasing growth of blanket bog and perhaps even climatic deterioration caused new low-lying lands, particularly wetlands, to be taken in for farming. Although the settlement landscape was largely based on permanently occupied, dispersed farmsteads, there may have been some local element of settlement mobility or seasonal movement of cattle herds.

Bronze Age lake settlements

Bronze Age lake settlement sites

Lake settlements are a vitally important element in Middle and Late Bronze Age settlement organisation and economy in Ireland. Middle Bronze Age sites have been excavated at Cullyhanna Lough, Co. Armagh (Hodges 1958), at Lough Eskragh, Co. Tyrone (Collins and Seaby 1960; Williams 1978), and at Moynagh Lough, Co. Meath (John Bradley, pers. comm.). Late Bronze Age lake settlement sites investigated include Lough Eskragh, Co. Tyrone (Collins and Seaby 1960; Williams 1978; 1988), Knocknalappa, Co. Clare (J. Raftery 1942), Clonfinlough (Moloney *et al.* 1993), Ballinderry no. 2, Co. Westmeath (Hencken 1942), Moynagh Lough, Co. Meath (J. Bradley 1997), Island MacHugh, Co. Tyrone (Davies 1950; Ivens *et al.* 1986), and Lough MacNean Lower, Co. Fermanagh (Mallory and McNeill 1991). There may also have been a lakeside settlement at Imeroo, Co. Fermanagh, where a worked oak timber from the edge of a bog has been dendrochronologically dated to 1478 ± 9 BC. This could also have been a trackway timber (Baillie 1985). A raised bog or fen site at Killymoon, Co. Tyrone, will be discussed below (Hurl 1995). There is a range of other evidence for Bronze Age settlement in lakeland regions, including the distribution of Bronze Age burials (Waddell 1990; B. Ó Ríordáin and Waddell 1993) and the incidence of numerous stray finds from lakes, bogs and rivers (e.g. R. Bradley 1990; Cooney and Grogan 1994; Eogan 1965; 1983). A Bronze Age post alignment at Lough Carra, Co. Mayo, may be some form of lakeland ritual structure or bridge (Lavelle 1992).

Middle and Late Bronze Age burnt mounds or *fulachta fiadh* seem to be one indicator of seasonal communal activities in river valleys, lakeshores and boggy ground. They have been found beside lakes, for example in south-east Clare (O'Sullivan and Condit 1995) and at Levallinree Lough and Lough More, Co. Mayo (Lawless 1992, 29). These sites consist of burnt mounds of stone, ash, charcoal and clay lying beside stone-built or wooden troughs. It seems certain that the mounds are spoil-heaps of burnt material, left after stones were repeatedly heated and dumped into the water-filled trough to boil water. Repeated heating and cooling shatters the stone, which is then cast up on the surrounding mounds. These sites have typically been dated to the Middle and Late Bronze Age and are now being found in ever-increasing numbers in the Irish landscape. There is some mild controversy as to their function. They may have served as cooking places, although it has been noted that animal bone is infrequent on excavated sites. An alternative explanation, inspired by early Irish texts, is that they were used as saunas or baths, for washing and cleaning. Whatever their actual function, archaeological survey has revealed that they are typically the product of many episodes of heating stone. This implies that they were visited and revisited on numerous occasions, perhaps over several seasons. These burnt mounds can be taken as an indicator of Bronze Age settlement in a region, supporting the idea of seasonal, communal gatherings in low-lying wetlands. They have often been found in association with barrows, standing stones and stone circles (e.g. at Drombeg, Co. Cork), possibly indicating a function in the ritual landscape (Brindley *et al.* 1989–90; Buckley 1990; O'Sullivan and Condit 1995).

Bronze Age hoards and single finds from lakes

The distribution and provenance of Bronze Age weaponry and tools provide several additional insights into lake settlement. Early Bronze Age axes, dirks and rapiers are known from across Ireland's lakeland regions (Harbison 1969a; 1969b; Burgess and Gerloff 1981). Late Bronze Age swords are widely distributed across the north-west lakeland region of Fermanagh and Cavan, and are also common across the west and through the midlands (Eogan 1965). Late Bronze Age hoards of weaponry, tools and ornaments are commonly found in wetland contexts in these regions (Eogan 1983). Bronze Age artefacts have occasionally been found on individual crannogs, islands and lakeshores, but archaeologists have generally made little or no attempt to investigate these findspots in detail. It is true that watery locations were often chosen for the deposition or concealment of such material, so that Bronze Age material need not always derive from settlement contexts (R. Bradley 1990; Cooney and Grogan 1994). However, it is possible to propose a number that almost certainly do.

At Monaltyduff, on Monalty Lough, Co. Monaghan, a range of Bronze Age artefacts were found 'on the surface of a crannog'. They included a stone axe, a hammerstone, two socketed bronze daggers, a tanged dagger, a tanged razor, a bag-shaped chape, a bronze gouge, a flesh-hook handle and possibly two rings (Lucas 1968). Eogan (1983) has suggested that this material may not be from an isolated hoard but may represent evidence for a Bronze Age lake settlement. The site is a large cairn, measuring 25–30m in diameter, and has also produced Early Historic material (Brindley 1986, 16). A large collection of Bronze Age and Early Historic artefacts were also reportedly gathered from a crannog site at Loughnaglack, Drummond Otra townland, Co. Monaghan. The finds included a flint thumb scraper, flakes, a slate spearhead, a stone disc, an Early Bronze Age halberd, a Late Bronze Age socketed bronze axe, three bronze daggers and a bronze ring (Lucas 1968). The site survives as a cairn, 18m in diameter, in the lake (Brindley 1986). Early and Middle Bronze Age finds are known from Lagore, the well-known Early Historic and Viking Age crannog in County Meath. These finds included a barbed and tanged arrowhead, a bronze double-edged knife-dagger with openwork handle and ring terminal (Eogan 1966), and a socketed bronze spearhead (Hencken 1950, 58). A wooden anthropomorphic figure from a sandy layer in the north-west part of the crannog has recently been radiocarbon-dated to 2135–1944 cal. BC (3650 ± 70 BP; OxA-1720) (B.J. Coles 1990, 326). Several crannogs on Lough Gara probably date from the Late Bronze Age, a site at Ross townland produced an intact coarseware pot, while Middle Bronze Age and Late Bronze Age tools, weapons and ornaments are known from elsewhere on the Lough Gara foreshore (J. Raftery, forthcoming a).

Eogan (1965, 178) has drawn attention to the antiquarian discovery of part of a sword mould on the 'surface of an ancient crannog associated with rude huts which were found at a depth of 21 feet (6.40m) under peat' in Fermanagh. He has suggested that the site may well be at Bohovny, Co. Fermanagh. At Ballycroghan, Co. Down, three bronze swords were found in 1949 on a small former lake island (Jope 1953, 37). The islands stood out as patches of clay and stones amidst the dark peats of the surrounding fields. On the island where the swords were found was a 'great deal of timber, both large and small, much of it bearing marks of apparent dressing with a gouge'. The site appears to have been a *fulacht fiadh* in a marshy landscape (Victor Buckley, pers. comm.). A bronze sword was found near the seventeenth-century Old Crom Castle, Co. Fermanagh, and others are known from the shore of Upper Lough Erne, Co. Fermanagh (Eogan 1965). Late Bronze Age swords were found 'in a crannog at Bohermeen, Co. Meath' (Wood-Martin 1886a, 171, pl. XXXVII), and on the 'plank floor of a crannog, at Furnish, Co. Tyrone' (Eogan 1965, 85). Oliver Davies investigated a small circular island or cairn in the shallow waters of Lough Oughter, where he found a pot which he dated to the Late Bronze Age (O'Donovan 1995, 183).

Bronze Age finds are also known from lakeshores and lake margins. These include the finds from the Lough Gara foreshore recovered during the 1950s. Bronze rings and bronze swords were found at Inch Island, Co. Sligo (Eogan 1983; B. Raftery, pers. comm.). A Late Bronze Age hoard, comprising a sword, a socketed knife, a socketed axe, a socketed hammer and three spearheads, was found on Boa Island, Co. Fermanagh (Wakeman 1879–82b). Two Bronze Age swords were found on the shore of Inisleague

Island, Lough Erne, Co. Fermanagh (Eogan 1965, 60), and on the shores of Drumcullaun Lough, Drumcullaun, Co. Clare (*ibid.*, 130). A Late Bronze Age sword was found in a field beside Cuilcagh Lough, Adlow townland, Co. Cavan (*ibid.*, 45), and on the foreshore near the ruins of the Anglo-Norman keep castle on Lough Oughter, at Clough Oughter, Co. Cavan (*ibid.*, 46). Another example was found 'in the wall of an old castle on Hog Island, Lough Mask' (*ibid.*, 75), which incidentally is also an early thirteenth-century masonry castle. A Late Bronze Age sword was found on the lakeshore at Kiltoom, Lough Derravarragh, Co. Westmeath (NMI files). Indeed, this part of Lough Derravarragh may have extensive Bronze Age lake settlement evidence. Another bronze sword, a socketed bronze spearhead and several stone platforms are scattered along this foreshore (NMI files; Victor Buckley, pers. comm.; Karkov and Ruffing 1997, 346). A large number of bronze weapons are recorded as having been found actually in lakes, such as a sword from Ladlestown, Lough Ennell, Co. Westmeath (Eogan 1965, 88). Bronze Age wooden dugout boats have been recovered from lakeshores at Ballagh Lough, Co. Monaghan (dendrochronologically dated to 999 BC) (Brindley and Lanting 1997), and Bronze Age dugouts are known from wetlands at Cuilmore and Tonregee, Co. Mayo (Robinson *et al.* 1996). There have been a number of archaeological excavations on Bronze Age lake settlements, which will now be discussed in detail.

Cullyhanna Lough, Co. Armagh

At Cullyhanna Lough, a Middle Bronze Age enclosed settlement was located in marshes on the north-east side of a small lake, overlooked by hills to the north-east, at the outlet of the Cullyhanna River (Hodges 1958; Mallory and McNeill 1991). The site was discovered through local drainage activities and excavated rapidly by a team of four to five archaeologists over a four-week period in June 1956. The excavation revealed that little attempt had been made to build up an artificial surface across the entire site, as only two low clay and stone mounds were created in the middle and north part of the site. The entire site was defined by an enclosing post palisade, 20m in diameter, of cleft oak timbers and an outer circle of birch roundwood (Pl. 6; Fig. 12).

The north mound was laid on a 'raft' of timber; it was encircled by six pairs of posts with a concentric outer circle of slightly smaller posts. A gap was noted on the eastern side, with sturdier timbers at it. Hodges interpreted this structure as a circular house about 6m in diameter with a central hearth and entrance. He reconstructed the house as having low walls, possibly built of turves, with the inner posts supporting cross-ties for the main rafters, and a medium-pitched roof. Finds from the mound included two thumbnail scrapers and two hollow scrapers. The second mound lay to the south, but appeared to have been the subject of rebuilding. A layer of clay capped a spread of charcoal on an underlying clay layer. The mound was defined to the east by a low stone revetment and to the west by a lightly constructed semicircular wicker structure. Upright posts were clustered around the central hearth. This was interpreted as a small wind-break structure with a spit. Finds from the south mound included a single sherd of very coarse undecorated pottery, a flint blade core and three hollow scrapers.

Hodges (1958) proposed that the woodworking evidence, the lack of pottery and the poor-quality flints suggested an Early Historic date. He compared the layout of the site with some raths and cashels rather than crannogs, and tentatively suggested a date between AD 500 and 1300. He proposed that a group of about twelve men equipped with iron axes could have built the structure in about five days. It is now known that the site is a Bronze Age occupation, as a timber was subsequently dated by Jennifer Hillam to 1526 BC (Hillam 1976). As the settlement was located in an area presumably prone to winter flooding and there were few finds from the site, Hodges proposed that it could only have been occupied in summer. He also believed that cattle could not have been corralled inside the damp conditions of the enclosure, indicating that it was not associated with booleying. He interpreted the site as a hunting camp, located to exploit the wetland resources of waterfowl and fish and also deer in the neighbouring

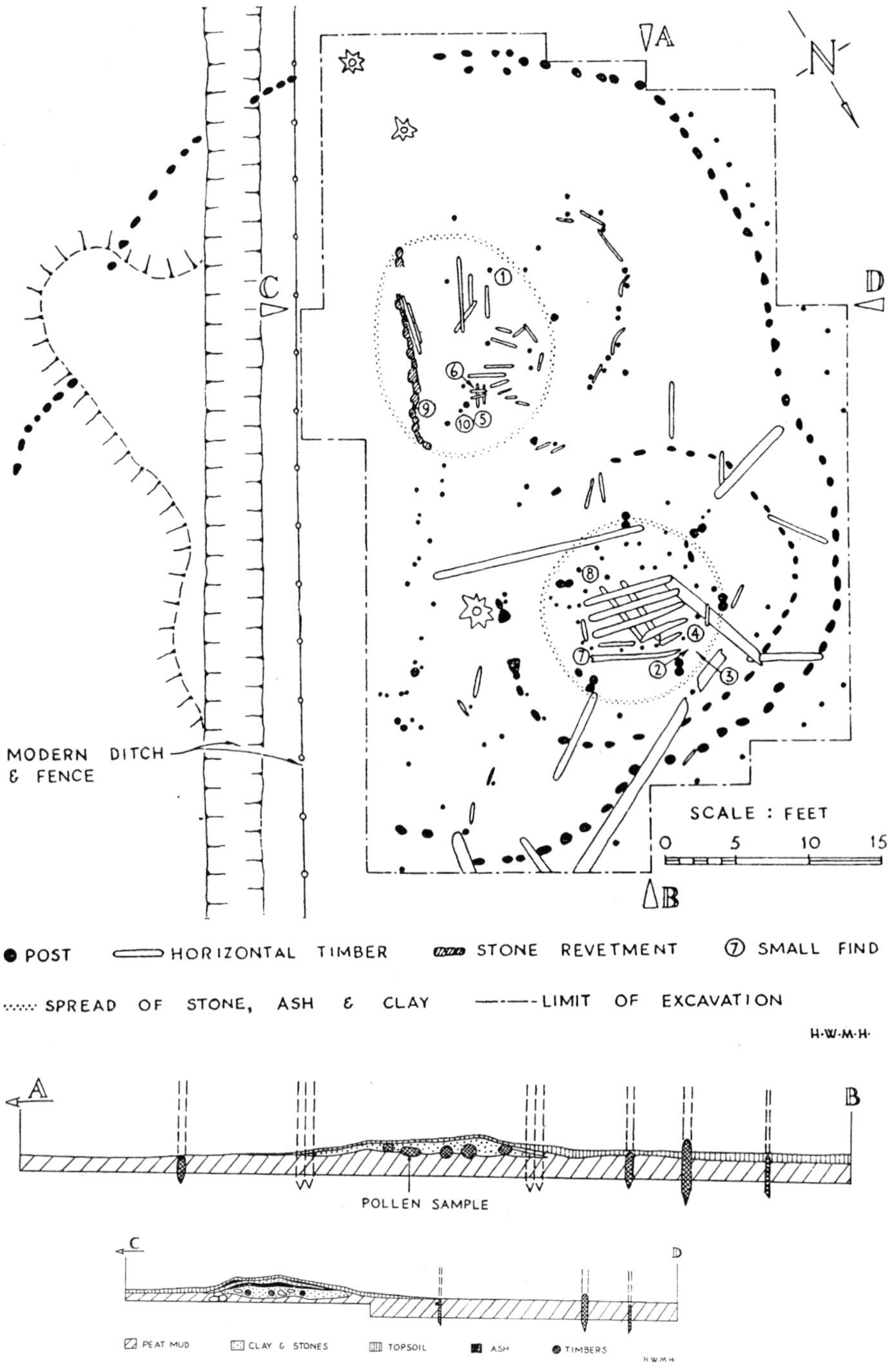

Fig. 12—*Middle Bronze Age lake settlement at Cullyhanna Lough, Co. Armagh: plan and cross-sections of excavated features (Hodges 1958).*

woodlands (Fig. 13).

The archaeological interpretation of the function of the site has not been greatly modified since Hodges's original publication (Herity and Eogan 1977; Cooney and Grogan 1994; Mallory and McNeill 1991). It is still interpreted as an isolated settlement, occupied for only a brief period or periodically over several seasons. The site may have been used as a defended refuge, as a hunting or fowling camp, or as a base for cattle transhumance. The economy of the site is barely understood, as soil acidity prevented any animal bone surviving and palaeobotanical studies apparently carried out were not published.

Lough Eskragh, Co. Tyrone

The Bronze Age lakeshore structures located at Lough Eskragh, Co. Tyrone, appear to have been multiperiod in date and varied in form and function. The structures were first exposed in 1953, when the lake levels at Lough Eskragh were lowered as water was drained off for use in a local textile mill. The lakeshore was then investigated by Pat

Fig. 13—*Reconstruction drawing of Middle Bronze Age lake settlement at Cullyhanna Lough, Co. Armagh (Hodges 1958).*

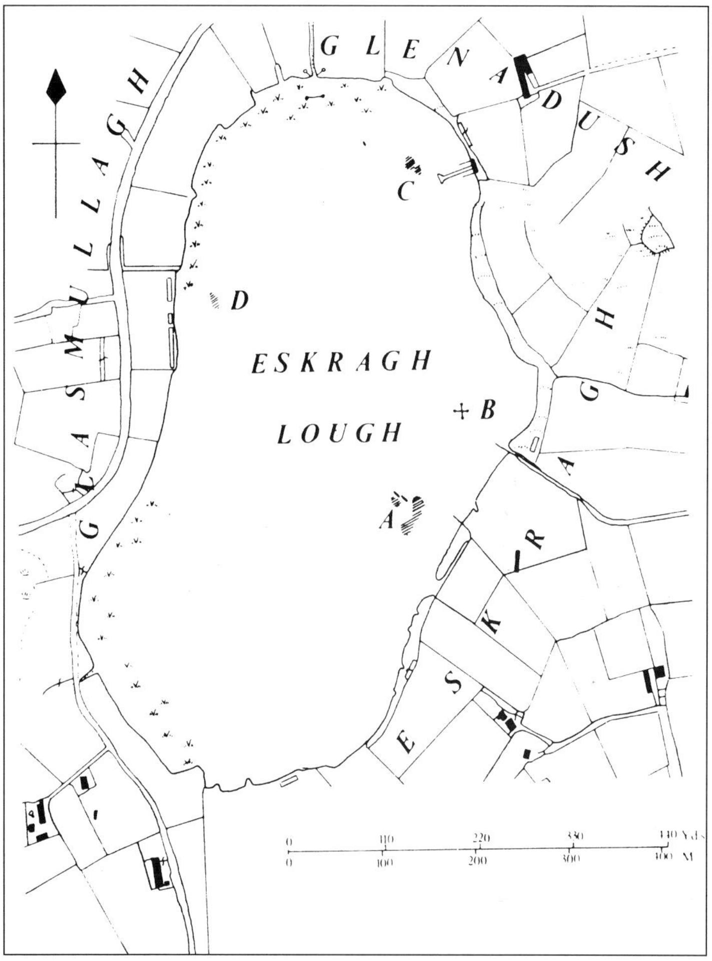

Fig. 14—*Late Bronze Age lakeshore settlements at Lough Eskragh, Co. Tyrone: location of Sites A, B and C (after Collins and Seaby 1960).*

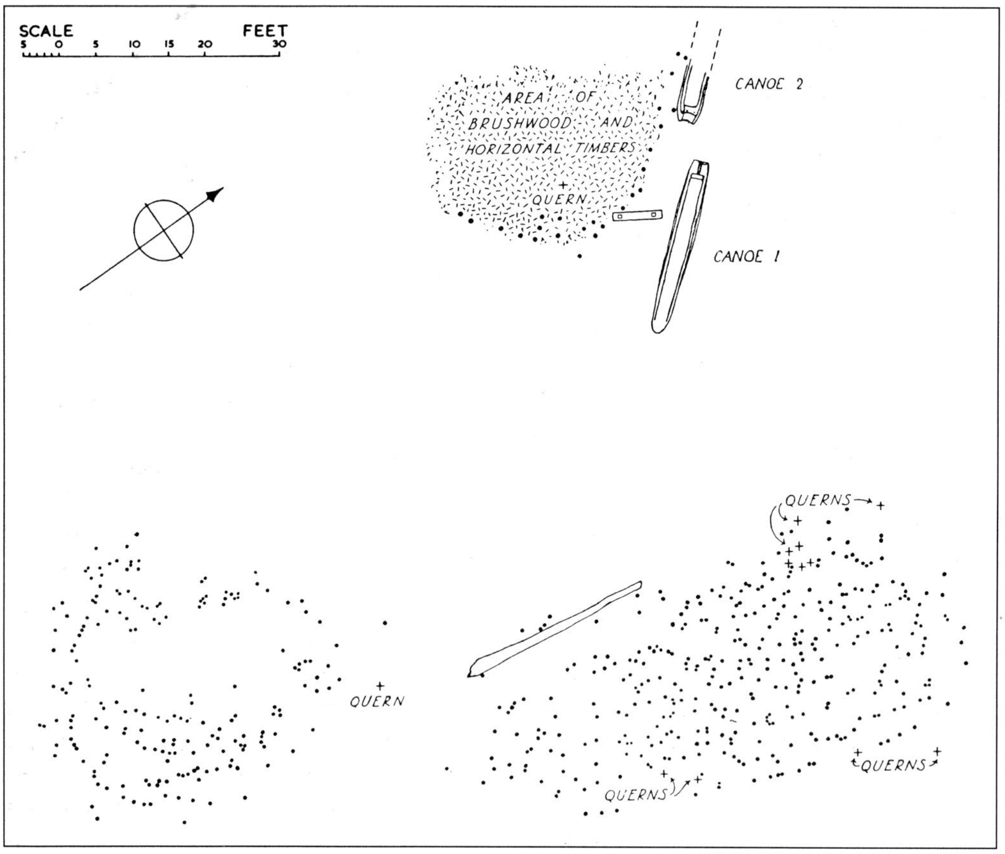

Fig. 15—*Late Bronze Age lakeshore settlements at Lough Eskragh, Co. Tyrone: plan of piled area and 'crannog' at Site A (after Collins and Seaby 1960).*

Collins and William Seaby, who recorded several different sites (Collins and Seaby 1960) (Fig. 14). In 1973, another phase of low lake levels caused fissuring of the lake muds and placed the site again under threat, leading to a second investigation of two sites (Williams 1978). There appear to have been two main phases of Bronze Age activity at Lough Eskragh, a Middle/Late Bronze Age metalworking site (Site B) and a Late Bronze Age lake settlement (Site A) (Mallory and McNeill 1991).

Site B was a Middle/Late Bronze Age platform on the eastern foreshore. It was defined in the 1960 investigations by a small spread of vertical posts and charcoal and was interpreted as a bronzesmith's working area, with finds including clay moulds for a leaf-shaped bronze sword and a large anvil stone. A bag-shaped socketed axe was also picked up from the lakeshore (Collins and Seaby 1960). The excavation of Site B revealed that it was a platform, 10.5m in diameter, of brushwood and horizontal birch logs laid on a bed of peats, constructed on a natural muddy rise in the lakebed. The foundation layer produced two finds, a fragment of sword mould and a broken saddle quern. There are problems with the chronology of this layer, as an unusually early radiocarbon date of 3105 ± 80 BP (1520–1140 BC; UB-948) was obtained from it. The next layer (layer 2) was a deposit of brushwood, twigs and pebbles which covered the whole area. Wooden posts and horizontal roundwood defined the perimeter of the site (about 9m in diameter), and burnt clay bearing the impression of wattles may have derived from a fence at the perimeter. Most of the Site B finds were found at this level, including about a dozen clay moulds for the casting of socketed axes and swords, and several small crucible fragments, a bronze ring and the remains of eight saddle querns. A deposit of fine yellow sand lay over the final occupation level.

Site A was situated 130m to the south. It had two Late Bronze Age features, a continuous area of piles running along the shore and a possible lake settlement platform to the north-west (Fig. 15). The area of piling measured 40m by 10m. It was thought

Pl. 22—*Late Bronze Age dugout boat found beside 'crannog' at Site A, Lough Eskragh, Co. Tyrone (from Collins and Seaby 1960).*

after the 1953 investigations to be two structures (Collins and Seaby 1960) but was later confirmed to be a single continuous feature (Williams 1978; O'Kelly 1989). There were about 600 birch and ash posts and it was recognised that many of the posts had been trimmed by the same bronze axe (Williams 1978, 38). Seventeen saddle querns, coarseware pottery and a bronze axe were recovered from amongst these piles. The piling produced a radiocarbon date of 2475 ± 45 BP (790–400 BC; UB-965). A 'crannog' structure lay about 11m to the north-west of the piled area. This was a circular platform, *c.* 10.5m in diameter, constructed of horizontal layers of timber and brushwood and defined by a revetment of small birch posts. A mortised plank was found on the north-east side of the platform. A radiocarbon date of 2690 ± 45 BP (960–800 BC; UB-1472) was obtained from an oak plank, and a dendrochronological date in the tenth century BC was obtained from one oak timber. A length of post-and-wattle was recorded on the west side of the 'crannog'. The finds from the Site A 'crannog' included two whole coarseware pots, several sherds of other pottery vessels, seven saddle querns, a jet bracelet, a stone axe and a carved two-piece alder tub (Williams 1978, 39). There were two large dugout canoes adjacent to Site A, one of which had previously produced two wooden tubs (Mallory and McNeill 1991) (Pl. 22).

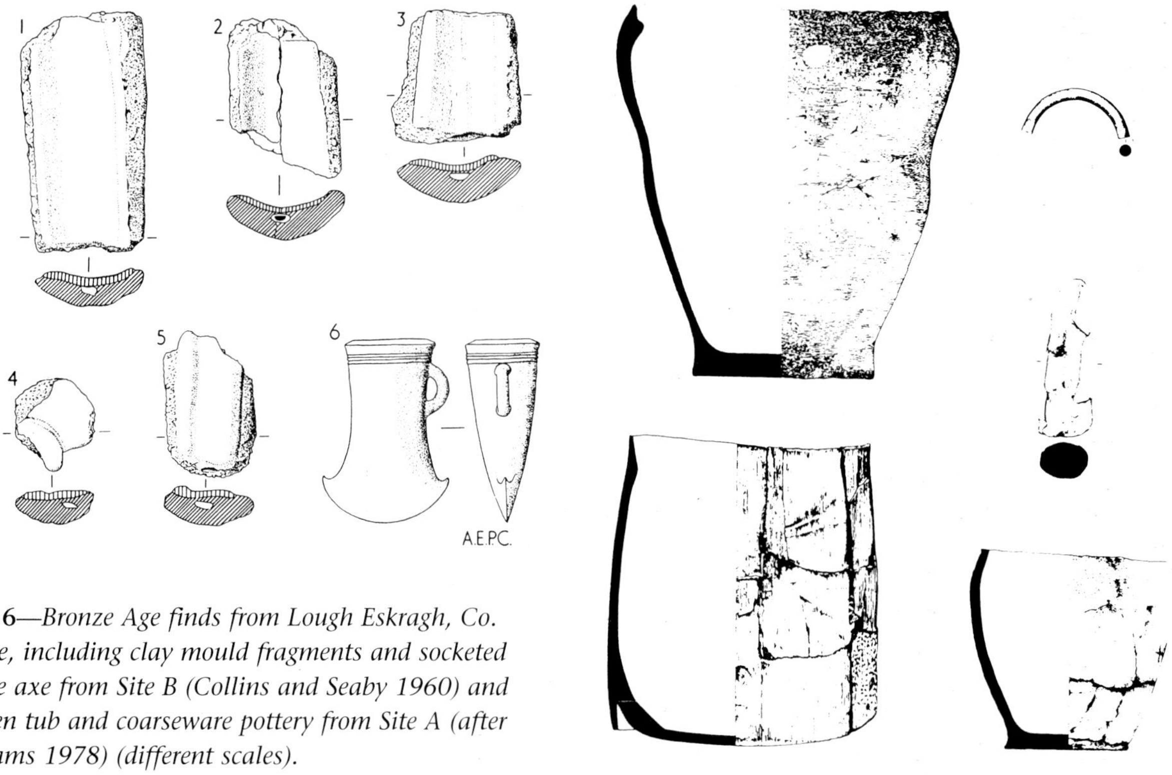

Fig. 16—*Bronze Age finds from Lough Eskragh, Co. Tyrone, including clay mould fragments and socketed bronze axe from Site B (Collins and Seaby 1960) and wooden tub and coarseware pottery from Site A (after Williams 1978) (different scales).*

Site C consisted of two Bronze Age platforms or low mounds surrounded by rings of posts and burnt clay or daub from wattlework. It had been almost completely destroyed by the time of Brian Williams's (1978) excavations. Two piles remained, and one was radiocarbon-dated to 2360 ± 45 BP (750–290 BC; UB-950). Site D was a possible Bronze Age post alignment, consisting of a linear arrangement of piles, 15m in length and 5m wide, on the western shore of the lake. Three saddle quern fragments were recovered from the lakeshore at these posts. The site was not investigated in detail.

Site B and Site A may have been occupied at different times. It is possible, despite the early radiocarbon dates from Site B, that the metalworking site and the occupation site were inhabited at the same time. Site A may have been the domestic settlement, with finds including pottery, wooden vessels, ornaments and dugout canoes. Site B may have been restricted to metalworking, with its mould fragments and crucibles indicating the production of bronze swords and socketed axes, the anvil stone used for pounding the primary ores, and the saddle querns used for physically reducing them down and for grinding down the lake clays for use in moulds (Fig. 16). If this latter interpretation is true, then it seems that the metalworking site was deliberately separated from the domestic area, either as a precaution against fire or as a social barrier between bronzesmiths and other people.

Killymoon, Co. Tyrone

Recent excavations at Killymoon, Co. Tyrone, have also produced an intriguing range of evidence for a Late Bronze Age wetland or raised bog metalworking site (Hurl 1995). Killymoon townland is known to have been the location of an early nineteenth-century discovery of a Late Bronze Age dress-fastener found in a wooden box, possibly in a bog (Eogan 1983). In recent years, cattle trample on an oval rise at the western edge of the bog revealed saddle querns, hammerstones and worked flints. An associated radiocarbon date in the tenth century BC was produced from organic material. In summer 1995, an excavation was carried out on the site by Declan Hurl of the Environment Service (Hurl 1995). A brushwood trackway, consisting of vertical stakes and horizontal brushwood, ran across the peats at the southern end of the site. This was dated to about 1100 BC and apparently represents the earliest activity on the site. The trackway may have led towards a hilltop enclosure to the west.

The Bronze Age occupation site was defined by a layer of grey ashy soil, measuring 23m (north-west–south-east) by 12m and up to 5m thick. This directly overlay the peat and may have been defined by stones around the edge. Several spreads of charcoal and large deposits of charred barley lay on top of this ash layer. The site produced three mounds, about 5m apart. The largest, central mound measured 3.5m in diameter and 50cm in height. It was composed of twelve convex layers of baked clay and charcoal over a domed setting of sandstone slabs. It may have been enclosed by a wooden windbreak. A smaller mound to the south consisted of four layers over limestone boulders. The smallest mound to the north consisted of four layers over burnt planks. The material suggested repeated episodes of industrial, rather than domestic, activity. Finds recovered from the grey, ashy soil included two clay mould fragments for a stick-pin and a spearhead, a socketed bronze axe, hammerstones, saddle querns, rubbing stones, coarseware pottery, spindle-whorls and stone axes. Human and animal hair, woollen twine, cloth and worked wood were amongst the other organic finds. A Late Bronze Age gold dress-fastener and a gold sleeve-fastener were found under a spoil-heap west of the central mound. The processing of grain may be indicated by the saddle querns, rubbing stones and some spreads of charred barley. Radiocarbon dates suggest multiphase occupation up until the end of the Late Bronze Age, *c.* 800 BC.

Killymoon appears to have been primarily a Late Bronze Age metalworking or industrial site. There was little evidence for house structures, animal bone or other domestic refuse, suggesting that its inhabitants came to the site from elsewhere. The spreads of ash, clay and mould fragments suggest that the mounds were being used for

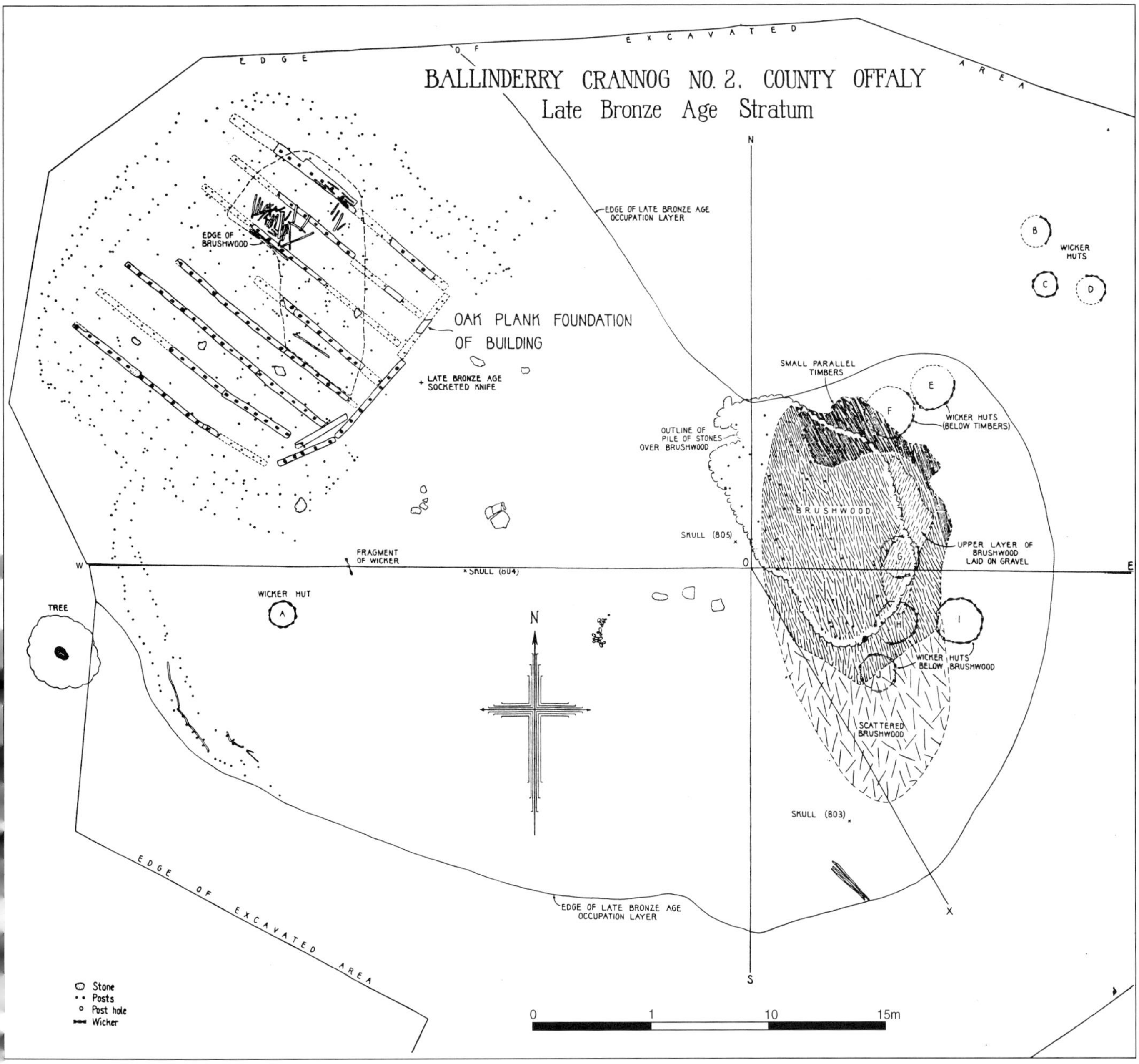

Fig. 17—*Late Bronze Age lake settlement structures at Ballinderry no. 2, Co. Offaly (Hencken 1942).*

Pl. 23—*General view of Late Bronze Age timber structure at Ballinderry no. 2, Co. Offaly (Hencken 1942).*

some industrial activity, either metalworking or the firing of pottery. The site may have been isolated for several reasons—to prevent fire in the domestic settlement, to provide access to peat and clay, or to preserve the secrets of the metalworker's trade—and may be associated with an enclosure on the hill. The discovery of gold on the Killymoon site raises possibilities of other associations. At Mooghaun, Co. Clare, the place of ritual deposition or concealment of a gold hoard in the lake may be deliberately linked to the nearby hillfort (Cooney and Grogan 1994).

Ballinderry crannog no. 2, Co. Offaly

Ballinderry crannog no. 2 was situated at the edge of Ballinderry Lough, Co. Offaly, and Moyvoughly Bog, Co. Westmeath. Excavated by the Harvard expedition in 1933 (Hencken 1942), it proved to be a multiperiod site, with a Late Bronze Age lake settlement underlying an Early Historic crannog (Herity and Eogan 1977; O'Kelly 1989; Harbison 1988; Cooney and Grogan 1994). Recently the site has been substantially reinterpreted by Conor Newman (forthcoming), who has made important suggestions as to its structures, phasing and function on the basis of the site plans and stratigraphy.

Hencken (1942) proposed that the Late Bronze Age settlement comprised a single large rectangular structure, several post clusters, a stone and brushwood feature, and a number of circular wicker structures in a thin black deposit of lake muds (Fig. 17; Pl. 23). The finds from this phase included bronze and stone artefacts and sherds of several pottery vessels. The animal bone from the site included cattle, pig, sheep/goat, horse, red deer, badger, otter, crane, wild duck, scaup, and cat. The site was then partially covered by a layer of white marl, prior to its use as an Early Historic crannog. Newman suggests, on the basis of a complex reinterpretation of the site stratigraphy, that the stone and brushwood feature and the circular wicker structures are later, intrusive features which derive from an Early Historic pre-crannog occupation (probably late sixth-century in date). The Early Historic crannog itself was probably constructed and occupied in the eighth century AD. He has also proposed that a second, substantial rectangular wooden structure can be traced in the grid-like alignment, spacing and orientation of posts at the opposite side of the site. Indeed, the majority of the Late Bronze Age finds (i.e. most of the coarseware pottery, all the amber beads and lignite bracelets) came from this area, suggesting that it was an area of intense activity around a former structure. This second timber structure may have rotted away (C. Newman, pers. comm.) or may have been disassembled, possibly because the wooden beams were better preserved on this higher part of the site (a knoll) and could be reused elsewhere.

Newman's reinterpretation implies that the Late Bronze Age lake settlement had two substantial wooden structures and a possible pathway linking them, with the buildup on the site of an occupation layer. Finds from the site included bronze knives, awls, a flesh-hook and a possible sunflower pin shaft. Other finds included spindle-whorls, a saddle quern, stone rubbers, wooden artefacts and leather. Three human skulls were found in the black layer beneath the wooden structures. While Hencken (1942) suggested that there were eight or nine pots amongst the 300-plus sherds, Newman's recent examination of the rim profiles indicates that there may have been as many as seventeen vessels.

Late Bronze Age finds are known from several places in the immediate vicinity of the Ballinderry 2 site. A hoard of bronze objects (including a socketed looped spearhead, two socketed gouges, a socketed and tanged chisel, a socketed knife and three large rings) was found in 1944 at a depth of 2.5m in peat, possibly in Moyvoughly Bog (Eogan 1983). More recently, a Late Bronze Age cup-headed pin and a bronze ring were recovered, possibly in association with cremated bone, from a site 400m to the north of Ballinderry 2. Various other items of Late Bronze Age date, including tools, weaponry and ornaments, have been reported from the site, although some of these may have been deliberately misprovenanced in order to increase their value (Newman, forthcoming).

Ballinderry crannog no. 2 seems to have been more than an ordinary domestic settlement site. The occurrence of three human skulls in its foundation layers seems to indicate a ritual origin for the site or the deliberate creation of a ritual ethos prior to its construction. The occurrence of metalwork hoards at the site and in its vicinity may also indicate the ritual importance of Ballinderry Lough to Bronze Age communities. There certainly seem to have been large timber-built structures on the site, but their reconstruction as conventional Bronze Age houses needs to be addressed. Nevertheless, there does appear to have been some measure of on-site settlement activity, with coarseware pottery, wooden artefacts and saddle querns found. It may be that Ballinderry 2 was a high-status settlement or a site associated with cult or ritual activities.

Pl. 24—*The Late Bronze Age levels under excavation at Moynagh Lough, Co. Meath (photo: John Bradley).*

Moynagh Lough, Co. Meath

The Moynagh Lough excavations have produced evidence for Mesolithic, Neolithic, Early/Middle Bronze Age, Late Bronze Age and Early Historic occupations (J. Bradley 1991; 1996; forthcoming). The first Bronze Age activity on the site was towards the end of the Early Bronze Age, when a layer of stones and sand was laid over the site's natural knolls (Pl. 24). On top of this sand was an occupation layer, 15cm thick, consisting of dark, charcoal-flecked earth. A radiocarbon date of 1510 BC (3460 ± 35 BP) was obtained from the occupation layer. This layer contained two wooden houses. The earlier was house 1, which consisted of a circular group of posts with a diameter of 6m. It had an occupation layer of peat and ash 6cm thick, with finds including burnt flint and grain. House 2 was also round in plan, with a diameter of 6.8m. It had a thicker occupation layer, 15cm deep in the centre. Finds included a large number of sherds of cordoned urn pottery, deriving from about twelve vessels. Worked stone included a barbed and tanged arrowhead, rounded scrapers, two worked flints and three struck flakes. Two plano-convex knives were found in the lake mud. Pointed bone objects and saddle quern fragments were also recovered. The settlement may have been surrounded by a light wooden palisade.

The Late Bronze Age occupation appears to have started about 700 BC, when lake levels fell, drying out a ridge running across the site. The earliest phase consisted of four stone scatters or gravel spreads which provided firm ground on the lake mud. One spread had the appearance of a platform (1.5m in diameter) constructed of carefully

Pl. 25—*Late Bronze Age socketed spearheads from Moynagh Lough (photo: David Jennings, courtesy of John Bradley).*

laid slabs. A small hearth, 20cm in diameter, was found. The second phase was represented by four large stone spreads, varying in size from 4m to 7m across. Most of the stones showed evidence for heat fracturing, while many had decayed to sand. The stone spreads were covered by a layer of charcoal-flecked peat, 1–20cm thick. At the edge of the layer, embedded in peat against the water's edge, was a series of wooden posts. A circular structure (6.5m across) with a hearth placed off-centre was discovered during the 1996 season and further explored during 1997 (John Bradley, pers. comm.). Apart from the hearth and spreads of ash, no occupation layer had survived within this structure.

This level was covered by a layer of heat-cracked stones, mixed in with charcoal and other debris. Finds from the layer of stone included the remains of at least four coarseware pots. Antler and bone objects included two spindle-whorls and a handled bone comb. There were 22 saddle querns (some fragmentary), three rubbing stones, three stone hones, three burnishers and an antler cheek-piece. There were also 32 amber beads, part of an amber ring, one glass bead, five bracelets and two small rings of lignite or shale. There were a surprisingly large number of bronzes on the site, including eight pins (with globular, nail and slightly expanded heads and a possible sunflower pin), two tweezers, two bronze spearheads (Pl. 25), a circular bronze disc and part of a bronze rod. There was also much animal bone, a spread of burnt grain and tiny fragments of burnt bone.

The Early/Middle Bronze Age phase seems most comparable with Meadowlands, Co. Down (Pollack and Waterman 1964), and Cullyhanna Lough, Co. Armagh (Hodges 1958). It appears to have been a high-status settlement, possibly enclosed by a palisade. Bradley (1996, 26) has explored a number of explanations for the Late Bronze Age site, stating that the activities included cooking, the grinding of grain and wool-carding, and that the inhabitants, with their amber, pins and spearheads, were of high social status. He compared the site to Knocknalappa, Co. Clare, and Killymoon, Co. Tyrone. The absence of large domestic structures and a palisade may have meant that the site

Fig. 18—*Reconstruction drawing of the Late Bronze Age lake settlement at Clonfinlough, Co. Offaly (drawing by Margaret Keane, courtesy of the Irish Archaeological Wetland Unit).*

served a function in the wider landscape. Bronze Age *fulachta fiadh* are known from the vicinity of Moynagh Lough (Corlett 1997), and the Late Bronze Age ritual site at Raffin is located one mile away (Newman 1995).

Clonfinlough, Co. Offaly

The Bronze Age lake settlement at Clonfinlough, Co. Offaly, seems to have been an isolated, defended farmstead located deep within a wetland landscape (Moloney *et al.* 1993). It was formerly located in a reed-swamp at the southern edge of a small lake, overlooked by a steep esker slope some distance to the north and backed by a raised bog to the south. There is some evidence for Bronze Age settlement on the esker drylands to the north and east. The Clonfinlough stone, possibly Bronze Age in date, is intervisible with the lake settlement, and several barrows and mounds are also apparently known in the vicinity (O'Brien and Sweetman 1997; Moloney *et al.* 1993). The River Shannon is a short distance away over the esker hills to the west. The site was partly excavated by the Irish Archaeological Wetland Unit in 1990 and 1991, mainly in the north-eastern part of the site, where most features were already exposed by peat-milling.

The site was enclosed by a large wooden palisade, a slightly irregular oval in plan and constructed entirely of stout ash roundwood posts, 16–20cm in diameter. The enclosed area measured 50m east/west by 40m north/south. There were occasional gaps between the posts in the palisade (up to 40cm on the west side) and it may have been open to the lakeshore on the southern side. Excavation indicated that the posts had been driven at a slight angle into the underlying marls, to depths of 2.65m. There were a number of structures inside the enclosure. These were interpreted as the remains of two substantial houses built on raised platforms, a smaller hut and a working surface (Fig. 18).

House 1, at the eastern edge of the enclosure, was built on a wooden and stone structure (platform 1). Its section, exposed in the peat drain face, revealed a complex construction of a roundwood substructure (of wattle 'boxes'), stone slabs, brushwood matting and finally split oak planks, creating a slightly domed disc up to 9.35m in diameter and up to 60cm thick. A large hearth (5.5m^2 in area) at the centre of this wooden platform was built of stone flags with several layers of ash and charcoal. A double wattle wall enclosed the platform, with an entrance feature to the north-eastern side. Traces of an occupation layer of crushed stone and gravel produced burnt and unburnt fragments of animal bone. Finds from the upper layers of the hearth included an amber bead and a quantity of coarseware pottery (mostly concentrated at the centre of the house) from six pottery vessels. Dendrochronological dating of the oak planks from the upper part of the platform suggested that it was constructed between 917 and

Pl. 26—*Clonfinlough hut 3 (the smallest structure), showing its wooden floor, central hearth and wall posts (photo: Irish Archaeological Wetland Unit).*

899 BC. A timber trackway running to the north of the platform, and contemporary with it, provided a dendrochronological date of 908 ± 9 BC.

House 2 was placed on a similar raised structure (platform 2) measuring 7.2m in diameter and 60cm in height. It was also built of roundwood, stone, brushwood and split oaks, although it was slightly smaller than platform 1 and may have taken less material to construct. Only a small part of the hearth had survived a modern drain; it covered an area of at least $1m^2$ and was constructed of slabs and stones, with a thin layer of ash and charcoal. A possible wooden floor surrounded the hearth. Platform 2 also had wooden and stone foundations, with an internal wattle substructure, an enclosing wall and an elaborate entrance feature. Its upper level produced a date of 886 BC. Two wooden paddles and a wicker object were found beside the entrance, as well as a possible saddle quern and several ground stones. A coarseware pot was broken on the platform, its sherds scattered about. There were also a number of other structures on the site.

Hut 3 lay only a few metres to the west of platform 2. This was a circle of vertical posts, 5.2m in diameter. Its floor was made up of layers of timbers, gravel and slabs. A hearth survived at the centre. A further wooden structure or working area to the north of platform 2 was probably an open-air platform, as no vertical posts or hearth were found. There was instead a buildup of organic material, charcoal and animal bone. Scattered around the site were trackways and dumps of worked timber in waterlogged hollows (Pl. 26).

The site appears to have been occupied sometime between about 917 and 886 BC. It is likely that the houses, the hut, the open-air wooden platform, the trackways and the palisade were built at the same time. Platform 1 and a wooden trackway were probably built sometime between 917 and 899 BC. There is also evidence that the platforms were repaired soon after their construction, the upper level of platform 2 producing a date of 886 BC. The houses were large enough (platform 1 measured at least 9m in diameter), with complex layers of timber and stone raising their floors above the wet peats. They were probably roofed with reeds and wooden spars. The archaeological evidence supported the idea of repairs soon after its initial construction, while the hearths had clearly been rebuilt on several occasions. The site was undoubtedly always wet so

Pl. 27—*Clonfinlough: wooden paddles lying on surface of platform 2 (photo: Irish Archaeological Wetland Unit).*

that structures had to be repaired on a number of occasions. While evidence for lake flooding was found, it was unclear whether this was the reason for the site's abandonment. It was also unclear whether the site was occupied on a permanent or a seasonal basis, but the size and solidity of the houses certainly suggest long-term occupation.

Clonfinlough appears to have been an enclosed farmstead with principal dwellings and smaller associated huts, perhaps occupied by a small social group or extended family. A small quantity of animal bone was found, mostly burnt, fragmented and unidentifiable. Cattle was the dominant species in the livestock economy, followed by pig, and sheep/goat played a minor role. In fact it is likely that not more than one sheep/goat was present. The dog may have been either a working animal or a source of food, but only one tooth was found. This dominance of cattle has been recognised on other Bronze Age settlement sites, such as Haughey's Fort, Co. Armagh, and Ballyveelish 2. At Clonfinlough it is uncertain whether dairying or beef production was the more important. It was suggested that the palisade or stockade was used for keeping in cattle but it may also have been used to define the settlement space. Butchery marks were present on the cattle bone, indicating that cattle were certainly used as a food source. In fact, the bones were even shattered for marrow, suggesting that food was in short supply on the site. However, there was no bird or fish bone, which suggests either that the wetland's resources were not being exploited or that such evidence lies elsewhere on the site. Finds from the site that appear to support an interpretation of agricultural activity and a basic domestic economy on-site included saddle querns, grinding stones, a possible churn piece, a possible basket baseboard and some heavy basketry. Two amber beads were found, as well as at least seven vessels of coarseware pottery. Two large paddle-like objects may be evidence for Bronze Age boats and navigation on the nearby River Shannon (Pl. 27). In conclusion, although the site was well preserved and produced evidence for substantial wooden structures, coarseware pottery and some artefacts, it produced no metalwork (in contrast to Moynagh Lough, Ballinderry crannog no. 2, Knocknalappa and Lough Eskragh). Might this lack of metalwork be taken to indicate that this was not a high-status settlement, or that it was abandoned in good order by its inhabitants, who left little of value behind them?

Knocknalappa, Co. Clare

Knocknalappa lies on the level marshy east bank of Rosroe Lough, in the rolling drumlin hills and lakelands of south-east Clare. The first discoveries at Knocknalappa were made in the summer of 1936 by local amateur archaeologists, when the lake level

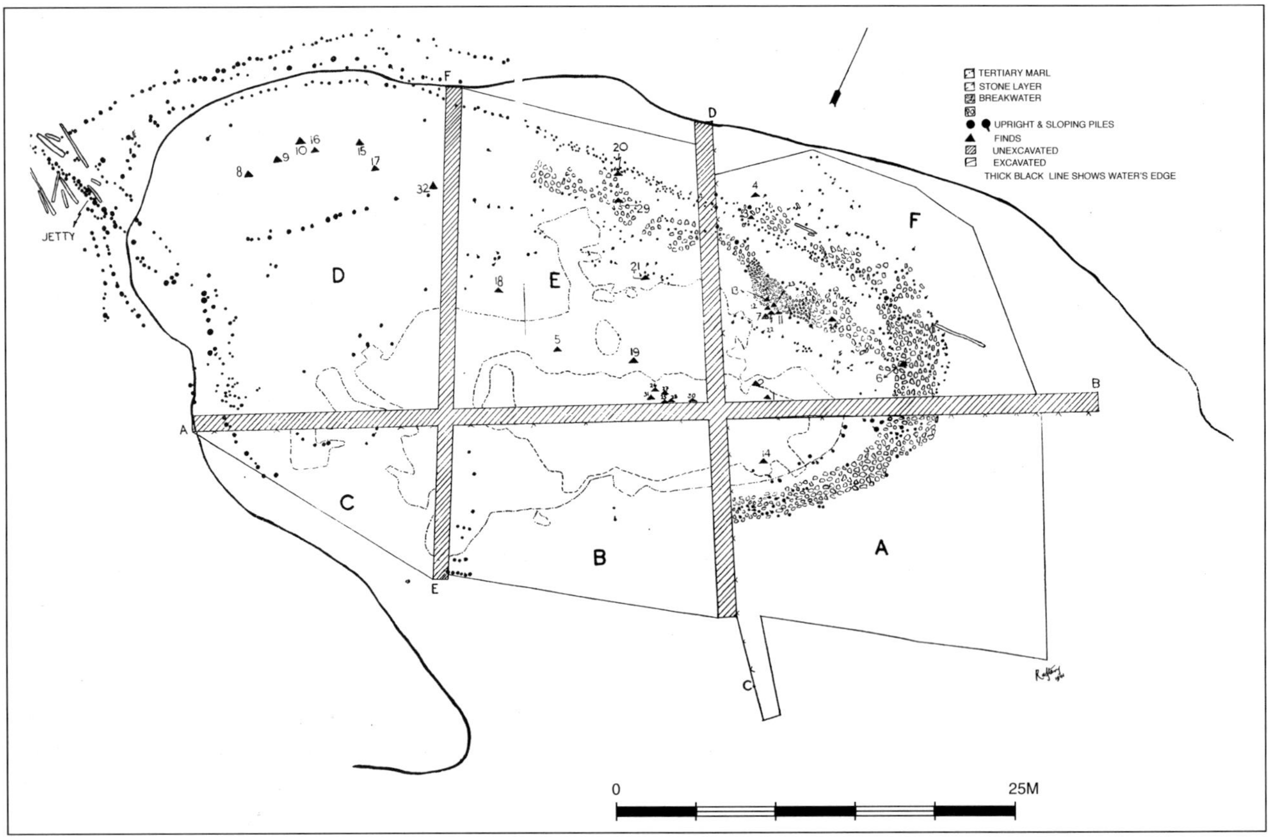

Fig. 19—*Late Bronze Age lake settlement at Knocknalappa, Co. Clare: plan of site (after J. Raftery 1942).*

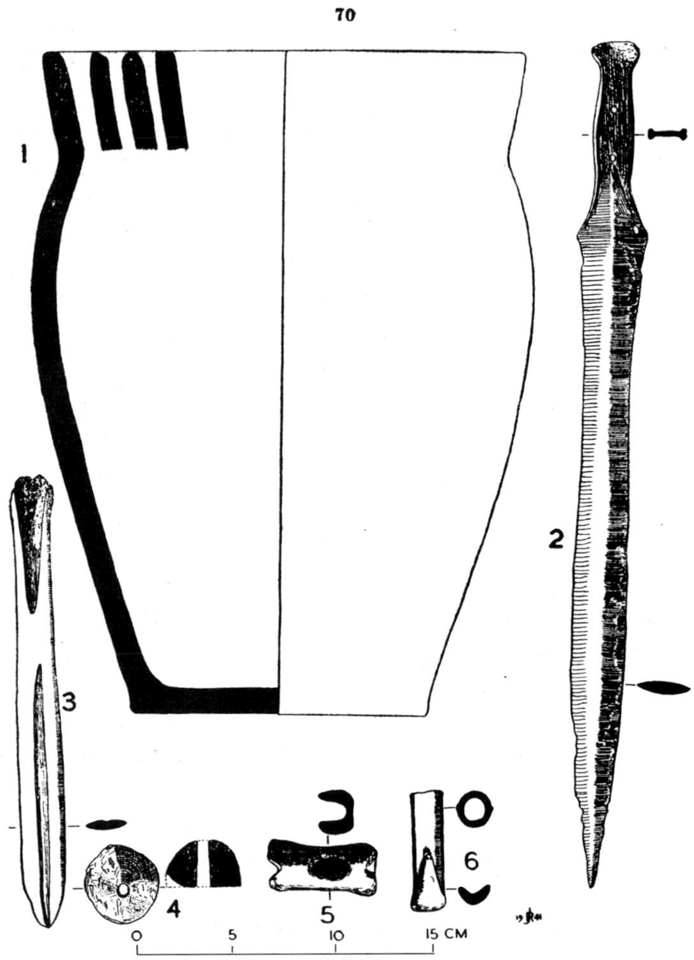

Fig. 20—*Late Bronze Age pottery, weaponry and other finds from Knocknalappa, Co. Clare.*

had been lowered through drainage. Their finds included a bronze flange-hilted sword, a bronze socketed gouge and a polished stone axe, stated to have been picked out of the marl, as were some bones and fragments of wooden vessels which decayed before inspection. These finds seem to have been made on the west side of the mound, possibly eroded out of its side or alternatively located on an exposed area of open lake marl. The site is located at the lake edge of a broad marshy foreshore, which is seasonally flooded. Overlooking this shore is the western slope of a drumlin, one of the more prominent hills in a generally low-lying landscape.

Excavation was carried out by Dr Joseph Raftery over a two-month period in the late summer of 1936. Before excavation the site appeared as a low, oval mound, 40m long and 15–20m wide, aligned roughly east/west. The excavation revealed that a natural shoal or rise of lake marl formed the foundation for the mound. Thereafter a thick layer of peat was laid down, within which were found a layer of brushwood and a narrow wooden platform. The platform was formed of half-split trunks, laid closely side by side. At each corner was a small roundwood stake. Lying on this platform was a thin spread of charcoal and stones.

The next layer within the peat was a discontinuous level of brown peaty soil, within which was found a lignite object, a flint chip, a bone knife, an antler tine and half a pottery vessel. The peat was then partly covered by a mixed layer of stones, animal bone and charcoal. This stony layer contained a bronze ring, a bronze sunflower pin, a lignite bracelet, two saddle querns, three 'hammerstones' and 157 pottery sherds. Above this was a layer of marl, deliberately redeposited onto the stony layer, containing a single amber bead. A thin layer of humus, within which was found an amber bead, covered the mound. Animal bone throughout the site included mainly cattle, sheep, pig, hare and a dog. Bird bone included raven, cormorant, tufted duck and lapwing. Surrounding the mound was an arc of vertical posts to the north and west, supplemented by a stone breakwater to the east. Raftery adjudged this to be the revetment for the mound material. Finds from the breakwater included three amber beads, a bronze bead, a bone spindle-whorl and 27 sherds of pottery. Finds from around the wooden piles and the area of the foreshore included about 116 sherds of pottery, a wooden disc and a thin bronze band.

The artefacts from the site were found either in structural layers or in positions possibly suggesting their erosion from the body of the mound. Lynn (1983) has suggested that the site may actually have been an Early Historic crannog, and that the finds derived from an adjacent Bronze Age midden which was dug up to provide material for the platform. However, recent wood technology studies and radiocarbon dates from the site confirm that it is a Bronze Age lake settlement. A Late Bronze Age radiocarbon date of 2795 ± 35 BP (1033–848 cal. BC; GrN-19692) has been obtained from a sample of carbonised material from the outside of a complete coarseware pot (J. Lanting, pers. comm.). More recently, the North Munster Project reidentified and sampled the palisade, obtaining a radiocarbon date of 1887–1671 cal. BC (GrN-23461). This raises the possibility that Knocknalappa was first occupied in the Early Bronze Age, with a Late Bronze Age occupation phase leading to the deposition of pottery, metalwork and amber beads (Figs 19 and 20).

Knocknalappa has been the subject of various interpretations. Such a quantity of animal bone, of both wild and domestic species (cattle, sheep/goat and pig) in the same contexts, suggests that the bulk of this material should be regarded as domestic refuse. The coarseware pottery, because of its general uniformity and spatial association with virtually all of the other finds, supports the view that all the material belongs to the same Bronze Age horizon. No evidence of any kind for house structures or hearths was found, leading Raftery to the conclusion that the site had no habitation importance. He instead interpreted the site either as a temporary platform used for fishing or fowling or as a refuge to be used in times of danger. It should be pointed out that turf-built or light wooden structures may not have been recognisable in the excavation.

Two Bronze Age *fulachta fiadh* have been located close to the site on the lakeshore.

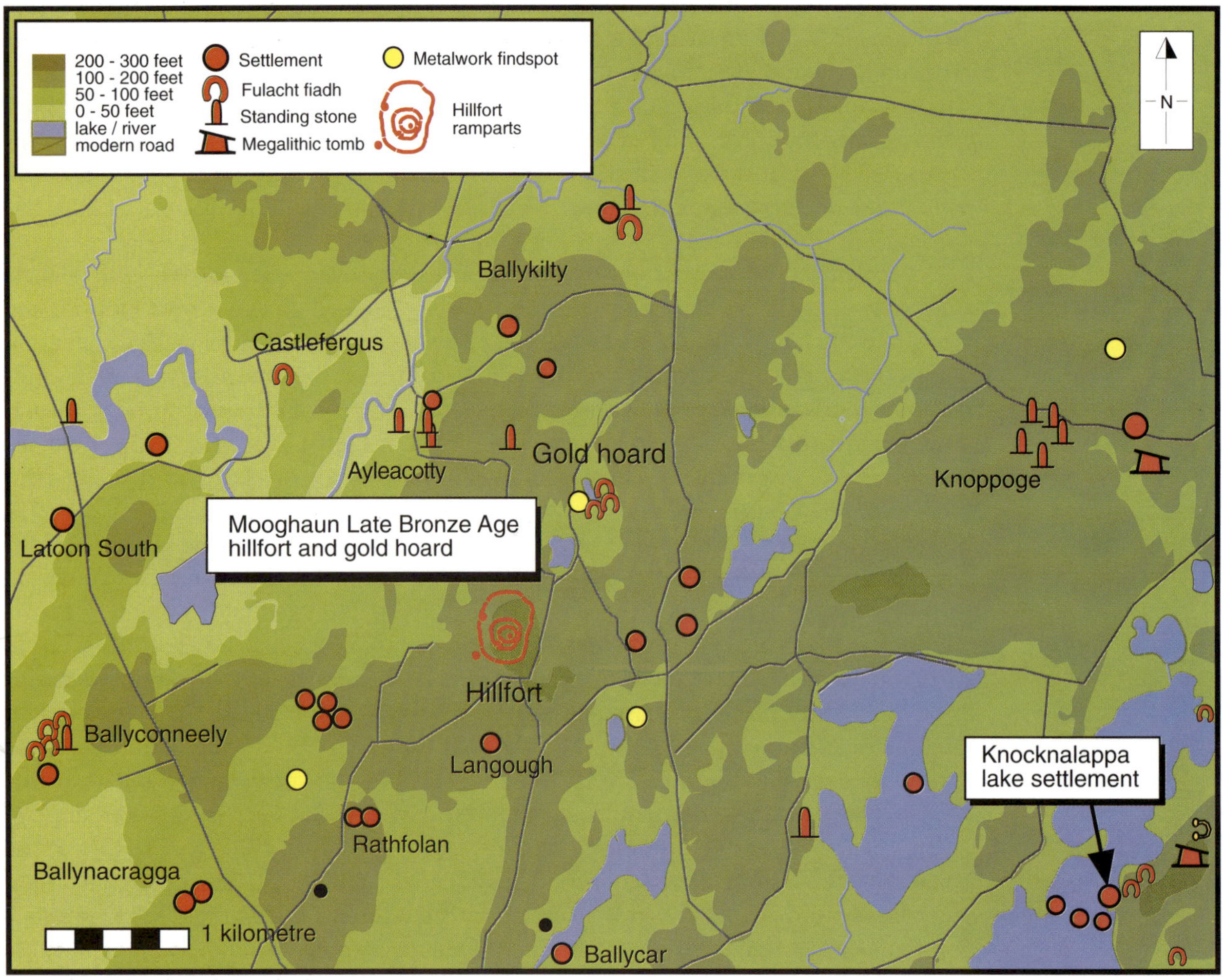

Fig. 21—*The Late Bronze Age lakeshore settlement of Knocknalappa in its regional setting of south-east Clare. Late Bronze Age hoards, stray finds, settlements and a hillfort are other elements of the contemporary landscape (map by Aidan O'Sullivan, reproduced courtesy of the North Munster Project).*

A wedge tomb on the crest of the drumlin hill which overlooks the Knocknalappa lake settlement seems to have become the focus of ritual activities in the Late Bronze Age. Thomas Westropp, the nineteenth-century antiquarian, reported that a gold object had been found beside the tomb; it was described as being 'three inches across, as thick as a cedar pencil, [with] slightly expanded ends, but no cups'. A drawing of the object was published by Scott (1905–8, 32); it is clearly a Late Bronze Age gold bracelet with expanded terminals, datable to *c.* 900 BC.

Knocknalappa in its regional landscape context

Knocknalappa is set in a landscape of rolling drumlin hills, interspersed with lakes, turloughs and bogs. The archaeological evidence of metalwork hoards, single finds, settlement sites and pollen studies indicates that the region was first intensively settled in the Middle Bronze Age (Grogan *et al.* 1995; 1996; Grogan and Condit 1994a) (Fig. 21). By the Late Bronze Age, gold and bronze hoards were deposited in Mooghaun Lough and Lahardaun bog. There are also a number of socketed bronze axes, spearheads and swords from the area. Bronze Age settlements, including hillforts, hilltop enclosures and small domestic enclosures, have been identified in this landscape. Mooghaun hillfort, a massive trivallate hillfort at the western edge of the lakeland zone, has been excavated; substantial defences and entrances, house sites, and domestic and industrial debris were discovered. The site appears to have been constructed between 1159 and 917 BC (Grogan and Condit 1994b). This is contemporary with a major phase of woodland clearance identified in a pollen core from Mooghaun Lough (Molloy 1997; Eoin Grogan, pers. comm.). It appears that the landscape was largely empty prior to this Bronze Age settlement activity.

Bronze Age domestic enclosures or farmsteads have also been found on exposed rocklands or limestone outcrops. These enclosures are defined by a low stone kerb enclosing an area about 20m in diameter, and are typically found in association with small field systems. The siting of these enclosures is interesting in that they are frequently found on rockland terraces overlooking lakes, bogs and coastal marshes. At Ballycar Lough a fine example of a stone enclosure is situated on a ridge overlooking this large lake, and at Ballynacragga a complex of stone enclosures and field systems overlooks extensive views of the Fergus estuary marshes (O'Sullivan and Condit 1995). The Knocknalappa Bronze Age lake settlement can be seen to be part of this settlement system, possibly representing a high-status or élite settlement. The discovery of a bronze sword and gouge on the site seems to indicate the relative wealth of its inhabitants. Knocknalappa is intervisible with Mooghaun hillfort and can be spatially linked to nearby Bronze Age artefactual findspots, *fulachta fiadh* and possible settlement sites. The value of the North Munster Project's research is that it indicates that Bronze Age lake settlements can be usefully investigated through a regional landscape project.

Rathtinaun (Crannog 61), Lough Gara, Co. Sligo

A Bronze Age lake settlement is also known from Rathtinaun, Lough Gara, Co. Sligo. This was exposed after drainage operations in 1952 led to the discovery of large numbers of archaeological sites along the lake margins (Cross 1953; J. Raftery 1957; Evans 1966). Rathtinaun (Crannog 61) was situated on the eastern shore of the lough, at the mouth of the River Boyle. The site was totally excavated between 1952 and 1955. It was selected for excavation owing to the discovery of several Late Bronze Age objects in its vicinity (B. Raftery 1994, 32–5).

The site appeared as an oval mound of stones, 29m by 34m by 2.5m in height. Excavation indicated that a natural mound had been levelled and a central depression filled by piling timbers and brushwood above it. The crannog was further raised with layers of timber and brushwood. A single possible hut, 9m in diameter, represented by vertical oak piles, was associated with a timber trackway. Several 'firebaskets' were also found. These were circular, built of post-and-wattle and lined with a protective yellow clay (Pl. 28). Finds from this lower level included coarseware pottery, a disc-headed pin,

Pl. 28—*Late Bronze Age 'firebasket' being excavated at Crannog 61, Rathtinaun, Co. Sligo (photo: Joseph Raftery, reproduced courtesy of Dept of Archaeology, UCD).*

a pair of tweezers, several rings, a possible cauldron fragment and a gold 'hair-ring'. Clay mould fragments and wooden containers were also found. Period 1 probably dated to the Dowris period of the Late Bronze Age.

The site was then covered by lake levels, sealing it under a layer of sand. In period 2 the crannog was reoccupied. Layers of brushwood were laid down around a central area of cobbling. There were no clear house structures, but there were six large hearths. These hearths were also in firebaskets, 2.5m in diameter, with hearthstones. One hearth reused a firebasket dating from period 1. There was no great chronological gap between period 1 and period 2, and the finds from the latter were also of Late Bronze Age date. Finds included two disc-headed pins, a pair of bronze tweezers, a bifid razor, a tanged chisel, a phalera, coarseware pottery and wooden vessels. A hoard of objects found in a box, apparently in the floor of the period 2 occupation, included a necklace of amber beads, rings of bronze and pure tin and three of lead with gold-foil cover. There was also a pair of tweezers, a bronze pin and, unusually, six boar tusks. The hoard appears to have been marked by narrow vertical stakes. A number of iron objects were also found in the period 2 level, including a pin, a possible sickle fragment, a fork-like implement, a shafthole axehead and a fragment of iron. Until recently this material was seen to represent the transition between bronze and iron tools and implements. Most recent radiocarbon dating indicates that this material is intrusive in period 2 and dates to the Early Historic phase of occupation (Barry Raftery, pers. comm.). The Late Bronze Age lake structures at Rathtinaun appear to have been the permanent settlement site of a small community, engaged in metalworking on a large scale. The finds from the period 1 and period 2 occupations are unusually rich, including bronze, gold, amber and other objects. It is likely that these finds indicate the high social status of Rathinaun's Bronze Age inhabitants, or alternatively that it was some form of trading or redistribution centre.

Island MacHugh, Co. Tyrone

Island MacHugh, Co. Tyrone, a crannog situated on the north-west shore of Lough Catherine, was excavated both by Oliver Davies (1950) and by Richard Ivens and Derek Simpson (Ivens *et al.* 1986; Ivens and Simpson, forthcoming). The site had a complex series of Neolithic, Late Bronze Age and Early Historic occupation layers. The Late Bronze Age site was defined by an irregular post revetment, several posts in depth, driven into the peat. Brushwood, rubble and peat and a paving of flat slabs were placed within the enclosed area. Finds from this deposited material suggested that it was introduced from another settlement. These finds included burnt pig and cattle bone, coarseware pottery, an amber bead, a hollow scraper and a flint knife (possibly derived from the Neolithic layer). Radiocarbon dates from the ninth and fourth centuries BC were obtained from timbers. A bronze sword was picked up on the shore of the island (Simpson 1986). Otherwise, the Bronze Age activities at Island MacHugh remain poorly understood.

Lough Carra, Co. Mayo

One further Bronze Age lake structure remains to be discussed. This is a Bronze Age post alignment from Lough Carra, Co. Mayo. Lough Carra is a large but shallow lake in the west of Ireland, to the north of Lough Mask, with crannogs, island cashels and promontory forts around its shores (e.g. Knox 1902). In autumn 1991, a Bronze Age post alignment was discovered in the lake by a local fisheries officer, and subsequently underwater diving surveys were carried out by local divers (Lavelle 1992; 1994). The structure is composed of a double line of posts driven vertically into the lake marls at a narrow part of the lake, with two opposing lengths of causeway running out from Kilkeeran and Ballycally townlands. The post alignments do not entirely cross the lake. On the west shore, the Kilkeeran post alignment measures 124m in length, and is composed of 84 posts set 2–4m apart. On the eastern shore, the Ballycally post alignment measures 93m in length and 7m in width. The posts follow a double pattern with a cluster of posts at the mid-point. Dendrochronological dates of about 1101 BC and 1571 BC were obtained from the Ballycally section, indicating its periodic reconstruction in the Middle Bronze Age and Late Bronze Age.

The Lough Carra Bronze Age post alignment is unique in Irish archaeology. It has been interpreted as a causeway or fishweir (Lavelle 1992). However, similar Bronze Age post alignments have been found in Britain and have been interpreted as ritual features or territorial boundaries, being locations for the deposition of pottery, metalwork and human bone. Bronze Age post alignments in Britain include sites at Flag Fen, Cambridgeshire (Pryor 1991, 74–121), Caldicot, Gwent (Nayling and Caseldine 1997), Harter's Hill and Greylake, Somerset (Brunning 1997), Testwoods Lakes, Hampshire, and Shinewater Park (R. Brunning, pers. comm.). There is a remarkable consistency in the form and chronology of these double post alignments. They frequently produce Middle and Late Bronze Age metalwork, including swords, spearheads, axes and other objects. Human skull fragments are also often found. The Lough Carra structure may simply be a bridge, but it could be a ritual post alignment or some other type of territorial boundary. It is also unlikely that the Lough Carra Bronze Age post alignment is the only example in the country, but other examples would require underwater diving surveys to locate them.

Chronology, occupation and abandonment

What is the origin and chronology of Bronze Age lake settlement in Ireland? While Early Bronze Age and Middle Bronze Age occupation phases are known from Moynagh Lough, Co. Meath, Cullyhanna Lough, Co. Armagh, and Knocknalappa, Co. Clare, most Bronze Age lake settlements date to the end of the period, between 1200 and 800 BC. Intriguingly, it was at this time that most Bronze Age metalwork hoards were put in lakes, bogs and rivers, and wooden trackways were being constructed across the midland bogs (Cooney and Grogan 1994; B. Raftery 1996). There may also have been a climatic downturn, possibly caused by the Icelandic Hekla volcanic eruption of 1159 BC (Mitchell and Ryan 1997). If uplands were being abandoned and arable crops were failing, then the pastures and grasslands of lakeshores, river valleys and bog islands may have become increasingly important in the economic landscape. However, it is also possible that environmental determinants were not the main reasons for change (Cooney and Grogan 1994; Cooney, forthcoming). Developments in Late Bronze Age society, such as the emergence of regional identities, tribal hierarchies, the new role of a warrior élite and a phase of increased warfare and conflict would have had an impact on the settlement landscape.

Little is understood about the processes by which Bronze Age lake settlements were occupied and abandoned. Some may have been occupied permanently, for a generation or more. Others may have been used for short durations, such as in the summer and autumn, when lake levels would have been lower, or were only visited periodically at particular times of the year. It is possible that settlements were abandoned for economic reasons, such as low food availability, or for social reasons, such as a death in the family making the site unclean or spiritually unsafe (Andersen 1997). The site chronology of most lake settlements is too crude to offer more than suggestions. Clonfinlough, Co. Offaly, has produced dendrochronological dates which suggest its construction, occupation and abandonment over a relatively short period, between 917 and 886 BC. This short period of occupation, perhaps for only a single generation, is a common feature of European wetland settlements, presumably because the sites became waterlogged and uncomfortable (e.g. J.M. Coles and Coles 1996).

Bronze Age lake settlements have produced some good archaeological evidence for house structures. At Cullyhanna and Clonfinlough, clay platforms or wooden rafts were constructed of timber, brushwood and clay, and served as the foundations for circular houses. These houses were relatively substantial, 6–8m in diameter, with central supports, post-and-wattle walls and thresholds. The roofing was probably of reeds or turf. It is possible that the use of such platforms meant that the houses were isolated just above water, surrounded by waterlogged vegetation and reeds. Smaller, peripheral structures were also found at Cullyhanna and Clonfinlough; these may have been storage buildings or animal shelters, or may represent the houses of socially less important individuals or family groups. Moynagh Lough has produced three houses, dating from the Early/Middle and Late Bronze Age phases of occupation. Hearths are typically centrally placed in lake settlement houses, but there is little other evidence for the internal ordering of space (work areas, sleeping arrangements, furniture).

Other Bronze Age lake settlement sites have produced only scanty evidence for houses, while still others have produced structures which may not be houses at all. Does this mean that these were not occupation sites, but served some other function? It is possible that houses were built of sods, turf or blocks of clay, or were tent-like structures of wooden poles and textile coverings that could easily be moved away. The well-known rectangular structure at Ballinderry 2 was probably not a house at all; such a structure would be entirely unlike any other excavated houses of the period. The circular wicker structures at Ballinderry 2 are intrusive features from the overlying Early Historic crannog (Newman, forthcoming). Some lake settlements, such as Knocknalappa, Killymoon and Lough Eskragh, appear to have produced little or no house evidence. There was a wooden 'raft'-like structure at Knocknalappa, upon which there was charcoal, stone and a layer of turf. It is hypothetically possible that a turf-built house with a reed roof was constructed on this wooden raft. If such a structure collapsed after abandonment, the only remains would be peat and clay over the wood. At Lough Eskragh, Site A produced a large circular structure which yielded an array of finds, but no clear house structure was recognised by the excavator. At Rathtinaun (Crannog 61), there was a possible circular wooden structure or hut in period 1, while period 2 did not produce any house structures, but several hearths.

A range of other structures are associated with Bronze Age lake settlements. Lightly built palisades are common: Clonfinlough, Ballinderry 2, Knocknalappa and Cullyhanna Lough have produced light, roundwood palisades. At Knocknalappa, stone breakwaters or kerbing are found at the margins, and a possible boat jetty was found at the waterside. Brushwood trackways are occasionally found, either running between the house platforms (e.g. Clonfinlough) or running away from the sites themselves (e.g. Killymoon). In some cases, while there are large numbers of posts, such as at Lough Eskragh, little structural pattern can be recognised.

Bronze Age lake settlements as agricultural farmsteads

A clue to the particular function of Bronze Age lake settlements lies in understanding the Irish Late Bronze Age agricultural landscape, which seems to have been largely based around permanently occupied dispersed farmsteads engaged in mixed farming on light, well-drained soils, with arable crops being cultivated in small garden fields and cattle herds managed in the surrounding landscape. There may also have been some element of localised settlement mobility or seasonal movement of cattle herds. Middle and Late Bronze Age *fulachta fiadh* could certainly indicate such seasonal communal activities in river valleys, lakeshores and boggy ground, while Bronze Age coastal shell middens, coastal marshland occupations and raised bog trackways indicate economic activities in wetlands.

It is likely that many Bronze Age lake settlements were the wetland agricultural homesteads of extended families (e.g. Herity and Eogan 1977; Eogan 1993). They also produce what might theoretically be expected to be found on domestic settlements, such as a certain range of artefacts and structures, tools and implements, pottery (mostly broken), quernstones, carbonised grain, food debris and animal bone, and a proximity to a water supply. There should also be the remains of fires, possible storage areas and a range of domestic and other structures. Cullyhanna Lough, Clonfinlough, Lough Eskragh Site A and Moynagh Lough have all produced structures, saddle querns, coarseware pottery, flint objects, wooden artefacts and some metal artefacts. Intriguingly, many Bronze Age dryland settlements, such as Chancellorsland, Ballyveelish and

Curraghatoor, yielded very little in the way of material culture despite producing domestic houses and much animal bone (M. Doody, pers. comm.). It may be that lake settlements were generally higher in social status than dryland sites. The absence of material culture on dryland settlements might be explained by the fact that people abandoning a homestead in good order take most of their tools and implements away with them. Wetland settlements might have been abandoned much more quickly, owing to rapid flooding. Admittedly, the lake settlement of Cullyhanna Lough was very poor in terms of its material culture, while Clonfinlough, which appears to have been a farmstead of several families, also produced relatively little (coarseware pottery and two amber beads). On the other hand, the Late Bronze Age lake settlement at Moynagh Lough, with its saddle querns, amber, gold ornaments and bronze weaponry, appears to be entirely different in character. Some of the Bronze Age lake settlements could be the enclosed habitations of small extended family groups engaged in wetland agriculture and exploitation of the surrounding landscapes. Clonfinlough appears to have been the settlement of a larger group of people, possibly inhabiting the location for an extended period, after which the site was finally abandoned.

Is it possible that these were the settlements of pastoralists or cattle-herders temporarily occupying lakeshores, fens and marshes? If there was an element of mobility in Bronze Age settlement and agriculture, then perhaps some lake settlements were occupied only seasonally (summer and autumn being the least difficult times of the year for wetland life). It is unlikely that such semi-nomadic or transhumance settlement sites would produce a lot of material culture, perhaps explaining why some sites have yielded relatively few artefacts. It is also possible that the Bronze Age lake enclosures were used as cattle corrals. At Clonfinlough, the enclosed area lies open only to the lakeshore and thus could have been used for holding cattle, while still allowing them access to drinking water. Cattle could have been grazed on the marshes and taken into the enclosures at night for protection from predators. The lake settlements could also have been where cattle were branded by their owners, castrated and exchanged with other farmers. It is possible that palaeoenvironmental studies on a Bronze Age lake settlement could identify the presence of dung-beetles and other insects associated with cattle. European wetland settlements are known to have been used as cattle byres and sheds, such as Site Q on the Assendelver Polders (Therkorn *et al.* 1984) and Goldcliff, Gwent (Bell 1993).

Bronze Age lake settlements as high-status residences or central places of assembly

Can high-status residences be identified on lakeshores or have the sites any functions outside the domestic sphere? Some Bronze Age lake settlements have produced a range of what might be expected to be high-status goods, such as bronze axes, rings, swords and spearheads, imported amber and lignite bracelets and beads, large amounts of coarseware pottery and large wooden structures. This is in contrast to dryland settlements, which rarely produce metalwork. The Late Bronze Age lake settlement at Rathtinaun had several phases of occupation, and finds included gold and bronze objects, amber and lignite. Ballinderry 2 produced several bronze implements and ornaments and as many as seventeen coarseware pots. The Late Bronze Age phase at Moynagh Lough yielded a large number of amber beads, lignite, bronze pins and bronze spearheads. For some social or symbolic reason, lakeshores could have been perceived as ideal locations for the occasional residences of the élite in society. Once established, lake settlements may also have attracted gatherings of large groups of people for short periods of time, such as at harvest or cult occasions, and could therefore be interpreted as central places of assembly in the surrounding landscape.

This might be supported by the fact that several Late Bronze Age lake settlements, such as Knocknalappa and Moynagh Lough, have been found to be spatially associated with *fulachta fiadh* on lakeshores. The role of *fulachta fiadh* in the Bronze Age landscape is not yet fully understood, but they may have served as cooking troughs or bathing places for surrounding communities. There are certain indications that these sites were used episodically. Every burning episode produces only a certain amount of shattered stone, which is then thrown up on the mound. The size of these mounds suggests that *fulachta fiadh* may have been used tens or hundreds of times. While this could have happened over a few days, it is as likely that people returned to them over months, and perhaps every year, before the trough was abandoned and another *fulacht fiadh* was started. It may be that they were primarily used in the summer and autumn, when local communities assembled for feasts or the exchange of goods. Consequently, lake settlements may in some way either be a replacement for these sites, establishing a more fixed residence at a familiar location, or have been occupied at the same time as the *fulachta fiadh*.

A high-status settlement or a central place would probably be defined by its location, high visibility, restricted access, and the presence of certain unusual structures or features. Exotic goods (amber, bronzes, textiles), food, drink and raw materials could have been brought to these sites at specified times of the year and exchanged for other goods. Other materials that could have been exchanged might leave less archaeological trace, such as slaves, sexual partners, stories or songs and dances. There may have been social gatherings, to inaugurate a leader, confirm trade agreements and define cultural or tribal units. How might such central places be recognised in the archaeological record? It might be expected that they would produce a diverse range of objects, many probably of high status, and that there might be little evidence for long-term habitation. Some Bronze Age lake settlements appear to fit this picture. If used as places of assembly, they could have been located on neutral ground between territories. Lakeshores may have been defining elements in territorial boundaries, and people could have come there by boat with less fear of attack.

Bronze Age lake settlements as defended refuges

Were lakeshore settlements used as defended refuges? Late Bronze Age society in Ireland certainly witnessed several important transformations, particularly the emergence of a stratified, hierarchical society increasingly focused on warfare and the strengthening of regional identities towards the end of the period. Late Bronze Age hillforts such as Haughey's Fort, Co. Armagh (Mallory 1995), Mooghaun, Co. Clare (Grogan 1996b; Grogan and Condit 1994b), Rathgall, Co. Wicklow (B. Raftery 1972), and the cliff fort at Dun Aonghusa (Cotter 1996) were probably used as regional centres of power and status or temporary defensive structures at times of political and social unrest. Burial practices and artefact hoards also indicate a stratified social ranking, probably based on familial descent, age, gender, and perhaps prowess in crafts or combat.

Late Bronze Age warfare in Ireland could have involved warrior groups acting together in well-organised groups, either fighting to enhance the status of individual leaders or raiding other settlements. Periodic raiding, ritual combat, warrior élites, and complex and varying tribal alliances and enmities may therefore have been significant elements in Bronze Age social organisation, so it behoves us to trace their impact on the settlement as well as the artefactual record. While archaeologists have tended to view Bronze Age weaponry in terms of its symbolic or prestige value, it is also true that bronze swords or spearheads were well suited for killing and maiming. It is possible that many Bronze Age lake settlements were actually primarily used as defended refuges rather than as farmsteads. Late Bronze Age swords suitable for both slashing and thrusting have been found on lake settlements (e.g. Knocknalappa). Bronze spearheads have also been found in lake settlements (Ballinderry 2, Moynagh Lough, Killymoon) and may have been used in a variety of ways, e.g. hafted on long wooden shafts and used as lances in close combat. It is also possible that horses were used in Bronze Age warfare, perhaps not for cavalry purposes but for rapid movement of warriors. Small bone objects, interpreted as horse harness components, have been found on several lake settlements (e.g. Knocknalappa, Moynagh Lough). It might be suggested that defended refuges were built in bogs or marshes as a useful means of defence against mounted warriors (Billy O'Brien, pers. comm.).

Bronze Age lake settlements are located in marshes, in bogs and on lakeshores. They could have been hidden amongst dense carr woodland, thus enhancing their defensive function. Alternatively, if they were located on more open lakeshores, they would have been highly visible from the surrounding countryside and thus a confident statement of power for miles round (a kind of wetland 'hillfort'). In either case, one could suggest that siting was an important aspect of their use. Bronze Age lake settlements typically have an enclosing palisade or stockade feature. The defensive effectiveness of these lightly built palisades can be questioned. They hardly seem to be very stoutly built or intended to withstand any forceful attack. It has been proposed that the enclosures of Bronze Age settlements merely served as boundary features, designed to define and separate the settlement space from the outside world (Cooney and Grogan 1994). However, this does not take into account the nature of 'primitive' warfare, which can be as much to do with display and symbolic aggression as with actual combat. It is also true that there were evidently close links between weaponry and watery places in Late Bronze Age Ireland (Eogan 1983; R. Bradley 1990; Cooney and Grogan 1994). Wetlands may therefore have been perceived as appropriate places for temporary warrior residences. Bronze Age lake settlements may have been used for gathering young men and women together in preparation for battle. They have produced both dugouts and large paddles (e.g. Clonfinlough), and boats may have been used for transporting warriors to battles and raids. Ballinderry 2 and Moynagh Lough have also produced human skulls, apparently hacked with swords, which may have been personal trophies or votive offerings thrown into wetlands after combat. It is also possible that the weaponry and skulls are propitiatory offerings after battles, intended to normalise relations with otherworldly forces and to return the community to a domestic state.

Crafts and industry

What was the role of Bronze Age lake sites in crafts and industrial production? Lough Eskragh Site B, Rathtinaun and Killymoon certainly appear to have been occupied by bronzesmiths. The finds from these sites include clay mould fragments for making bronze swords and socketed axes, crucibles, saddle querns (often in great numbers), firebaskets (Rathtinaun) and thick spreads of ash and burnt clay which indicate repeated use of industrial hearths and fires. It may be that such lakeshore settlements were production sites occupied by craftsmen working in isolation from neighbouring communities. By these means, metalworkers and specialists can keep the skills of their trades secret from the general population (Hodder 1982). Lakeshores would have provided various resources for the metalworker, such as wood for fires, clays for moulds and kilns, and water. These metalworking sites may also have been usefully situated by water for travel and communications, or to be at places between territories for trade and exchange. It is possible that other domestic and industrial activities were carried out on these lakeshores, such as the production of pottery from lake marls and other clays and the manufacture of saddle querns and rubbing stones. Moynagh Lough and Lough Eskragh Site A produced an inordinate amount of saddle querns. The production of wooden and reed baskets, wooden artefacts and thatching could also have been carried out using local wetland raw materials, such as reeds, sedges, alder and willow wood.

Cult or ritual sites

It seems likely that Bronze Age societies, like many other 'primitive' communities, had a highly complex cosmology, with supernatural entities and forces active in the landscape, and an abundance of spirits and other otherworldly creatures inhabiting rocks, springs, trees and lakes. It is important to remember that the sacred and the profane were not separate aspects of the landscape, but were interlinked in the daily and seasonal rhythms of life and played a role in settlement organisation. Indeed, it is known that agricultural peoples can have as many as 200 ceremonial occasions during the year (Andersen 1997). The use of watery places—lakes, rivers and bogs—seems to have been of central importance to Late Bronze Age societies in Ireland. At the King's Stables, it appears that an earthen pond was actually constructed for ritual purposes (Mallory and McNeill 1991). Other lakes and ponds were also used for ritual purposes, such as Mooghaun Lough, Co. Clare, and the Bog of Cullen, Co. Tipperary (Cooney and Grogan 1994). Several Bronze Age lakeshore settlement sites have produced swords, spears, tools and personal ornaments. A Late Bronze Age hoard was deposited in a pit at Rathtinaun, its location possibly marked by stakes. Late Bronze Age tool and weapon hoards are also known from the environs of Ballinderry 2 and Knocknalappa. Swords, spears and other objects may have been brought to the site and ceremonially deposited in the water or reeds. Human skulls are also known from Bronze Age lake sites, such as Ballinderry 2 and Moynagh Lough; these may have been deposited in similar rituals. It is possible that these lake settlements became the focus for ritual activities on the lakeshores, associated with certain events, such as harvests, deaths in the community or particular ritual festivals.

In conclusion, it is most probable that Bronze Age lake settlements retained a range of functions, not just one or two. Lake settlements were used for social, economic and ritual reasons, for crafts and production, and as a means of isolation, defence and proximity to waterways. For example, the placing of skulls and weaponry in water or in the foundations of the site may not have been part of some separate ritual practices but could have been considered a normal feature of the initiation of domestic settlement. Individual sites could have been multipurpose, fulfilling social, ritual, domestic, economic and defensive roles at the one place in the landscape.

Iron Age lake settlement

Introduction

The evidence for Iron Age (500 BC–AD 500) settlement of any form in Ireland is extremely scarce. The Iron Age remains an enigma in many ways, with little known about its people, settlement and economy (B. Raftery 1994; Cooney and Grogan 1994). There is little archaeological evidence for an invasion of 'Celtic' peoples; if anything, the record testifies to many social and ritual continuities with the Late Bronze Age (Cooney and Grogan 1991; B. Raftery 1994; Waddell 1995). Most archaeological evidence for the Iron Age is limited to ceremonial sites and metalwork (which is dominated by La Tène-style decorated bronzes), much of it unprovenanced with little contextual information (B. Raftery 1983; 1984). Several Iron Age ritual sites or ceremonial wooden structures have been excavated, such as the '40-metre' structure at Emain Macha, Co. Armagh, dated to 95 BC (Waterman 1997). Iron Age objects were also thrown into the small lake or pond of Loughnashade, situated to the east of the Iron Age enclosure (B. Raftery 1983; 1984), and the spatial association between the two suggests some form of structuring of the ceremonial landscape. The Iron Age ceremonial structures at Dun Ailinne, Co. Kildare (Wailes 1990), and Raffin, Co. Meath (Newman 1995), indicate that various scales of regional and local ritual sites can be expected. The 'royal sites' of the Hill of Tara, Co. Meath (Newman 1997), Uisneach, Co. Westmeath (Grogan and Donaghy 1997), and Rathcroghan, Co. Roscommon (Waddell 1983), were also probably used as ceremonial sites in the late Iron Age. The Hill of Tara has produced late Iron Age ceremonial and settlement evidence from the Rath of the Synods (Cooney and Grogan 1994), and more recently an Iron Age metalworking surface was found beneath the bank of Ráith na Ríg (Helen Roche, pers. comm.). The evidence for Iron Age burial is scarce, mostly involving the insertion of cremated deposits or inhumation burials into Neolithic or Bronze Age barrows, tumuli or cairns (B. Raftery 1994).

In terms of Iron Age settlement, there is some evidence for limited activities on a few hillforts, such as Freestone Hill, Co. Kilkenny, Rathgall, Co. Wicklow (B. Raftery 1994), and Haughey's Fort, Co. Armagh (Mallory 1995), while there may have been some Iron Age occupation on Dun Aonghusa, Co. Galway (Cotter 1996). At Scrabo Hill, Co. Down, there is evidence for an Iron Age settlement, including hut sites, inside a hilltop enclosure (Mallory and Hartwell 1997, 27–8). Iron Age houses may have been identified recently inside a later enclosure at Lislackagh, Swinford, Co. Mayo (Walsh 1995). Iron Age territorial boundaries or defences are known in the form of lengthy linear earthen or wooden structures, such as at the Doon of Drumsna, Co. Roscommon (Condit and Buckley 1989), the Dorsey, Co. Armagh (Lynn 1989), the Black Pig's Dyke, Co. Monaghan (Walsh 1987), and the Claidh Dubh, Co. Cork (Doody 1995). These earthworks appear to define regional boundaries, possibly controlling access into Connacht and Ulster. Iron Age timber trackways have been excavated at Corlea, Co. Longford (B. Raftery 1996), and in Lisheen Bog, Co. Tipperary (Gowen 1997), also indicating substantial community investment, probably associated with an individual's or tribe's prestige and status. It has been suggested that some crannogs have Iron Age levels; for example, the presence of Romano-British pottery in the primary occupation at Lagore crannog formerly led some archaeologists to date its origins to the Iron Age (Caulfield 1981; J. Raftery 1981). Until recently it was believed that Crannog 61 at Rathtinaun, Co. Sligo, had an Iron Age level, but recent radiocarbon dating now suggests that this is definitely not the case (Barry Raftery, pers. comm.).

Iron Age agriculture, as indicated from faunal studies from excavated sites, seems to indicate the raising of cattle, pigs and sheep/goat. However, most of the evidence comes from ceremonial sites, so it is possible that these assemblages give an unbalanced picture of Iron Age farming (Mitchell and Ryan 1997). Cereal cultivation, as indicated by beehive querns and recently discovered wooden ard-heads, may have been of some importance in the farming landscape (Caulfield 1981; B. Raftery 1996). However, a striking feature of recent Iron Age palaeoenvironmental studies is the constant identification of an 'agricultural lull' in the pollen record between about 100 BC and AD 340, when there is widespread evidence for large-scale woodland regeneration and a fall in cultivated land plant indicators (Weir 1993; 1995). There may also have been a climatic downturn at about 540 BC (Baillie 1995b; Mitchell and Ryan 1997, 246). What are the reasons for this lack of Iron Age settlement evidence and the increase in woodland cover? Did some major catastrophe (climate change, widespread disease) have a malign affect on Iron Age population levels? Is it due to social changes leading to a low archaeological visibility for much of the population? It is possible that Iron Age societies in Ireland focused on power and warfare to such an extent that virtually all energy and wealth was invested in high-status ceremonial structures and high-status metalwork (Tom Condit, pers. comm.). People living in simple huts with a material culture based entirely on leather and wood (there is no Iron Age pottery in Ireland) will leave very little archaeological trace.

Iron Age metalwork on lake islands and lakeshores

Are there any hints that Iron Age lake settlements may yet be discovered? Iron Age finds from lake and river contexts are relatively common in Ireland. The deposition of weaponry and metalwork in watery places in the Iron Age may be a replication of the archaeological evidence from across Europe, from La Tène itself to Llyn Cerrig Bach, where metalwork hoards and artefact collections were thrown into lakes as propitiatory donations (Cooney and Grogan 1994; R. Bradley 1990). It has been suggested that these lakes were identified with otherworld forces. Lisnacrogher, Co. Antrim, and Loughnashade, Co. Armagh, appear to be prime candidates for the identification of Iron Age sacred waters in Ireland. It is difficult to assess the relationship between Iron Age finds from lakes and settlement patterns, but presumably there are some, as sacred lakes gradually became identified with local tribes or social groups. In any case, it may yet be possible to identify Iron Age settlements by means of these metalwork deposits. A few crannogs have produced possible Iron Age finds, although their relationship with

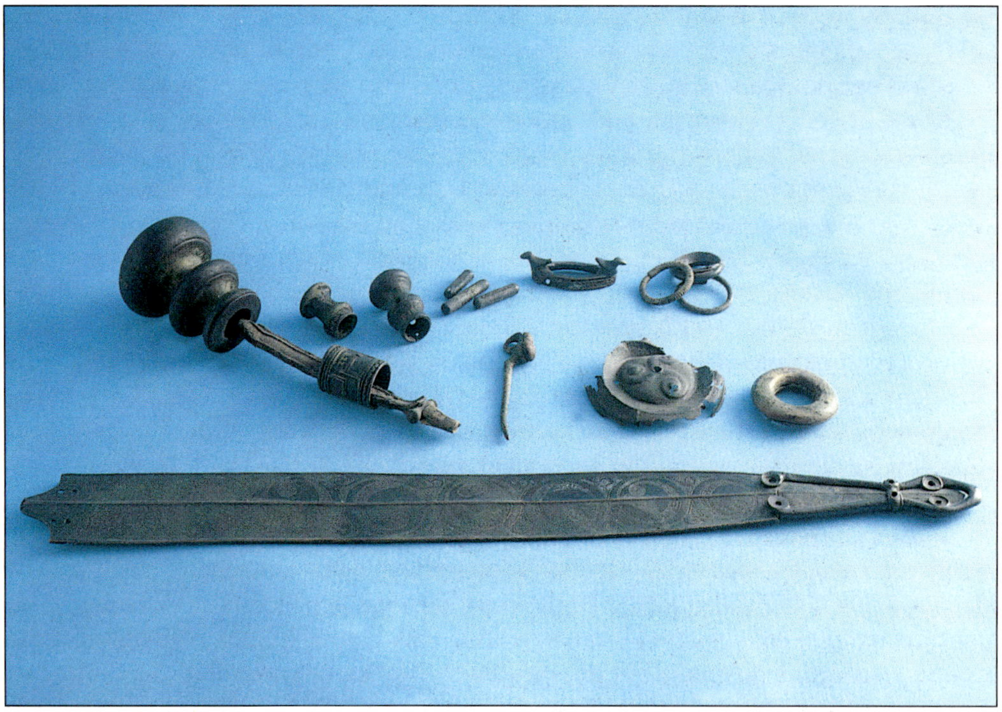

Pl. 29—*Iron Age finds from Lisnacrogher, Co. Antrim (photo: Ulster Museum).*

the particular sites is uncertain. A La Tène sword was recovered from Ballinderry 2 (B. Raftery 1983, 91). A globular iron cauldron was found during peat-digging beside a crannog on the shore of Drumlane Lough, Co. Cavan, at a depth of 2.5m in the peat (*ibid.*, 208). The crannog was a small subrectangular island, with vertical piles, horizontal timbers, stone and animal bone (O'Donovan 1995, 185).

Iron Age finds are also known from lake islands and lake foreshores. A Halstatt C sword of bronze is known from Lough Gill, Co. Sligo (B. Raftery 1994, 29). An Iron Age spearbutt and a Nauheim-derivative fibula were found on the exposed foreshore of Derrymore Island, Lough Gara, Co. Sligo (B. Raftery 1983). A Type 2a pendant was found with a bronze horsebit on Duck Island, Lough Allen, on the rocky foreshore of the lake (*ibid.*, 72). A Type B horsebit was found in Loughbeg, Co. Antrim (*ibid.*). A large number of prehistoric artefacts were found during dredging at Toome, on the north-west corner of Lough Neagh, on the east side of the exit of the River Bann. Iron Age finds included an iron La Tène sword (*ibid.*). At Loughnashade, bronze trumpets and other Iron Age objects were apparently cast into the lake for ritual purposes. Two possible chariot mounts were apparently found 'on a fort on an island in Lough Gur, Co. Limerick' (*ibid.*, 81). A La Tène iron horsebit and iron spearhead were found in Inchiquin Lake, Co. Clare, where wooden piling was recorded on the lake foreshore (*ibid.*, 109; MacNamara 1901, 349).

Iron Age discoveries at Lisnacrogher

Lisnacrogher, Co. Antrim, is one of the most significant sites of the Irish Iron Age, the place of discovery in 1882 of a massive collection of high-status weaponry, ornaments, tools and other objects (Pl. 29). The site was found by local men cutting turf, after a local lough had been partially drained. The turf-cutting apparently exposed oaken timbers laid in regular order. By 1883, when wider antiquarian attention was focused on the site, most of these timbers had been removed. William Wakeman (1883–4), who was taken to the site by Canon Grainger, described the crannog as being situated within the boundary of a now nearly drained lough, in the townland of Lisnacrogher. He observed large quantities of timber, some with mortised ends, and encircling stakes, and noted a considerable quantity of rough basket-like work (presumably post-and-wattle). There was little chance of establishing the relationship between the metalwork and the wooden structures. Lisnacrogher also produced souterrain ware (Ryan 1973), so on balance this was probably an Early Historic crannog.

The Lisnacrogher finds included four iron swords, four bronze scabbards, spearheads, spearbutts, ring-headed pins, a ribbon torc, a bronze necklet, bronze bracelets, spiral rings, penannular rings, stone beads, a bronze bowl, an iron axe, an iron adze, an iron sickle, an iron billhook, a wooden knife, decorative bronze mounts, rings, bronze strips and a range of other objects (Wakeman 1883–4; B. Raftery 1983; 1984). Wakeman (1889) published a further note on the site, stating that it was not totally destroyed, as Canon Grainger was continuing to get antiquities from turf-cutting, and made a final comment on other discoveries from the bog, including wooden vessels and other objects of later date (Wakeman 1890–1). It is not clear if the finds came from a single deposit or if they were spread over a large area. It also seems likely that many of the finds ascribed in collections to 'Lisnacrogher' were not actually found there. Unscrupulous dealers were known to be in the habit of labelling an antiquity as being from the site to increase its value (B. Raftery 1983).

Knowles (1897) explained that Lisnacroghera crannog was located in Carcoagh townland, although this name may be related to the nearby Lisnacrogher townland. Croghery Bog, a modern name for the site, straddles the boundary between Carncoagh and Lisnacrogher townlands. Although the site has been subject to extensive reclamation, it is possible that archaeology lies hidden under the modern grassland and within the remaining areas of bog. It seems likely that the Iron Age finds at Lisnacrogher were actually the result of ritual wetland deposition, in the manner of Llyn Cerrig Bach in north Wales and various Celtic ritual deposits in Europe. The wooden structures may have been the remains of an Early Historic crannog. Certainly this was proposed by the Scottish antiquary and expert in lake settlements, Robert Munro, on his visit in 1886 (Lynn 1983; B. Raftery 1994).

Iron Age boats on lakes

Iron Age boat planks from a vessel built using sewn planks and mortise and tenons have been found at Cummerstown, on Lough Lene, Co. Westmeath (Ó hEailidhe 1992; Brindley and Lanting 1991). The planks, which had been known to local people for many years, lay in 4–5m of water about 70m from the shore. The remains of the boat

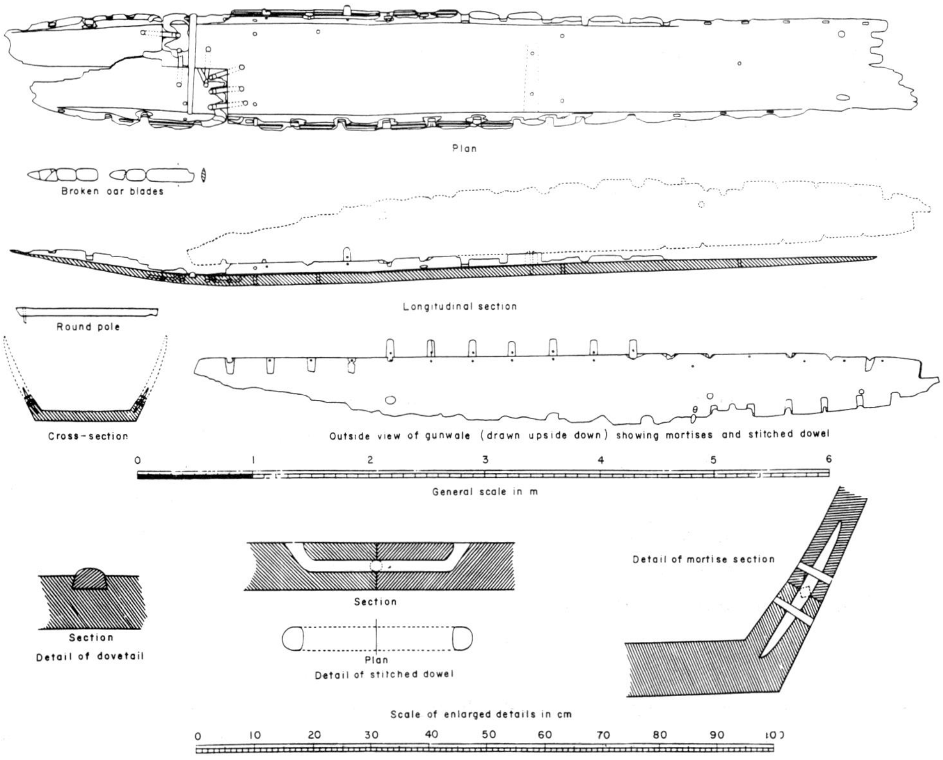

Fig. 22—*Iron Age plank-boat timbers found at Lough Lene, Co. Westmeath (after Ó hEailidhe 1992).*

consisted of one long oak plank and one short oak piece, skilfully scarfed together, which formed the bottom, as well as one oak plank from the side (Fig. 22). The boat was broken at the prow and stern, so its length cannot be reconstructed, but it was certainly in excess of 7.9m. At the time of its discovery, two carved willow oars were found underneath the planks. The surviving portion of the hull indicated that it was a flat-bottomed vessel with straight sides, and that the oak planks were assembled using yew-wood free-tenons in mortises and yew-wood treenails. The scarf joints also utilised dovetails and withy stitching, and were luted with wood resin or linseed oil. The boat was carvel-built in the manner of Mediterranean boats, using mortise and free-tenon techniques which had died out in Europe by the seventh century AD (Ó hEailidhe 1992; B. Raftery 1994). The plank was radiocarbon-dated to between AD 180 and 540 (2195 ± 25 BP; GrN-17263), or the later Iron Age (Brindley and Lanting 1991). It is possible that the sample, taken from slow-grown yew wood, is younger than the boat, which may therefore be dated to the Roman era. The scarce archaeological and historical evidence for early boats in Ireland suggests that plank-built boats were not part of the Irish tradition prior to the introduction of Viking ships, but that native craft were of wicker, lathe and skin construction, much like modern coracles (Colin Breen, pers. comm.). It has been suggested that this narrow, low vessel was constructed for the use of Roman traders navigating the Irish midland lakes and rivers. The excavation of a barrow overlooking the lake produced an imported Iron Age bronze Somerset bowl with cremation dating to the last few centuries BC (E.P. Kelly 1995). This raises intriguing possibilities for the presence of Iron Age settlement in the region. However, the Lough Lene boat need not indicate the presence of Roman shipwrights or traders. The presence of such an exotic item in an Irish midland lake could be explained by the presence of a local shipwright versed in European ship-building skills. However, this still leaves open the question of why local groups would demand such an unusual craft (B. Raftery 1994). A few Iron Age dugout canoes are also known, such as that from Gortgill, Co. Antrim, dated to 350 BC–AD 70 (*ibid.*, 111).

Iron Age linear earthworks in lakelands

Linear earthworks are an important archaeological feature of Iron Age Ireland. The Dorsey, the Black Pig's Dyke, the Claidh Dubh and the Doon of Drumsna have all produced radiocarbon dates in the last few centuries BC or early centuries AD (Mitchell and Ryan 1997, 243). A few linear earthworks run through lakelands, occasionally employing open bodies of water as an additional demarcation feature. In particular, the Dunclaidh linear earthwork runs from Lough Kinale to Lough Gowna, Co. Longford, possibly demarcating the territory between the midlands and the Cavan area (B. Raftery 1994, 88). It is possible that linear wooden features could be traced in these lakes, in the manner of the Bronze Age post alignment already described from Lough Carra, Co. Mayo. Otherwise, it is possible that the two lakes were important in some other symbolic sense in the Iron Age, with the deposition of metalwork in their waters. It is also possible to view linear earthworks as routeways or ritual structures running through the landscape, and not only as divisions between two regions. The earthworks could have served as a processional routeway between the two lakes. Underwater diving surveys at either end of the Dunclaidh linear earthwork may yet throw light on its date and function.

Iron Age promontory forts in lakelands

Promontory forts in Ireland, on account of their size and impressive defences, have typically been seen as tribal centres or refuges rather than domestic residences. The dating of promontory forts remains highly problematical, since almost none have been excavated. While they have often been seen as dating from the Iron Age, there is little archaeological evidence to support this (B. Raftery 1994). A coastal promontory fort at Loughshinney, Co. Dublin, has produced Gallo-Roman Samian ware of first- to second-century AD date, and there are also records of Roman coins and Romano-British copper ingots in the vicinity of the fort (Mitchell and Ryan 1997; B. Raftery 1994). It is therefore possible that some lake promontory forts date from the Iron Age. Promontory forts have been identified on several lakes in Mayo, Sligo and Roscommon (e.g. Rindoon, Lough Ree). The large lakes of Mayo have produced several examples of promontory forts, such as at Treanbeg on the eastern shore of Lough Feeagh, at Errew and Ringall on Lough Conn, and at Doon Point and Castlecarra on Lough Carra. These lake promontory forts are typically situated on narrow headlands, occasionally with multivallate stone-built ramparts with rock-cut ditches cutting off large enclosed areas (Gibbons and Condit 1991; Gibbons *et al.* 1991).

Iron Age crannogs in Scotland

Is it possible to use the archaeology of Scottish crannogs to gain insights into potential Iron Age lake settlements in Ireland? In contrast to the Irish archaeological record, many Scottish crannogs are known to have construction and occupation phases from the Late Bronze Age and pre-Roman Iron Age period, while others have been dated to the Roman Iron Age in the early centuries AD (Morrison 1981; 1985; Dixon 1981; 1984; 1991; Barber and Crone 1993, 520; Crone 1993). Scottish crannogs that have been excavated in recent times include the underwater site at Oakbank, Loch Tay (Dixon 1982a; 1982b; 1984), and 'dryland' excavations at Milton Loch, Dumfriesshire (Piggott 1953), Loch Glashan, Argyllshire (J.G. Scott 1960), Loch Arthur, Dumfriesshire (J. Williams 1971), and Buiston, Ayrshire (Barber and Crone 1993). Scottish archaeologists have also led the field in the underwater archaeological survey of lake settlements (Morrison 1985; Dixon 1982b; Henderson, forthcoming a). Scottish crannogs, typically built at loch edges, consist of layers of brushwood and rubble, revetted around with vertical piles and surfaced with oak timber. They can also be constructed on raised platforms, mortised to upright piles, with houses thus elevated to some height above the water surface. Causeways are frequently found leading to the drylands. A single house is frequently placed in the middle of the crannog, covering most of its surface area. Recently, Historic Scotland commissioned a radiocarbon-dating programme of crannogs in south-west Scotland. Milton Loch 1, Milton Loch 2, Loch Arthur, Erskine Bridge (on the River Clyde), Barean Loch and Buiston have all produced radiocarbon dates between 850 BC and AD 200, the pre-Roman and Roman Iron Ages in Scotland. Indeed, it has been proposed that this earlier dating of Scottish crannogs indicates that the very concept of crannog-building was introduced from Scotland into Ireland in the late sixth century AD (Crone 1993, 246, table 1; see below for detailed discussion). While the fact that Iron Age crannogs exist in Scotland does not mean that they are found in Ireland, it can be pointed out that Irish archaeology has not carried out the neccessary investigations to prove or disprove the case. The hints offered by the few Iron Age finds from lakeshores and islands should certainly be followed up.

Early Historic and Viking Age lake settlement

Introduction

The Early Historic and Viking Age settlement landscape in Ireland was intensively managed, with farmsteads, field systems and routeways dispersed through a largely open agricultural background. Early Historic (AD 400–800) and Viking Age (AD 800–1100) settlement studies have typically been dominated by the archaeological excavation and geographical analysis of ringforts, crannogs, monastic sites, and monastic or Viking towns (de Paor and de Paor 1960; Edwards 1990; Mytum 1992). Early Historic settlement studies have also traditionally been paralleled, or led, by historical studies of the politics and events of the period (Ó Corráin 1972; Ó Cróinín 1995). Early Irish laws, hagiographies, annalistic references, genealogies and other historical texts have been used to construct models of social organisation and political and kinship relationships (MacNeill 1923; F. Kelly 1988; 1997). These social models of kings, nobles, wealthy farmers, abbots and bishops have often dominated discussion of contemporary settlement organisation (Mytum 1992; Mitchell and Ryan 1997, 260–1).

Ringforts, both raths and cashels, are typically seen as the settlement form *par excellence* of the Early Historic period. Their origins, distribution and function have been the subject of much discussion (Ó Ríordáin 1942b; O'Kelly 1970; Edwards 1990; Limbert 1996; Mitchell and Ryan 1997; Stout 1997). They are traditionally interpreted as the enclosed residences of the wealthy farmer and his family (the *bóaire* of the Irish law tracts). It has been proposed that some ringforts, particularly those with multivallate defences and a small enclosed area, were actually royal residences (Warner 1988). Some ringforts also served as centres for secular metalworking, such as Garranes, Co. Cork (Ó Ríordáin 1942b), and the seventh- to eighth-century site of Garryduff, Co. Cork (O'Kelly 1962). Ringforts have also been shown to be associated with field systems, as at Cush, Co. Limerick (Ó Ríordáin 1940), while upland enclosures such as those at Ballyutoag, Co. Antrim (Williams 1984), may have been summer transhumance sites. Ringforts probably have their origins between the fifth and sixth centuries AD and their heyday between the sixth and ninth centuries (Lynn 1983; Stout 1997). They could have been spatially organised in a hierarchical fashion, with smaller sites congregating around large, centrally placed multivallate ringforts (Stout 1997). They could have been occupied over hundreds of years (Stout 1991) or for only a generation or two (Mytum 1992). In any case, they are the most common archaeological monument type in Ireland, with at least 50,000 examples (Stout 1997).

There is a range of evidence for other forms of secular settlement. Promontory forts, although probably originating earlier, are also known to have Early Historic settlement evidence, such as at Larrybane, Co. Antrim (Mitchell and Ryan 1997, 264), and Dunbeg, Co. Kerry (Barry 1981). Promontory forts may also have been some form of élite settlement or temporary place of refuge. Souterrains, stone-built underground passages with chambers, are also common during this period. These are occasionally found within ringforts, but are also known on their own or associated with single houses which may have been unenclosed settlements (Mitchell and Ryan 1997, 281). The settlements of the 'unfree or the merely ordinary' are rarely clearly identified (Brady 1994a). Finally, apart from Hiberno-Norse Dublin and a few possible ringforts and crannogs, there is little good archaeological evidence for settlement in the tenth and eleventh centuries AD.

The settlement landscape of the Early Historic and Viking Age church should be considered as integral to the secular settlement landscape (Mitchell and Ryan 1997, 288–96; Bitel 1990; Swan 1988; Manning 1995). It is possible to identify spatial associations between ringforts and early church sites (Stout 1997). The early church in Ireland was diverse in character and had a range of secular, economic and political functions in the settlement landscape. Ecclesiastical settlements ranged in size and importance from small churches operating within local territories to larger centres controlled by bishops, to the even larger monastic towns, with their populations of abbots, bishops, monks and craftspeople, which were centres of political power. The earliest church settlements were simple, often only a wooden or stone church with cross-inscribed pillar stones set within a small, stone-built enclosing wall. The larger monastic sites, such as Clonmacnoise, Co. Offaly, and Kells, Co. Meath, were typically strategically located on important routeways, such as roads and rivers. Monastic settlements were centres of learning, craftsmanship and production, and it is likely that they were important in terms of trade and exchange across the country. Abbots were often men from local and regional political dynasties, and they exercised military power and administered large farmed estates. Towards the end of the period, these monasteries had their own monastic tenants in lands often at some distance from the town. The organisation of the settlement landscape thus needs to take the church into account.

Early Historic and Viking Age agriculture in Ireland included both pastoral farming (with the herding of cattle, pigs, goats and sheep) and intensive arable agriculture. Early Irish laws commonly describe the use of the plough and draught animals and the construction and ownership of horizontal watermills for grinding grain. There were field systems enclosed by stone walls and wooden fences. Cattle were of prime importance, in terms of both the economic landscape and social organisation (Lucas 1989; McCormick 1995; Patterson 1994; F. Kelly 1997), and ringforts were probably situated within extensive grazing lands. It has also been proposed that they were used as corrals for protecting valuable cattle from raids and wild animals, and there is supporting ancient beetle evidence from the ringfort at Deer Park Farms, Co. Antrim, that cattle were kept inside the fort (McCormick 1995). Early Irish law divided up agricultural land in terms of its suitability and its proximity to such things as a road, a river mouth, a pond, mountain grazing and woodland. In the earlier part of the period, land was owned in common by the *deirbfine*, the common male descendants of a great-grandfather, although privately owned land was also known. During the latter part of the period, a simpler, closer kindred emerged, and privately owned land became more and more common (Mitchell and Ryan 1997, 282).

Indeed, Irish society was transformed during this period from one based on kinship and reciprocity to a hierarchical, ranked society with lords and clientship. It has been strongly argued that early Christianity had a major impact on the social and settlement landscape from the fifth and sixth centuries AD (Mytum 1992), and that Viking raiders and settlers had a major impact in terms of warfare, trade and urbanism after the early ninth century. However, internal change was an equally important factor in the development of Irish society. Profound social changes can be linked to ongoing economic changes, with the emergence of a redistributive economy controlled by both a secular and an ecclesiastical social hierarchy. It has been argued that these early changes represent in essence the gestation, by about AD 800, of feudalism in Ireland. By the eleventh century Ireland had lordships that were remarkably similar to those of contemporary Europe (Graham 1993, 23). It has also been argued that the period witnessed the emergence of central places in the settlement landscape—towns, villages and fortifications—from where the social and economic landscape was controlled. In fact, it may be that settlement, as in earlier periods, was structured in terms of social hierarchy (Mallory and McNeill 1991). Early Historic and Viking Age lake settlement in Ireland can usefully be investigated within all of these settlement, social, ritual and economic themes.

Early Historic and Viking Age lake settlements

Lake settlement studies for the Early Historic period are dominated by the study of crannogs. Indeed, Early Historic crannogs are amongst the most recognisable and evocative features of the Irish landscape. However, there is also a range of other evidence for settlement on lakeshores, islands and in lakelands, such as lake promontory forts, island duns ('water-cashels') and cashels and ringforts on lakeshores and islands. There are also numerous small cairns and mounds in lakes, many potentially associated with metalworking activities on crannogs. The potential for rural Viking settlement has also perhaps been underemphasised (J. Bradley 1988). Viking Age annalistic references abound with documentary evidence for naval fleet activities by both the Irish and the Vikings on Lough Ree, Lough Erne and Lough Derg. It is possible that temporary and seasonal Viking settlements (e.g. camps, longphorts, boat-harbours) may yet be located in the Irish midland lakes and river valleys. There is also the entire ecclesiastical range of settlement evidence, including church sites and hermitages on lake islands and monastic sites on islands and lakeshores.

Early Historic and Viking Age crannog excavations

The crannog is a classic Early Historic settlement form (Wood-Martin 1886a; Ó Ríordáin 1942a; Edwards 1990; E.P. Kelly 1991a; 1991b). Archaeological excavation of crannogs has typically revealed well-preserved houses, pathways, fences, working areas, metal, bone and wooden artefacts, food and industrial debris, and a wide range of environmental evidence in the waterlogged deposits. A crannog can be defined as:

> 'an island, wholly or largely artificial, usually circular, built up of layers of dumped peat, brushwood (often woven), heavier timbers, stones, soil, rubbish, etc., whichever material was most readily available. The chief characteristic is that the island was originally surrounded by a retaining ring of close-set vertical timber piles' (Lynn 1983, 50–1).

Crannogs, like some ringforts, are generally interpreted as the homesteads of strong farmers or lower nobility, or as 'royal centres'. However, there is a good deal of variation in the form, size and material assemblage of crannogs, suggesting a more complex hierarchy of social status, economy and function. It can also be pointed out that the number of crannogs investigated in any systematic fashion is actually quite low, and that in any case most archaeological excavations have concentrated on the larger sites, which are likely to be high-status in origin. Over the last 150 years Irish crannog studies have waxed and waned, but their contribution to our understanding of the Early Historic period has been immeasurable.

Crannogs are widely distributed across the midlands, north-west, west and north

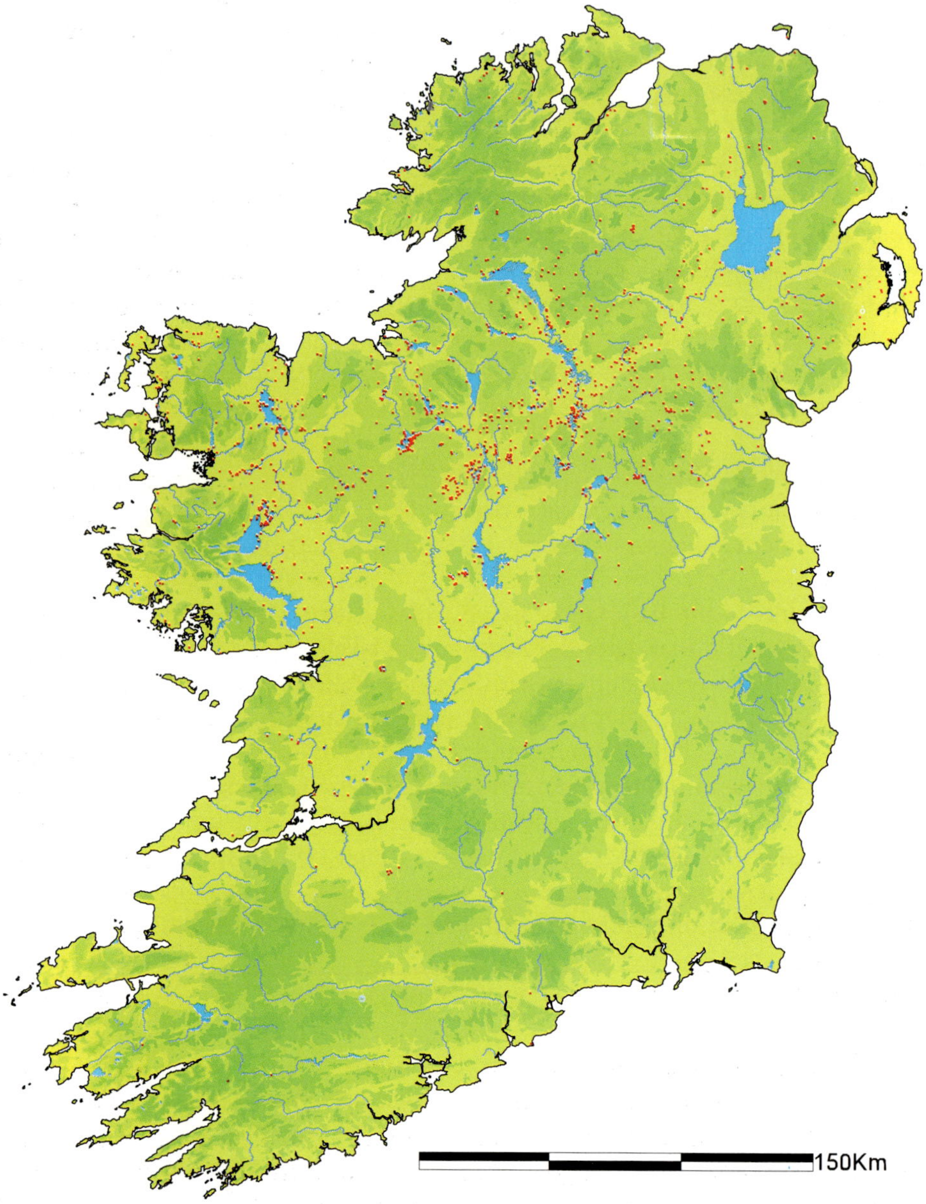

Fig. 23—*Distribution of crannogs in Ireland, based on the records of the National Monuments Service, Dúchas—The Heritage Service, and the Environment and Heritage Service, DOE(NI).*

of Ireland (Fig. 23). They are particularly concentrated in the drumlin lakes of Cavan, Monaghan, Leitrim, Roscommon and Fermanagh. They are more dispersed across the west and north-east, although concentrations can be identified, such as in Lough Conn, Lough Cullin and Castlebar Lough, Co. Mayo. Crannogs are known in every county of Northern Ireland, but are particularly concentrated in a belt stretching from Fermanagh through south Tyrone and Armagh to mid-Down. Other regions have smaller numbers widely dispersed, but a few crannogs have been identified in the south and east. Crannogs tend to be found on the smaller lakes, being infrequent or rare on large midland lakes of the River Shannon system, such as Lough Ree and Lough Derg, while there are also few on Lower Lough Erne and Lough Neagh. There are particular concentrations on Lough Carra and Lough Conn, Co. Mayo, Lough Gara, Co. Sligo, Drumhallow Lough, Co. Roscommon, and Lough Oughter, Co. Cavan. Smaller lakes can have either one crannog or a small group of them, such as on Lough Eyes and Drumgay Lough, Co. Fermanagh. On some larger lakes, such as Lough Derravarragh, Co. Westmeath, and Lough Sheelin, Co. Cavan, they are distributed along the shoreline at regular intervals. Crannogs are found in both deep and shallow lake waters, on lakeshores and in peatlands. A smaller number have been found in rivers, estuaries and coastal wetlands. They can be recognised in drained land as tree-grown hummocks, or as grassy knolls in reedy land. It is difficult to distinguish between entirely artificially built islands and those natural islands or shoals that were used as lake settlements. The distinction is probably academic anyway, as the Early Historic Irish texts do not distinguish between crannogs and occupied natural islands.

There have been a relatively small number of Early Historic or Viking Age crannog excavations, and most of these were carried out by nineteenth-century antiquarians whose records are inadequate for modern studies. An exception is George Coffey's excavation of Craigywarren, Co. Antrim, the report of which can be used to reconstruct the plan and occupation of a small single-phase crannog. In modern times, several Irish crannogs in the midlands and north-east have been the subject of detailed archaeological investigation. The following discussion will initially focus on Moynagh Lough, Co. Meath, Newtownlow, Co. Westmeath, Ballinderry 1, Co. Westmeath, Ballinderry 2, Co. Offaly, Lagore, Co. Meath, Clea Lakes, Co. Down, Lough Faughan, Co. Down, and Bofeenaun, Co. Mayo. These particular sites give valuable insights into the chronology, construction and settlement history of the larger types of sites especially. This will then be followed by a broader discussion of the archaeology of Irish crannogs.

Moynagh Lough, Co. Meath

Moynagh Lough, Co. Meath, is the most completely excavated crannog of recent times (J. Bradley 1982–3; 1984; 1985–6; 1990–1; 1991; 1993; 1994–5; 1996; 1997). The site had been occupied in the Late Mesolithic and the Early and Late Bronze Age (J. Bradley 1996; see discussion in Mesolithic and Bronze Age sections above) (Fig. 24). In the Early Historic period, there were several phases of occupation from the late sixth to the ninth century AD. The site was enclosed by a series of palisades and contained substantial circular houses; there is ample evidence for on-site metalworking, the trade of exotic goods, and diet and economy on the site (J. Bradley 1991; McCormick 1995). Moynagh Lough may well have been a 'high-security island industrial estate' (Morrison 1996; J. Bradley 1993; Youngs 1989). More recently, historical research by Edel Bhreathnach (1998) suggests that Moynagh Lough may be identified as the place known as *Loch Dé Mundech,* and that its crannog may well have been a 'royal site' of the *Mugdorne*.

The Early Historic crannog was situated at the southern edge of a former lake on the River Dee, overlooked by hills and slopes to the south and west (J. Bradley 1991; 1994–5; 1997, 58–60). It was sheltered from south-west winds and was snugly placed inside one corner of the lake with good views to the north and north-east. It seems that the muddy knolls and artificially constructed mounds of peat occupied in the Mesolithic and Bronze Age remained as lake shallows beside the deepest part of the

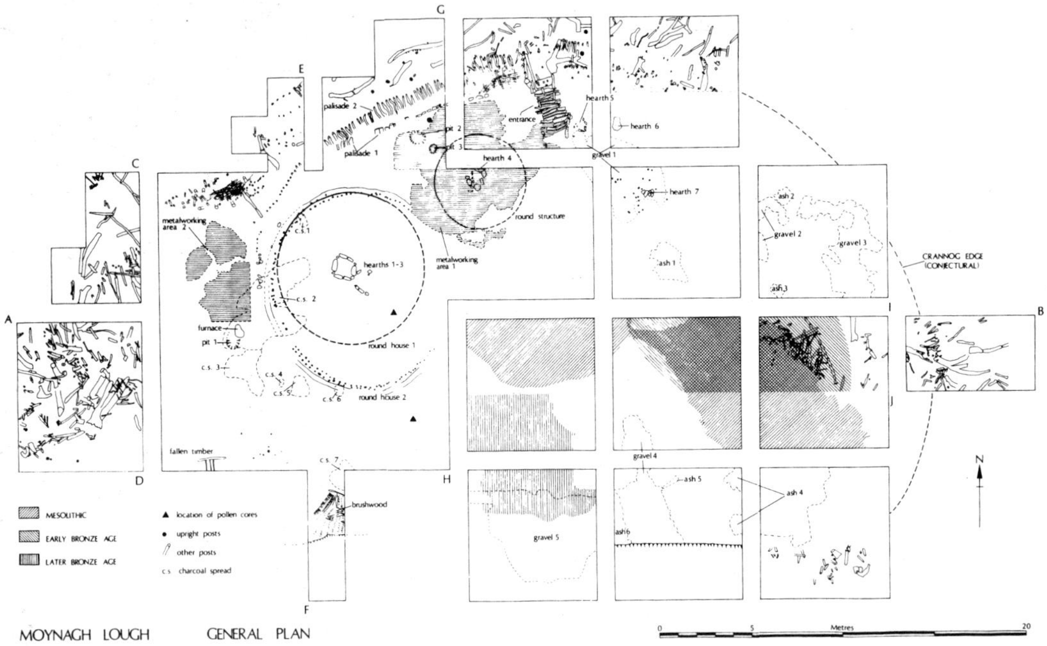

Fig. 24—*Plan of excavated multiperiod lake settlements and crannog at Moynagh Lough, Co. Meath (after Bradley 1991).*

lake, making it a good location for crannog construction. There were at least five phases of occupation in the Early Historic period, each marked by a redeposited layer of peat and possibly representing a generation of activity. The crannog varied in form through these five phases of occupation, but in general terms it measured 40m east–west by 32m north–south. The substructure consisted of stones, gravelly earth, timbers, brushwood and redeposited peat. Piles were driven into the ground both outside the crannog (to a distance of 10m out from the western side) and within to retain the foundation layers.

The earliest phase, Phase V, is represented by a group of refuse layers, but no structures are yet reported. Finds included a rimsherd of E-ware, a bronze disc-pendant pin, a bronze penannular brooch with bird's-head terminals, bone combs, glass beads and a leather shoe. The phase is now interpreted as dating from the late sixth to early seventh century AD (J. Bradley 1997, 60). The next known phase in the Early Historic period, Phase W (from the late seventh to the early eighth century), witnessed the use of a pit, a hearth and a furnace and the deposition of refuse layers outside the crannog. A layer of gravel was spread over the pit and a stone-lined rectangular hearth was built upon it. The hearth was surrounded by post-holes, probably from a spit with a pit to one side. A small circular wooden house, possibly a workshop or store no more than 3m in diameter, is also reported from these early phases. E-ware, an iron shield-boss and a bronze mount were found near this structure. Other structures included a wooden trackway (J. Bradley 1997, 58). Two Merovingian glass vessels and a bronze spatula were found under gravel in this phase. Other finds from Phase W included a penannular brooch, gold filigree and a separate-bladed shovel (J. Bradley 1991; 1994–5, 165; 1997).

In the next phase, Phase X (*c.* 720–48), a basal layer of redeposited peat was laid on the site and a roundhouse was located between two metalworking areas. The house was circular and double-walled and measured about 7.5m in diameter. A timber pathway led in from an entrance to the north-east, one reused timber providing a dendrochronological date of AD 625 (J. Bradley 1994–5, 164). Metalworking area 1 was situated between the house and the entrance. Metalworking area 2 was larger and lay to the west of the house. It produced four major features—a furnace, a stone-lined area

Pl. 30—*View of the large eighth-century roundhouse from Phase Y, Moynagh Lough, Co. Meath (photo: John Bradley).*

of clay, a spread of compacted pebbles and a dump of metalworking debris. There was also a cesspit, recut on two occasions, which produced layers of dung interspersed with layers of straw and leaves. Finds from this phase included sheet-metal beating tools, crucible fragments, heating tray fragments, hundreds of fragments of two-piece clay moulds and motif-pieces. The moulds were used for the production of brooches, mounts, studs and other decorated objects. Ingots were introduced onto the site, placed in crucibles, melted in the furnace and poured into the moulds. The furnace was used on at least eight occasions. The moulds may have been cooled nearby on the pebbled area; post-casting work and mould-making may have been carried out on a pink clay and cobbled spread. The spatial organisation of the metalworkers' areas can thus be recognised.

In Phase Y (*c.* 748–80) there were two roundhouses, a large oak palisade and a furnace pit, with finds including crucibles, a clay mould, clay nozzles and a bronze ingot. The palisade was of hewn and cleft oak, tightly placed together in a U-shaped trench. Its construction has been dated to AD 748, at least 150 years after the first occupation of the site. The palisade revets a layer of redeposited peat upon which the houses were constructed. The largest house (roundhouse 1) was a substantial circular structure, 11.2m in external diameter (10m in internal diameter), with double walls and a laid foundation of reddish-brown gravel. There were at least 250 internal posts, probably deriving from internal partitions, beds and benches. There were several phases of hearths, and twenty spreads of ash and animal bone were scattered through the occupation layer, which was 12cm thick. Substantial stone-lined hearths of rectangular form were constructed, and the spreads of animal bone were usually in their vicinity (Pl. 30). The second house was smaller, approximately 5.2m in diameter, and also had a stone-lined hearth, but the occupation layer was less apparent. There was a bowl-shaped furnace to the west of the house, lined with lake marls. Finds from the large roundhouse included iron knives, key handles, a spearhead, stone hones, iron nails and spindle-whorls, bronze pins, bronze finger-rings, bone combs, glass beads, jet bracelet fragments, gaming-pieces and flint strike-a-lights. Finds associated with the furnace included three complete crucibles, 50 crucible sherds, three heating trays, a clay mould fragment, baked clay nozzles and a bronze ingot. Many of the crucibles bore evidence of being held by iron tongs.

Phase Z, the uppermost surviving layers of occupation, had been greatly disturbed by modern bulldozing during attempted land reclamation. There were the remains of a palisade, a foundation layer of redeposited peat and a single charcoal spread. The palisade was constructed of young oak roundwood trunks. These posts probably had wattles woven around them where they stood above the ground. The crannog would have been 36–40m across. Finds from this layer included three tanged iron knives, two complete crucibles and sherds of others, part of a rotary quernstone, a bone comb fragment, a glass bead, a chunk of amber and four jet bracelet fragments. The phase probably dates from *c.* 780–810.

Moynagh Lough is both a well-preserved multiperiod archaeological site and a remarkable example of an Early Historic Irish crannog. Its long-term excavation has revealed several important things about Early Historic settlement continuities, on-site domestic and industrial activities, and the status and lives of its inhabitants. The crannog was apparently occupied continuously between *c.* 600 and 810, a period of some 200 years. Although there may have been short phases of abandonment, it seems that every generation or so the entire crannog was reconstructed and ever-larger houses placed upon it. The site seems to have been used both for domestic occupation and for various metalworking practices. The presence of furnaces, copper ingots, crucibles, heating trays and baked clay nozzles strongly indicates on-site metal production (melting bronze and smelting copper and tin), and the numerous clay mould fragments indicate that a wide range of bronze artefacts were actually being made there. Amber, gold wire and enamel found on the site indicate the production of fine jewellery. There was also some iron-working on the site: slag, a furnace base and hydrated ferric oxide were found within the large house. Other crafts practised on-site include the working of wood, leather, bone and antler; there may also have been glass-working, as glass rods, a vitrified glass bracelet and an unfinished glass bead are known. The crannog-dwellers obtained several other fine items through long-distance trade networks, such as the Merovingian glass vessels, jet bracelets, amber and tin.

The archaeological evidence of a large house, fine metalwork and imported items suggests that Moynagh Lough was a high-status settlement; this is supported by historical references which tentatively suggest that it was an actual 'royal site' of the *Mugdorne*. What was the role of the crannog in the wider settlement landscape? The economy of the site is revealed by the large faunal assemblage. There were large numbers of cattle, pig and sheep, with smaller numbers of horse, red deer, cat and dog. Dairy cows predominated in the bovine bone record and were killed only when they had passed their prime, while male calves were slaughtered at a young age. Most of the cattle were slaughtered off-site. The crannog-dwellers clearly had their own herds on the neighbouring drylands, and only meat was taken on to the site. It is clear that the surrounding rolling hills were well supplied with good grazing land for large herds of cattle (McCormick 1983; 1985–6; 1995). The presence of rotary querns on the crannog also suggests some measure of arable farming. There are several substantial Early Historic ringforts on the neighbouring drylands, notably those to the immediate west at Lissanard, Lissnacross and Cherbourg Wood (Fig. 25). A motte at Nobber to the north may also have its origins in the Early Historic period (Edel Bhreathnach, pers. comm.). Other sites in the environs include several crannogs (Eogan 1957), a potential unenclosed settlement at a souterrain at Ballynee (Eogan 1990) and possible horizontal mills on the River Dee (Corlett and Shanahan 1998). The crannog of Moynagh Lough was set in a prosperous, well-populated landscape of farms and lakelands, and its inhabitants probably controlled much of this territory.

Craigywarren crannog, Co. Antrim

The small Early Historic crannog at Craigywarren, Co. Antrim, provides useful contrasts with the larger 'royal sites'. It was located at a depth of 6ft in a bog, about 80 yards out from the former western shore of the original lake. About half a mile to the

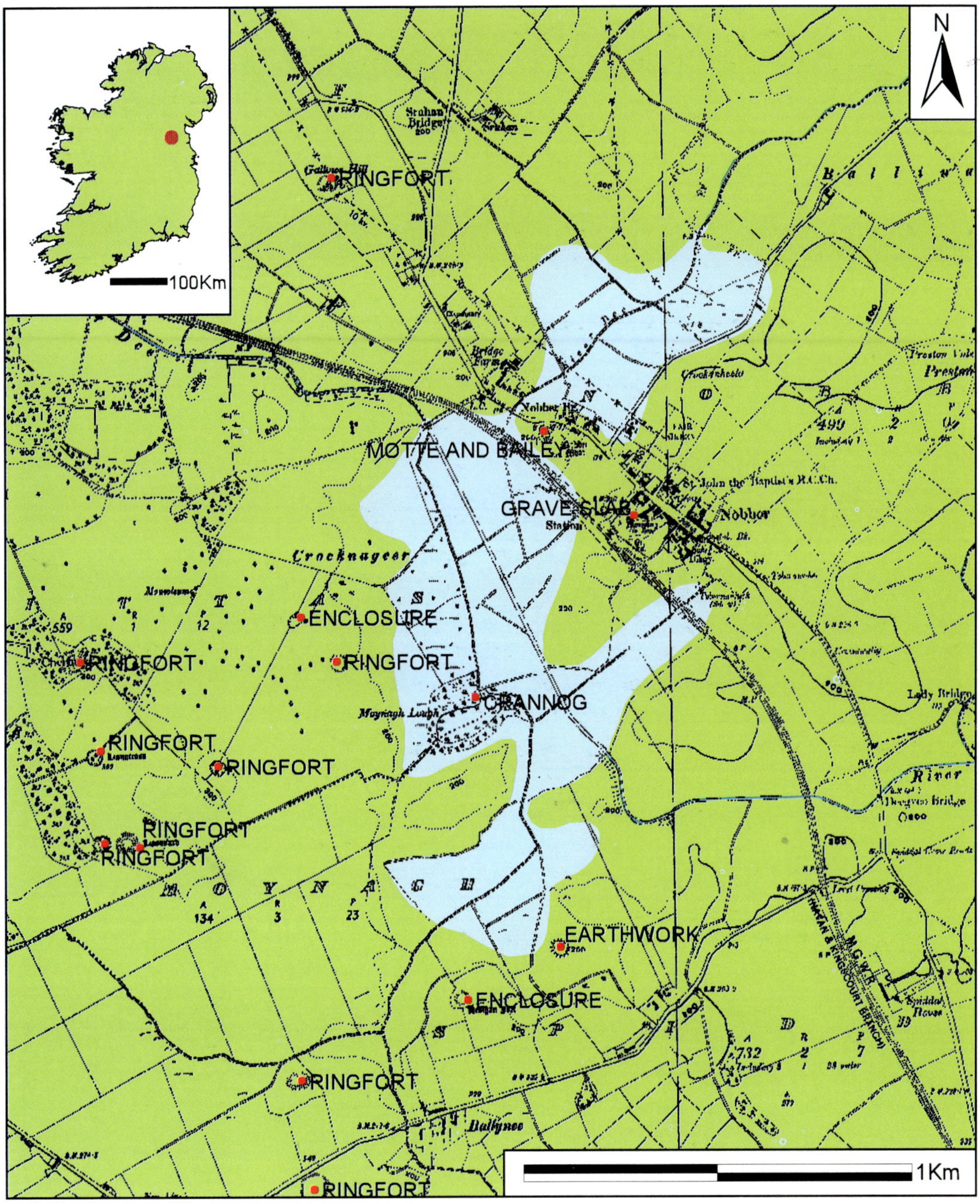

Fig. 25—*Map of Moynagh Lough crannog, Co. Meath, in its reconstructed lake landscape. Several Early Historic ringforts are situated on the neighbouring drylands (map by Paul Synnott, after Bradley 1991).*

north was Lisnacrogher crannog, the reputed nineteenth-century findspot of an assemblage of La Tène metalwork. Craigywarren crannog was almost totally excavated by W.J. Knowles, George Coffey and a team of nine assistants over a two-week period in August–September 1901 (Coffey 1906).

The crannog was small and circular, measuring only about 14m in diameter. It was defined at its edge by a lightly built palisade. The habitation was constructed of a primary layer of heather and small branches on the underlying black mud, followed by a second layer of horizontal trunks and branches, followed by another layer of heather. Spreads of stone and several adzed planks and mortised timbers were found within, and on, this surface. In particular, the excavators proposed that a spread of mortised beams adjacent to the 'kitchen-midden' at the north-east corner of the crannog was the remains of a hut site (Fig. 26).

Craigywarren produced a range of lithic finds, including flint flakes, scrapers, an

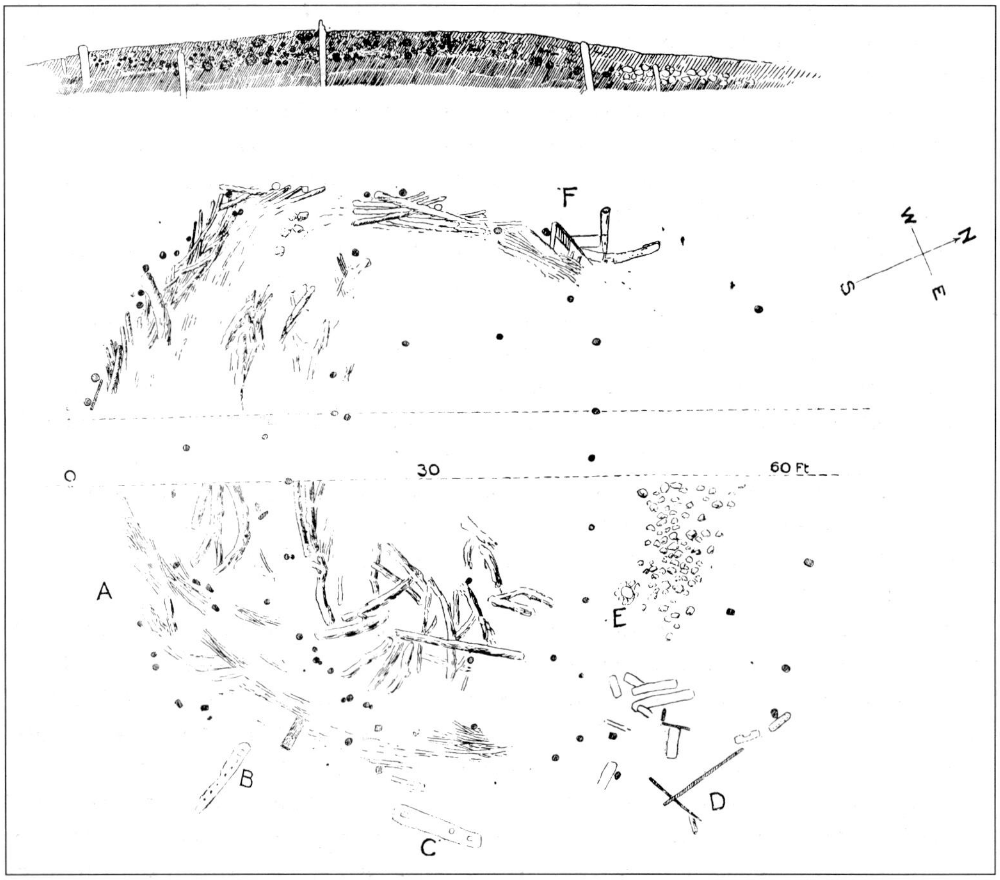

Fig. 26—*Plan of Craigywarren crannog, Co. Antrim (from Coffey 1906).*

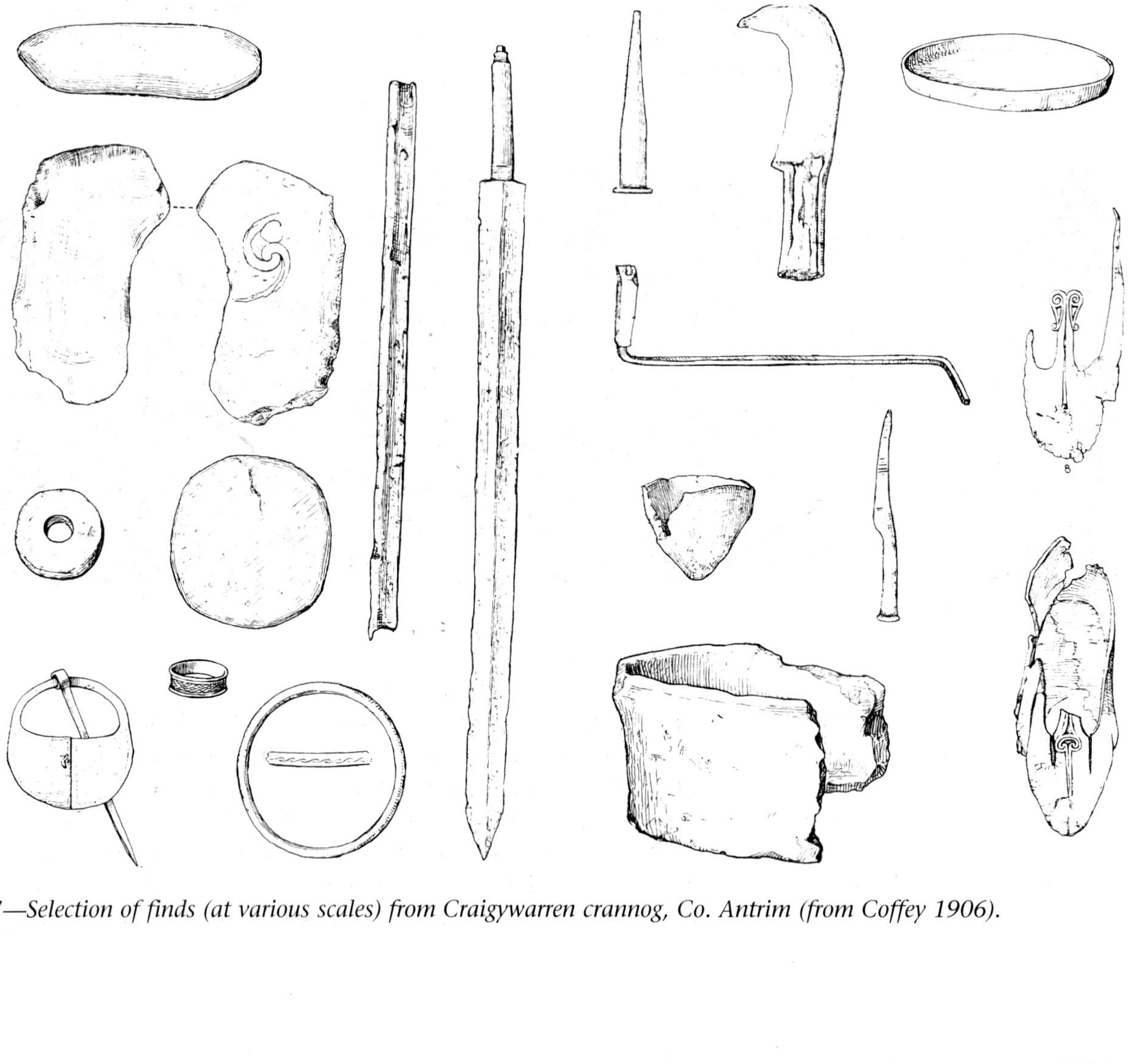

Fig. 27—*Selection of finds (at various scales) from Craigywarren crannog, Co. Antrim (from Coffey 1906).*

arrowhead, three polishing stones, spindle-whorls and a stone axe fragment. The excavators decided that the flints were not strike-a-lights. However, because there were no cores to indicate on-site flint-working, they felt that the flints were introduced on to the site with stone and gravel during its construction, but it is also possible that they represent an unrecognised Neolithic or Early Bronze Age occupation phase. Bronze finds included a silvered, plain penannular brooch, a brooch pin fragment, bracelet, disc and ring. An iron sword was found below the hut timbers, and other iron finds included a possible spearbutt, two billhooks, a chisel, an iron pan and an unknown object, which may have been a barrel-padlock key. Plain souterrain pottery and clay crucibles were recovered; one of the latter had red vitreous matter on its surface, possibly the remains of melted enamel. A bone trial-piece and a bronze bracelet were also found. Portions of decorated leather shoes and a bag were recovered. Animal bone from the site included red deer, cattle, sheep/goat, pig and three horse skulls. The finds indicated to the excavators the presence of both craftworkers and relatively wealthy inhabitants, and the site was dated, on the basis of the penannular brooch, to the tenth century AD. It is likely that this date is much too late. The brooch, the plain souterrain pottery and the decorated leather shoes could be dated to as early as the sixth to seventh century AD (Fig. 27) (Ryan 1973, 625).

Craigywarren seems not to have been the site of either long-term or high-status settlement. There is little clear evidence for a house structure, unless the entire palisade itself is a house. It is also possible that the site was not actually a domestic residence at all, but a focus for some craft activities (such as enamelling and metalworking), though it produced little industrial waste. Craigywarren, like the ninth-century site at Bofeenaun, Co. Mayo (see below), seems to have had only one occupation phase, and it may have been for a period the wetland equivalent of a wealthy farmer's ringfort. Presumably many such crannogs were constructed and either were abandoned for social, political or environmental reasons, or never became centres for long-term settlement. Understanding the process by which this abandonment happened may be as interesting as tracing long-term continuities.

Pl. 31—*General view of Early Historic crannog at Ballinderry no. 2, Co. Offaly (Hencken 1942).*

Ballinderry crannog no. 2, Co. Offaly

Ballinderry crannog no. 2, Co. Offaly, was excavated by the Harvard expedition in 1933 (Hencken 1942). The site was first constructed as a Late Bronze Age lake settlement (see above), later to be occupied as a crannog during the Early Historic period. The crannog was constructed in the seventh or eighth century AD on a naturally raised area in either shallow water or marshy, swampy ground (Pl. 31; Fig. 28). It had a palisade of oak, birch and ash, enclosing an area 35m in diameter, constructed of sharpened posts driven into the muds. It only partly survived on the north and had a possible entrance or gate to the north-east. There was a second possible palisade inside the

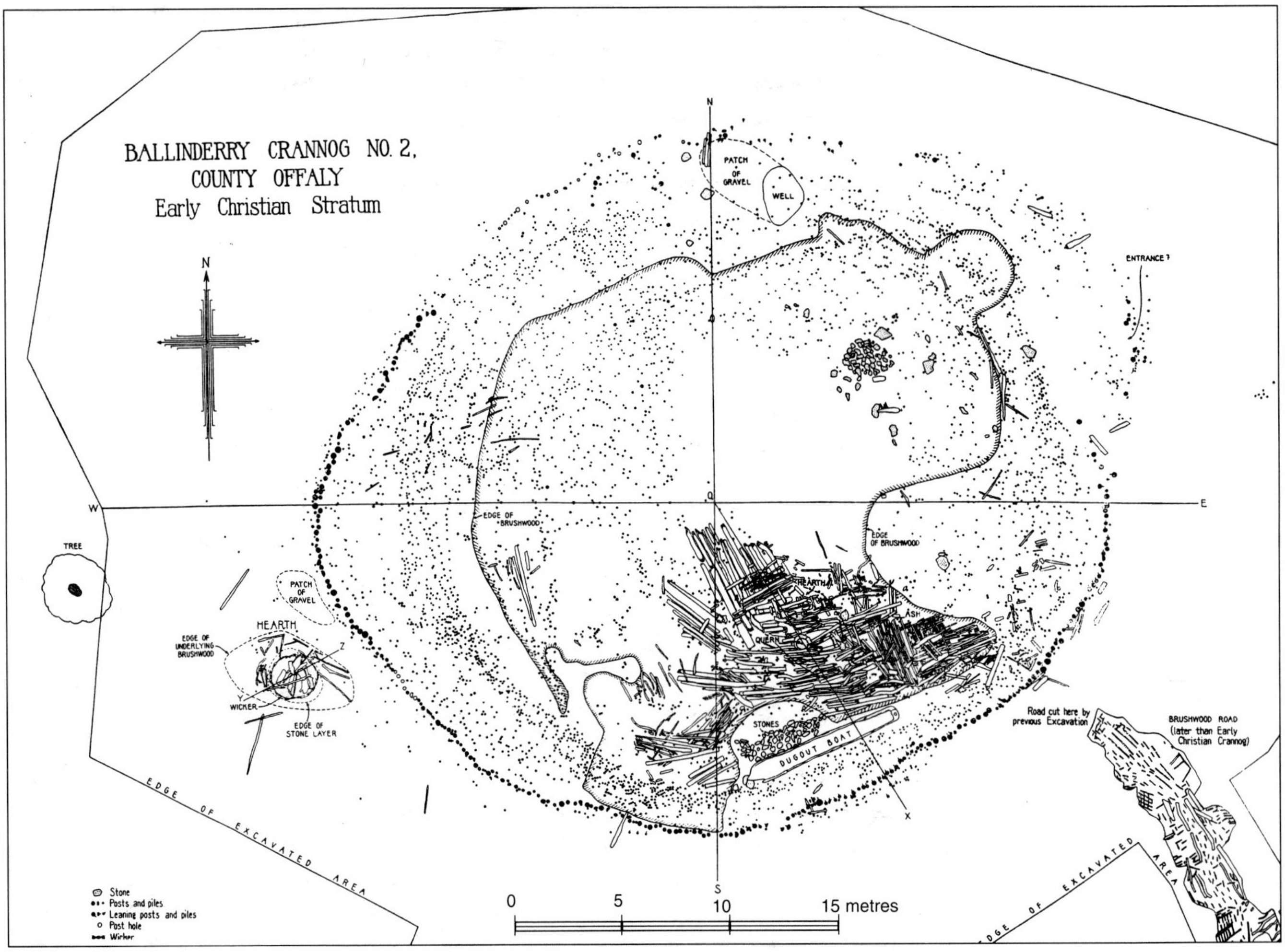

Fig. 28—*Plan of Early Historic crannog at Ballinderry no. 2, Co. Offaly (after Hencken 1942).*

main one, represented by a dense concentration of posts encircling the crannog. The internal area was densely piled with smaller posts to consolidate the marshy ground. The crannog had a well-preserved timber floor on the southern side, where there was a large hearth with several layers of ashes. A dugout canoe and a rotary quern were found in the southern area. Elsewhere the natural lake muds were covered with a dark clay and a thin layer of brushwood, in which animal bone was common. There were up to four layers of wood in places, although Hencken considered that these were the product of one phase. The area outside the crannog had 'an enormous accumulation of food bones, chips and fragments of wood, and other debris', an outer hearth and a brushwood trackway (possibly medieval in date). At least ten circular wicker structures were excavated in the north-east area of the crannog, believed by Hencken (1942) to be Late Bronze Age in date but shown by Newman (1986) to date to the initial phase of Early Historic occupation.

Ballinderry crannog no. 2 produced large numbers of finds. There were four zoomorphic penannular brooches (one of them found under the timber floor), several bronze pins (including two ringed pins), a bronze torc, an escutcheon from a hanging bowl, a hollow bronze armlet decorated with iron and copper wire, and a drinking-horn terminal. It is likely that metalworking was being practised on-site, as there were several whole crucibles and crucible fragments, ingot moulds, moulds and trial-pieces. Finds of iron weaponry included a sword, two spearheads, two spear ferrules and a possible shield-boss. There were five iron knives, two iron ladles, iron shears, a possible spade or hoe, an iron handled bowl, and several pieces of possible iron slag or bog ore. Decorated glass beads of various types were recovered, as well as amber beads and an amber stud and ring. Bone combs, pins, gaming-pieces and worked antler were also amongst the finds. Finds of leather included a number of decorated shoes, shoe soles and other fragments. There were two woven textile fragments. Wooden objects included lathe-turned wooden vessels, bucket and barrel staves, a vessel base, wooden spindles, a dugout boat and a wooden oar. There was also a wooden mallet, ladles and a number of peculiar wooden implements possibly associated with weaving. A number of flint scrapers and blades and a portion of an arrowhead were recovered, as well as two Early Historic rotary querns. Some sherds of later Romano-British pottery were also found on the site.

Ballinderry crannog no. 2 was probably occupied by fairly wealthy inhabitants from the eighth century AD, people who had access to high-status metalwork, glass and amber and who themselves engaged in a small amount of metalworking, woodworking and perhaps textile production. The crannog may not have been rebuilt many times before its abandonment. The economy of the site was reconstructed from the faunal assemblages. There were only two rotary querns, suggesting the relative unimportance of tillage and arable crops. A large assemblage of cattle bone was taken to indicate the importance of grazing; pig and horse bones were also plentiful. In fact, horse may have been eaten. Sheep/goat bones were also found. There may have been some limited hunting of wild animals, such as red deer (which was also very common in the pre-crannog lake muds), hare, badger, otter, fox and marten. There were also dog and cat bones, probably from domesticated pets. There may have been some poultry on the site, but there seems to have been relatively little exploitation of wildfowl or fish.

Lagore, Co. Meath

Lagore crannog, Co. Meath, was first discovered in 1839, when local labourers digging a drainage ditch exposed wooden structures, huge amounts of animal bone and numerous finds of metalwork at the site. The subsequent antiquarian investigations at Lagore can safely be considered to mark the beginnings of research on Irish crannogs (Wilde 1840; Wood-Martin 1886a, 23–5; Talbot 1849; Macalister 1928, 301; Hencken 1950, 36; de hÓir 1990, 112). The site was later excavated by the Harvard Archaeological Expedition between 1934 and 1936 (Hencken 1950). The stratigraphy of the crannog was complex and badly obscured by the earlier diggings, so that its dating and structures have been the subject of much reinterpretion (J. Raftery 1981; Lynn 1985–6; Warner 1985–6). The crannog survived as a large mound, 41m across, consisting of a 3m thickness of peat, brushwood and timber at the eastern end of a now-drained lake (Fig. 29). It was occupied between the seventh and early eleventh centuries AD, and historical sources have traditionally been used to identify it as the actual historical site of *Loch Gabor*, the Early Historic residence of the kings of Brega of the Southern Uí Néill (Price 1950; Warner 1985–6).

The richness of its archaeological deposits has meant that Lagore has provided the data for many debates on Early Historic and Viking Age chronology, royalty, iron-working, artefactual assemblages, agriculture and economy (Edwards 1990; Warner 1994, 66). In particular, several archaeologists have attempted to push back the date of the start of Lagore to before the fifth century AD (e.g. B. Raftery 1972; J. Raftery 1981), but most recent commentators have accepted a seventh-century origin for the site (Lynn 1983, 52–3; Warner 1985–6; Edwards 1990). Lagore crannog was certainly occupied over a long period, and reconstructed and rebuilt on several occasions. Indeed, Hencken (1950), strongly influenced by the constraints of the historical references, identified three separate, consecutive palisades of firstly piles, then posts and finally planks. Lynn (1985–6, 71) has suggested even more phases of occupation. The palisades probably defined the outer defences of the crannog, although Warner (1994, 66) has recently raised the intriguing possibility that these post circles were instead the remains of massive 'royal' houses (Fig. 30).

Hencken (1950) suggested that the crannog-builders first placed a layer of animal bone, brushwood and peat on the lakebed, as a foundation to work from in building

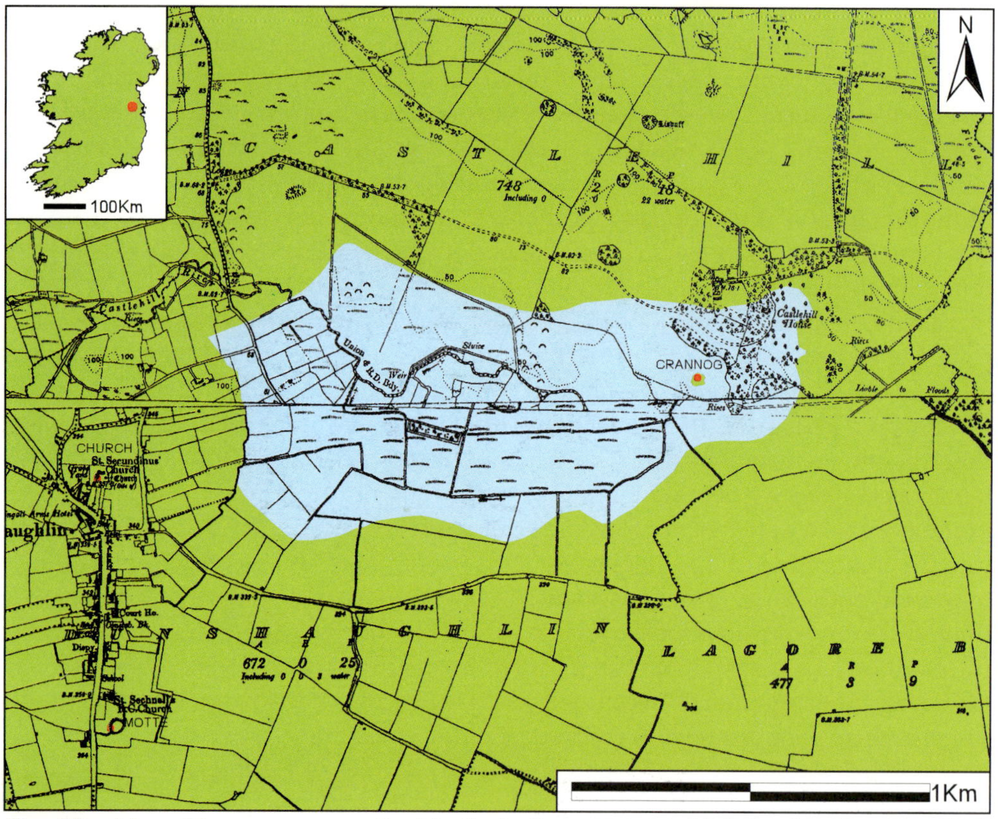

Fig. 29—*Map of Lagore crannog, Co. Meath, in its reconstructed lakeland setting. The Early Historic church at Dunshaughlin can be seen to be situated directly opposite the crannog, on the other side of the lake (map by Paul Synnott, based on Hencken 1950).*

the main crannog. This layer he designated as his Period Ia, which he considered to precede the use of the crannog proper. Lynn (1985–6) has suggested that the Period Ia material is itself evidence of a lake settlement, rather than the debris and working platform of crannog-builders. This occupation phase, compacted and driven into the lake muds by the weight of the later crannog, may have had houses, hearths, piles, wooden platforms, brushwood and wattle mats and occupation debris. This earliest phase of occupation produced some Roman pottery (including *terra sigillata*) and post-Roman material. The latter included seventh- to ninth-century pottery, an iron sword, a seventh-century gold ornament and a seventh- to eighth-century horsebit. Period Ib was taken by Hencken to represent the first main phase of occupation, but it was probably just one of several successive phases after the first occupation. It produced Romano-British pottery, evidence for a seventh- to eighth-century workshop for making glass studs, and a seventh- to eighth-century bronze disc.

Hencken (1950, 7) believed that historical references to the destruction of the crannog could be identified in the archaeological record. He thought that the Period I occupation was abandoned after the event referred to in the Annals of Ulster for AD 850, when Cinaed son of Conaing, king of Cianacht, rebelled against Máel Sechnaill, plundered the Uí Néill and 'deceitfully sacked the island of *Loch Gabor*, levelling it to the ground' (*corro ort innsi Locha Gabur dolose corbo comardd fria lar*), while also burning the nearby church of Treóit. Period II and Period III produced few finds to enable close dating of the site. Hencken felt that the Period II occupation probably ended with the destruction of Lagore in 934 (AU), when 'the island of Loch Gabor was sacked by Amlaíb, grandson of Imar' (*Inis Locha Gabhar do thogail la hAmlaibh h. nImair*). There are no historical references to the site after 969. The end of Period III and the probable abandonment of the site probably occurred in the late tenth or early eleventh century. More recently, archaeologists have pointed out the circular arguments that lie behind Hencken's use of historical references to phase the various occupations but accept his

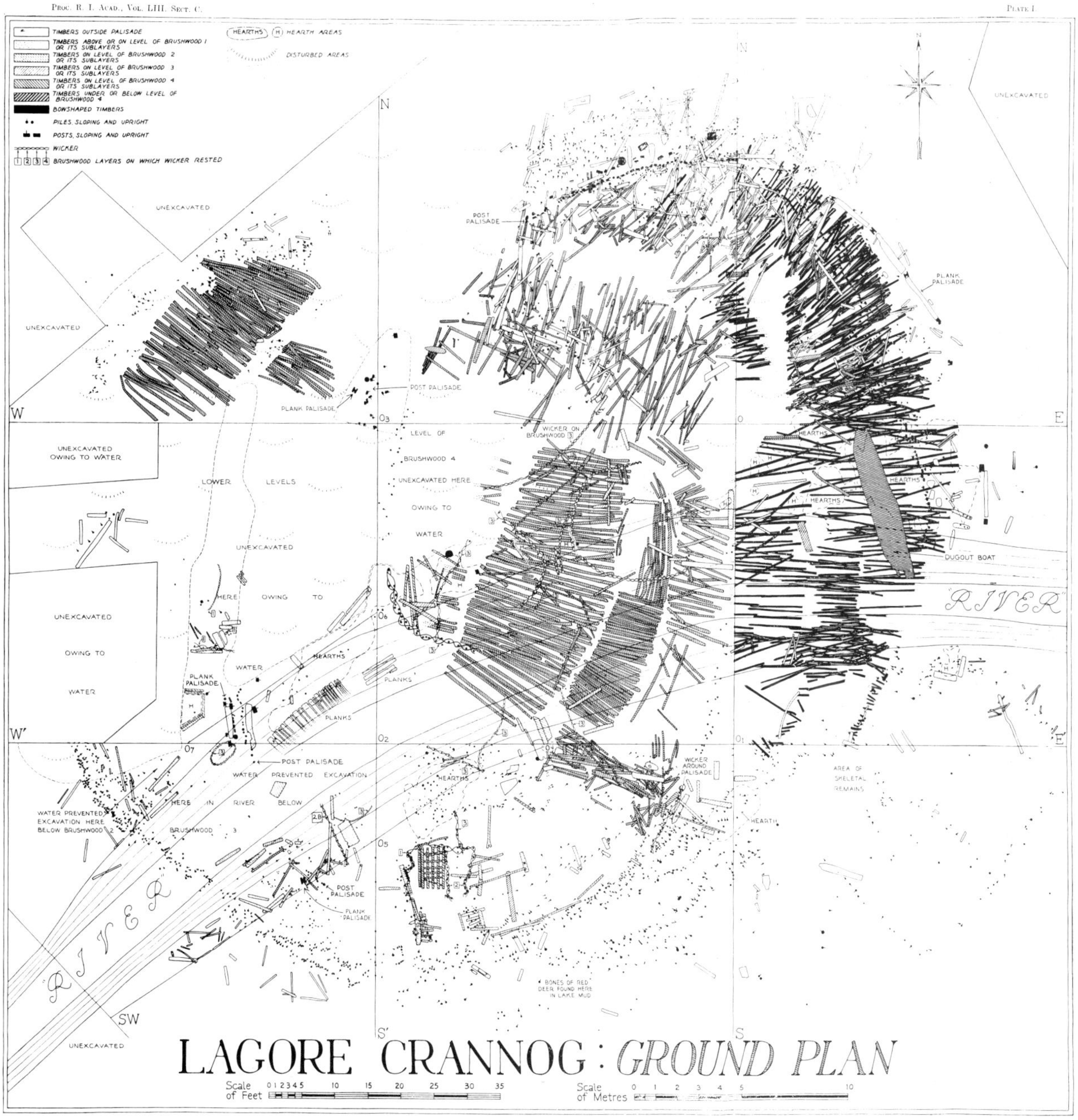

Fig. 30—*Plan of Early Historic crannog at Lagore, Co. Meath (after Hencken 1950).*

general dating of the site (Warner 1985–6). It is also worth pointing out that other potential phases of prehistoric and medieval occupation at Lagore have rarely been described. Later medieval artefacts from the site were largely ignored by the excavator, and a wooden anthropomorphic figure from a sandy layer in the north-west part of the crannog has recently been dated to the Early Bronze Age (B.J. Coles 1990, 326).

The Lagore excavations produced huge numbers of Early Historic and Viking Age finds, described in detail in the original report, within which the nineteenth-century discoveries from the site are also incorporated. The stratigraphy and dating of these finds are a complex subject, and a reinterpretation of them will not be attempted here. Instead the site economy and crafts will be discussed in general terms.

There was extensive evidence for bronze-working at Lagore, particularly in the seventh-century and tenth-century phases of occupation. The site produced pieces of copper ore, sandstone ingot moulds and moulds for bronze rings, clay crucibles, tuyères, spilt bronze waste and scrap pieces of sheet bronze. There were also bone and stone trial- or motif-pieces, indicating the preparation of designs on-site. Bronze artefacts included penannular brooches (Pl. 32), zoomorphic penannular brooches,

Pl. 32—*Gilt bronze brooch from Lagore, Co. Meath (photo: National Museum of Ireland).*

decorated belt-buckles and strap-ends, pins and ringed pins, bowls and rings. There were also some on-site blacksmithing and iron-working, with large amounts of iron slag in the Period II occupation and iron-working floors in the Period II and Period III phases. Iron penannular brooches and pins may have been made there. Objects of finer metals included gold filigree ornament and silver bracelets. There was also evidence for glass-working, with moulds for glass studs occurring, but other finds included glass bracelets and armlets, glass rods, millefiori, enamel and a large number of glass beads. The glass beads were decorated in a range of ways, in blue, white, yellow, khaki and green, and varied in shape from annular to segmented, dumb-bell and melon-shaped. There were also large numbers of lignite bracelets. Imported European objects included Roman glass fragments, amber and E-ware pottery. Animal bones were used as motif-pieces to work out designs for metalworking (Fig. 31).

A range of other domestic crafts were also practised on the site. Leather shoes, scraps of leather and a wooden shoe-last probably indicate the manufacturing of shoes on-site, while an iron leather-working tool, similar to an example from Ballinderry crannog no. 1, was also found. Wooden spindles, spindle-whorls, fleece and animal hair were found, along with uncarded wool and numerous pieces of textiles. Spinning and possibly weaving on a simple loom were probably carried out in the crannog. Bone-working resulted in bone combs, pins, a possible nail-cleaner, gaming-pieces, bone dice and a possible dice-box. There was a wide range of woodworking equipment, including iron axes, an adze, a wooden mallet, knives, gouges, awls, a punch, two small saws, a draw-knife and iron nails, as well as whetstones for sharpening them. Wooden artefacts produced on-site included stave-built buckets, lathe-turned bowls (including some which replicate E-ware pottery), ladles, spindles and various other domestic utensils.

It is clear that Lagore was witness to several violent episodes. The excavations produced 200 human bones from lower levels or the seventh-century Period Ia occupation of the crannog; many were from headless bodies. Fourteen human skulls with cut occiputs indicated the beheading of victims, while other bodies were scattered about the edge of the site. Two iron collars with chains, a possible leg-iron and an iron trident have been interpreted as means of controlling hostages or slaves (Byrne 1973, pl. 13; Hencken 1950, 115; Warner 1994). It is also possible that these iron chains, similar to the examples found in a canoe near a crannog at Ardakillen, Co. Roscommon, were used as dog collars, perhaps for large hunting dogs (B.G. Scott 1978, 228). Weaponry included a range of different types of iron swords. There were twelve iron spearheads, leaf-shaped and shouldered, including a Viking spearhead with an ornamented socket. There were spearbutts, ferrules and iron shield-bosses, while iron horsebits were also found.

Lagore crannog produced huge amounts of animal bone: 50,000 pounds of bone were recovered from the excavations, and the nineteenth-century antiquarian accounts describe similar huge amounts being removed for fertiliser. Cattle easily predominated (much of it slaughtered) in the faunal assemblage, but pigs and sheep/goat were also kept. Horse was fairly infrequent, although certainly present in small numbers. Dog, cat and fowl were also present. There may have been some limited hunting of deer, hare, wild geese and wild duck. Hencken's impression was that meat-eating predominated over grain, although he paid little attention to the use of dairy products. Agricultural tools included iron ploughshares, plough-coulters, sickles, billhooks and a few rotary querns. Wheat straw (*Triticum* sp.) was identified in a mass of plant remains.

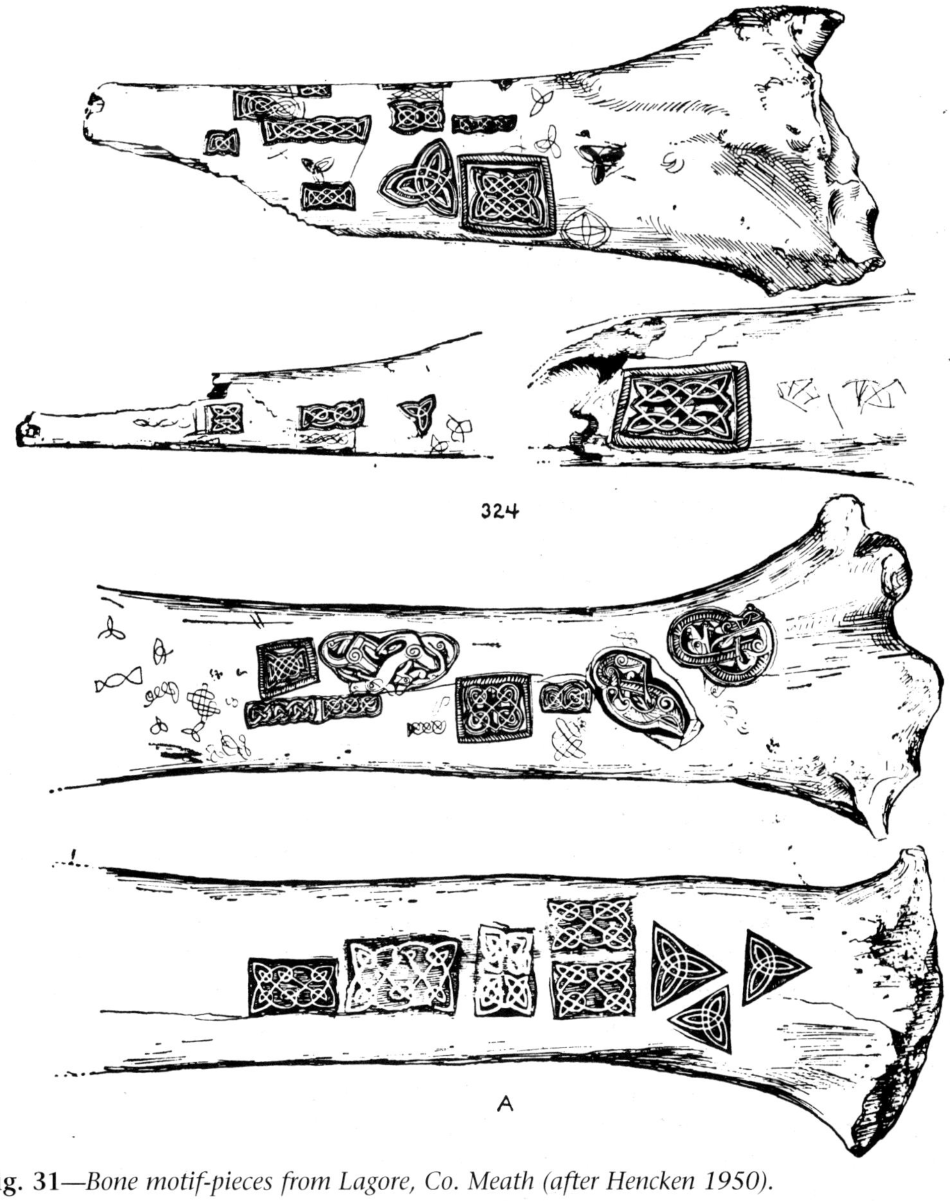

Fig. 31—*Bone motif-pieces from Lagore, Co. Meath (after Hencken 1950).*

Pl. 33—*Crannog 61, Rathtinaun, Co. Sligo. Detail of revetment piles and house posts on lakeshore side of site (photo: Joseph Raftery, reproduced courtesy of Dept of Archaeology, UCD).*

Pl. 34—*Wooden dugout boat found lying on lakebed beside Crannog 61, Rathtinaun, Co. Sligo (photo: Joseph Raftery, reproduced courtesy of Dept of Archaeology, UCD).*

There were also iron shears, although these may have been used for textile-working. Other evidence for textile production included spindle-whorls, fleece and goat hair, and woven textiles.

Rathtinaun (Crannog 61), Co. Sligo

Crannog 61 at Rathtinaun, Co. Sligo, was first recognised in 1952 after artificial lowering of the water-level of Lough Gara. The site appeared as a large cairn or mound, 36m by 29m and 2.5m in height, in a sheltered bay on the eastern side of the lake, about 30m from the drylands. Initial discoveries of some Late Bronze Age artefacts on the site indicated its late prehistoric origin (see above). The site was totally excavated between 1953 and 1955 by Joseph Raftery. It remains largely unknown in Irish archaeology, and the following description is taken from Joseph Raftery's final report, shortly to be published (J. Raftery 1957; forthcoming a; forthcoming b; Barry Raftery, pers. comm.). The site had two Late Bronze Age phases of occupation (Period I and Period II), followed by a period of abandonment and concealment by lake sands. A dugout boat was found on the lakebed beside the crannog (Pl. 34).

The Early Historic occupation began with the Period III level. This was the richest period of activity, probably dating from between AD 600 and 750. A large mound of stones, 11.5m in length, was placed on the sands and retained by a wooden revetment. Peat, logs and stone were heaped against and around the sides of this mound and were in turn retained by a timber revetment, increasing the size of the crannog to 28.5m by 21m. A layer of brushwood, gritty yellow sand, flagstones and timber were laid over this at about the same time. The crannog was retained by a vertical pile palisade, probably built in two phases. There were no recognisable houses, but a large, centrally placed hearth was in use over an extended period, while a layer of brushwood and peat may have served as a house floor. Finds from the Period III occupation included various stone objects, including two polished stone axes, flint flakes and scrapers, hones and four rotary querns. There was a bronze penannular brooch, bronze pins, rings and an armlet, an iron spearhead, a shield-boss, iron ferrules, iron ladles (Pl. 35), a billhook and an iron barrel-padlock fragment. There were also clay crucibles and bone pins, combs, beads and spindle-whorls. Glass pieces included a fragment of a Merovingian glass vessel, greenish-yellow in colour. A layer of sand indicated lake flooding and temporary abandonment of the crannog, which had slumped to the south.

The Period IV occupation began with the levelling of the crannog surface by placing grassy turfs and stones over the Period III remains. This was held in position by a stout revetment and two rows of squared oak posts running along the eastern side of the crannog. It is interesting to note that the strongest defences faced the land. The initial phase of occupation in Period IV produced scanty evidence for a house, although the Period III hearth continued in use. The latter stages produced definite house evidence, in the form of a large circular house, 10.5m in diameter, of carefully sharpened stout oak posts spaced at intervals of 20–35cm (Pl. 33). It may have been

Pl. 35—*Early Historic iron ladle from period III occupation on Crannog 61, Rathtinaun, Co. Sligo (photo: David Jennings, reproduced courtesy of Dept of Archaeology, UCD).*

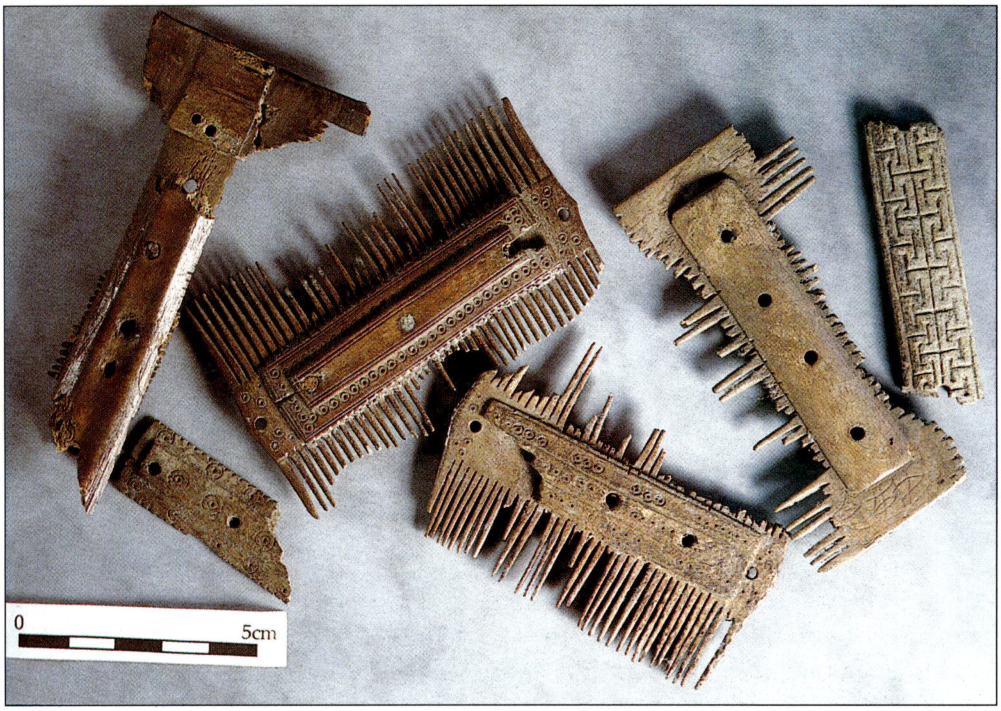

Pl. 36—*Early Historic bone combs from several phases of occupation on Crannog 61, Rathtinaun, Co. Sligo (photo: David Jennings, reproduced courtesy of Dept of Archaeology, UCD).*

demolished on the north side, where no posts remained. There was a central hearth area and a possible entrance to the east, facing the land. The final phase of Period IV occupation saw the crannog being extended to the south-west. Finds from this occupation included hammerstones, stone scrapers, flakes and a rotary quern. There were also iron pins, ferrules, knives, and a hoard consisting of a rotary quern, an iron horsebit and a wooden pin. Pins of bone and antler handles were common, as were stave-built and lathe-turned wooden vessels. There were also clay mould fragments for casting copper-alloy rings. Period IV occupation was ended by a lake flood which deposited water-washed sands over the site.

The Period V occupation began with the raising of the level of the crannog, with a solid deposit of stone heaped over the whole site. This deposit, 1.5m thick, measured 26m north–south and 20.5m east–west, forming an oval plan. However, all superficial features had practically disappeared. A small stone setting, 10m long, may have been the curving arc of a wall, while a tight concentration of fourteen narrow stakes may have formed some structure. A layer of clay and ash could have been a floor. The Period V finds included the usual stone axes, pebbles, scrapers, hones, rotary querns and flint strike-a-lights. There was a bronze ring-pin and strap, as well as an iron socketed spear-head, shield-boss, knives, nails, sickles, bone pins, combs and spindle-whorls. Wooden vessels included stave-built buckets, bases, barrel hoops, carved tubs and a spoon. The crannog was then abandoned for a considerable period, allowing the buildup of a turf layer and natural vegetation across the site, forming a 10–15cm depth of dark soil.

In Period VI, the inhabitants of the locality decided to reuse the old crannog site, extending it with a heap of stones, twigs, peat and grassy sods on the existing mound and beyond the perimeter of its eastern side. It was supported by a double-row revetment of wooden posts along its eastern side, strengthened on its outer side by a layer of sandy and peaty material sloping down to the water's edge. This may have been a palisade rather than a revetment; the lines of posts ran for about 31m along the side of the site. The western side of the crannog had been largely washed away by wave erosion. Traces of occupation were meagre, apart from artefacts and a layer of ash and clay on the north-east side of the site. Finds included the usual stone objects, as well as bronze decorated discs and ring-pins, and iron socketed spearheads, knives, nails, rings, slag, bone pins, combs (Pl. 36) and wooden artefacts.

The final phase of occupation, Period VII, was scanty and barely traceable. A small area on top of the mound had a thin layer of black soil over it, covered by small angular stones. The finds included stone axes, hammerstones, hones, chert flakes and stone discs. There were also bronze penannular rings, discs and pins, iron nails and rods, bone pins and combs, beads and a glass gaming-piece. The full interpretation of the chronology, function and economy of Rathtinaun must await its publication (J. Raftery, forthcoming b). However, it is clear that this was again an unusually rich settlement, whose inhabitants had access to a range of both luxury and exotic goods and resided on the site through the Early Historic period and Viking Age.

Bofeenaun, Co. Mayo

Recent investigations of a ninth-century lake settlement at Bofeenaun, Lough More, Co. Mayo, raised interesting questions about the interpretation of Irish crannogs. This was a largely artificially constructed islet with enclosing wooden palisade, yet its date, size, form and on-site activities confound the conventional definition of an Early Historic or Viking Age crannog. The site was located on the south shore of a small lake in a hollow basin between glacial ridges and hillocks in a landscape then clothed in blanket bog. It was first discovered and recorded by local amateur archaeologists, Michael Flynn and Christy Lawless (Lawless 1992), and thereafter investigated by the Irish Archaeological Wetland Unit over a two-week period in October 1992 (Keane 1995). The crannog was only one of a number of prehistoric and historic period archaeological sites exposed on this lakeshore, which included two *fulachta fiadh*, eighteen linear wooden structures (interpreted as deer-traps), a submerged pine forest, quarries and a natural spring which emits iron ores.

The crannog was situated on a natural knoll of peat jutting out into the water (Pl. 37). There was a substantial depth of peat (over 6m) under the site, which stood only 46cm above the drained level of the lake. It was separated from the dryland by a stretch of swampy ground, but a possible stone and wooden jetty may have provided access to the site. It was defined by a wooden palisade, enclosing an oval area measuring 14.6m by 11.8m. The palisade was gapped and irregular and was typically constructed of roundwood oak, birch, hazel and willow posts. Lawless (1992, 14) suggested that the variation in construction of the palisade indicated multiperiod origins, but the subsequent excavations revealed that the crannog was a single-phase, single-function site. A dendrochronological date of AD 804 ± 9 was obtained from a single oak timber (Keane 1995).

Pl. 37—*Viking Age iron-working site or 'crannog' on Lough More, Bofeenaun, Co. Mayo (photo: Irish Archaeological Wetland Unit).*

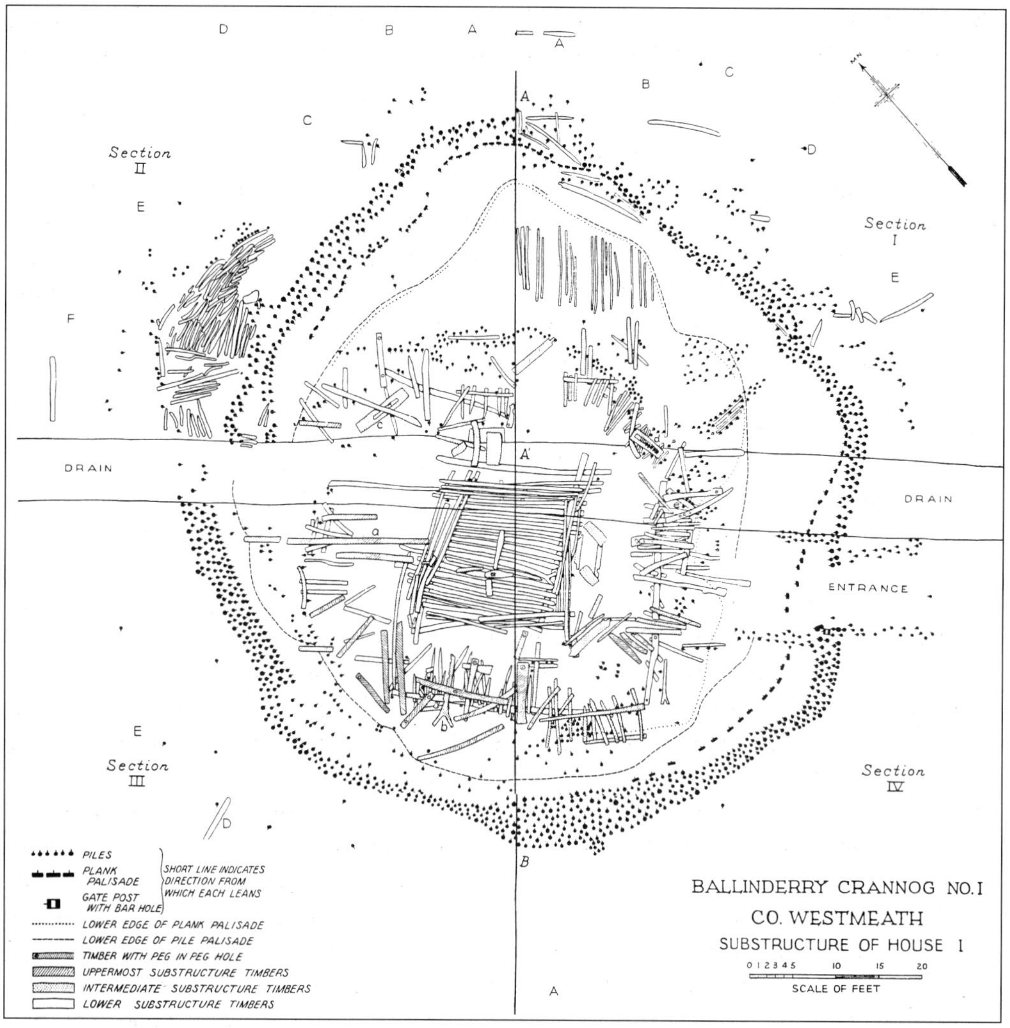

Fig. 32—*Plan of earliest layers at Ballinderry crannog no. 1, Co. Westmeath: interpreted by the excavator as a foundation layer, since reinterpreted as a rectangular house with occupation horizon dating to the tenth century AD (after Hencken 1936).*

The surface of the crannog was defined by a single layer of stone flags, which had been partly eroded away. Finds from this surface included two stone mortars, a grinding stone, a hammerstone and two iron objects. The site was covered in a large quantity of metal slag. Analysis of a sample (74kg) indicated that it had been produced during metalworking activities, with such diagnostic forms as tapped slags and furnace lining fragments. The only structural evidence is the palisade and the stone paving, while the only finds are related to iron-working. The crannog is highly unusual in that it appears to have been exclusively an iron-working site. There were no traces of occupational structures or any other form of domestic or industrial activity. The heavy concentration of slag, the presence of possible furnaces and the hollowed stones used as crushers suggest that its inhabitants were smelting iron from the ores found in the nearby bogs. The present lake is coloured rusty red in the spring, and small quarries in the gravel ridge at the west end of the lake may be evidence for early open-cast mining. There is little other evidence for contemporary settlement in this immediate setting, although there are large numbers of ringforts and stone cashels several miles to the north-east (Margaret Keane, pers. comm.). Bofeenaun provides many contrasts with such larger sites as Moynagh Lough, Lagore and Ballinderry. It was entirely industrial in function, focused only on iron production from local ores. Furthermore, it seems to have been used for only a short time, as there was little evidence for long-term occupation. It is possible that it was not occupied at all, being only a work-site for people living elsewhere. It confirms that not all crannogs were domestic habitations; many of the crannog-cairns and small sites may also have been industrial production centres.

Ballinderry crannog no. 1, Co. Westmeath

Ballinderry crannog no. 1 produced occupation evidence from the tenth and eleventh centuries AD, with activity on the site continuing intermittently until the seventeenth century. The crannog survived as a large, weed-covered hillock, 33m by 20m, at the north-west end of a lake that formerly lay between glacial moraines. At the time of its investigation this had been drained to marshy and boggy land. The discovery of a Viking sword in 1928 had brought the site to the attention of Adolf Mahr of the National Museum. It was excavated by the Harvard expedition in 1932 (Hencken 1936), and has been the subject of various reinterpretations (Lynn 1985–6; Newman 1986; Johnson 1997). The following description will take account of each of these.

Hencken (1936, 107–8) interpreted the site as a large circular crannog built on a large raft-like central foundation, with an internal plank palisade and an outer pile palisade, a large entrance, a wooden quay and a series of three houses, the earliest of which occupied most of the island. He believed that the archaeological evidence represented two main phases of occupation, in the latter part of the tenth century and through the eleventh century. The rectangular raft-like structure of thick oak logs which lay in the centre of the site he took to be the foundation layer. It measured 6m square and was constructed of heavy logs laid directly on the lakebed, probably during a dry period. The platform had raised sides and pegs driven deeply into the clays. The raft was enclosed by small posts describing a circular structure, and timbers were laid radiating out from the centre. Many of these timbers had complex joints and peg-holes, suggesting that they derived from a reused wooden structure (Fig. 32). Most of the artefacts associated with the raft structure can be dated to the tenth or early eleventh century AD. The finds from the lowest layers associated with the raft structure included two iron socketed and riveted Viking spearheads, an iron billhook with a decorated socket, some nails, hones, a decorated bone comb plate, some wooden implements, and a large wooden tub. There was also a small carved and dowelled wooden 'knee', possibly from a dugout boat. Finds from the next layers, also apparently below House I, included a tenth-century bronze ring-headed pin, iron knives, some decorated wooden vessels, a possible wooden motif-piece and a possible pack-saddle. An ornately decorated gaming-board may have been designed for playing the Viking wargame *Hnefatfl*. It probably dates from the tenth century and was decorated in the west Viking tradition, typical of the Scandinavian colonies in the Irish Sea region. A Viking battleaxe found outside the crannog may date from these earliest layers. Human remains are also known from the site.

Hencken (1936) interpreted this raft-like platform (and the associated layer of peat, brushwood, animal bone and ash spreads which covered it) as the foundation for a subsequent large horseshoe-shaped structure, and indeed the entire crannog. This horseshoe-shaped structure was interpreted as the earliest house (House I), for which the crannog was built. A large hearth was in use at its centre. The finds from the layers apparently comprising the floor of House I included a fine iron Viking sword, its handle decorated with silver and its blade inscribed with the letters VLFBEHRT. This sword is of a type produced in the ninth century in the Rhineland and exported throughout Europe. There was also a yew-wood archer's bow, a type of weapon more typical of Viking than of Irish warfare (Andy Halpin, pers. comm.). Other finds from this level, but from outside the house, included an iron plough-coulter, iron rings, and objects of leather, lignite, bone and antler. There were also some wooden buckets and lathe-turned bowls.

Hencken believed that after a brief period of occupation House I sank into the lakebed sediments and was covered by more layers of peat and brushwood. Two further houses (Houses II and III) were then constructed at one corner of the site, but the central hearth continued in use. Finds from these layers included a Viking silver kite-shaped brooch, bronze pins, iron chain-links, a millstone, bone comb fragments, a wooden dugout boat and wooden tubs and hoops. The only find from the floor of House II was an iron knife. House III produced a bronze pin, a bone needle and a wooden dugout boat. Finds from the central hearth included a bronze penannular brooch and pin, and bone, iron, glass, wood and antler objects. The wooden quay structure outside the crannog produced an iron woodworking axe and a wooden tub.

The excavator believed that Houses II and III then fell out of use and were covered with a layer of clay; some planks on this surface may indicate the construction of a fourth house (House IV). There were two hearths and ash spreads at this level. Finds from these strata included bronze pins, buckles, querns, a large iron side-axe or hewing axe (probably of medieval date), hones, bone combs and pins, and objects of wood and leather. The site was covered by a layer of gravel and another deep layer of soil. A hearth was found in this top layer, with finds of coins indicating seventeenth-century occupation. Ballinderry crannog no. 1 produced an interesting range of seventeenth-century objects, such as pottery, several coins dating to about 1690, a brass button, glass linen smoothers, lead bullets (some of which were probably being made there), and several fragments of clay pipes. There were also a range of metal and organic finds from unstratified deposits outside the palisade, the most important of which were a tenth-century copper-alloy hanging lamp and an array of wooden objects.

Chris Lynn's (1985–6) stratigraphical and structural reinterpretations of the early phases of the site were that it actually comprised two crannogs. In his opinion, Hencken's 'House I' was itself the primary crannog (Lynn's crannog 1), defined by the horseshoe-plan area of timbers strengthened by small piles, with a smaller, roughly circular wicker house (Hencken's 'hearth surround', measuring 5m in diameter). The horseshoe timbers were actually the open-air decking around the circular house. Lynn believed that the outer pile palisade derived from a later period of occupation and was not contemporary with this early crannog (Pl. 38). This later period of occupation involved the construction of a second, larger crannog (Lynn's 'crannog 2') directly over 'crannog 1'. 'Crannog 2' had a larger palisade and two rectangular houses built near the edge of the site, while a large open-air ash spread accumulated across the centre. This enlargement could have come shortly after the construction of 'crannog 1'. Newman (1986) came to a similar conclusion through his reanalysis of the site and the typological characteristics of its finds. He also proposed that House I was itself a crannog and that the circular hearth was a round house. In his opinion, the crannog had a pile palisade, which was later reinforced by a plank palisade at the same time as one entrance was blocked up. Ruth Johnson (1997) has also recently carried out a detailed re-evaluation of the early layers of the site and has re-examined the finds, particularly in terms of their stratigraphical context.

The cultural associations of Ballinderry crannog no. 1 have attracted much attention. Hencken noted the number of Viking tools and weapons on the site, but took them simply to mean that the crannog's Irish inhabitants were in contact with Scandinavian settlements of the period. It is also likely that Viking raiders in the Irish midlands would have had to rely on local alliances to spend the winter on Lough Ree. Most recently, Johnson (1997) has explored the cultural and chronological origins of the site. The quality of the carpentry and the assembly of the raft-like structure suggest that this was actually a house, not merely a foundation layer. It was constructed of tightly placed, half-split and hewn timbers, some of which have complex joints and notches. This 'raft' may be the remains of a Hiberno-Scandinavian rectangular house, possibly built in the 930s or 940s, perhaps using stave-building techniques. The range of Viking artefacts, such as the decorated items, the iron axe, the imported iron sword (Pl. 39), the wooden bow, the gaming-board (Pl. 40) and the ship's timber suggest the presence of a cultural grouping with close ties to the Scandinavian world. Johnson also suggests that the latter phases of the site represent a conventional Irish crannog, whose inhabitants remained in close contact with Hiberno-Norse Dublin. Further historical

Pl. 38—*View of Hencken's 'House 1' at Ballinderry crannog no. 1, Co. Westmeath, since reinterpreted as a crannog itself, with a smaller house in the centre (Hencken 1936).*

Pl. 39—*Decorated hilt of Viking Age sword from Ballinderry crannog no. 1, Co. Westmeath, imported from northern Europe (photo: National Museum of Ireland).*

Pl. 40—*Decorated tenth-century wooden gaming-board from Ballinderry crannog no. 1, Co. Westmeath (photo: National Museum of Ireland).*

and archaeological research on the surrounding social, political and settlement landscape could reveal more about this intriguing crannog.

Newtownlow, Co. Westmeath

Newtownlow crannog, Co. Westmeath, was occupied between the tenth and thirteenth centuries AD. The site had been discovered after machine damage during land reclamation and was excavated over two seasons (Bourke 1986; 1987). The crannog had a habitation area, 20m across, on a timber platform enclosed by an oak palisade. The substructure consisted of layers of timbers and brushwood, with several larger trunks resting on a timber beam. There were two conjoined open-air hearths and a large destruction layer of burnt red ash which sloped down around the sides of the site. Several timbers in this ash were interpreted as the burnt remains of a substantial wooden structure. Finds from this area included bone spindle-whorls, a bone toggle, an iron adze and a segmented bead. A layer of black organic midden material was found. A D-shaped wooden structure, 14m by 5m, represented by oak stakes may be associated with the midden layer. The encircling palisade was of large cleft oak timbers. At a later stage, the palisade was mantled with a layer of stones and the centre of the site was covered with a layer of fairly sterile clay.

A hoard of early tenth-century Anglo-Saxon coins was found on the site (after the machine damage), probably deposited during the 950s (Kenny 1984). A range of copper-alloy pins and objects dating from between the tenth and twelfth centuries were also found. Finds from peat outside the palisade included stave-built vessels, an iron ladle and a shaft-hole carpenter's axe, bone combs and a bone toggle. There were large amounts of animal bone, including cattle, pig, sheep, goat and horse, as well as wild species such as red deer, hare and fox. A sherd of green-glazed pottery discovered in the stony layer dates it to the late twelfth or thirteenth century. This agrees with the broad range of finds from the site, suggesting occupation from the tenth to the thirteenth century.

Lough Faughan, Co. Down

The Early Historic crannog of Lough Faughan, Co. Down, was excavated in 1951–2 (Collins 1955), primarily because of the antiquarian discovery of a medieval glazed jug on the site (Wood-Martin 1886a, 92). The excavations indicated that the site was mostly Early Historic in date, occupied at some unknown period between the seventh and tenth centuries AD. There was also evidence for medieval occupation in the form of pottery and a coin. The crannog was constructed on a substratum of hazel, alder and birch brushwood and peat over a marshy deposit. The 'peat' was often composed of heather, bracken and scrub, and there were several layers of bluish or yellowish clay and a few heavy timbers. The upper surface of this substructure was covered with woven wattle panels, interpreted as the beginning of the occupation layer. The occupation layer consisted of brown peaty deposits within which were several clay hearths surrounded by stone kerbing and associated with spreads of timbers. Some of the hearths were industrial rather than domestic, as iron and bronze slag, crucibles and a clay mould for casting bronze pins were found in them. Some finds in the substructural levels were probably derived from domestic refuse from another settlement transported onto the site.

The crannog occupation layer produced iron tools, axes, knives, shears, two bronze pins, bone pins, glass and amber beads, spindle-whorls, numerous sherds of plain, cordoned and decorated souterrain ware, and some imported Samian ware. There was also some medieval pottery on the site, probably dating from the thirteenth century, while an early thirteenth-century coin was later found on the crannog. Rotary querns and whetstones were used on-site. Animal bone included mostly cattle, with some pig, fish and bird (possibly from a fighting cock). One slightly rectangular platform may have been either occupational or a building platform. A layer of burnt material, containing carbonised oats and barley, covered much of the site, suggesting a widespread fire

Pl. 41—*Aerial photograph of Clea Lakes, Co. Down. The excavated crannog is the small tree-clad island on the lake in the middle distance (CUCAP; reproduced with the permission of the Cambridge Committee for Aerial Photography).*

(Collins 1955; Evans 1966). The site economy was based on mixed farming in the surrounding landscape, with the slaughtering of cattle at a young age probably indicating a preponderance of dairying (see below). Lough Faughan appears to have been a crannog whose inhabitants were engaged in both bronze-working and iron-working. Indeed, the site had a largely industrial function, with several hearths and little evidence for house structures.

Clea Lakes, Co. Down

Clea Lakes crannog, Co. Down, was excavated in June 1956 as part of the County Down Archaeological Survey research programme. It was situated in a small lake lying in the drumlins to the west of Strangford Lough, two miles north-west of the coastal town of Killyleagh (Pl. 41), and had already been excavated in the nineteenth century, when bronze pins, a stone disc and both Early Historic souterrain ware and medieval coarseware were found. Collins and Proudfoot's (1959, 92) excavations were limited to a narrow trench. The site was artificially constructed by depositing subsoil, freshly quarried rock-chips and a thin layer of peat over the natural boulder clay. The occupation layer comprised a 3ft-thick deposit of rubbish, within which were the footings of a stone building and most of the artefactual finds. This was covered by a brown loam and stone, within which there was a hearth with ash. The uppermost surface of the crannog was enclosed by a stone wall in the manner of a cashel.

The artefactual assemblage from the modern excavation was all of Early Historic date. It included souterrain ware, two crucibles used for bronze-working as indicated by their staining, a bronze fragment, an iron socketed gouge, three bone pins, a glass bead, lignite bracelets, a stone rotary quern, a perforated stone disc, two spindle-whorls, a whetstone, 36 pieces of flint (including a thumbnail scraper and Mesolithic Larnian flakes), a tracked stone and a stone pebble used as a 'linen polisher'. The flint objects were clearly used as 'strike-a-lights'. The Clea Lakes crannog excavations were limited in extent, but produced the typical range of material found on other crannogs. Although the size and status of the original crannog is unknown, it is interesting that bronze-working on some scale was being practised on the site (Collins and Proudfoot 1959).

Stone crannogs and island cashels

In Connemara and Donegal, crannog sites commonly consist of stone-built mounds in the shallow water of small peaty lakes. There are at least 25 crannogs and lake settlements in the lakes of Connemara, Co. Galway. Most of these are island cashels; a further eleven are either crannogs or are unclassified. It is likely that many more examples exist (Gosling 1993). At Gortacarnaun, on Lough Naneevin, there appears to have been a conventional crannog. The site was excavated by the antiquarian George Kinahan, who identified a roundwood palisade, a brushwood floor, a hearth and post-and-wattle screens. Finds included a stone arrowhead and animal bone (Kinahan 1866–9). On Lough Mask and Lough Corrib, Co. Mayo, crannogs typically were built largely in stone, although wooden posts have been found (Lavelle 1994). The Donegal crannogs are also mostly built in stone, often set in bleak, isolated landscapes in which there is little other settlement evidence (Lacy 1983). This predominant use of stone slabs and rubble may well be due to the original nature of the topography, where stone may have been in far greater supply in the past than timber. For this reason, stone-built crannogs are commonly seen as the western version of the classic midland crannog, and are regarded as also being probably Early Historic in date. It could be pointed out that stone foundations are commonly also found on the midland crannogs (e.g. at Cró-Inis, Co. Westmeath). It has been suggested that their morphological similarity to the stone-built crannogs of the Scottish lochs might suggest that they too date from the Iron Age (Robinson 1997). However, in contrast to Scottish crannogs, there is little artefactual or other dating evidence yet available to support this. It has also recently been suggested that these stone-built islets post-date the classic wooden crannogs, being constructed of stone because of a shortage of mature oak timber by the ninth century (Mitchell and Ryan 1997, 262). This interpretation is not supported by any dating evidence either. However, it might be borne out by evidence from several excavated crannogs. Ardakillen crannog, Co. Roscommon, apparently showed two phases of use. The lower layers were of the classic crannog type, built of peat, brushwood and timber enclosed by a palisade. The upper layers, in contrast, were of a dumped stone fill with an encircling stone wall (Wilde 1857) and may date from the medieval period (Edwards 1990, 37). At Lough Faughan, Co. Down, a stone revetment or wall was also constructed on the upper layers of the site (Collins 1955, 53). Similarly, at Clea Lakes crannog, Co. Down, a stone wall was built to enclose the upper surface of the island (Collins and Proudfoot 1959, 92).

Stone forts or cashels on natural lake islands are another common settlement feature of the north-west and western lakelands. In west Galway there are two stone-built crannogs but twelve island cashels. Furthermore, it has been stated that since the appropriate fieldwork has only been started in south Connemara, there may well be two to three times that number of lake-dwellings there (Gosling 1993, 32). In south Connemara, notable island cashels include Lough na Scannive, identified by Edgar Layard at the end of the nineteenth century (Layard 1897). Island forts are also found on Lough Corrib (Gosling 1993), on Lough Carra (Lavelle 1994) and on Lough Cullen, Co. Mayo (Layard 1899). In Donegal, the well-known O'Boyle's Fort encloses an entire island (49m east–west) in Doon Lough. The wall is massively constructed, being 4m wide at the base and 4.8m in height; although reconstructed like many western stone forts, it has internal passages, steps, a parapet and a narrow entrance. A second possible cashel is situated on a small island to the west (Lacy 1983).

Lough-na-Cranagh, Co. Antrim, a small, shallow lake by the coast of north-east Antrim, near Fair Head (Pl. 64), contains an island artificially constructed on a rock outcrop by laying layers of boulders on the lakebed. The island is enclosed by a stone revetment, of double kerb and rubble fill construction, and rises 1.5m above the lake water. The site was excavated in 1886, producing animal bone and stone artefacts. The surface was covered with stone slabs and a possible hearth was found ('in the centre of the crannog black charred sand occurs several inches in thickness') (M'Henry 1886). Recent underwater surveys on the site revealed several jetties, slips and other stone features possibly intended for boats (Donnelly 1997, 70–3). These stone forts may range widely in date of occupation, from Late Bronze Age origins (or at least settlement history) to the medieval period, but their main period of use is probably in the Early Historic period. Their role in lake settlement may be seen as complementary to the more classic wooden and stone-built crannogs. In addition, the presence of ringforts, cashels, watermills and unenclosed settlements by lakeshores needs to be assessed in any lake settlement projects.

Early Historic and Viking Age crannog regional studies

Fermanagh lakes, Co. Fermanagh

Crannogs are only one element in Early Historic and Viking Age settlement organisation, but there have been few attempts to study patterns in their regional distribution. The Fermanagh crannog survey carried out in 1977 revealed several interesting patterns of siting and location (Claire Foley, pers. comm.). The following account is based on the field notes of the survey prepared by Claire Foley. The lake margins were walked during a hot summer and a dinghy was used to get access to the islands. The crannogs were mostly located in the small lakes in the vicinity of Upper and Lower Lough Erne and in the drumlin lakes to the south of the county. They avoided the large lakes with their open stretches of water, but were typically found in small isolated lakes drained by unnavigable streams. If the lakes were small, the crannogs were found to be centrally placed, thus making them as inaccessible as possible. In larger lakes, such as Lough MacNean, they were closer to the shore, often found in sheltered bays and inlets. Crannogs were found in clusters in six lakes. The Fermanagh crannogs ranged in diameter from 8m to 34m and typically rose to a height of 3m above the lake surface. Horizontal and vertical timbers were commonly found, along with stony layers. Early Historic and medieval finds from Fermanagh crannogs (during nineteenth-century investigations and the crannog survey) included fragments of rotary querns and crannog ware pottery, iron slag, crucible and mould fragments, bronze pins, jet bracelets and beads, and iron tools and weapons. The crannogs were typically found to date from between the ninth and the eleventh centuries AD, while sixteen radiocarbon dates from the fifteenth to the seventeenth century were also obtained, supporting the model of extensive post-medieval crannog use in Fermanagh.

Lough Ennell, Co. Westmeath

The archaeological and historical evidence for Lough Ennell, Co. Westmeath, suggests that between the ninth and twelfth centuries AD local secular and ecclesiastical politics led to the formation of a complex settlement system based on the lake (Farrell and Buckley 1984; Karkov and Ruffing 1990–1; E.P. Kelly 1991a; Karkov and Ruffing 1997). This settlement evidence includes ringforts, crannogs, metalworking and monastic sites, and coin hoards around the lake (Fig. 33). Historical references suggest that several of the ringforts and crannogs were used as royal sites or high-status settlements. It is suggested that in the eighth or ninth century the Clann Cholmáin kings of the Southern Uí Néill moved their base from the Hill of Uisneach to Lough Ennell (Karkov and Ruffing 1997, 338). It was a move of some miles, but Lough Ennell was certainly more strategically placed, lying on the River Brosna/River Inny drainage which leads to the River Shannon and north of the major dryland routeways of the *Slige Mór*.

There may also be prehistoric settlements on Lough Ennell. Small, heavily concreted cairns of stone, 10–12m in diameter, are found at Inchacrone, Wren Point and

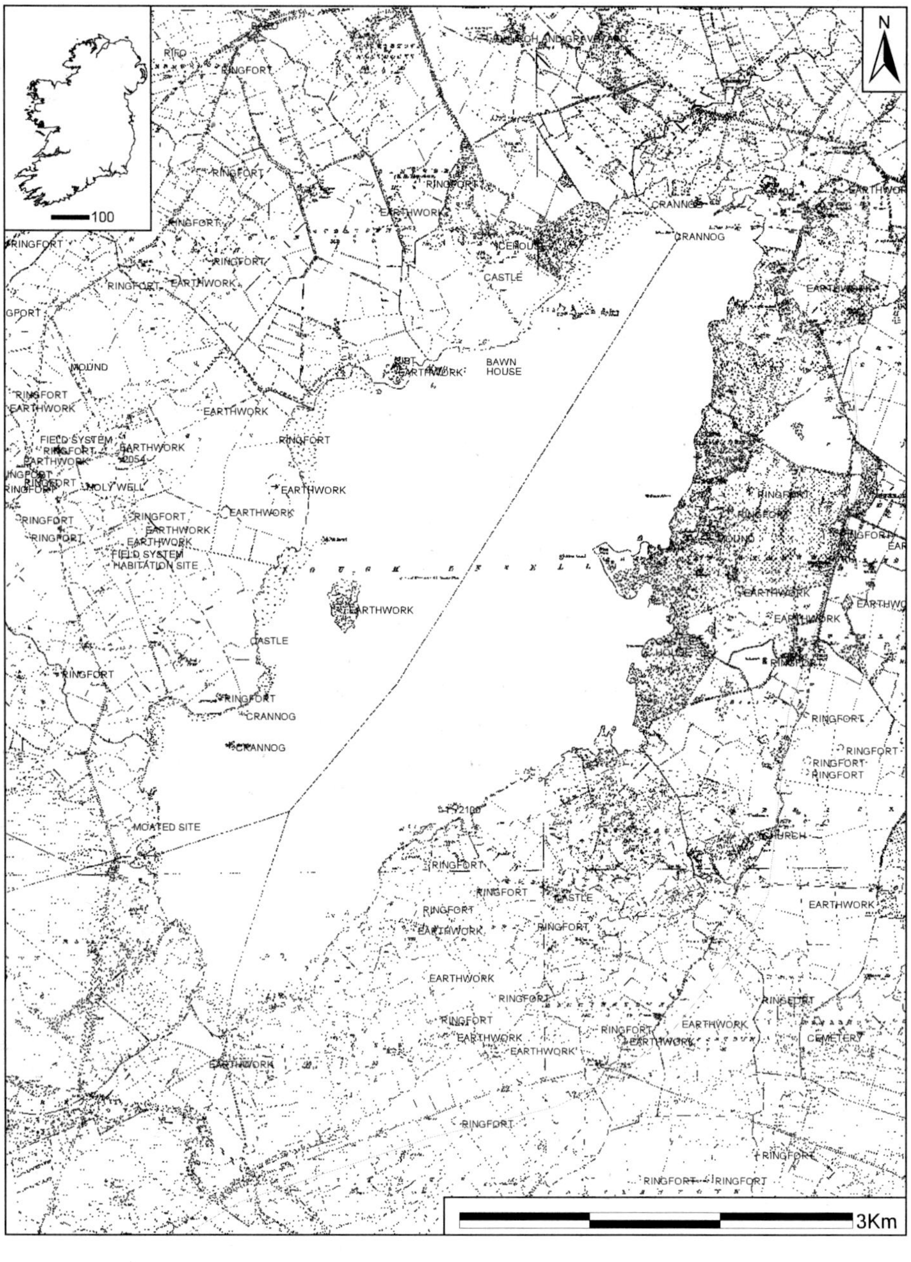

Fig. 33—*Map of Lough Ennell, Co. Westmeath, where crannogs, cairns, ringforts and monastic sites and hoards of silver attest to its political importance in the Early Historic period and Viking Age (based on the records of the National Monuments Service, Dúchas—The Heritage Service).*

Goose Island (Farrell 1991; Karkov and Ruffing 1990–1). Similar stone cairns, platforms and jetties have also been located underwater around several crannogs along the eastern shore of the lake (Farrell 1991). There is little dating evidence for these as yet. Their spatial association with the crannogs may suggest that they were Early Historic or Viking Age platforms from which fishing or fowling was carried out, but they could well be prehistoric in date. Similar mounds at Lough Gara, Co. Sligo, produced Mesolithic, Neolithic and Bronze Age assemblages (J. Raftery 1957).

Cró-Inis, the best-known crannog in Lough Ennell, is historically attested as the royal residence of the Clann Cholmáin of the Southern Uí Néill. It lies on the south-west shore, and Dún na Sgiath, a multivallate ringfort also historically identified as a royal seat of the Clann Cholmáin, is located on the neighbouring dryland (E.P. Kelly 1991a; 1991b; Warner 1994). Cró-Inis was briefly excavated in 1938 by R.A.S

Macalister, who discovered a large stone structure, a boat slipway, a stone pavement and a pit associated with an ash spread (Macalister 1938). The Crannog Archaeological Project's investigations in the vicinity of the site revealed two to three concentric rows of roundwood partly enclosing the site, dated to *c.* AD 850, and a plank palisade dendrochronologically dated to *c.* AD 1100–25. Eleventh- to twelfth-century bronze pins were also found in the muds (Farrell and Buckley 1984; Farrell 1991). It has been suggested that the site was first constructed in the ninth century and refortified in the twelfth, and a tower-house was built on the island in the fourteenth century. The early monastic site of Dysart is situated directly to the north of Cró-Inis and Dún na Sgiath. It is only preserved by its enclosure, although an early cross-base is found there. Three Viking Age silver hoards (Dysart 1, 2 and 3) have been recovered on Dysart Island, and a hoard of two silver ingots was recovered from a 'submerged crannog' at Dysart (Ryan *et al.* 1984; Farrell 1991).

Goose Island crannog, on the eastern shore of Lough Ennell, is built up of boulders and smaller stones with an encircling roundwood palisade which is open towards the mainland. Timbers provided radiocarbon dates between the late ninth and mid-tenth centuries AD. Some form of medieval stone building or tower-house may have stood on the island, as worked stone is presently scattered around its surface (Karkov and Ruffing 1990–1). Two ringforts which command good views of the crannog and its neighbouring stone platforms are situated on the adjacent dryland in Belvedere.

Cherry Island is an enhanced natural island, situated to the south of Carrick Bay on the south-eastern shore of the lough. It has a stone cashel on its surface and is overlooked by a ringfort on the dryland. The island may be Inis na Cairrge, which can be linked in historical references to Dún na Cairrge, a ringfort on the shore of Carrick Bay known to have been a residence of the Fir Thulach kings. Viking Age silver has been found on Cherry Island, and a Viking Age silver hoard was found on the dryland at Carrick (Ryan *et al.* 1984; E.P. Kelly 1991b).

Rushy Island and School Boy Island lie at the mouth of the River Brosna at the north end of the lake. Archaeological surveys in this area have also indicated similar associations between settlements on the dryland and the lake archaeology (Farrell and Buckley 1984; Farrell 1991). At Rushy Island, a possible crannog now set in marshy ground has produced Viking Age silver and a possible bone midden (Karkov and Ruffing 1992–3). Two crannogs, two islands, two underwater cairns, a few stone platforms and one partially submerged platform have been recorded in the vicinity of School Boy Island, and it is known that two Viking Age ecclesiastical handbells were found in the water off the island (Karkov and Ruffing 1990–1). It has been suggested that Rushy Island and School Boy Island were defensive sites at the outlet of the River Brosna and that there were links between these crannogs and the early monastery of Lynn, which is situated at the north-east corner of the lake (Karkov and Ruffing 1997). Lynn was certainly an important monastic and economic centre in the region, as claimed by the twelfth-century hagiography of its founder, Colmáin Maic Lúacháin.

Origins and chronology

What are the origins and chronology of crannogs in Ireland? Although enclosed lakeside settlements were used in Ireland in the Late Bronze Age, there is no evidence for their continuity through the Iron Age into the Early Historic period (Lynn 1983; Crone 1993). Most of the evidence for the dating of crannogs is based on artefactual material, typically metalwork, not always from secure contexts. Indeed, there are a range of artefacts, such as spindle-whorls, iron tools, quernstones and glass beads, which are not particularly closely dated within the Early Historic period (Lynn 1994, 83). Our best chronological evidence remains the results of the dendrochronological sampling programme carried out in the 1970s and 1980s by Michael Baillie of the Palaeoecology Centre at Queen's University, Belfast (Baillie 1979; 1982). This produced a series of 'spot dates', mainly in the late sixth and early seventh centuries AD, from crannogs in the north-east.

Island MacHugh, Co. Tyrone, produced predominantly early seventh-century dates (AD 594 ± 9, AD 608, AD 616 ± 9, AD 619, AD 622 ± 9 and AD 627 ± 9) (Ivens *et al.* 1986). Three crannogs in Antrim have produced late sixth- and early seventh-century dates: Midges Island was dated to AD 570 ± 9, Lough Tamin to AD 618 ± 9 and 584 ± 9, and Teeshan crannog probably to AD 581. An early fifth-century phase was formerly proposed for Teeshan crannog, but the timbers that produced these dates had no sapwood and were probably derived from the heartwood of large oak trees felled in the late sixth century AD (Baillie 1995a). A single crannog at Kilnock, Co. Antrim, produced a slightly later date of AD 722 ± 9 (Baillie 1979). Two Fermanagh crannogs have produced mid- to late sixth-century dates: Mill Lough has been dated to AD 553 ± 9 and AD 643 ± 9, and one crannog at Ross Lough produced dates of AD 570 ± 9 and AD 614. Three crannogs in Connacht have also produced slightly later dates. A crannog at Levallinree Lough, Co. Mayo, which had dugout boats, an iron felling axe, a fish-spear and a socketed iron blade on its surface, also produced a dendrochronological date of AD 609 or 610 (Lawless *et al.* 1989). The Swedish Carrowmore Project's test excavations on a crannog at Cloverhill Lough, Co. Sligo, produced two calibrated radiocarbon dates of AD 883–1024 (1085 ± 90 BP; St-7622) and AD 886–992 (1120 ± 50 BP; Lu-1841) (Burenhult 1980, 29–33). Recent archaeological investigations of a metalworking site at Bofeenaun, in Lough More, Co. Mayo, produced a dendrochronological date of AD 804 ± 9 (Lawless 1992; Keane 1995). In Leinster, at Moynagh Lough, Co. Meath, oak timbers have been dendrochronologically dated to AD 625 and AD 748. If this sample can be taken as representative, then it appears that the oak palisades were first being constructed on Irish crannogs over an 80-year period in the late sixth and early seventh centuries AD. It has been suggested that the increase in crannog construction in the sixth and seventh centuries was due to some political or social upheaval or an increase in surplus wealth. Indeed, it is at this time that ringforts, crannogs and defended monastic enclosures first appear (Edwards 1990, 37). It is possible that a combination of climatic deterioration (caused by a comet or some other cosmic event) and famine destabilised early Irish society to the extent that defended settlements became vital (Warner 1993; Baillie 1995b). However, it may be that crannogs were built as part of a fashion, or as a new means of displaying wealth or power. Perhaps it is as simple as this—people lived on the water because they wanted to.

In contrast, many Scottish Dark Age crannogs were being built at an earlier period, in the third to fifth century AD (Crone 1993). It has therefore been suggested that the 'crannog concept', the idea of building and living on an artificial defended islet, was introduced into Ireland from south-west Scotland by returning Irish migrants. Warner (1983) has explored a range of evidence for links between south-west Scotland and northern Ireland at an earlier period in the Iron Age. He notes that Irish artefacts have been found on several early Scottish crannogs and suggests that Irish settlers and craftsmen settled in lowland Scotland in the first few centuries AD, bringing with them certain artistic styles and technical skills. These settlers may later have returned to the north of Ireland, bringing with them Scottish objects and settlement concepts. It has also been suggested that the 'crannog concept' was part of a package of new agricultural ideas introduced from Roman Britain. Graham (1993) has suggested that Irish migrants from Wales would be a logical source of this introduction. However, as Llangorse is the only known Welsh crannog (Redknap 1991; Redknap and Lane 1994), Wales is unlikely to have inspired Irish crannogs. In fact, the reverse may be the case: Llangorse may be of Irish origin (Campbell and Lane 1989, 679). It might be worth remembering that lake settlements were common in various parts of Europe, usually serving as fortified military sites. Fortified lake settlements should be seen as a common response to particular environmental or social conditions, with little need for a diffusionist model to explain their distribution.

Is the currently accepted chronological model of Irish crannogs proven? There are a few outstanding problems. Firstly, it would be wrong to say that the dendrochronological programme has provided a random sample of Irish crannogs, as these were mostly 'spot dates' from oak palisades. The construction of the oak palisades represents only one particular woodworking phase on these crannogs, not always the original construction phase. It may well yet prove to be the case that oak palisades are a secondary addition to most Irish crannogs. It is possible that there were cultural reasons (such as the owner's status and prestige, or a period of increased conflict) for the construction of oak palisades. It was, after all, a high-status building material, the use of which was tightly controlled in early Irish law (O'Sullivan 1994a). At Moynagh Lough, Co. Meath, the original palisade was of roundwood and could have preceded the oak palisade by many years. At Lagore, Co. Meath, the oak palisade certainly occurs later in the occupation history of the site. The first palisade at Ballinderry crannog no. 1 was of roundwood piles, and was also later replaced by an oak plank palisade. Interestingly, radiocarbon dating of non-oak structural timbers on many Scottish crannogs has provided significantly earlier dates there (Barber and Crone 1993). The Irish chronological model also emphasises only the large crannogs, whereas the chronology of many other potential lake settlements has yet to be established. The date of most stone cairns, causeways and lakeshore mounds is unknown, while stone-built crannogs in the west of Ireland may well be earlier.

However, the origin of crannogs is only one interesting aspect of their archaeology. The history of their use across time and ultimate abandonment also needs to be explored. In some cases, although absolute chronology is lacking, it appears that crannogs were constructed, occupied and abandoned within a single generation; Craigywarren and Bofeenaun crannogs appear to have been single-phase sites. Artefactual evidence suggests that other crannogs were occupied over considerable periods, certainly from the sixth to the twelfth century and beyond. Ballinderry crannog no. 2 was occupied between the sixth and eighth centuries, Lagore was occupied through at least three phases between the seventh and early eleventh centuries, and Ballinderry crannog no. 1 had at least two periods of occupation between the tenth and eleventh centuries. Crannogs on Lough Ennell and Lough Kinale are known to have been constructed and repaired over centuries. The Early Historic/Viking Age period is one of profound internal social and economic change in Ireland, and there may well have been significant differences in the social function and economic role of crannogs at different times. It is also true that several crannogs were occupied up to and during the medieval period. The process by which individual sites were repaired, reconstructed, occupied and abandoned over considerable periods deserves greater attention.

Structures, palisades and houses

The complex nature of the structures found on and around Irish crannogs has rarely been a subject of interest in recent years. Crannogs were built in a variety of locations, such as natural knolls or shoals in lakes, or in deeper water through deposition of layers of timber, stone, brushwood and peat. Crannog-builders obviously made use of earlier features. Mesolithic, Neolithic and Bronze Age lake settlement mounds were also often the location for Early Historic crannogs, the elevated platforms over the marshy ground or water providing a useful base to start from. Substantial timber rafts of mortised planks (often possibly reused) and cleft beams were anchored or retained in place by vertical piling. The crannog occupation layer was then built up by depositing peat, heather, brushwood and timber on the surface. These mounds are often revetted by low, encircling rows of piling, while larger enclosing palisades are also common. Occasionally there are also enclosing circles of piles several metres out from the crannog, acting as breakwaters against wave action or as additional defensive features. It has been suggested in reconstruction drawings that many Scottish crannogs (e.g. Oakbank, Milton Loch) were constructed as raised platforms on piles, upon which a dwelling-house is constructed. This interpretation has only rarely been proposed in Ireland (Warner 1994, fig. 2).

A classic feature of the Irish crannog is the timber palisade, built either as a structural revetting feature or possibly as a defensive enclosing element. At Ballinderry

Pl. 42—*Crannog in the Rosses, Co. Donegal. A stone causeway can be seen zigzagging out to the site (photo: Victor Buckley).*

crannog no. 2 there was a single post and pile palisade; at other sites, such as Lagore, there were certainly a number of palisades of piles, posts and planks. It has been noted that the crannogs at Cró-Inis, Goose Island and Lough Kinale did not have palisades in the shallows facing the shore (Farrell 1991). It may be that the horseshoe-shaped palisades at these sites were designed as breakwaters to protect the crannogs from wave erosion. It is also possible that they forced boats approaching the crannog to come up to it from the landward side (Eamonn Kelly, pers. comm.). An unusual palisade was identified at Crannog no. II, Cuilmore Lough, Co. Mayo, where a natural promontory of ground was fortified by erecting a double palisade in the manner of a promontory fort embankment. A possible gate or tower may have been situated in the middle of the palisade. The inner, enclosed area contained a possible circular structure (Rynne and MacEoin 1978). The site would require underwater investigation to establish the nature of this palisade, but it seems similar to the larger lake promontory forts described below.

There are a range of other stone and wooden structures associated with many crannogs. Many, such as landing stages, jetties, causeways and breakwaters, may have been for boat navigation and storage. Stone causeways or pathways approaching the crannog from the land are often constructed as zigzag lines, presumably to baffle attackers and make their approach slower (Pl. 42). Defended entrances with pathways leading in to the settlement are also known, such as at Moynagh Lough. Entrances can be at the eastern, north-eastern or northern side. However, this pattern is based on the limited evidence of a few excavations, and it is more likely that palisade entrances simply faced the land, although at Moynagh Lough it probably faced towards the lake. Certain crannogs have quays or slipways for dugout boats, coracles and plank-boats. At Ballinderry crannog no. 1, a substantial slipway of oak planks overlain by peat and brushwood was found in the pile palisade at the north-west side of the site. Dugout boats are a common find on crannog excavations, such as Lagore and Ballinderry crannog no. 2, and it is likely that more are preserved underwater at unexplored sites. For example, there are six dugout boats lying at a depth of about 1.5m on the lakebed around a crannog in Lough O'Flynn, Co. Roscommon (Donal Boland, pers. comm.). It is possible that even larger boats docked at crannogs. A wooden knee from a plank-boat was found in the Ballinderry crannog no. 1 excavations, and a wooden object which has the appearance of an oar (rather than a paddle) was found at Ballinderry crannog no. 2. Archaeological surveys have also produced evidence for stone cairns and platforms close to larger crannogs which could be ancillary structures to the main settlement, used for fishing, metalworking or some other activity.

The character of the internal settlement space of Irish crannogs remains a puzzle in many respects. This is unfortunate, as it has rightly been proposed that the house is a key feature for the study of past societies. The size, shape, form, location, function and internal spatial variations of houses are amongst the best methods of assessing the social organisation, way of life and culture of past peoples (Lynn 1994, 82). Houses have been identified in only a few Early Historic and Viking Age crannog excavations—possibly at Ballinderry crannog no. 1 (Hencken 1936; Lynn 1985–6), definitely at Moynagh Lough (J. Bradley 1991) and possibly at Lagore (Lynn 1985–6). The smaller house at Moynagh Lough, 7.5m in diameter, was constructed of a double wall of vertical posts and was associated with a cesspit and two metalworking areas, found to either side of the structure. Some crannogs, such as Bofeenaun, have little or no evidence for house structures. Craigywarren may or may not have had a house, and it is unknown what was found at Moylarg. However, most antiquarian excavations were too rapidly carried out to clarify the occupation of crannogs. In contrast, the modern excavations at Moynagh Lough uncovered one house which survived only as post-holes, features that were probably overlooked in early crannog excavations. In any case, there have been relatively few attempts to reconstruct the form of the houses found on crannogs. Kinahan (1866–9, 31) ventured an unusual house reconstruction. Wakeman's well-known reconstruction drawing of an Irish crannog has had a major impact (Wood-Martin 1886a), while more recently John Bradley (Cotter 1986, cover illustration) and Richard Warner (1994) have depicted quite different interpretations of the types of houses found on crannogs.

There are several potentially interesting aspects to the archaeology of houses on crannogs, such as the social and domestic organisation of the internal space. Lynn (1994) has identified important changes in house-building in Early Historic ringforts: round houses are found in central locations between AD 500 and 800 but thereafter rectangular houses are found to the sides and at entrances (between AD 800 and 1000). Interestingly, he suggests that the hypothetical Ballinderry 1 circular post structure placed over the rectangular 'raft' may have been a high-status house. On the other hand, the unenclosed marshland settlement at Tivannagh, Co. Sligo, may have had a large rectangular house towards the end of the Viking Age.

It has been suggested that the presence of large houses on crannogs is evidence for 'royal occupation' (Warner 1994). At Moynagh Lough a particularly large house was excavated, measuring 11m in diameter with a double post wall, two hearths and demarcated sleeping areas. Recent historical research suggests that Moynagh Lough was possibly a 'royal centre' (Bhreathnach 1998). At Lagore, which is definitely a 'royal site', the only houses identified were post-and-wattle structures under 10m in diameter. However, Warner (1994, fig. 2) has recently suggested that some Irish crannogs could have been totally dominated by a single massive house structure, encompassing the entire island in the manner of the Scottish Milton Loch and Oakbank crannogs. In other words, what we usually interpret as the crannog palisade may in fact be the house wall. This model, largely based on the original interpretation of Lissue, has the advantage of explaining why houses have proved so difficult to identify in the internal areas of many crannog excavations (Richard Warner, pers. comm.). It is worth pointing out that Lynn (1985–6, 73) has already dismissed this avenue of interpretation; in his opinion, the Lissue structure was a 'totally unsuitable design for a soft, artificial island site'.

Other aspects of the settlement space of crannogs also require more detailed study. How are houses, huts and working areas organised in relation to each other, to pathways through the site, to the entrance features and to the enclosing palisade? It would be interesting to explore patterns in the location and organisation of hearths and cooking areas, metalworking surfaces and furnaces, bone-working and woodworking areas and food-processing. Do the entrances of houses face the crannog entrance and the land, or do they look out across the lake to other settlements? How are the food middens and industrial waste pits situated in terms of the domestic space? Does the distribution of finds tell us anything about the use, occupation and abandonment of crannogs?

Crannogs as 'royal centres'

Clearly this debate over the significance of large houses on crannogs leads to an exploration of the social status of their inhabitants. It is generally thought that these were the settlements of wealthy or powerful kings, nobles or craftsmen. Warner (1988), in his review of the archaeology of Irish kingship, suggested that some crannogs, like multivallate ringforts of small internal dimensions, may have been regional or local royal centres. The social organisation of early Irish society meant that there were a large number of kings, lords and other nobles resident in the Irish landscape. The precepts of Irish kingship required that certain features be present on a 'royal site'. There should be a 'royal' house (*rígtheach*), a great house (*tech mór*) or a feasting house (*tech midchuartha*), a place of proclamation and outer buildings for clients and artisans (Byrne 1973; Warner 1988; 1994). Historical sources suggest links between many crannogs and kingship, while the excavation of some crannogs has certainly revealed large amounts of bronze and silver metalwork, exotic imports and weaponry. These crannogs were undoubtedly high-status centres in some form. Lagore, Co. Meath, Cró-Inis, Co. Westmeath, and Island MacHugh, Co. Tyrone, have all been historically identified as royal centres (Hencken 1950; E.P. Kelly 1991a; 1991b; Ivens *et al.* 1986), while the artefact assemblage from Moynagh Lough and the emerging historical evidence for the region suggest that it too was a royal site. Most recently, Warner (1994) has explored the royal associations of crannogs in more detail. In some cases, he suggests that it is the lake itself which was identified with royalty; alternatively, the main royal site may in fact have been a ringfort on the drylands. A close spatial relationship between a large ringfort and a crannog can be seen at Dún na Sgiath ringfort (the royal seat of Máelsechnaill, the king of Clann Cholmáin) and the Cró-Inis crannog (E.P. Kelly 1991a; 1991b) (Pl. 43). A royal ringfort of the Fir Tullach, Dún na Cairrge, is situated on the opposite, eastern shore of the lake. Warner has also identified a possible link between Island MacHugh crannog and a ringfort known as Lislear at the opposite end of Lough Catherine, Co. Tyrone (Warner 1994).

It is possible to point to a range of other possible spatial and social associations between crannogs and ringforts. At Lisleitrim, Co. Armagh, a crannog with oak palisade is overlooked by a large, trivallate ringfort with souterrain on the neighbouring drumlin (Evans 1966; Mitchell and Ryan 1997, fig. 145) (Pl. 44). At Levallinree Lough, Co. Mayo, there is an interesting archaeological complex of an Early Historic cashel, a ringfort and hut sites situated on slopes by the lake. The cashel is sited on a hilltop with commanding views of the countryside and the lake to the north-west. There are at least six crannogs in the lake, some submerged, one of which has produced a dendrochronological date of AD 609. It has been suggested that this is a royal settlement complex, as the name of the lake and the adjoining townland (*Leath Bhaile ar Rí*) may be translated as 'half quarter of the king' (Lawless 1993; Lawless *et al.* 1989). At Coolure Demesne, on the north-east shore of Lough Derravarragh, Co. Westmeath, a large earthen enclosure, possibly of Early Historic origin, lies on the lakeshore. The nearest

Pl. 43—*The 'royal' ringfort of Dún na Sgiath, with Cró-Inis crannog out on the water, Lough Ennell, Co. Westmeath (photo: Richard Warner).*

Pl. 44—*Multivallate ringfort and crannog at Lisleitrim, Co. Armagh (photo: Environment and Heritage Service, DOE(NI)).*

archaeological site is a crannog directly opposite it in the lake. Interestingly, this crannog has produced a large amount of Viking Age silver, including weighing-scales, weights, a hoard containing Viking hack silver, bracelets and an enamelled bronze plaque from an Early Historic shrine (E.P. Kelly 1991a; 1994, 215).

While some 'royal crannogs' may indeed have been permanently occupied royal 'seats', some were lake-dwellings only occupied by the king at certain times of the year, and others may simply represent strategic refuges or bolt-holes. Island MacHugh crannog, previously occupied in the Neolithic and Bronze Age, was again the focus of lake settlement in the early seventh century (timbers were dated to AD 608–19; Ivens *et al.* 1986, 102). It was excavated by Oliver Davies (1950) and more recently by Richard Ivens, Derek Simpson and D. Brown (Ivens *et al.* 1986), but very few Early Historic artefacts were found on the site. Warner (1994) has suggested that this indicates that the crannog was only periodically occupied. He believes that it may be more useful to think in terms of royal complexes in the vicinity of lakes, with the crannog being only one of the royal settlements. The king may well have visited the crannog as part of his tour through the territory, to assemble an army or to attend the rituals and banquets associated with kingship on occasions when the nobles and wealthy farmers of the surrounding landscape gathered at the crannog. The association between crannogs, royal tours and military assemblies is indicated by the twelfth-century (but based on earlier texts) hagiography *Betha Colmáin Maic Lúacháin*, which states that the

> 'King of Meath is not entitled to demand a troop from Fartullagh to accompany him on his round, except a lad for his horses, when he is in Cro-Inis for the purpose of collecting the troop to accompany him' (Meyer 1911).

The large amounts of pig and cattle bone from crannog excavations at Lagore and Moynagh Lough may be evidence for communal feasting associated with royalty. However, while the king may only have been 'on-site' at certain times of the year, it is worth emphasising that the 'royal crannog' could still have been the permanent dwelling of the king's retainers, herdsmen and artisans. In other words, it was still a permanent residence. It is important, then, to see the king as only one aspect of a 'royal crannog'; the presence and activities of the members of other social classes on the site are an equally important factor in the occupation of the site. Indeed, it could be pointed out that studies of Early Historic social organisation tend to concentrate on the upper classes, ignoring the 'unfree or the merely ordinary' (Brady 1994a). This emphasises even more the importance of viewing crannogs within a wider landscape context. If 'royal crannogs' were temporary occupation or summer lodges, where did the king come from and go to during the rest of the year? There is clearly great potential for historical and archaeological research on the relationship between crannogs and political territories.

Defended settlements

Crannogs have clear defensive capabilities. They are difficult of access and easy to defend against attack, and the surrounding water provides an additional protection against wild animals and fire. Indeed, in the seventeenth century, the many difficulties in successfully attacking Gaelic Irish crannogs are described by English commentators (see below). Crannogs are often sited in areas of good natural defensibility, whether in open water or at the edge of wetlands. Stone causeways were constructed to provide access to the sites, but their narrowness and unpredictable turns and weaves were also meant to control such access. The enclosing revetments out in the water may have been to protect against attacks by boat, while the palisades were probably also seen as an additional defensive feature. Crannogs are often compared with ringforts, but they would have been rather more difficult to build than dryland sites (thus requiring a large labour force) and would have afforded better protection to their inhabitants. There is a range of historical evidence which suggests that many crannogs were defended sites with potential military associations. Certainly they were attacked by armies. The Annals of Ulster for the year AD 985 state that Máel Sechnaill 'ravaged Connacht, plundered its islands (*do thogail a n-innseadh*) and killed its chiefs'. It is obvious that such islands were raided by boat, probably light, coracle-like craft (Colin Breen, pers. comm.) which could be carried across land, as indicated by an annalistic reference in AD 961:

> 'an unusual thing was done by King Domhnall, son of Muircheartach, namely he brought vessels over Dabhall [Blackwater] and across Slaibh Fuaid, to Loch Ainninn [Loch Ennell] so that the islands of the lake were plundered by him' (AFM, 961).

Human bones, some bearing evidence of hacking or wounding, have been found at Lagore, Co. Meath (Hencken 1950, 198–203), Ballinderry crannog no. 1, Co. Westmeath (Hencken 1936), Ardakillen, Co. Roscommon (Wood-Martin 1886a, 237–8), and Killyvilla Lake, Co. Monaghan (D'Arcy 1897, 397). Lagore, the royal site of the kings of southern Brega of the Southern Uí Néill dynasty, is known from the historical sources to have been attacked on a number of occasions (Price 1950). The site produced an unusually large number of weapons, including swords, spearheads, axes and shield-bosses. A shield-boss was also found at Lough Faughan, Co. Down. There were also huge numbers of human bones at Lagore, many belonging to decapitated bodies. Two iron collars with chains and a possible leg-iron may have been used for holding prisoners or slaves (although, as previously noted, they might have been dog collars). A possible 'slave collar' was also found in a canoe at Ardakillen crannog, Co. Roscommon (Wood-Martin 1886a, 237). It has been suggested that the human bones from crannogs which show pre-mortem violence are evidence for the ritual killing of slaves or hostages and the deposition of partial human remains in a watery environment (Ó Floinn 1995, 144). The occurrence of human bone on crannogs certainly testifies to violence carried out there, whether during attack on the sites or as part of political action against hostages. It is likely that crannogs were occasionally used as strongholds or military settlements in the Early Historic period and the Viking Age.

High-status metalwork and imported items

Crannogs were probably occupied by a range of social classes—slaves, craftsmen, farmers and their families, and aristocracy. There is a tendency to emphasise the upper classes in settlement studies, mostly because they are more visible in the archaeological record. Certainly, the presence of the aristocracy on several midland crannogs is probably indicated by the quality of the metalwork found by treasure-hunters in recent years. Viking Age silver and coin hoards in Ireland are mainly distributed in the midlands and have frequently been found on crannogs and lakeshores (Kenny 1987). Anglo-Saxon, Viking and Kufic coin hoards and Viking Age hack silver and silver ingots are also known from several crannogs and islands. In particular, there is an unusually high concentration of Viking silver hoards along the shores of Lough Ennell, in proximity to several known crannogs, islands, ringforts and monastic sites. At Carrick on Lough Ennell, a huge hoard of Viking silver ingots was recovered from the foreshore, while a smaller hoard of silver ingots was found on Rocky Island (Ryan *et al.* 1984). A hoard of Hiberno-Norse and Anglo-Saxon coins was found by treasure-hunters on a crannog at Lough Lene, Co. Westmeath (E.P. Kelly 1994, 215). Weighing-scales, weights, a hoard containing Viking hack silver and bracelets and an enamelled bronze plaque from an Early Historic shrine were found on a crannog at Coolure Demesne, Lough Derravarragh, Co. Westmeath (*ibid.*, 215). The presence of Viking metalwork in Irish midland crannogs has generally been interpreted in terms of trading contacts between Hiberno-Norse Dublin and the political territories of the Southern Uí Néill. Kelly (1991a) has proposed an interesting model for this distribution. He notes that the finds from ninth- and tenth-century occupations on crannogs in the territory of Mídhe are similar to those from Hiberno-Norse Dublin (e.g. ringed pins, iron swords, decorated metalwork). He contrasts this with the pattern from north Louth (the buffer zone between the Uí Néill and Ulaid territories), where settlement sites have produced native souterrain ware but no Viking finds. Kelly (1991a, 87) suggests that the archaeological record confirms that the Southern Uí Néill were looking towards Dublin, perhaps controlling trade with its hinterland, while the Conaill Muirtheimne of north Louth looked north for their cultural orientation. It may be that some of this scrap silver was being used for the production of ecclesiastical metalwork for presentation to the church by its powerful secular patrons (E.P. Kelly 1991a; 1994; pers. comm.).

Crannogs often produce high-quality ecclesiastical and monastic metalwork associated with the early church's liturgical rituals. This metalwork may have been kept on crannogs for its protection during the turbulent years of the early Viking raids. It is also possible that such lake settlements acted as stores for ecclesiastical metalwork because, as the high-status residences of the local secular patrons of the church, they were considered an appropriate place to keep such items. Several fragments of a large eighth-century book-shrine were picked up on a crannog in Lough Kinale, Co. Longford, while an eighth-century silver chalice paten and Viking Age hack silver are also known from this lake (E.P. Kelly 1993a; 1994, 215; Farrell *et al.* 1989). An eighth-century processional cross was found by treasure-hunters beside a crannog at Tully Lough, Co. Roscommon (E.P. Kelly 1994, 218). Moylarg crannog, Co. Antrim, produced an intricately decorated bronze sieve, possibly a wine-strainer used in the mass, dated to the eighth to ninth century AD (E.P. Kelly 1991b). Two Viking Age ecclesiastical hand-bells were found in the water off School Boy Island, which is located near the early monastic site of Lynn, Co. Westmeath (Karkov and Ruffing 1990–1).

Pl. 45—*Imported E-ware pottery sherd from Lagore, Co. Meath (photo: National Museum of Ireland).*

Pl. 46—*Imported Merovingian glass vessels found at Moynagh Lough crannog, Co. Meath (photo: National Museum of Ireland).*

Early Historic and Viking Age Ireland was also involved in long-distance trade with Britain, Gaul, Aquitaine and beyond to the Mediterranean. Crannogs (like some ringforts) have produced a certain amount of imported, exotic material. Mediterranean (A and B-ware) and western French pottery (E-ware) has been found on several crannog excavations. E-ware has been recovered from Lagore (Pl. 45) and Moynagh Lough crannogs and from the monastic island of Inis Cealtra. These may have carried wines to the aristocratic dwellers on crannogs and to early church settlements for use in the liturgy (Edwards 1990, 68–73). Indeed, the wooden barrels represented by large hoops and staves found at Lough Faughan and Lagore may themselves be imports, wine vessels from Europe, a possibility which could be tested by dendro-provenancing of the timber. The sherds of Roman Samian wares found on several crannogs may have been imported into Ireland during the Early Historic period for symbolic or medicinal reasons. Imported Frankish glass vessels have been uncovered at Moynagh Lough, Co. Meath (Pl. 46), at Rathtinaun crannog, Co. Sligo, Corraneary crannog, Co. Cavan, Ballinderry crannog no. 2, Co. Offaly, and Lagore, Co. Meath (E. Bourke 1994). Some of the iron swords and a horsebit from Lagore may have been imported from northern Europe, while the Viking Age sword from Ballinderry crannog no. 1 is certainly an import. Alternatively these weapons could suggest the presence of Frankish mercenaries or Viking warriors on crannogs. It may have been that some crannogs served as centres for the production and redistribution of goods, making them significant non-urban markets in the wider settlement and economic landscape. Nobles and wealthy farmers on crannogs may have sought to transform their wealth into high-status objects of copper alloy, glass and bone. It is also possible that some of these crannogs were neutral meeting places for travelling merchants, where local kings attracted trade goods into a region. Obviously, the raw material for many of these crafts and industries would have had to be brought onto the site by boat, while foreign imported goods may also have been transported by boat up the navigable rivers. Artisans and craftworkers may have been resident on the crannog or monastic island, though perhaps they could have been living in unenclosed settlements on the neighbouring drylands. The protection and patronage of such craftworkers indicate the social status of the main crannog resident. The metalwork and glass would also have had to be dispersed out through the wider community by some means. It is likely that the distribution of goods through the social and settlement landscape was carried out from crannogs largely for reasons of gift-giving, reciprocity and clientship.

Crafts and industry

Crannogs were not only refuges or royal sites, but were also centres of craft production. While the waterlogged nature of many crannogs must have enhanced the preservation of finds, it is evident that the artefactual assemblages from some crannogs are unusually rich. Some crannogs, like some ringforts and monastic sites, appear to have been centres for bronze-working (Ryan 1988). Craftsmen may have been gathered together on crannogs or ringforts to control trade or because of royal patronage. Craftsmen themselves were often of high status (F. Kelly 1988), so it is possible that they owned crannogs as well. The evidence for bronze-working is abundant on crannogs, although it was also practised in ringforts and monastic settlements. Lagore has produced waste from the smelting of copper ores; crucibles used for purifying the copper and for adding tin to make bronze are common finds on crannogs (Edwards 1990, 90). Mould fragments, in which rings, pins and ornamented objects were cast, are also a familiar find from crannog sites, and motif-pieces show how designs were worked out. At Moynagh Lough, Co, Meath, it is possible to draw this evidence together, as there was extensive evidence for ornamental metalworking, with spatial organisation of two metalworking areas with their pits and furnaces across the site. There were also crucibles and moulds for brooches, mounts, studs and other decorated items. Indeed, it will be possible from this evidence to reconstruct the working patterns of metalsmiths at Moynagh Lough (J. Bradley 1991). Lagore, Ballinderry 2 and Lough Faughan crannogs also produced such crucibles and moulds. Moylarg crannog, Co. Antrim (Buick 1893; 1894), may also have been a bronze-working site; its excavation produced a finely made decorated bronze sieve of eighth- to ninth-century AD date (E.P. Kelly 1991b), a lead model of a decorated ring for a brooch, and a copper ingot with its own mould. Brooches, pins, buckles, studs, strap-ends and rings are very common on crannog habitations. Ringed pins are known from crannogs throughout Early Historic and Viking Age Ireland; a ninth-century example was found on the crannog at Lough Ravel, Derryhollagh, Co. Antrim (Bourke 1988). Glass and enamels may also have been used for the decoration of bronzes, as the necessary raw materials and heating trays are known from Lagore, Ballinderry crannog no. 1 and Moynagh Lough. The iron pans from crannogs may have been used for heating glass. Lagore may have been a glass-working site, producing moulds for glass studs, glass bracelets and armlets, glass rods, millefiori, enamel, amber, and a large collection of coloured and decorated glass beads.

Crannogs were also used for blacksmithing and iron production. It is not known whether these were permanent 'forges', as most of the evidence could have been left by periodic visits by smiths. Iron-working is not peculiar to crannogs, as evidence is also known from several ringforts and other settlements. Nevertheless, unprocessed iron ore, slag and iron bloom were found at Lough Faughan, iron slag was recovered from Ballinderry crannog no. 1, and iron furnace bottoms were found at Lagore. Indeed, a crannog at Bofeenaun, Co. Mayo, seems to have been used solely for iron production and could be considered as an entirely industrial, rather than domestic, site (Keane 1995). This crannog may have been situated to exploit local bog ores (possible quarries are also known in the vicinity) and it was probably never inhabited in the conventional sense. It may be that proximity to water was important in iron-working, or that iron-working was carried out on isolated sites for protection against fires or to control access to its products. The location of small stone mounds beside larger crannogs (e.g. at Lough Ennell and Lough Gara) may also be explained by this practice. Morrison (1985) has suggested that iron-working was carried out on such smaller mounds in Scottish lochs. At Barnagrow Lough, Co. Cavan, there are two such crannogs beside each other. The larger crannog was circular, defined by stakes, with a house site, hearthstone and quernstones. The smaller crannog site, 70m to the south-west, was also defined by posts (O'Donovan 1995).

There is also abundant evidence from crannogs for the production of wooden artefacts, such as lathe-turned bowls (some of which imitate imported E-ware pottery), carved tubs, stave-built buckets and occasionally decorated wood (e.g. Earwood 1993). Turned bowls are known from Ballinderry crannog no. 1, Ballinderry crannog no. 2, Lough Faughan and Moynagh Lough. Interestingly, a few crannogs, such as Lagore and Moynagh Lough, have also produced some evidence for lathe-turning waste (the wooden 'cores' left after the bowls are complete). These were also found on the Early Historic ringfort at Lissue, Co. Antrim (Bersu 1947), and at the early monastic site at Iona (Barber 1981). It may be that such wooden bowls were actually produced on-site, using easily assembled pole-lathes (Earwood 1991–2). Wooden bucket stave blanks found at Moynagh Lough suggested that some element of coopering was being carried out on the site (J. Bradley 1982). It is known that Early Historic carpenters were proficient at large-scale structural woodwork, such as horizontal mills, churches and wooden bridges (e.g. Boland and O'Sullivan 1997). The quality of the carpentry used on crannogs is not particularly high, although complex grooved, jointed and drilled timbers were found at Ballinderry crannog no. 1 and Lagore, possibly reused from other structures. There is good evidence for carpentry tools from crannogs, Lagore in particular producing a wide range of woodworking tools, such as felling and hewing axes, an adze, a wooden mallet, knives, gouges and awls. Lough Faughan produced an interesting range of woodworking tools and some well-made wooden artefacts, including a lathe-turned wheel hub from a cart or wheeled vehicle. Wooden dugout boats may also have been made in the vicinity of such lake settlements.

Other finds from crannogs include bone, bronze and iron pins, bronze brooches and souterrain ware (a coarse native pottery). Souterrain ware has been found on several crannogs in the north-east, such as Lough Faughan, Moylarg and Craigywarren, while coarse blackened potsherds have also been found at Lagore and Moynagh Lough. Moylarg, in particular, produced a wide range of plain and undecorated souterrain pottery. These coarsewares were probably used for cooking (Ryan 1973). However, it should be emphasised that there is no reason to consider these wares as specific to crannogs, since they are as often found on other settlement types. Bone-working and antler-working were also apparently common crafts on crannogs, the known low status of comb-makers perhaps suggesting the range of social classes present on these sites. Lagore produced a fine collection of bone combs, and the large bone assemblages in crannog middens were probably treated as a ready supply of raw material. Antler would have been gathered in the surrounding landscape, or indeed supplied to the crannog by the surrounding communities, and there is much evidence for antler waste. Textiles were obviously produced from wool and hair on crannogs, using distaffs, spindles or simple looms. A possible loom fragment was found at Lough Faughan crannog, while tablet weaving implements were found at Lagore. Indeed, Lagore produced a large assemblage of well-preserved textiles. Leather-working may have been practised on some sites, as shoes, scraps of leather and a wooden shoe-last were found at Lagore, while iron leather-scoring tools are known from Lagore and Ballinderry crannog no. 1. It is also possible that the large numbers of calf and cattle bones from crannogs are a result of the production of hides and skins for use in manuscripts.

Agriculture and economy

What was the role of crannogs in the agricultural landscape? The Early Historic Irish agricultural landscape was complex and intensively managed. Farmsteads, field systems and routeways were dispersed through a largely open, cleared countryside (Edwards 1990, 49–56; Mitchell and Ryan 1997), although discrete areas of managed woodland remained, as well as wastelands of bog, marsh and uncultivable uplands (F. Kelly 1997; MacNiocaill 1971). Palaeoenvironmental studies also indicate a large-scale clearance of woodlands in the fourth and fifth centuries AD, suggesting the exploitation of new land (Weir 1993; 1995). The early Irish law tracts and hagiographies are often used to reconstruct the social and economic organisation of farmland; they testify to the importance of milling, water-power, ploughing and brewing, and also indicate the range of dairy foods and meats eaten (MacNeill 1923; Ó Corráin 1972; F. Kelly 1997). Early Historic ringforts are typically seen as the defended homesteads of wealthy farmers who were at the heart of this economic landscape (Proudfoot 1961; MacNeill 1923; Patterson 1994). The role of monastic centres in the transformation of the land and the reclamation of woodlands and marshes is now also being explored. Stout (1997) suggests that ringfort-owners were primarily occupied with cattle-herding and dairying, while the monastic centres were more active in arable agriculture. Ryan (1997) recently pointed out that this model of complementarity between secular and monastic settlements oversimplifies the evidence. He notes that ringfort inhabitants probably also raised arable crops and used grain, while monasteries, as the centres of farmed estates, probably controlled cattle herds. Ironically, while crannogs are recognised as an important element in Early Historic and Viking Age settlement systems, there has been little attempt to explore their role in the exploitation and management of the wider agricultural landscape, to identify the farm unit of a crannog or even to investigate whether they had any social and economic function in the farmed landscape (Pl. 47). In contrast, recent landscape studies have shown that Scottish crannogs

Pl. 47—*Crannog at Kilcorran, Co. Monaghan. The siting of such lake settlements in relation to neighbouring cattle pastures needs to be explored (photo: Dúchas—The Heritage Service).*

are deliberately situated in the lake shallows adjacent to the best agricultural land (Morrison 1985). In general, the study of the subsistence economy of crannogs is dominated by Lagore, Ballinderry 1 and 2 and Moynagh Lough, although the use of these crannogs for occasional communal or 'royal' feasting may have skewed the evidence in favour of high-status foods and delicacies.

Cattle-herding and pastoral farming were clearly of great social and economic importance in the Early Historic and Viking Age landscape. They formed the basis for land classification, and the cattle herd was the measure of a farmer's status (Stout 1997; Lucas 1989; Patterson 1994). The large quantities of cattle bone and agricultural implements recovered from excavated crannogs certainly suggest that they played some role in the agricultural landscape. McCormick (1983) has examined the faunal assemblages from Lagore and Moynagh Lough and suggests that dairying was of prime importance. Indeed, the early Irish sources testify to the popularity of milk, butter, cheeses and other dairy products (Ó Corráin 1972, 55–6). Although it would have been impossible to house cattle within crannogs, these sites may still have been positioned at particular parts of lakes to control prime pasture on the neighbouring drylands. Cattle were grazed outside throughout the year, with pastures carefully maintained for the winter by fences and transhumance in the summer. Indeed, wetland meadows and marshes would have provided good grazing in the summer and autumn, and in the lowland around lakes the practice of booleying may have been carried out, not in far-off uplands but along river meadows and lakeshores. The lake would have supplied a ready source of drinking-water. The ringforts and enclosures that are frequently paired with crannogs may not have been settlements but byres and corrals for the protection of the cattle (from wolves and raiding rivals) of the crannog-dwellers (McCormick 1995, 34).

Sheep and pig were also an important aspect of stock-raising on crannogs; the large assemblages of cattle bone on crannogs may be misrepresentative owing to past sampling techniques and the fact that cattle produce more bone than smaller animals. At Moynagh Lough, although cattle predominated slightly, there were also large numbers of pig and sheep/goat. Pigs were kept for pork, bacon, puddings and sausages. Ballinderry crannog no. 2 produced a number of young pigs. Small wicker structures have commonly been found on crannogs, and these may have been occasional pigpens for young animals. Otherwise pig herds could have been allowed to roam in the woodlands around the lakes. Sheep were kept for their wool, meat, milk and skins, while goats may also sometimes have been kept on crannogs. Horses may occasionally have been eaten, but the presence of horsebits at Ballinderry 1 and Lagore and the large amount of weaponry at Lagore may suggest their use in hunting and warfare. The wheel hub from Lough Faughan may have been from a chariot drawn by horses, while a wooden artefact from Ballinderry 1 may have been used as a pack-saddle. Chickens may have been kept on some crannogs. Lagore and Lough Faughan produced bones of domestic fowl, though the presence of particularly large bird bones with well-developed spurs may indicate the practice of cock-fighting. Bones of wild animals (e.g. red deer) and wildfowl are occasionally found on crannogs, suggesting some measure of hunting, but by and large wild foods were not as important as domesticated animals and crops.

There are also indications that arable farming and tillage were an important element in the farming landscapes around Early Historic and Viking Age crannogs. Ploughing, the production of crops of wheat, oats, barley and rye, and the communal use of watermills are frequently mentioned in the early Irish law texts and hagiographies. Vegetables such as onions, leeks, celery, kale and peas were also grown (Edwards 1990, 62; F. Kelly 1997). However, there have not been sufficient palaeobotanical studies carried out on the waterlogged deposits of crannogs to assess the presence of cereal foods. In addition, there has been little attempt to locate field systems associated with crannogs, or to explore how crannogs spaced along lakeshores may have controlled their own strips of arable land. Plough irons, including both coulters and ploughshares, have been found at Rathtinaun, Co. Sligo (Pl. 48), Lagore and Ballinderry 1. Reaping

Pl. 48—*Early Historic ploughshares from Crannog 61, Rathtinaun, Co. Sligo (photo: David Jennings, Dept of Archaeology, UCD).*

hooks or sickles and billhooks have been found at Lagore. A wooden shovel is known from Moynagh Lough (J. Bradley 1982), while a possible iron spade-tip was found at Ballinderry 2 (Hencken 1942). A deposit of carbonised oats and barley was found at Lough Faughan, Co. Down (Collins 1955), suggesting that they were stored on the site and burnt by accidental fire. Wheat straw, possibly used for flooring, was found in a mass of organic debris at Lagore. Stone rotary querns, whole and fragmentary, are a common find on excavated crannogs, no doubt used for preparing flour for the crannog inhabitants. They have also been identified during archaeological survey on the surface of many other crannog sites (E.P. Kelly 1991a; Kieran O'Conor, pers. comm.).

It might also be assumed that crannog-dwellers made much use of the rich, bountiful harvests of the surrounding wetlands, such as berries, nuts and plant foods. Unfortunately, the detailed palaeobotanical studies of waterlogged occupation deposits necessary to prove or disprove the case are lacking. Red deer bone is fairly uncommon and they may have only been hunted for sport. Bird bones are rather more plentiful on excavated crannogs, suggesting wildfowling on lakes and their margins. Lagore crannog in particular produced a large amount of bird bone, including wild goose, wild duck, raven, swan, great-crested grebe, coot, moorhen and corncrake. Wild geese and wild duck were the most common, indicating that the crannog-dwellers were expert fowlers. There is little empirical evidence for fishing from crannogs; only a few fish remains were found at Lagore, although iron eel-spears are occasionally found on crannogs. However, the hagiographies and law texts leave little doubt as to the importance of coastal and riverine fisheries, which were owned and protected by law by the eighth century (F. Kelly 1997; O'Sullivan 1994b; 1993–4).

Marshland settlements

It has already been shown that natural islands were used as settlements, often through the construction of large stone cashels (Pl. 49). There are also a number of other marshland or lakeshore settlements which cannot be strictly defined as crannogs. These were similar in form to crannogs but with few artificial foundations or palisades, and they served as unenclosed, although isolated, settlements. Bofeenaun was built on

Pl. 49—*O'Boyle's Fort, Lough Doon, Co. Donegal (CUCAP ALQ-81; reproduced with the permission of the Cambridge Committee for Aerial Photography).*

a natural peat knoll, although this was enclosed with a wooden revetment. There were no houses on the site and it is unlikely that it was ever inhabited in the conventional sense. At Crannog no. II, Cuilmore Lough, Co. Mayo, a natural promontory of ground was apparently defended by a double palisade at the landward side (Rynne and MacEoin 1978). This is reminiscent of the later stages of Crannog 61, Lough Gara, which was defended by a double post row at its landward side (J. Raftery, forthcoming b). At Tivannagh, Co. Roscommon (Crannog 124), a ninth- to tenth-century marshland settlement at the mouth of the River Boyle was excavated by Joseph Raftery and produced several phases of early prehistoric and historic occupation (J. Raftery 1957). It was situated on a narrow spit of land on the lakeshore which appeared to have no continuous palisade or formal defences. A layer of brushwood was laid down and a large rectangular house, 10m by 8m, and an oval-shaped house, 5m by 2m, were built. The oval house or shed walls had fallen over, and the upper structure and wattle were preserved. There were also a number of smaller circular structures, perhaps houses or possibly wattle-lined pits. There were indications of repair and reconstruction, with a second rectangular house built over the earliest one. The landward side of the settlement was defended by a strong palisade of oak posts.

The artefactual evidence included bone pins, combs, glass beads, bronze ornaments, wooden pins, a carved wooden trough and numerous finely turned wooden bowls. A large amount of woodworking debris was scattered about the site. A rotary quern, an iron billhook, and cattle, pig, sheep, horse and deer bone were also retrieved.

A range of bronze objects were found, as well as a clay mould for a rectangular-headed pin, numerous clay crucibles and blue glass beads. Evidently metalworking was being practised on the site. The artefacts suggest a ninth- or tenth-century AD date (Barry Raftery, pers. comm.).

Tivannagh 'crannog' is interesting for a number of reasons. It appears to be a ninth- or tenth-century unenclosed lakeshore settlement with a rectangular house. It has been proposed that this form of open, unfortified settlement was the dominant settlement form after AD 1000, possibly relating to the replacement of the *túath* social structure by the feudal system of administration (Stout 1997). It is also significant that a rectangular house was used, tallying with Chris Lynn's theories on house evolution after *c.* AD 800 (Lynn 1994).

Lake promontory forts

Promontory forts have been recorded on the large lakes of north Mayo, on Lough Feeagh, at Errew Point and Rinagall Point (on Lough Conn) and Doon Point and Castlecarra (on Lough Carra) (Gibbons and Condit 1991). They have also been noted in the Sligo lakes and possibly at Rindoon, Co. Roscommon, on Lough Ree (Condit *et al.* 1991; K. O'Conor, pers. comm.). They have been found in the Cavan lakes, on Dungummin Lough, Milltown Lough and Mullagh Lough (O'Donovan 1995, 37). Lake promontory forts are typically sited on narrow headlands, with multivallate stone-built ramparts with rock-cut ditches cutting off large enclosed areas (up to 400m by 100m). Promontory forts, on account of their size and impressive defences, have typically been seen as tribal centres rather than domestic residences (Gibbons and Condit 1991, 39). Coastal promontory forts have been variously ascribed to the Late Bronze Age (e.g. Barry 1981), the Iron Age (B. Raftery 1994) and the Early Historic period (Mitchell and Ryan 1997, 247). The emerging Late Bronze Age date of Irish hillforts may suggest that the lake promontory forts also have early origins, while late Iron Age occupation has been suggested for coastal promontory forts (B. Raftery 1994). The reuse of lake promontory forts in the Anglo-Norman period can also clearly be seen at Rindoon, Co. Roscommon, where a town was established in the early thirteenth century.

In contrast to coastal and inland sites, the lake promontory forts are all situated on low-lying headlands or peninsulas projecting out into the lakes. This makes them less easy to defend than the typically isolated coastal types. However, there was also an advantage to their defenders, who could easily have made their escape by boat across lake waters, an option not available on the high rocky cliffs and headlands of the Atlantic coast. The construction of a promontory fort on a lake peninsula therefore seems to indicate a concern for both landward defence and controlled access to the lakeshore. A lake promontory fort's rampart and ditch must be continued onto the lake foreshore and out towards the deep water to prevent attackers from simply going around the defences. At Rinagall Point, Lough Conn, the rampart can be seen as a collapsed rubble mound on the lakeshore (Gibbons and Condit 1991, 40). Undoubtedly, underwater survey in the waters off these ramparts could produce interesting archaeological evidence, such as wooden palisades or stone-built walls. The survival of slipways, boat-harbours and boats also remains a possibility. In fact, lake settlement research could easily make a major contribution to our understanding of the chronology and cultural background of Irish promontory forts, whether coastal, inland or lakeshore. It would also prove interesting to investigate the potential social and political relationships between such promontory forts and other settlements in these lakelands.

Monastic and pilgrimage sites on lake islands

Early Historic and Viking Age lake settlement studies need to integrate both the secular and the ecclesiastical organisation of the surrounding landscape. The settlements of the early church in Ireland are important in the secular context because of the complex familial and political relationships between ecclesiastical authorities and local kings. The earliest Irish monasteries were often placed in peripheral or marginal areas, as indicated by the use of the word *dísert* (wasteland) in their placenames, and may have been responsible for the opening up of new agricultural land and the clearance of woodland (Ó Corráin 1972, 49). While most island monasteries are maritime and situated off the west coast, there are also important monastic and pilgrimage sites on inland lakeshores and islands (Manning 1995). Lake promontory forts also have early monastic remains, such as at Errew Point, Co. Mayo, on Lough Conn (Gibbons and Condit 1991, 40). Early Historic crannogs are often situated near apparently contemporary church sites and ecclesiastical metalwork has occasionally been found on crannogs, such as the eighth-century book-shrine from a crannog on Lough Kinale, Co. Longford, and the ecclesiastical handbells from School Boy Island on Lough Ennell, Co. Westmeath. Metalwork may have been stored on such islands after the instability of the early Viking raids (E.P. Kelly 1993b, 174).

Lough Ree, on the upper River Shannon, has a number of monastic and pilgrimage sites on the small islands along the eastern shore (Harbison 1991). The most important is the monastic site of Inchclearaun or *Inis Clothrann*, Co. Longford, situated at the northern end of the lake. A large fort at the highest part of the island is associated with the pagan mythology of Medb of Connacht and the sixth-century Christian saint Diarmaid. The island also had a number of Early Historic cross-inscribed slabs. There are several surviving stone churches on the island, from the probably Early Historic *Teampull Dhiarmaida* to the medieval Augustinian *Teampull Mór,* with its sacristy, chapter house and cloister garth. A fourteenth-century poem states that the island had 'seven churches and a steeple', a common feature of pilgrimage sites, and it was locally known in the nineteenth century as *oileán na seacht dtempull* ('island of the seven churches'). The twelfth-century *Féilire Óengusa* refers to Inis Clothrann as a port (Edel Bhreathnach, pers. comm.). Several other islands on Lough Ree have ecclesiastical remains. Inisbofin, historically associated with the sixth-century St Rioch, has several Early Historic grave-slabs, and was raided by the Vikings in the ninth century. Two Viking Age objects (a ring-pin and a fragment of cast bronze) were recovered from the island during renovations by the Board of Works in 1911 (de Paor 1962). More recently, a ninth-century decorated bronze book-cover was found on the island (E.P. Kelly 1994, 218). Inisbofin also has Romanesque and late medieval church buildings. The island monasteries and church sites of Lough Ree were clearly of some regional importance. The Annals of the Four Masters state that in 1089 a fleet under the leadership of Muircheartach Ua Briain arrived upon Lough Ree. They plundered the churches of the lake, namely *Inis Clothrann, Inis Bó Finne, Inis Ainginn* (Hare Island) and *Cluain Eamhain* (Cloonoun).

Lough Derg, on the lower River Shannon, has a number of important Early Historic and Viking Age ecclesiastical sites on the lakeshore and on its islands. An eighth- or ninth-century *Céli Dé* monastery was situated at Terryglass, Co. Tipperary, at the northeast corner of the lake. The best-known monastic island is *Inis Cealtra*, situated at the mouth of a bay on the western side of Lough Derg. The island is associated with Mac Creiche, possibly a pagan deity (Harbison 1991). The monastery may have been founded by St Colum of Terryglass in the sixth-century, or by St Caimin, with whom the largest church on the island is associated. A large slab-shrine, known as 'the confessional', near the church was the focus of pilgrimage. Liam de Paor's excavations on the island indicated that a wooden structure, a mud-walled oratory and several houses may have preceded it. The island has at least five churches, a round tower, a number of high crosses and cross-decorated slabs. A series of earthwork enclosures on the island appear to have been built after the decline of the monastery after 1200. It has been suggested that they can be associated with later medieval pilgrimage activities on the island.

Lough Erne, Co. Fermanagh, also had a number of important ecclesiastical lake settlements, including Devenish (Ralegh Radford 1970), White Island (Wakeman 1879), and Boa Island. Devenish is the best known of the Lough Erne monasteries, and was probably founded by St Laisre or Molaisse in the mid-sixth century. An eighth-century wooden and bronze shrine found in Lough Erne between Belleek and Enniskillen may be associated with it. The island has a large circular earthen enclosure which is probably the remains of the monastic vallum. Otherwise there is little trace of the earliest foundation, but it may have been a *Céli Dé* monastery in the ninth century. Devenish was raided several times by the Vikings. In 836, all the churches of Loch Erne, together with *Cluain Eois* (Clones, Co. Monaghan) and *Daimhinis,* were destroyed by the Vikings (Annals of Ulster). In 923, 'naval force of the foreigners went on Loch Éirne and they ravaged the islands of the lake and the surrounding peoples' (Annals of Ulster). Devenish has several twelfth-century ecclesiastical structures, including a round tower and a stone oratory (St Molaisse's House). The twelfth-century monastic community may have been responsible for the production of the *Soisceal Molaisse,* an ornate bookshrine now in the National Museum of Ireland. The island probably had an Augustinian abbey and associated churches in the fifteenth century. In addition to large-scale monastic sites, there must also have been smaller church sites and hermitages on other islands and along lakeshores. It has already been pointed out that the monastic sites of Dysart and Lynn are found on the shores of Lough Ennell, which has abundant evidence for secular settlement (ringforts, crannogs, island cashels). On Lough Owel there is even better evidence for monastic settlement on the lakeshore and islands. At Portloman, Co. Westmeath, on the north-western shore, there is historical evidence for a monastery dating to the seventh century. There may also have been an ecclesiastical settlement on Church Island and on the eastern shore at Portnashangan (Swan 1988; Karkov and Ruffing 1997, 344).

These lake monasteries should be regarded as having an important function in Early Historic and Viking Age settlement organisation, being centres of farmed estates, ecclesiastical authority and secular pilgrimage. They managed their own agricultural lands, presumably with tenant farmers and settlements scattered in the landscape around the lakes. They also served as important centres for communications, as hostels for travellers up and down the rivers and lakes, and as proto-urban markets or redistribution centres for local and regional products. They may have been closely enmeshed in the secular political territories of surrounding communities.

Irish and Viking naval warfare on lakes

There are a range of ninth- and tenth-century historical references to the activities of Irish and Viking boats and ships on Lough Ree, Lough Erne and Lough Neagh. In 838 a Viking fleet was based on Lough Neagh (*Loch Eacthach*), whence various locations in the north were attacked. By 845 the Vikings were sailing up the River Shannon, establishing a *dúnadh* on Lough Ree and raiding various sites in the midlands (E.P. Kelly 1991a). The Irish may have adopted Viking naval tactics. In 905 two Irish fleets battled on Lough Derg. The Annals of the Four Masters state that in AD 902

> 'an army was led by Cormac and Flaithbheartach against the Uí Néill of the south, and against the Connaughtmen; and they carried away the hostages of Connaught in their great fleets on the Shannon and the islands of Lough Ree were plundered by them'.

A Viking fleet from Limerick was active on Lough Ree during the 920s and 930s. There is a range of potential archaeological evidence for their presence, possibly at the south-east end of the lake. A large tenth-century Viking silver ingot and arm-ring hoard was found in 1820 on Hare Island at the south-east end of Lough Ree. A Viking gold hoard, of late ninth- to early tenth-century date, was also found on the island (Graham-Campbell 1974), while a Viking silver ingot was found recently at Coosaun Point, Co. Westmeath, within sight of Hare Island (Sheehan 1989–90). It has been suggested that these metalwork finds can be related to the events of 937, when control of the lake was wrested from the Vikings (Smyth 1979, 252). It is probable that a Viking longphort or settlement was established somewhere around Lough Ree. Fanning (1983) believed that a substantial earthen enclosure at Ballaghkeeran Little, on the edge of the lake to the south-east of Hare Island, was a Viking settlement. He carried out a short series of excavations on the site and found that the enclosure was defined by a substantial earthen bank on its landward side. A number of hollows on the lakeshore adjacent to the mouth of the Breensford River may have been for sheltering plank-boats; their excavation produced iron slag and fired clay, but there was little clear evidence for a Viking occupation (Fanning 1983). Lough Erne was also a location for Viking Age naval fleets and battles. In 922 (AFM) there was 'a fleet of foreigners upon Loch Eirne [Lough Erne] so that they plundered the islands and islets of the lake, and the districts on every side of it; and they remained on the lake till the ensuing summer'. In 931, 'the foreigners took up their station upon the lakes of Erne; and they spoiled and plundered many districts and churches, as far as Loch Gamhna'. In 927 (AFM), 'the foreigners of Luimneach went upon Loch Oirbsen [Lough Corrib, Co. Galway], and the islands of the lake were plundered by them'. In 928 the same group met with defeat, when 'a slaughter was made of the foreigners who were on Loch Oirbsen by the Connaughtmen'.

There is also evidence for Irish naval warfare on Lough Ree. The Annals of the Four Masters state that in 960 'Inis-Mor [Inch-More, an island situated between Hare Island and Inisbofin] in Loch Ribh was taken by Murchadh Ua Ceal-laigh from Ceallach . . . and he was carried as a prisoner with his fleet into Ui-Maine'. The Annals of Inisfallen state that in 988 Brian Boraimhe put a large fleet on Lough Ree: 'a fleet, viz 300 boats was put on Loch Ree by Brian and they harried Mide and went to Uisneach'. Other fleets were put on Loch Ree by Brian in 992 and 993. There is historical evidence that Irish fleets raided the lake's monastic islands. In 1016 there was 'a great hosting by Brian's son to Loch Ree and he plundered Inis Clothrann and Inis Bo Finne'.

Is there any archaeological evidence for this phase of nautical activity on the inland waterways? It is possible that temporary encampments, harbours, boat-yards, and even longphorts were constructed on islands and lakeshores. Underwater archaeological survey and remote sensing may yet uncover such evidence. There is also some faint evidence that midland crannogs were actually used as temporary Viking bases. Ballinderry crannog no. 1, Co. Westmeath, produced an unusual amount of Viking weaponry, such as an imported Viking iron sword, a decorated Viking iron axe, a wooden bow (more typical of Viking warfare), a decorated iron billhook, and several decorated wooden objects such as a gaming-board, a bowl and a trial-piece. A wooden knee, possibly from a dugout boat, was also found in the excavations. However, the presence of these objects does not mean that Ballinderry 1 was a Viking settlement. Such objects could easily have been captured by the Irish during a battle in the vicinity, or they could have arrived on the crannog as part of ongoing trade between the kings of the Southern Uí Néill and Hiberno-Norse Dublin.

Medieval lake settlement

Introduction

Gaelic Irish society had already undergone crucial changes before the Anglo-Norman invasion in 1169. The eleventh- and twelfth-century Irish settlement landscape was controlled by lordships similar to those of contemporary Europe, and the new religious orders, the Cistercians and Augustinians, were already in place (Graham 1993, 23; Mallory and McNeill 1991). However, it is certainly true that in the late twelfth and thirteenth centuries the Anglo-Norman invasion and colonisation had a major impact on the Irish landscape. Nucleated settlements were established and a manorial economy introduced which led to increased woodland clearance, more emphasis on arable agriculture and a burgeoning economy in the intensely settled lands of the east. The Anglo-Norman economy also meant that towns, markets and fairs were of increased importance. After the initial invasion there came a wave of new settlers, from peasants and craftspeople to soldiers, merchants and clerics (Barry 1987; O'Conor 1998). The Gaelic Irish continued to live on the conquered lands of the east, some working as 'betaghs' on the Anglo-Norman manors and farms. In their own lands further to the west, it is likely that there were strong elements of settlement continuity, although profound social and cultural changes were probably set in train there too.

In the Late Middle Ages, in the late fourteenth and fifteenth centuries, the Gaelic Irish experienced a revival in military power, giving rise to what is commonly known as the 'Gaelic Resurgence', with increased raids on the richer English settlements and a state of endemic warfare across the country. The 'Resurgence' was due to a cultural and military renewal amongst the Gaelic Irish, the continued Gaelicisation of the Anglo-Norman lords (the *Gaill*) (Frame 1981, 111–35), and a discernible economic decline in both the Gaelic Irish economic landscape and in the English settlements of the Pale and elsewhere (Lydon 1987, 241–3). In addition to a European climatic deterioration, there were the debilitating effects of the great European famine of 1315–17, the Bruce Invasion, and the Black Death of 1348–9. Historians have also recognised social transformations, with the dissolution of feudal social and property relationships in the late fourteenth and fifteenth centuries (Barry 1993). By 1500, Ireland was comprised of a number of virtually independent Gaelic Irish and Anglo-Norman lordships (Richter 1988, 191–2). By the end of the Middle Ages the Gaelic Irish were living within and at the edges of the English colony and its lordship, and there was a complex social and economic relationship between the ascendant Gaelic Irish, the Anglo-Irish and the settlements of the Pale (Barry 1992).

Prior to the coming of the Anglo-Normans, the Irish landscape was largely structured around a dispersed settlement pattern. Although the countryside was certainly intensively managed, with farmsteads, field systems and routeways, most people lived in ringforts and cashels, crannogs, royal sites, monastic or church enclosures, and other types of dispersed settlement. The only towns were situated at ports, such as the Hiberno-Norse towns of Dublin, Waterford, Limerick and Cork, while some monastic sites such as Clonmacnoise, Co. Offaly, or Glendalough, Co. Wicklow, may also have served as towns (Edwards 1990). In the twelfth and thirteenth centuries, the Anglo-Normans introduced a system of nucleated settlement into the country, establishing towns, rural boroughs and manorial villages in the lands they had conquered in the south-east and east of the island. Anglo-Norman manors and granges, both secular and ecclesiastical, were important elements in the settlement landscape. They engaged primarily in arable production and a market economy (Barry 1987; Graham 1985; 1993). English peasant farmers were brought in to populate the manorial farms, which were centred around a manor house and a church (Glasscock 1993, 214; Mitchell and Ryan 1997). The new Anglo-Norman farms at the periphery of the colony may have been mostly worked by Irish tenants, who lived away from the manor house and church, and therefore nucleated settlements may have been scarcer there (McNeill 1980, 84–8; O'Conor 1998). Thus dispersed settlements may have been the norm at the edges of the Anglo-Norman territory, with farmsteads scattered through the landscape around moated sites (dispersed defended farmsteads), as well as fortified settlements such as mottes and ringwork castles (Barry 1987; Glasscock 1993, 217). Although the new monastic orders had been introduced before the Anglo-Norman invasion, many new Cistercian, Benedictine and Augustinian abbeys and monasteries were founded in the twelfth and thirteenth centuries. These monastic houses served as the centres of farmed estates, and large stone abbeys and cathedrals were built throughout the country (Glasscock 1993, 220–1).

The nature of Gaelic Irish settlement in the medieval and late medieval periods is still not fully understood, but ringforts and crannogs certainly seem to have continued in use as occupation sites for the upper classes (e.g. Proudfoot 1970, 40–5; Barrett and Graham 1975; Glasscock 1993, 225–7; O'Conor 1993, 257–8; 1998), and tower-houses served as residences for the upper classes of Gaelic Irish society from the fifteenth century onwards (Barry 1987, 186; Cairns 1987, 8–9; McNeill 1997, 228–9). The Cisterican and Augustinian monasteries, abbeys and churches in the west and north-west remained the focus for significant ecclesiastical and secular settlement (Barry 1987). In the late Middle Ages, the patronage of Gaelic and Gaelicised lords was also attracting Franciscan and Dominican orders into the country (Nicholls 1993, 402, 437–8). However, the settlements of ordinary people in Gaelic Irish society remain to be discovered. They may have lived in timber and earthen houses or 'creats' gathered together in small nucleated settlements or 'clachans', but definite archaeological evidence for these has resolutely failed to appear (Glasscock 1993; Nicholls 1993). The Gaelic Irish economy probably remained largely dependent on pastoral farming, although oats, barley and wheat were also cultivated (Nicholls 1993, 398, 411). Indeed, by the late medieval period the Gaelic Irish of west Ulster were apparently moving continuously through the countryside with their cattle herds and cruchs, in a nomadic settlement system (K. Simms 1986; A. Simms 1983). In any case, simple transhumance with the herding of cattle to uplands and other grasslands continued in Gaelic Irish areas (Nicholls 1993, 413). Presumably riverine water-meadows and lakeshore grasslands were seen as valuable, self-renewing resources by local farmers.

Medieval and late medieval lake settlements

There is a range of archaeological and historical evidence for lake settlement in the medieval period (*c.* 1100–1350) and the late medieval period (*c.* 1350–1534). Historical references clearly indicate that crannogs and islands were used both as permanent settlements and as temporary fortifications by the Gaelic Irish in the thirteenth, fourteenth and fifteenth centuries. This was largely due to the military tactics of the Gaelic Irish, who did not use masonry castles, employing instead the natural defensive features of lakes, islands, woodlands and bogs. Although the contemporary historical documents do refer to certain Gaelic Irish fortifications, it seems that these were crannogs, longphorts, ringforts or other earthen fortifications rather than masonry castles (O'Conor 1993; 1998). In the medieval period, Anglo-Norman ringworks, moated sites and mottes are known from throughout the midland lakes region and occasionally in the north-west. Late medieval Gaelic Irish and Anglo-Norman castles and tower-houses are also commonly found on crannogs, lake islands and lakeshores. Medieval and late medieval monasteries and abbeys are found on lakeshores and islands, often continuing in use from earlier monastic foundations. They include the Augustinian abbeys at Tristernagh, on Lough Iron, Co. Westmeath, and at Inchcleraun on Lough Ree, the Premonstratensian foundation on Lough Oughter, Co. Cavan, and the Fratres Cruciferi church at Rindoon, on Lough Ree, Co. Roscommon (Barry 1987). These abbeys were well sited for trade and traffic on the lake waters. A few medieval boroughs and towns are also known from lakelands, such as Rindoon, Co. Roscommon, on the western shore of Lough Ree, Cong on Lough Corrib and Antrim on Lough Neagh (Barry 1987, fig. 28).

Medieval crannogs

Crannogs as medieval Gaelic Irish settlements

There is good archaeological and historical evidence that crannogs were occupied, reconstructed and strengthened in the medieval and late medieval periods (e.g. Barry 1987, 18–20; E.P. Kelly 1991b; O'Conor 1998; Wood-Martin 1886a, 146–56, 236–8). In fact, the Gaelic term *crannóg* does not come into use in the Irish annals until after the twelfth century. Prior to this, a lake settlement was typically referred to as an *inis* or *oilean*. Crannog excavations have often produced medieval and late medieval pottery, metalwork, weaponry and other artefacts. However, the interest in the Early Historic origins of crannogs and the earliest settlement of these sites has tended to greatly reduce the attention paid to this later material. A brief review of some medieval archaeological evidence from crannogs will be presented here. Island MacHugh, Co. Tyrone (Davies 1950; Ivens *et al.* 1986), Ballinderry crannog no. 1 (Hencken 1936, 160) and

Lagore (Hencken 1950, 7) have all produced medieval Irish and imported pottery, coins and metal artefacts. Newtownlow crannog, Co. Westmeath, produced a sherd of green-glazed pottery from the uppermost stony layer, dating it to the late twelfth or thirteenth century (Bourke 1986; 1987). It also produced a thirteenth-century ring-brooch (Deevy 1998). It seems likely that this was a Viking Age crannog, occupied into the medieval period. At Lough Atrain, Co. Cavan, it appears that a crannog was occupied in the medieval period, as suggested by the thirteenth-century silver coin recovered from the site (Davies 1946a, 32–4). The crannog of Lough Faughan, Co. Down, was excavated in 1951–2 after the discovery of a medieval glazed jug on the site (Wood-Martin 1886a, 92; Wilde 1857, 158) which seemed to indicate a thirteenth-century occupation phase contemporary with castles in the region. The modern excavations indicated that the site was mostly Early Historic in date, but medieval imported pottery and an early thirteenth-century coin were also produced (Collins 1955). Clea Lakes crannog, Co. Down, was partly excavated in the nineteenth century, producing bronze pins, a stone disc and both Early Historic souterrain ware and medieval coarseware (Collins and Proudfoot 1959).

Fig. 34—*(1) Late medieval everted-rim ware from crannogs in County Fermanagh (after Wood-Martin 1886a).*

Medieval everted-rim ware and crannog ware have been found on several crannogs in the north, and are probably the best archaeological evidence for occupation on these sites between the thirteenth and sixteenth centuries (McNeill 1980, 107–13; Ivens 1988; Ó Floinn 1988; forthcoming). This crude, hand-made cooking pottery is distinctive for its dark, unglazed appearance and heavy, gritty inclusions and texture. It frequently has geometric designs on the rim and supports rounded handles (Fig. 34). In terms of origins and date, it was probably being made from the early thirteenth century onwards, and either derives from the native souterrain ware tradition (McNeill 1980, 109) or was inspired by Anglo-Norman styles of pottery (Ó Floinn, forthcoming). It was probably the most commonly used cooking ware in Ulster in the thirteenth and fourteenth centuries (McNeill 1980, fig. 21), but its use on many Gaelic Irish crannogs in west Ulster may be later in date, probably from the fifteenth or sixteenth century.

William Wakeman found large fragments of everted-rim ware or crannog ware during his crannog surveys in County Fermanagh, on the Ballydoolough, Drumgay, Lough Eyes and Drumdarragh crannogs (Wakeman 1870–1a; 1870–1b; 1870–1d, 561; Wood-Martin 1886a, 92–9). More recent archaeological surveys in County Fermanagh also produced everted-rim ware or crannog ware on exposed crannog surfaces (Claire Foley, pers. comm.). Significantly, the Fermanagh crannog survey has also produced a range of late medieval radiocarbon and dendrochronological dates from wooden structures and palisades on these islands. Corban Lough crannog was dated to 1476 and Killyfoal crannog in Mill Lough to *c.* 1530 ± 9. A crannog in Lough Eyes was dated to 1510 ± 9, and one in Carrick Lough to 1536 (Baillie 1979). D'Arcy's excavations of crannogs at Killyvilla, Co. Cavan (1897, 397), and Drumacrittin, Co. Monaghan (1900, 222), also produced everted-rim ware or crannog ware. Davies's (1950) excavations at Island MacHugh, Co. Tyrone, and in various crannogs in Cavan (Davies 1942) also uncovered sherds of this pottery. Clearly this is good evidence for late medieval settlements on crannogs and islands. There are also other medieval finds from crannogs and lakeshores. Medieval ring-brooches were found on crannogs in Lake Ervey, Co. Meath, Lake McHugh, Co. Leitrim, and Lough na hIncha, Co. Roscommon (Deevy 1998). A medieval ring-brooch is known from Lough Sewdy, where a possible crannog (Sallow Island) is overlooked by a large Anglo-Norman motte at Ballymore on the hill to the south. Another ring-brooch was found somewhere on Lough Ree, Co. Westmeath. These brooches probably date to between the thirteenth and fifteenth centuries (Deevy 1998).

Crannogs as medieval lordly residences

There are a range of historical references to Gaelic Irish occupation on crannogs and islands, but tracing the location and character of these sites would require more detailed historical and placename research than can be presented in this study. It is apparent that crannogs continued to serve as Gaelic Irish lordly residences in the thirteenth, fourteenth and fifteenth centuries. In 1187, MacDermot, lord of Moylurg, died 'in his own mansion' (*ina tigh fein*) on Claenlough (Annals of the Four Masters). This royal residence may have been a crannog. A poem lamenting the death of Brian O'Neill, king of Tír Eóghain, in 1260 calls him 'Brian of Lough Laoghaire' (*Briain Locha Laoghaire*) (O'Conor 1993). This association of kingship could be either with the lake itself (possibly the modern Lough Catherine), a settlement on its margins or an actual crannog on the lake (Warner 1994). Lough Laoghaire crannog, Co. Tyrone, is mentioned in several historical references. It was burnt in an internal O'Neill dispute in 1456 (Annals of Ulster), one of the O'Neill kings died there in 1325 (Wood-Martin 1886a, 155–6, 179), and it was burnt again by Hugh Roe O'Donnell during raids in 1500 (Annals of the Four Masters). Oliver Davies (1950, 57) identified the site as being Island MacHugh, the crannog excavated by him in the 1940s on Lough Catherine, Co. Tyrone. The crannog certainly produced a considerable amount of evidence for thirteenth- and fourteenth-century occupation (Davies 1950, 45–56, 92; Ivens *et al.* 1986). Island MacHugh continued to be inhabited throughout the fifteenth and sixteenth centuries (Davies 1950, 56–85). A tower-house was probably built on the crannog in the early sixteenth century (Ivens *et al.* 1986, 99). The Annals of Ulster record that in 1388 Donnell O'Conor burned both the fortress of Ard-an-Choillin and the adjacent 'island' of Lough Cairrgin (Ardakillen Lough, Co. Roscommon). This seems to indicate a continuing 'royal' link between dryland ringforts and lake crannogs, a pattern recognised on several Early Historic crannogs (Warner 1994; see above). The islands of Lough Cairrgin are mentioned several times in the medieval annals (O'Conor 1998).

Fig. 34—*(2) Late medieval everted-rim ware from crannogs in County Fermanagh (after Wood-Martin 1886a).*

Crannogs as medieval fortified settlements

Crannogs were obviously used by the Gaelic Irish, and perhaps occasionally even by the Anglo-Normans, as defended or military settlements in the thirteenth, fourteenth and fifteenth centuries. They offered a degree of inaccessibility and a measure of natural defensiveness by means of their isolation on the water, and continued to be used in the midlands, west and north-west even after the introduction of native tower-houses in the fifteenth and sixteenth centuries (O'Conor 1993, 238–42). In the Annals of Loch Cé, *sub anno* 1220, there is a reference to an attack by Walter de Lacy, lord of Meath, on a crannog on Lough Oughter belonging to the O'Reillys. In 1247, 'Milid Mac Gosdelb . . . took the crannog of Claenloch and left a garrison of his own men on it' (Annals of Connacht). The crannog, which was probably somewhere in south Leitrim, was quickly retaken by its owner Mag Ragnaill, with the help of Cathal and Toirrdelbach O Conchobair (Annals of Connacht; Annals of the Four Masters; Annals of Loch Cé). A crannog in Lough Leisi (Kilglass Lough, Co. Roscommon) is mentioned as being the site from which Toirrdelbach mac Aeda Ua Conchobair escaped in 1246. The same site is mentioned again in 1452, when 'Lochainn Oc O hAinlige . . . was treacherously killed in the crannog of Loch Leise' (Annals of Connacht; Annals of Loch Cé) (Fig. 35). Clearly, crannogs were being used as residences into the late fifteenth century. The Annals of Connacht describe 'a great wind . . . which demolished many stone and wooden buildings and crannogs and ricks all over Ireland' in 1477. In the following year, 1478, there was another mighty wind, which caused a night of destruction 'owing to the number of men, cattle, trees, lake and land buildings which it laid low' (Annals of Connacht). The 'lake buildings' (*crainnuib*) were certainly crannogs. The crannog of Loch Bethad (Lough Veagh, Co. Donegal), the residence of Niall Garb O'Domnaill, was burned by Eogan O'Domnaill in 1524 (Annals of Connacht). It was the residence of Caffar O'Donnell in 1559 (Annals of the Four Masters).

It is possible that some crannogs were constructed by Anglo-Normans. The Annals of Loch Cé state that the crannog of Inis Laodhachain, built in 1223 by William Gorm de Lacy, was attacked shortly after its construction by the Connachtmen. O'Conor (1993, 240) has suggested that this 'crannog' may actually be Clough Oughter castle (see below), which is known to have been built about this time (Reeves-Smyth 1995,

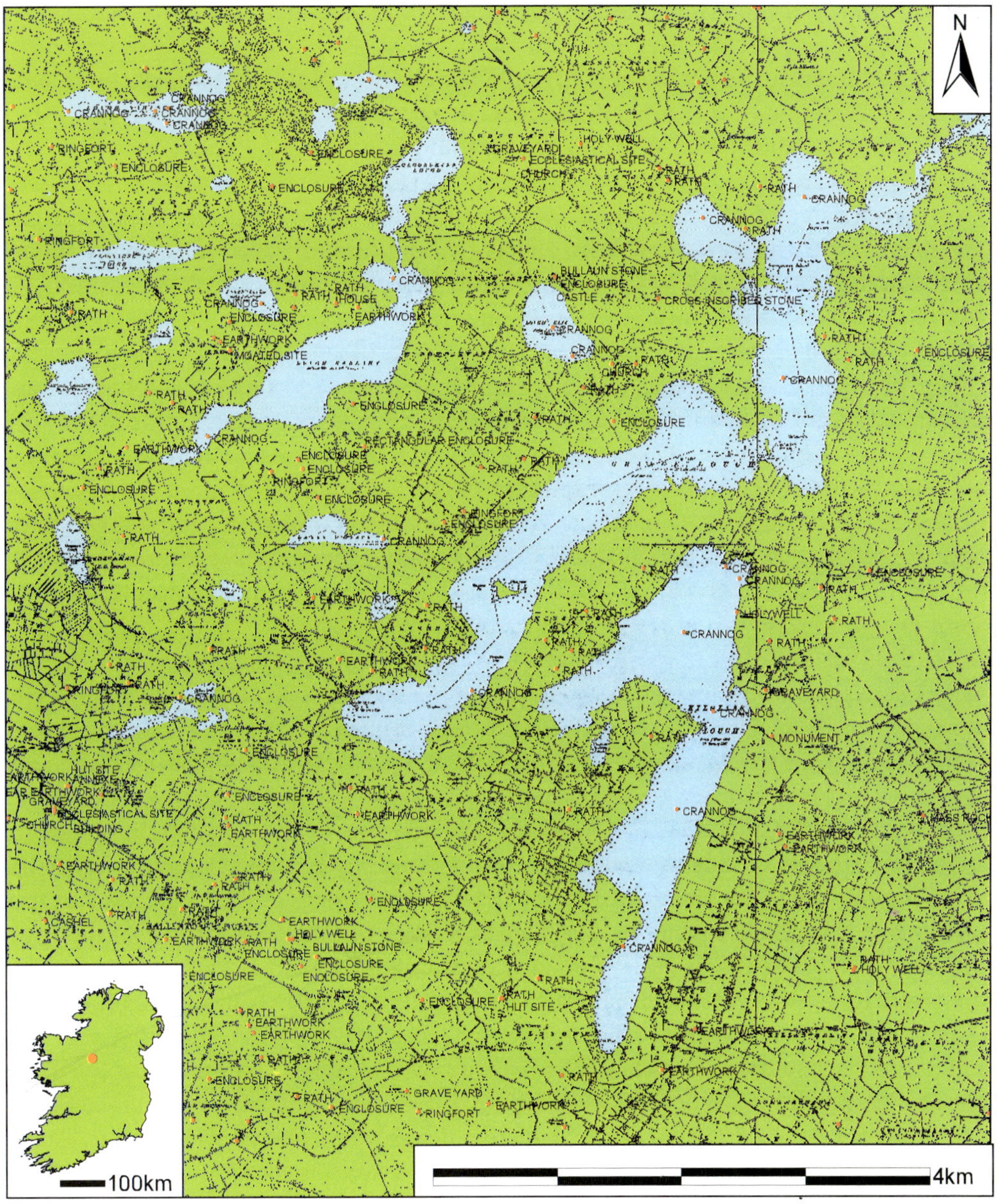

Fig. 35—*Map of Kilglass Lough and other lakes, Co. Roscommon. Annalistic references attest to medieval Gaelic Irish occupation on these crannogs (map by Amanda Kelly, based on the records of the National Monuments Service, Dúchas—The Heritage Service).*

12). Medieval ring-brooches have been found on crannogs at Lough Ervey, Co. Meath, Lake MacHugh, Co. Leitrim, Newtownlow, Co. Westmeath, and Loughnahincha, Co. Roscommon (Deevy 1995). Interestingly, as these brooches are generally found on Anglo-Norman settlements and are not typical of Gaelic Irish dress, they may indicate the presence of Anglo-Norman soldiers, settlers or merchants on crannogs. Deevy (1995, 56; 1998) also suggests that they could represent the process of acculturation between the Gaelic Irish and the Anglo-Norman population in the thirteenth and fourteenth centuries, with the exchange of gifts in alliances or other social ties.

Lake island or *inis* settlements

While there are a few annalistic references to crannogs in the late thirteenth and fourteenth centuries, most accounts of lake settlements refer to an island (*inis*) in Gaelic hands (O'Conor 1993, 242). It is likely that many of these *inis* sites were actually crannogs, but others could have been other forms of island or lake settlement, such as cashels on natural islands or unenclosed settlements. Giraldus Cambrensis, in his twelfth-century account of Ireland, *Topographia Hiberniae*, stated that Irish lakes

> 'contain islands rising to some height and very beautiful. The lords of the land usually appropriate them as places of safety and refuge, as well as of habitation. They are inaccessible except to boats' (O'Meara 1982, 37).

There are a range of *inis* sites which were certainly crannogs (O'Conor 1993, 242–3). The Annals of Ulster for 1170 refer to a recently built 'island' called Inislachain 'upon' Loch Ruidhe. The 'island' of Lough Cairrgin (Ardkillen Lough, Co. Roscommon) is referred to several times in the thirteenth and fourteenth centuries. 'The islands (*insi*) of Loch Ardakillen were taken from the garrison left there by O Conchobair Donn' in 1467 (Annals of Connacht). Several crannogs were excavated in Ardakillen Lough during the nineteenth century; one had a possible medieval stone cashel on its upper surface (Wilde 1857). Domnaill O Cobthaig and his two sons were treacherously killed by Máelsechlainn on Cró-Inis in Loch Ennell (*Croinis Locha hAndind*) in 1446 (Annals of Connacht; Annals of the Four Masters). This was the crannog of Cró-Inis, certainly built in the Early Historic period and occupied through the medieval period, at the latter end of which a tower-house was built on the site (Farrell and Buckley 1984; E.P. Kelly 1991a; 1991b).

O'Conor (1998) has proposed that some *inis* sites were natural islands or islands with earthen or stone fortifications. For example, O'Donnell plundered 'Eo-inis' in 1231 (Annals of the Four Masters). This is probably Eonish, a natural drumlin island on Lough Oughter, Co. Cavan, which is the site of a ringfort and medieval church. A crannog is situated at the west end of the island, where there is a narrow strait on the course of the River Erne (O'Conor 1993, 243; O'Donovan 1995). In 1244, 'Tadc son of Aed mac Cathail Chrobdeirg was blinded and emasculated . . . on Inis na Connire', a small natural island on Lough Allen, Co. Leitrim (Annals of Connacht; Annals of the Four Masters). In 1245 Farrell Mac Tagadain was killed on Inishfree (Annals of the Four Masters), a small natural island on Lough Gill, Co. Sligo. Other references to *inis* sites may be to either natural islands or crannogs. The Annals of the Four Masters state that O'Gara was killed in 1435 on Inis Bolg, an island on *Loch Techet* (Lough Gara, Co. Sligo). Lough Gara has a range of natural islands and crannogs, and the site of the murder was presumably one of these. The likelihood is that most *inis* sites were actually crannogs, but detailed historical and topographical surveys will be necessary to establish this. It is also possible that small natural islands were enclosed by stone walls and cashels in the medieval period.

Marshland ringforts

It is generally believed that ringforts were constructed, occupied and abandoned entirely within the Early Historic period (Stout 1997, 22–31; Edwards 1990, 18–19; Lynn 1975), but there have been several attempts by historical geographers to suggest that ringforts were occupied in the medieval period (e.g. Proudfoot 1970, 40–5; Barrett and Graham 1975). More recently, O'Conor (1993, 257–8; 1998) has re-explored the evidence for medieval occupation on ringforts. He agrees that archaeological evidence for medieval ringfort occupation is slight, but points out that few archaeological excavations of ringforts have been conducted in the areas controlled by the Gaelic Irish in the medieval period. It is also possible that many Anglo-Norman mottes or ringworks were built on ringforts. Ringforts are commonly found on the drylands around lakes, but there are also examples on lake edges and in wetlands which could be called 'marshland ringforts' (Victor Buckley, pers. comm.). While the best-known example, a marshland enclosure at Antiville, Co. Antrim (Waterman 1971), probably dates to the Early Historic or Viking Age, there is also a potential medieval marshland ringfort at Loch Pairc, Co. Galway.

Loch Pairc 'crannog', Co. Galway, appears to have been some type of marshland settlement or ringfort (Macalister *et al.* 1914). The site was rapidly excavated in 1913 by R.A.S Macalister, E.C.R Armstrong and R. L. Praeger, and interpreted as a crannog. It was located in an area of waterlogged marshland and appeared as a low circular mound enclosed by a ditch. The mound measured 36m (110 feet) in diameter, while the entire site, including the ditch, measured 48m (146 feet) across. It had a low depression on the north side, suggested to have been the location of a 'landing stage'. The site appears to have been constructed in a shallow lake or turlough, possibly at a period of low water-levels. The mound may have been constructed from the fill of the ditch, which was dug into the marl. The excavators stated that the site was constructed using a wooden palisade which retained the thrown-in fill of large stones, marl, peat and animal bone. The faunal assemblage included cattle, pig, red deer, sheep/goat and some bird bone (Macalister *et al.* 1914). A continuous layer of stones and rubble which lay on the sloping, outer face of the mound suggested to the excavators that the site had been enlarged at a later date. No internal structures were noted. James Lyttleton (1997; 1998) has recently undertaken an important reinterpretation of the site and its finds. He notes that the artefacts from the site included whetstones, polishing stones, bone pins, needles and harp-pegs, antler handles and bone combs. There were also a range of iron artefacts—arrowheads (including a crossbow bolthead), spurs of the prick and rowel types, knives, awls, nails and a horseshoe. Bronze objects included ringed pins, stick-pins and tweezers. He proposes that most of the finds can be dated to the thirteenth or fourteenth century, apart from a seventeenth-century musketball and horseshoe. Lough Pairc may well have been a temporary military encampment or campaign stronghold in marshlands, as suggested by the crossbow bolthead, arrowheads and spurs.

Mottes and ringwork castles on lakes

The Gaelic Irish probably did not build castles in the medieval period (O'Conor 1998). However, masonry castles were certainly being built by the Anglo-Normans from the late twelfth to the early fourteenth century (Sweetman 1995; McNeill 1997, 17–55, 81–168), although most of their early fortifications were constructed of earth and timber (O'Conor 1993). Earthwork castles include two basic forms, mottes and ringwork castles.

Mottes are flat-topped earthen mounds with timber and clay defences, stockades and towers, often associated with a 'bailey' used as a defended enclosure for houses and other buildings. While there has been very little archaeological investigation of mottes in Ireland, historical sources suggest that they can typically be dated to between the late twelfth century and the early fourteenth century (Barry 1987; Sweetman 1995, 5–7; Mallory and McNeill 1991; O'Conor 1993; 1998). Mottes are typically found in the midlands and north-east, apparently constructed to defend the conquered lands from the Gaelic Irish (Stout and Stout 1997, fig. 58). However, it has also been suggested that several mottes found in west Ulster were constructed by the Gaelic Irish (Sweetman 1995, 7). An Anglo-Norman motte was constructed on Coney Island, Co. Armagh, at the south-west end of Lough Neagh. Two large iron-smelting furnaces were established near the motte to exploit the bog ores of the lake (Addyman 1965; Barry 1987, 109). There are several mottes in Westmeath, Cavan and Meath in the vicinity of midland and northern lakes (Graham 1980, fig. 1). At Knockatemple, Co. Cavan, a motte-and-bailey was constructed on a promontory jutting out into Lough Ramor, cut off from the mainland by a bank and ditch. A rectangular depression on the lakeshore may have been used as a slipway for boats (O'Donovan 1995, 225). There are numerous crannogs and islands on the same lake. A large motte-and-bailey is situated on the south shore of Lough Sewdy at Ballymore, Co. Westmeath (Pl. 50), on a hill with steep slopes overlooking the lake. There are a number of possible crannogs and island settlements in the lake; a Viking Age silver kite-shaped brooch was found on Sallow Island (Somerville 1993), as well as much other metalwork (Eamonn P. Kelly, pers. comm.). A medieval ring-brooch was also found at Lough Sewdy, possibly from the motte itself (Deevy 1998). There are other mottes in the Anglo-Norman liberty of Meath on lakes, such as

Pl. 50—*Anglo-Norman motte and bailey on the shore of Lough Sewdy, Co. Westmeath. Viking Age and medieval finds are also known from this lake (CUCAP AVH 29; reproduced with the permission of the Cambridge Committee for Aerial Photography).*

Portloman on Lough Owel, and in the vicinity of Lough Derravarragh and Lough Iron, Co. Westmeath (Graham 1980, fig. 2). Mottes are also concentrated at the north-east corner of Lough Neagh, Co. Antrim (Glasscock 1975).

Mottes were typically constructed rapidly at strategic locations to consolidate conquered lands and control communications. Anglo-Norman colonisers in Irish lakelands may well have built such fortifications to control the surrounding territories, possibly wresting political power from the inhabitants of the crannogs in the lakes. It is also possible that several of these mottes were constructed on Early Historic raised ringforts or other Gaelic Irish fortifications. The motte at Lough Sewdy may well have been placed on a ringfort or adjacent to an island settlement. Lough Sewdy was a focus for settlement in the Early Historic period, the Viking Age, the medieval period and the post-medieval period (when a seventeenth-century military encampment was constructed beside the motte).

Another form of Anglo-Norman fortification is the ringwork castle, defined by a circular or oval raised area enclosed by an earthen bank and ditch and possibly defended by a palisade. Ringwork castles probably also had timber gatehouses, wooden towers and internal buildings (Sweetman 1995, 7–8; O'Conor 1998). There are a few ringwork castles in the midland lakes region (Stout and Stout 1997, fig. 58).

Masonry castles and tower-houses on lakes

The earliest masonry castles in Ireland were probably built by the Anglo-Normans between 1190 and 1310, with the main period of construction at the turn of the twelfth and thirteenth centuries (Sweetman 1995, 5, 8). These castles were often very large in extent and frequently had keeps, mural towers, gatehouses and curtain-walls (Leask 1941, 12–74; Sweetman 1995, 11–36; McNeill 1997, 17–55, 81–168). It has been suggested that castles were not used by the Gaelic Irish prior to the construction of tower-houses in the fifteenth and sixteenth centuries (O'Conor 1993; 1998). A few Anglo-Norman castles are known from lakes. At Clough Oughter, Co. Cavan, a substantial circular tower was built in the early thirteenth century on a natural area of shallows or rocky islands on Lough Oughter. It was probably built by the de Lacys, but fell into the hands of the Gaelic Irish O'Reillys soon after its construction. The site was recently excavated, producing medieval, late medieval and post-medieval occupational evidence (Manning 1989–90; O'Donovan 1995, 227). A possible Gaelic Irish keep castle known as *Caisleán na Circe* is situated on a small island in the north-west corner of Lough Corrib, Co. Galway. It appears to have been built *c.* 1235 by Feidhlim O'Conor, and later passed to the O'Flahertys. It has a rectangular keep with corner-towers and entrance, and the structures show evidence of repair in the fifteenth or sixteenth century (Gosling 1993, 162).

In the late medieval period, the Gaelic Irish and the Gaelicised Anglo-Normans began to use tower-houses—square or rectangular stone towers, occasionally with side-turrets, with a vault typically over a ground floor and with upper floors marked by windows, fireplaces and staircases, and various external features (Leask 1941; Barry 1987; McNeill 1997). They have been described as 'the typical residence of the Irish gentry' in the late Middle Ages (Sweetman 1995, 36). The origins and chronology of tower-houses remain subjects of debate. A few may have been built in the late fourteenth century (O'Keefe 1987) but most probably date to the early fifteenth century, and they were probably built in lesser numbers through the early sixteenth century (Barry 1987, 186; Cairns 1987, 8–9; McNeill 1997, 228–9). They were mostly abandoned as dwellings by the early seventeenth century (McNeill 1997, 228–9). It is possible that many tower-houses would have had a bawn enclosing adjacent stone, clay and wooden domestic structures, although few archaeological traces of these have been found (Barry 1987; Cairns 1987, 17; McNeill 1997, 211–23). The defensive nature of the bawn has been questioned; it is likely that the tower-house itself was the real fortification. In any case, tower-houses should be seen not only as fortifications but also as domestic residences and the centres of farmed estates (O'Conor 1998). They are typically found in the south, west and midlands of the country, precisely the areas of greatest political instability and decline in centralised government in the late fourteenth and early fifteenth centuries (Stout and Stout 1997, 59). Probably the best-known lakeshore tower-house is the picturesque fifteenth-century Ross Castle, on the shore of Lower Lough Lene near Killarney, Co. Kerry (Reeves-Smyth 1995, 57).

Tower-houses are known to have been constructed on crannogs and lake islands. At Cró-Inis, Co. Westmeath, it is likely that a stone tower identified by Macalister (1938) is in fact the foundations of a tower-house (E.P. Kelly 1991a). At Island MacHugh, a possible sixteenth-century tower-house was constructed on an earlier crannog. The late medieval settlement produced a range of artefacts, including everted-rim ware (Davies 1950; Ivens *et al.* 1986). A tower-house at Lough Coura, Co. Offaly, was also built on a crannog (Nicholls 1993, 406). Tower-houses are also occasionally situated on lake islands or lakeshores in the vicinity of crannogs. At Crover, Co. Cavan, a tower-house was built in the early fourteenth century by Thomas McMahon O'Reilly on a small rocky island off the western shore of Lough Sheelin (O'Donovan 1995, 235). Interestingly, there are at least six possible crannogs in the vicinity of the island, possibly indicating settlement continuity between the Early Historic crannogs and the late medieval tower-house. At Ballynahinch, Co. Galway, a small sixteenth-century tower-house was built on an island in Ballynahinch lake, possibly on an earlier crannog or lake cashel (Gosling 1993, 158). A circular stone fortress known as Castle Hag was probably built on an artificially enlarged island on Lough Mask, Co. Mayo. Historical references attest to its use in the twelfth and sixteenth centuries (Lavelle 1994, 103). At Castleburke, on Lough Carra, Co. Mayo, a tower-house known as Kilvoynell served as the stronghold of Myles Mac Evilly in 1574. It overlooks a crannog in the lake, possibly the earlier residence of this family (Pl. 51) (Lavelle 1994, 107). At Parkes Castle, Co. Leitrim, a fifteenth- to sixteenth-century tower-house with a moat formerly stood right

Pl. 51—*Late medieval tower-house on the shores of Lough Carra, at Castleburke, Co. Mayo (photo: Chris Corlett).*

on the shore of Lough Gill. A survivor of the Spanish Armada, Francisco de Cuellar, resided for some time in this castle, commenting acerbically in his later writings on the mobile warfare tactics of the Gaelic Irish. Claire Foley's excavations revealed that it was demolished and replaced by a larger castle and bawn in the seventeenth century (Reeves-Smyth 1995; Barry 1987, 189). There are numerous other examples of tower-houses on lakeshores, islands and crannogs in Clare, Galway, Westmeath, Leitrim, Cavan, Fermanagh and Tyrone.

These masonry castles and tower-houses on lakes would primarily have been defended family residences, located to control the political territories around lakes and the boat routes through the waterways. Like earlier crannogs and fortified islands, they utilised the natural defensiveness of promontories, lake islands and marshlands. It is possible that medieval and late medieval plank-boats, boat-harbours and other outer defences (palisades or barriers in water channels) can be found in the vicinity of such structures. However, these castles and tower-houses would also have been the centres of manors and farmed estates, and it is likely that water-meadows were used for grazing cattle and that crops were grown on the neighbouring dryland. It is also probable that fish caught in rivers and lakes were a source of both food and revenue. The character of the surrounding settlement landscape would need to be investigated. It is likely that important aspects of continuity with earlier settlements can be traced. It will also be important to explore the less clearly evident medieval and late medieval lakeshore settlements of the lower classes, such as unenclosed farmsteads, hut sites and industrial working areas.

Manorial farms and moated sites on lakes

Anglo-Norman agriculture was primarily geared towards the production of a crop surplus for a market economy. In most of the colony, nucleated villages or manors were established, centred on a large manor house, church and surrounding houses and field systems. In the eastern part of the island, these farms were populated with English peasant farmers, living either in villages or in farmsteads close to the manor house (A. Simms 1983; Graham 1985). In the west midlands and north, it is likely that Anglo-

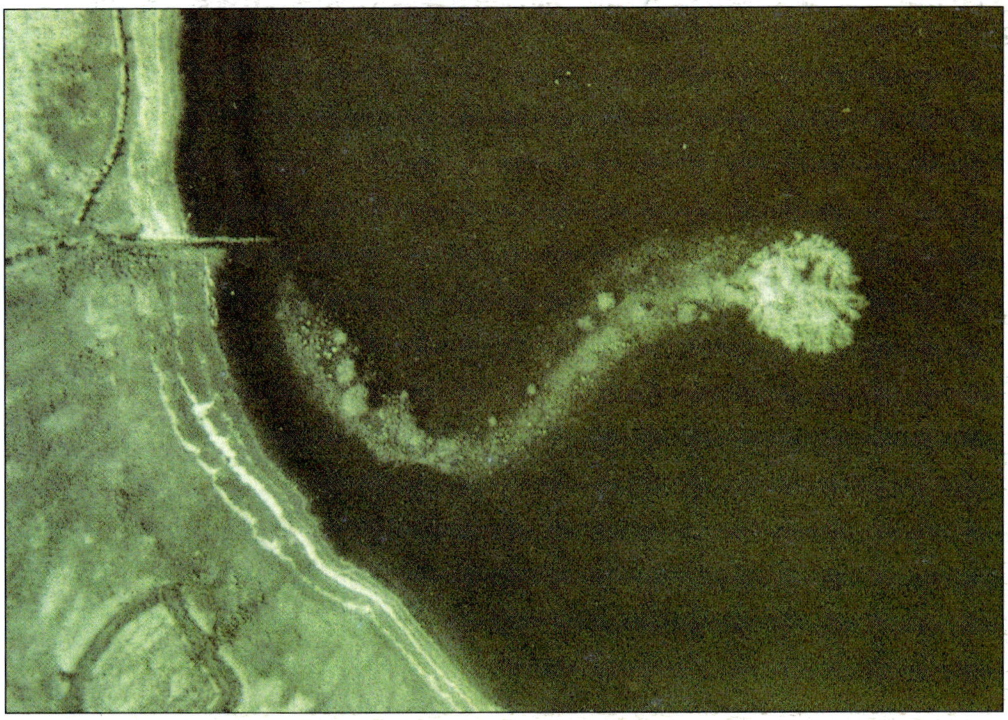

Pl. 52—*Cloonacleigha Lough, Co. Sligo. A medieval moated site is situated opposite a crannog with a well-made stone causeway leading out to it (photo: Ordnance Survey of Ireland).*

Norman farms were largely worked by the native Irish, who may have lived in houses further away from the manorial centre (McNeill 1980; O'Conor 1998). The manor houses of the Anglo-Norman lords and the farmsteads of strong peasant farmers may have been situated inside moated sites—large, rectangular earthen enclosures defended by deep ditches (Barry 1977; 1987; 1997). Moated sites may also have served as defended dispersed settlements in the borderlands between the Anglo-Norman territories and the Gaelic Irish lands. They appear to have been occupied from the end of the thirteenth century to the early fourteenth century and are more typically situated in the south-east of the country (Barry 1977). They are also known from the midland lakes region, in the vicinity of Lough Ennell, Lough Iron, Lough Derravarragh and Lough Lene, Co. Westmeath, Lough Gowna, Co. Longford, and Lough Carrafin, Co. Cavan. Rectangular earthworks which may be moated sites are known from the midland region too (Stout and Stout 1997, fig. 58). At Inismore, Co. Cavan, a possible moated site or large rectangular earthen fort formerly stood on the shore of Carrafin Lough (O'Donovan 1995, 222). Two moated sites may have formerly stood at Carrickabane and Lisnadarragh, immediately to the north of Lough Kinale and Lough Sheelin (*ibid.*, 222). It is possible that some moated sites were constructed and occupied by the Gaelic Irish (Graham 1988, 30–1; O'Conor, forthcoming) (Pl. 52).

Abbeys and monastic sites on lakes

The settlement of the medieval church has received relatively little attention in Irish archaeology; most studies concentrate on its architecture and sculpture, and there have been only a few archaeological excavations (Barry 1987). Medieval and late medieval monasteries, abbeys and friaries are certainly known from lakeshores and islands, often continuing in use from earlier 'Celtic' monasteries (Pls 53 and 54). Lough Ree, on the River Shannon, has a particularly interesting range of medieval and late medieval ecclesiastical settlements, which presumably dominated the lake. Inchcleraun had a medieval Augustinian abbey, the *Teampull Mór,* with its sacristy, chapter house and cloister garth. It is known to have had 'seven churches and a steeple' in the fourteenth century, a common feature of pilgrimage sites (Harbison 1991).

Pl. 53—*Aerial photograph of the monastic island of Devenish, Lower Lough Erne, Co. Fermanagh (photo: Environment and Heritage Service, DOE(NI)).*

Pl. 54—*Aerial photograph of the monastic island of Inchcleraun, Lough Ree (CUCAP AHM 19; reproduced with the permission of the Cambridge Committee for Aerial Photography).*

Saint's Island was also a monastic site, producing manuscripts and hagiographies in the thirteenth century (Henry and Marsh-Micheli 1993, 788, 792). Inisbofin has Romanesque and late medieval church buildings, the successors to its Early Historic and Viking Age monastic sites (see above). There are also a number of medieval churches around the lake, such as at Rindoon on the western shore (J. Bradley and Dunne 1988). An Augustinian abbey was located at Tristernagh, on Lough Iron, Co. Westmeath (Barry 1987; Swan 1988). Some of the houses of the smaller religious orders are also to be found by lakes, such as a Gilbertine foundation near Lough Sewdy, Co. Westmeath (Ballymore), and a Premonstratensian site on Trinity Island, Lough Key, Co. Roscommon (Barry 1987, 162). Several ecclesiastical settlements are to be found on islands on Lower Lough Erne, Co. Fermanagh. They include Devenish (Ralegh Radford 1970; Waterman 1979), White Island (Wakeman 1879), Boa Island and Inishmacsaint

(Barry 1987, 140). Devenish had several twelfth-century structures, including two round towers and a stone oratory (St Molaisse's House). The island probably had a twelfth-century Augustinian house (Pl. 53). The surviving church and cloister of St Mary's Priory probably date from the fifteenth century. Archaeological excavations at the site produced, amongst later material, medieval English pottery and a twelfth-century bronze ringed pin. There were also sherds of fine late medieval pottery from France, Germany, Spain and The Netherlands. Lough Erne was the route for foreign pilgrims travelling to St Patrick's Purgatory on Lough Derg, Co. Donegal—hence the presence of this pottery on the site (Waterman 1979; Harbison 1991; Barry 1987; Hamlin 1988; Donnelly 1997, 53–6).

Medieval church settlements on lake islands and lakeshores and smaller parish churches were not only centres of worship, pilgrimage, learning and ecclesiastical authority. They served as important economic centres as well. Presumably there would have been houses, barns, workshops and other structures around the ecclesiastical buildings on the islands. The communities living there had a ready supply of water for fishing and domestic purposes. They probably had their own manorial estates, managed at a distance by means of granges and smaller farmsteads scattered in the landscape around the lakes. Some were probably used as hospitals and places of refuge for the region. Placed centrally on nautical routeways, they provided ready waterborne access to large areas around the lakes. Indeed, long-distance shipping moving up and down the country by means of its rivers and lakes probably used these islands as hostels, markets and sources of food and trade goods. Church settlements on islands and lakeshores would also have been used as hostels by pilgrims moving along the waterways, as shown by the presence of late medieval European pottery at Devenish, Co. Fermanagh.

Boroughs and market towns on lakes

It is worth remembering that some Anglo-Norman boroughs were situated on or near lakes. There were medieval boroughs at Cong on Lough Corrib and at Antrim on Lough Neagh (Barry 1987, fig. 28). At Rindoon, Co. Roscommon, on the western shore of Lough Ree, an Anglo-Norman borough was established in the mid-thirteenth century on a narrow peninsula, known as the Warren peninsula or St John's Point, jutting out into the lake (Pl. 55). The borough may have been situated within a prehistoric promontory fort. There is also evidence for an Early Historic or Viking Age monastic

Pl. 55—*Aerial photograph of the site of the Anglo-Norman borough of Rindoon, Co. Roscommon (photo: Dúchas—The Heritage Service).*

site, as ecclesiastical handbells, a bronze Crucifixion plaque and a decorated cross-slab are known from the site (J. Bradley and Dunne 1988). It has been suggested that Rindoon was the site of the longphort established by Viking raiders on Lough Ree in the ninth century. Rindoon was used as a harbour in 1200–1, when a retreating John de Courcy ferried his army to safety out of Connacht. In 1227 a castle was built on the site by Geoffrey de Marisco as a base for his campaign west of the Shannon. The borough was evidently founded at this time. A bawn and ditch are mentioned in an account of an attack on the site in 1236 (Annals of Connacht). By the 1270s Rindoon was a vital emplacement in the wars against the O'Connors and a means of protecting ships sailing up Lough Ree. It was attacked on various occasions through the thirteenth and fourteenth centuries and was in Gaelic Irish hands by 1342–3. There are a number of other historical references to sites and activities at Rindoon up until the early seventeenth century, when it fell into decay as a town (J. Bradley and Dunne 1988; Reeves-Smyth 1995, 78).

A variety of archaeological sites survive at Rindoon, including a masonry castle within a possible ringwork castle, a parish church, several house sites, a town wall with a gatehouse and three mural towers, and a windmill. To the north-west, outside the town wall, is the site of the medieval hospital of St John, of the Fratres Cruciferi. A sheltered cove or small bay on the east side of the promontory may have been the site of the medieval harbour. Recent underwater archaeological survey at the site has identified boat slipways, 'hards' and jetties of probable medieval date (Colin Breen, pers. comm.). Rindoon was clearly an important military, ecclesiastical and secular settlement on Lough Ree, being an Anglo-Norman borough with a market, military defences and a harbour. It was obviously one element in a medieval settlement landscape based around Lough Ree, with contemporary ecclesiastical settlements on Inchcleraun and Inchbofin (J. Bradley and Dunne 1988; Barry 1987, 173–4).

Medieval boats and ships on lakes

There are numerous annalistic references to the use of boats and ships on Irish lakes between 1100 and 1534. Various terms are employed for these vessels. There was the *long,* which was probably a large boat or ship, occasionally capable of carrying at least 60 people. There was also the *bád,* a term probably used to describe various sizes of smaller boat. Finally, there was also the *coite* or 'cot' (Flanagan 1988, 500). There are also occasional references to wooden rafts or ferries of unknown form. Many of the cots referred to in the annals may have been either small dugout boats, wicker-built coracles or small plank-built craft. They were used for conveying people and small cargos around lakes. An unusual incident on a 'cot' led to a drowning in 1397:

> 'Dermot, the son of Ivor O'Beirne, was in a fever, and was conveyed in a cot on a lake from his own house, towards the house of Murrough, the son of Thomas (O'Beirne); and he leaped out of the cot, unobserved by any, into the lake, and was immediately drowned' (Annals of the Four Masters).

Although small plank-built vessels are not as yet known in the archaeological record, several Irish dugout boats have produced medieval and late medieval radiocarbon dates (Lanting and Brindley 1996). These smaller craft would have been used on a day-to-day basis by farmers and fishermen inhabiting lakeshores, although they could have been unstable on the choppy waters of windswept lakes. It is also likely that larger boats and ships were plying the waters of the Corrib, Shannon and Erne lake systems for reasons of trade and pilgrimage. Indeed, it seems that lakes like Lough Ree, Lough Erne, Lough Corrib and other lakes were teeming with craft of all sizes in the Middle Ages. These vessels would have sailed familiar routes, stopped at night in safe harbours and at settlements on the lakeshore, and probably travelled long distances from sea-ports into the country. The larger boats were also used for travel and communications around the smaller lakes, and occasionally came to grief on their waters. The following incident is recorded as having occurred during a boat journey from Hog Island on Garadice Lough, Co. Leitrim, in 1418:

> 'Owen, the son of Tiernan More O'Rourke, Tanist of Breifny, was drowned shortly after Christmas, as he was going (in a boat) from Inis-na-d-torc to an island in Lough Finvoy, to visit his father, who was then lying ill of a mortal disease' (Annals of the Four Masters).

Similarly, there are records of a boating tragedy on Lough Sheelin, the large lake on the borders of Cavan, Longford and Meath. The lake has several crannogs and tower-houses along its edge (O'Donovan 1995). The incident occurred in 1418:

> 'Richard, the son of Thomas O'Reilly, lord of East Breiffny, was drowned in Loch Silean . . . Many others were also drowned. Finola, however, daughter of MacRannall and wife of O'Reilly, escaped by swimming' (Annals of the Four Masters).

Larger plank-built boats and ships were also engaged in naval warfare, attacking crannogs, island and lakeshore settlements, and monastic sites. These probably derived from the Nordic shipbuilding tradition, being long, narrow craft with a single central mast. Some may have been galleys, large military craft with 40–60 oars and capable of high speed. Ships were largely used to transport troops up and down the waterways, thus providing an element of surprise in raids and attacks. However, smaller vessels may have been used to raid crannogs and castles on islands. In 1421 a night attack was made by Cathal O Ruairc and his sons against Mag Flannchaid on Iniskeen in Loch Melvin, Co. Leitrim, 'and the garrison of the lake . . . betrayed Mag Flannchaid and surrendered its vessels to Cathal and his sons' (Annals of Connacht).

Medieval naval fleets on the lakes could have been quite large, as indicated by various annalistic references to the activities of Ruaidhri Ua Concobhair in the late twelfth century. In 1157, 'such was the greatness of the frost, that Ruaidhri Ua Concobhair drew his ships and boats on the ice from Blean-Gaille to Rindoon and his fleet on the River Shannon the like of which was not to be found at that time for numerousness, and for the number of its ships and boats' (Annals of the Four Masters). Even these large ships were at the mercy of storms and winds on the large lakes. In 1190,

> 'O'Conor and the Sil-Murray went to Clonmacnoise on that night and early next morning embarked in their fleet, and sailed up the Shannon until they came to Lough Ree. A violent storm arose on the lake, by which their vessels were separated from each other; and the storm so agitated the vessel in which O'Conor was, that it could not be piloted. Such was the fury of the storm, it foundered, and all the crew perished, except O'Conor himself and six others' (Annals of the Four Masters).

There is also historical evidence for raids on island monasteries. In 1231, 'Domnall O Domnaill King of Tir Conaill and Aengus MacGilla Finnein raised an army against Cathal O Raigillig. They brought ships (*longius*) to Loch Oughter and plundered Eanish, where . . . they carried off precious objects and the wealth and treasure and good things there' (Annals of Connacht). Similarly, the islands of Lough Erne were ravaged by a fleet operating out of Lough Oughter in 1272:

> 'O'Donnell collected the vessels and boats upon Lough Erne, and (proceeded) thence to Lough Oughter. The goods and the valuables of the surrounding country (which were upon the islands of that lake) were seized on and carried off by him; and he acquired control and sway in every place in the neighbourhood on this expedition' (Annals of the Four Masters).

Medieval settlements on lakes

There are a range of research questions specific to medieval settlements on lakes. There are the ordinary questions of social and political history, settlement continuity and change, and landscape and economy. However, this concluding section will concentrate on aspects of the lakeland siting of medieval and late medieval settlements. Lake islands, lakeshores and lake margins may have been deliberately chosen for the construction of mottes, ringworks, moated sites, castles and tower-houses because a lake siting enhanced their defensive qualities. However, settlement continuity undoubtedly also played an important part in the location, construction and use of medieval settlements. The Early Historic or Viking Age settlement landscape may in most cases be a strongly influential factor in the organisation of medieval settlement patterns. Certain medieval lordly families and social groups may have continued to control and manage ancestral farmlands from castles which were built on or near Early Historic and Viking Age crannogs, ringforts and other settlements. These earlier settlements would have been a constant reminder of the legitimacy of power. Anglo-Norman fortifications may also have sprung from earlier settlements, either for practical reasons or as a means of taking over power and authority in a locality.

Castles, whether of masonry, earth or timber construction, were probably intended primarily to withstand a large-scale military attack and to protect the lord, his family and retainers; the lake waters provided an additional barrier to attackers. However, if that was the case then we might expect isolation and the hidden nature of a site to be obvious factors in settlements. The opposite is the case: lakeshore and island structures are highly visible from afar and were major statements of power in the landscape, controlling boat traffic and signalling ownership and status. Castles on lakeshores and islands may also have been sited for potentially aggressive reasons, as emplacements within rival territories or on boundaries. The added bonus of lakeshore settlement is the potential rapidity of movement and action across large distances. Territories could have been more easily captured and held from a site with easy access to a lake and the rapid transport and communications that waterways provide. It is undoubtedly the case that most lakeshore and island castles have the full set of nautical structures, such as slipways, landing places and harbours, but little has been done to trace them.

Lake island and lakeshore castles were probably also sited to control and manage local farmlands, estates or manors, and to exploit various lakeland resources. It has been suggested that most castles had adjoining clay and timber buildings, outhouses, field systems, mills, rabbit warrens, fishponds, enclosed woodlands and other agricultural features. Castles on lakes should be investigated in terms of their role in the management of the agricultural landscape. Lakes provide particular resources, such as fowl, fish, and water-meadows and marshes for grazing cattle. Fish were an important part of the medieval diet, given the religious restrictions on meat-eating during the year (O'Sullivan 1995b; 1997c). Fishponds are an important aspect of the rural landscape of medieval England, while a lakeland siting provides some measure of constant fishing. Local rivers and streams may also have been used for watermills.

In conclusion, what is needed is an integrated landscape study of medieval settlement around lakes. This should aim to examine the evidence for the original and continuing medieval Gaelic Irish settlement, as well as any evidence for Anglo-Norman mottes, moated sites or masonry castles. The relationship between these two elements should be explored. The nature of ecclesiastical settlement could also be linked with this secular evidence, as parish churches, monastic islands and church estates are known from around lakes. This would be linked to a programme of historical research. A study of medieval lake settlement archaeology should also trace changing agricultural patterns through detailed palaeoenvironmental studies in a lake setting.

Post-medieval lake settlement

Introduction

The post-medieval period (between 1534 and 1700) was one of great social, economic and political change in Ireland, witnessing religious and cultural conflict between the dispossessed Gaelic Irish, the Old English and the new Scottish and English colonists. By about 1515 the English lordship in Ireland had fallen into decay, and the area controlled had receded to a small area on the east coast known as the Pale. Outside this defended area and the few fortified towns in east Munster lay a landscape held by rebellious Old English lords, who had abandoned their allegiance to the London government, and the Gaelic Irish. The Tudor monarchs made some efforts to redress this decay of power in Ireland, but with little success. The religious reformation distanced the two countries further, creating tensions that were to culminate in a series of rebellions and bloody wars. By the mid-sixteenth century, English government in Ireland was gradually re-established and a system of settler plantations in the midlands was being implemented. After the failure of the Desmond rebellion in Munster in 1583, the confiscated lands of the earl of Desmond and his followers were taken into the plantation of Munster. In Ulster, the regions outside English control were also won after several years of military action against the earl of Tyrone's 'Great Rebellion' of 1595–1603. The defeat of the last of the Gaelic Irish chieftains at the end of the Nine Years' War in 1603, followed by their flight out of the country in 1607, enabled the crown to begin the plantation of Ulster. The granting of these lands to loyal Irish lords and English soldiers and the planting of new Scottish and English settlers in Munster, Ulster and the midlands were intended to promote new markets and towns, the construction of manor houses and castles, and the introduction of an English system of agriculture and landscape organisation (McCurtain 1972; Moody *et al.* 1976; Cullen 1981; Brady and Gillespie 1986; Canny 1987; Gillespie 1993; Loeber 1991).

Ireland was viewed by the English government as an unstable polity which needed to be improved through the creation of a new commonwealth, with one king, one law, one religion, one language, and an interdependence of master and man. The English were also being inspired by their creation of new colonies in America, so that Ireland became a place of experimentation in settlement. By means of plantations the Gaelic Irish would be absorbed, through settlement and interaction, within an English system. The English and Scottish settlers who came to Ireland brought with them an entirely new way of life, one very different to that of the native Gaelic Irish and the Old English. In many ways, the plantations initially proved too ambitious. British settlers were difficult to attract in numbers. However, the defeat of the Gaelic Irish rebellion of 1641 after twelve years of war enabled an even larger and more efficient English plantation scheme, with massive land confiscations which were often accompanied by major mapping surveys, such as the Down Survey implemented by William Petty in the 1650s (Andrews 1997). After the end of the short Williamite wars of English succession (1689–91), Ireland was finally under total English control and witnessed a prolonged period of social and economic stability. The Irish landscape was almost clear of woodlands and was organised into estates and fenced field systems; cattle meat was exported and sheep grew in importance. The growth of demesne and estate villages went hand in hand with ideas of agricultural improvement, largely creating the modern Irish rural landscape of dispersed farmhouses with large, enclosed fields, large estates and small villages and rural towns (Mitchell and Ryan 1997, 327; Stout and Stout 1997, 62).

A range of social and economic factors were to be important in the shaping of the post-medieval Irish landscape. The plantation system made important changes. However, Ireland was also affected by England's political and economic relationship with its American colonies, being drawn into an Atlantic and north European economy. Nevertheless, continuity in Gaelic Irish and Old English settlement and society was as important as change, in many ways making it difficult to draw a clear line between the late Middle Ages and the post-medieval period (Gillespie 1993). Most of the native

Irish population remained as tenants to the new lords. For the Scottish and English settlers, there were also the pervading influences of the traditional Irish economy and way of life and the realities of the Irish landscape. The early seventeenth-century settlers often built fortified residences in the manner of late medieval Irish tower-houses, sensibly reflecting the unsettled nature of the times. Cattle-raising was also found by the settlers to be more suitable for the landscape of west Ulster and Munster, while the Antrim and Down coast of east Ulster was naturally the region to be the most successfully settled because of its proximity to Scotland (Mallory and McNeill 1991). The economy of the post-medieval English settlers was one of embryonic industrialisation aimed at widening trade, the organisation of manufacture and the production of a substantial agricultural surplus. Woodlands were felled for industrial use and arable farming gradually replaced pastoral farming in many areas (Mitchell and Ryan 1997, 317–20).

Gaelic Irish society largely continued to be structured around a great number of lordships, the strongest overlords in Ulster being typically the O'Neills of Tyrone, but with competitors in the O'Donnells, Maguires, O'Cahans and O'Neills of Clandeboy (O'Dowd 1986; Mallory and McNeill 1991). Nevertheless, there were great social and economic changes in Gaelic Ireland, the waning of the Irish ways of life and the abolition of the native Brehon Laws in 1603, and the elegiac, lamenting poetry of the Irish bards paralleled a widespread introduction of English customs (McCurtain 1972). In terms of settlement and economy, the Gaelic Irish continued many of the practices of earlier times. Tower-houses continued to be built and occupied until the mid-seventeenth century. Some few ringforts may have been occupied (Hayes McCoy 1964), but crannogs certainly served as lordly residences and refuges (see below). Most people lived in small circular or oval huts, with walls of wattle and daub and roofs of thatch. These may occasionally have been gathered together in small, agglomerated settlements. Prior to 1600, most of the country was owned by the numerous Gaelic Irish clans or by the church, and rented out to tenants. Gaelic Irish lords had enormous herds of cattle, which were important in both social and economic terms. The herds and those who drove them were known as *caoruigheachta* or 'creaghts', and these were typically moved through the countryside as part of a booleying system. The herders probably lived in temporary wooden structures which could easily be taken down and moved. Indeed, in the seventeenth century the continuous movement of Gaelic Irish pastoralists with their cattle gave English writers the impression that Irish society was entirely nomadic. In reality, it was the unsettled nature of the times and the constant loss of arable crops in war which had exaggerated the normal tradition of cattle transhumance. As well as supplying dairy products, cattle provided hides for export (Aalen 1978; Nicholls 1972, 114). Arable agriculture was known amongst the Gaelic Irish, and landowners cultivated their own lands with the aid of labourers, who were probably paid with a share of the crops (Nicholls 1972, 115). Wheat and rye were grown on good land, barley harvested for brewing and distilling, and oats grown on the poorer lands of the west (Ryan and Mitchell 1997, 316). On the other hand, it has been pointed out that the Gaelic Irish lords also adopted several features of the new plantation settlements (Mallory and McNeill 1991, 311). The character of rural settlement during the period is barely understood, as little archaeological investigation has been undertaken. The following discussion of post-medieval lake settlement will therefore focus on crannogs and planter castles by lakes.

Gaelic Irish crannogs

Post-medieval Gaelic Irish settlement and society show much continuity from the late medieval period (Aalen 1978; O'Dowd 1986; Nicholls 1972). Certainly, there is plenty of archaeological and historical evidence that crannogs were constructed, occupied and used as places of rebellion and resistance in the sixteenth and seventeenth centuries (Wood-Martin 1886a, 146–54, 236–8; Hayes-McCoy 1964, 9–10, 16, 20). Wood-Martin (1886a) wrote: 'although we have no account of the first erection of crannogs in Ireland, and must therefore consider their origin to date back from prehistoric times, yet we have undoubted proofs of their continued use down to the close of the seventeenth century'. Some crannogs may have been occupied as late as the 1690s (Hayes-McCoy 1964, 20). English contemporary accounts refer to them as 'cronnocks', 'ffreshwater loghes', 'fortified islands' and 'lodgings in the fen' (Shirley 1846, 44). Crannogs were perceived by the English as hotspots of rebellion and resistance which would have to be demolished, one writer suggesting:

> 'That none of the Irish do build any houses on loughs, but be enjoined to build castles or houses upon the firm land, and those houses that now are built upon loughs to be defaced' (Hayes-McCoy 1964, 20).

Gaelic Irish crannogs: settlement and economy

Were crannogs permanent residences or only temporary refuges in the sixteenth and seventeenth centuries? The archaeological excavation of several crannogs in Cavan, Monaghan and the midlands has produced evidence for occupation, but it is uncertain how long people stayed there. Aghavoher crannog, Co. Cavan, was investigated by Oliver Davies, who described a small circular island constructed of timber, with finds including animal bone, hones, quernstones, iron and everted-rim ware. He suggested that the crannog's principal occupation was in the sixteenth century (Davies 1942; O'Donovan 1995, 175). More recently, it has been noted that sherds of sixteenth-century Mediterranean pottery are present in that assemblage (Ó Floinn, forthcoming). At Corraneary Lough, Co. Cavan, Davies excavated a crannog which produced two phases of occupation, one probably medieval, the second in the sixteenth century. This site also produced everted-rim ware (Davies 1942; O'Donovan 1995, 180; Ó Floinn, forthcoming). Several crannogs have produced seventeenth-century occupation evidence. At Deredis Upper, Farnham Lough, Co. Cavan, a circular island was shown to have a stone facing, wooden piles and seventeenth-century pottery (Bellarmine jars) (Davies 1942, 19). Lough Henney crannog, Co. Down, was occupied at the beginning of the seventeenth century. An Inquisition held at Ardquin in 1605 stated that Tool mcPhelim McIvor occupied the island. An iron helmet, forged from a single piece of metal with a fitted nasal guard, was found on the site before 1852. Helmets of this type are known from fifteenth- to sixteenth-century Europe. A mass of rusted chain-mail, again of fifteenth-century European type, was also found (Jope 1966, 185; Flanagan 1992). Ballinderry crannog no. 1, Co. Westmeath, produced an interesting range of seventeenth-century objects, such as pottery, several coins dating from about 1690, a brass button, glass linen smoothers, lead bullets (some of which were probably being made there) and several fragments of clay pipes (Hencken 1936, 165). It is possible that the site was occupied for some time, although the evidence of bullet-making might suggest only a temporary occupation during the wars at the end of the seventeenth century.

It is likely that crannogs continued in use as Gaelic Irish lordly residences. A map of the escheated territories made for the government in the Monaghan area, the 'Platt of the county of Monaghan', contains rough sketches of the dwellings of the chiefs of Monaghan which 'are in all cases surrounded by water'. Each barony had a site depicted as 'The Iland'; one at Lisnanisk in the barony of Farney was marked on the map as 'The Iland Ever M'Cooley's house' (Wilde 1857, 231). A 'gentleman's residence' at Monaghan was known to be in a crannog, being the chief dwelling-place of MacMahon, the lord of the district, and the crannog was protected by a wattle palisade, within which was a bawn and a house (Hayes-McCoy 1964). There is a crannog today in Convent Lough, in Monaghan town, which may well be this site (Victor Buckley, pers. comm.). Crannogs are depicted in Richard Bartlett's map of Monaghan town, which may also be the sites in questions (Hayes McCoy 1964). Some crannogs were occupied up until the eighteenth century and afterwards. They were used as fishing stations (Morrison 1985), as dog pounds (Kieran O'Conor, pers. comm.), as illicit stills for making *poitín* (Kinahan 1870–1, 461), and as 'kail gardens' for producing vegetables

(Wood-Martin 1886a). Indeed, the late occupation of crannogs has been recognised since the beginnings of research. One of the earliest researchers, E.P. Shirley (1846, 49), considered that the crannogs of the MacMahon country (Monaghan) were used by 'gangs of freebooters and *Tories*' (Roman Catholic Irish outlaws) in the seventeenth century.

Gaelic Irish crannogs as munitions and treasure stores, refuges and hospitals

During the wars of the sixteenth and seventeenth centuries, crannogs were occasionally used by the Gaelic Irish as places of defence and as munitions stores. Fynes Moryson's (1908) account of the English defeat of the rebellious earl of Tyrone includes the following reference to crannogs being used as ammunition stores:

> 'Then he tooke some of Tyrone's strongest Ilands, namely, one wherein he had a strong fort, where we recovered three peeces of his Majesties artillery, and another Iland called Magerlowni, which next to Dungannon was the chiefe place of his aboade, and magazins for his warre' (Moryson 1908; Hayes-McCoy 1964, 10).

Crannogs were also used as prisons and as safe places to store gold and silver plate. A sixteenth-century hoard of gold and silver coins and a gold ring found on Cherry Island, Lough Ennell, Co. Westmeath, may be archaeological evidence for this practice (E.P. Kelly 1994, 215). In May 1567, the English soldier Thomas Phettiplace, when asked by the lords of Queen Elizabeth's council what castles or forts O'Neill possessed, replied:

> '. . . that fortification that he only dependeth upon is in *ssartin ffreshwater loghes* in his country, which from the sea there come neither ship nor boat to approach them; it is thought that there in ye said *fortified islands* lyeth all his plate, wch is much, and money, prisoners, and gages, wch islands hath in wars before been attempted, and now of late again by ye Lord Deputy Sr Harry Sydney, wch for want of means for safe conduct upon ye water, it hath not prevailed' (Shirley 1846; Wood-Martin 1886a, 147).

In Marshal Bagenal's description of Ulster (1586), a description of O'Neill's condition refers to a wetland settlement: 'You shall do verie well to see his lodgings in the fen, where he built his lodging, and kept his cattell, and all his men'. Unusually, this seems to imply that cattle were kept in crannogs, although they may have been corralled on the dryland (Wilde 1857, 232). Crannogs were also used as places of refuge, as hospitals or as safe places for the wounded and injured. Thus in 1603 Hugh Boy O'Donnell, having been wounded, 'was sent to *Crannog-na-n-Duini*, in Ross-Guill, in the tuathas (Donegal), to be healed'. This island settlement was located in Mevagh, Co. Donegal (Wood-Martin 1886a, 150; Annals of the Four Masters).

Gaelic Irish attacks on crannogs

Gaelic Irish raids on other Irish lake settlements in the fifteenth and sixteenth centuries are occasionally described in the historical sources. There may be a strong element of settlement continuity in the reuse of earlier sites, but dendrochronological dating from some sites in Northern Ireland may indicate their actual construction in the fifteenth and sixteenth centuries (Baillie 1985; 1995a). Interestingly, the Fermanagh crannog survey produced sixteen radiocarbon dates from the fifteenth to the seventeenth century. It has been suggested that the fortification of crannogs at Mill Lough, Lough Eyes, Corban Lough and Carrick Lough, Co. Fermanagh, in the late fifteenth and early sixteenth centuries is related to warring between the O'Rourkes of Breffni and the Maguires of Fermanagh (E.P. Kelly 1991b, 122). Crannogs were also under attack further to the north-east. In 1540, the O'Donnells 'went into the crannoge of Loch

Pl. 56—*Richard Bartlett's seventeenth-century depiction of an attack on a Gaelic Irish crannog (National Library of Ireland).*

Pl. 57—*Detail of Richard Bartlett's map of Dungannon, Tullahoge and an attack on a crannog, showing various other sites and cruck houses around the lake (National Library of Ireland).*

Beiathaigh' (Lough Veagh, near Gartan, Co. Donegal), and 'O'Donnell broke down and demolished the crannoge' (Annals of the Four Masters). In 1544 O'Donnell marched through Antrim and took *Inis-an-Lochain, Baile-an-locha, Inis-locha-Burrann* and *Inis-locha-leithinnsi.* On these fortified islands and lake castles the loot included arms, armour, brass, iron, butter and provisions. In 1571 the Mac Dermots burned Inis Floinn and Inis-Mic-David, somewhere on the borders of Roscommon and Sligo (Wood-Martin 1886a).

English attacks on Gaelic Irish crannogs

Gaelic Irish crannogs were attacked by English forces on various occasions in the sixteenth and seventeenth centuries (Pls 56 and 57). These attacks were not always successful. Sir Henry Sydney wrote the following passages to Queen Elizabeth I on 12 November 1566, describing such a failed attack. The English attackers had to retreat from the island with a few casualties. The letter seems to describe a fortified lake island, about 100m from the shore, with a palisade of timber and stakes.

> 'So on the 21st of the same month, we removed and marched towards Ardmach, and in the way, having occasion to encamp hard by a logh, in which was an island, and in the same, by universal opinion and reports of divers of that country, a great quantity of the rebel's goods and victuals kept, only without guns, as it was thought, not greatly strong as it seemed but hedged about, and the distance from the main not being passed five-score yards, the army coming timely to the camp, divers soldiers were very desirous to attempt the winning of it, which was granted to them . . . They found the place better manned than it was thought, and they of better courage than before that time the like men had ever shewed themselves in the like place. They found the hedge so bearded around with stakes and other sharp wood, as it was not without extreme difficulty scaleable, and so ramparted as if the hedge had been burned—for doing whereof the fire-works failed—without a long time it was not to be digged down' (Wood-Martin 1886a, 148).

A crannog in Drumcaw, Co. Monaghan, was attacked by English forces in 1598. Prior to the rising, Maguire and Brian MacHugh Og had raised trouble in the region and a punitive force was sent north to deal with them. The Drumcaw crannogs were garrisoned by the rebels and had to be attacked by unusual means. The crannogs were out of musket range from the shore. Piles of brushwood and timber were collected on the windward lakeshore, set on fire and floated on the lake. The wind carried them down to the crannogs. Those of the garrison who escaped the fire were shot or drowned in the lake. The other crannogs in the area were then abandoned because of this successful attack (J. Smyth 1953–6).

Crannogs are depicted on early seventeenth-century maps of Ulster. These maps were the work of Richard Bartlett, a Norfolk cartographer engaged to supply military maps for Lord Mountjoy's campaign against Hugh O'Neill, earl of Tyrone, in 1601–3 (Hayes-McCoy 1964; Andrews 1997). The maps were based both on measured surveys from hilltops and on information gathered from soldiers. Map V illustrates, within three 'scrolls', the English-held Dungannon Castle, the Gaelic Irish Tullahoge royal inauguration site, and an attack on a Gaelic Irish crannog. The crannog is situated in a lake set amongst low hills with small patches of woodland. There is a second, abandoned crannog or lakeshore settlement with an unroofed house (hipped roofs) at the opposite end of the lake. The inhabited crannog is slightly angular in shape, with post-and-wattle enclosing fences and three circular thatched houses (Pl. 57). The crannog is being attacked by English cannon, musketry and a small force of infantry, while its inhabitants are also defending themselves with musket fire. In any case, it seems likely that the capture of the crannog on Map V marked a significant moment in the campaign (as important as the capture of Dungannon and the destruction of the inauguration chair at Tullahoge).

Historical accounts describe attacks on two crannogs at this time, at Roughan Lough, Co. Tyrone, and at Magherlocowe, Co. Armagh. Roughan Lough remained in the hands of O'Neill until 1 July 1602, while Magherlocowe was taken later in the campaign. Mountjoy described the attack on Roughan Lough crannog, stating that it was O'Neill's 'strongest island fort'. It was surrendered after the English forces started constructing earthworks on the drylands. The English attackers shown in the depiction seem to be within a rectangular enclosure which already has trees on its ramparts. Although this may be an English fortification, it is more likely to be a field or an abandoned Gaelic settlement. Fynes Moryson's account of the attack in April 1601 on Loghrorcan crannog (Lough Lorcan, Co. Armagh) states that 'a great house upon their (the English) side of the shoare was captured with it, and burnt'. It is apparent that crannogs were part of wider settlement systems, linked with dryland settlements and field systems (Hayes McCoy 1964, 8–10).

Bartlett prepared a second depiction of an attack on a crannog (Map XI) (Pl. 56). This depiction has distinct similarities to that shown on Map V. Hayes-McCoy (1964, 9) suggested that these two sites were one and the same. A crannog is again situated towards the end of a lake. A road runs along one side of the lake; on the other side is extensive woodland. The only other settlement is an isolated house on a nearby hill. The crannog has a post-and-wattle fence enclosure, the wattles again apparently woven around the actual palisade piles. Within the crannog there are three thatched rectangular houses; two have doors depicted. There is also an unusual rectangular wooden framework structure towards the back of the crannog, whose function is unclear. Hayes-McCoy (1964, 20) suggested that it could be a gallows, an unfinished house, or a structure for stretching and drying animal skins. This crannog is also being attacked by English troops with cannon and muskets from a rectangular earthen enclosure with adjacent banks or walls. This enclosure certainly appears to be a field with corn growing in it.

Bartlett also illustrates two crannogs on his map of Monaghan (Map IX), evidently intending to depict the local landscape before English occupation (Pl. 58). The map dates from some time after 1602 (Hayes-McCoy 1964). Two crannogs are situated in a

Pl. 58—*Detail of Richard Bartlett's map of Monaghan, showing crannogs in lake (National Library of Ireland).*

lake fed by a small stream and with low rolling hills, streams and woodland in the vicinity. The smaller crannog has a post-and-wattle palisade or enclosure with a single thatched house. The larger crannog also has a post-and-wattle fence. However, the house on this crannog is highly unusual, with a hipped roof of shingles and a cruciform plan with several gables.

There are several references to Ulster crannogs being used as Gaelic Irish fortifications during the wars of the 1640s, following the 1642 rebellion. A crannog on Lough Shillen, Co. Derry, was attacked in 1642 and 1643, and was abandoned and torched by the Irish defenders in 1645 because of their inability to hold out owing to lack of provisions.

> 'The Coleraine detachment came upon Cormac O'Neill, son of Fedhlim Oge, at Rayleagh and robbed and killed his people, namely the Clann William; thence they proceeded to Lough-Inis-olyn, and to Moneymore, until the two forces were near one another. They collected a great deal of spoil and the creaghts fled south to Dungannon. After plundering far and near, the English returned to Lough-inis-olyn. They sent Rory Ballagh O'Mellan to demand the island from Shane O'Hagan, son of John, son of Edmond Oge. It was refused them. They then fired three shots of a cannon, which they had with them, and departed the place . . .' (Annals of the Four Masters; Wood-Martin 1886a, 149).

Inis O'Luin was attacked again in 1643, when the English cannonaded the crannog and attempted to flood it by blocking up an exit stream in the lake. Finally, the Annals of the Four Masters record that in March 1645 'the people of O'Hagan burned Inis-O'-Lyn, for want of provisions, and followed the general eastwards'. The island was divested of its oak piles, being reduced to an 'unseemly bank, overgrown with reeds and bushes' (Reeves 1857–61a, 157; Wood-Martin 1886a, 149).

A crannog at Lough Annagh, Co. Offaly, seems to have been the location of a battle between the English forces and the Gaelic Irish in 1691. There is corroborative archaeological evidence for this action. Lewis's *Topographical dictionary,* published in

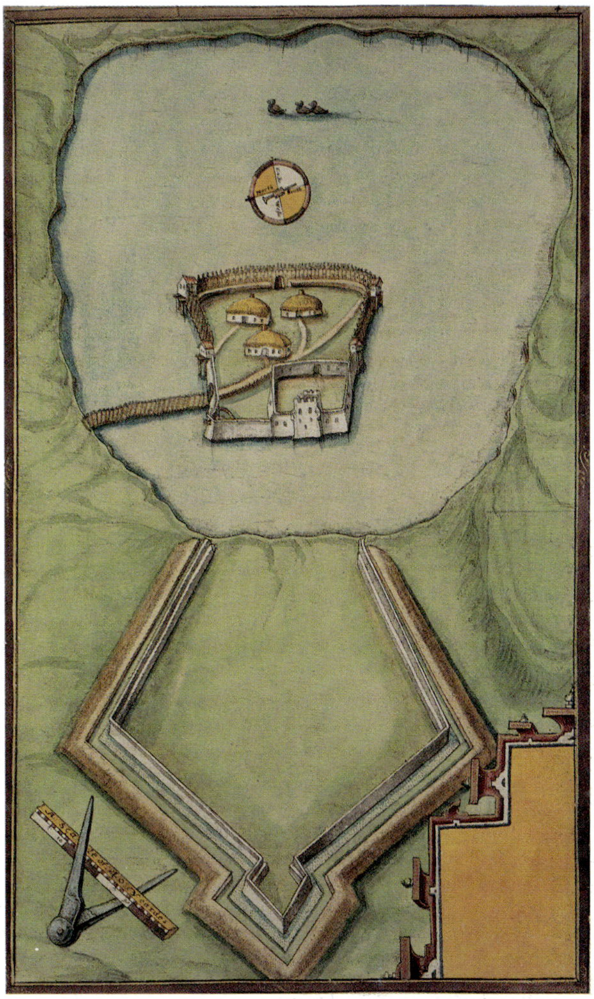

Pl. 59—*Richard Bartlett's map of Agher Castle, a captured Gaelic Irish tower-house and bawn with a star-shaped fort constructed on the drylands (National Library of Ireland).*

Pl. 60—*Parkes Castle, Lough Gill, Co. Sligo (photo: Chris Corlett).*

1837, has a reference to a crannog on the lake, stating that

> 'in the middle of this lake, where it is most shallow, certain oak framing is yet visible and there is a traditional report that in the war of 1641 a party of insurgents had a wooden house erected on this platform, whence they went out at night in a boat and plundered the surrounding country' (Lewis 1837, 175).

The crannog and other finds were described by one T. Stanley, who visited the site in 1868 and 'observed an island-like patch rising a little above the water level; of piles... upwards arranged in lines', with broken querns, burnt brick and stone in the shallow water off the crannog. A wooden road ('a curious bog-pass, made like an American corduroy road') was found on the mainland and may have been the site described as 'the tougher of Malahone', mentioned by Major Edward Wood in his account of a battle between his forces and the Irish army on the neighbouring hill on 4 May 1691. Finds from the crannog included seventeenth-century armour (a iron cuirass), an iron halberd, iron swords, a matchlock and a gun-barrel of small calibre, apart from some other finds of likely Early Historic date. It seems likely that the crannog was either the Irish headquarters or a place of retreat at the time (Wood-Martin 1886a, 208–10).

Gaelic Irish, English and Scottish planter castles on lakes

The Gaelic Irish continued to live in tower-houses and defended residences in the sixteenth century, although they were probably being built in lesser numbers (Pl. 59) (Barry 1987, 186; Cairns 1987, 8–9; McNeill 1997, 228–9). It has been proposed that they were abandoned as dwellings by the early seventeenth century (McNeill 1997, 228–9). However, the English and Scottish planters were also constructing large defended houses and masonry castles in the escheated lands, in architectural styles that were broadly similar to those found in Tudor England and lowland Scotland. These planter castles were occasionally built on earlier Gaelic Irish castles. A large planter castle was built in 1610 on the shores of Lough Gill, at Parkes Castle, Co. Leitrim (Pl. 60), on the site of an earlier fifteenth- to sixteenth-century O'Rourke moated tower-

Pl. 61—*Tully Castle, Lower Lough Erne, Co. Fermanagh (photo: Environment and Heritage Service, DOE(NI)).*

house (Reeves-Smyth 1995, 64; Barry 1987, 189). In Fermanagh, such masonry castles were being placed along both Upper and Lower Lough Erne, occasionally close to the lakeshore (Johnston 1980). At Tully, Co. Fermanagh, a planter castle was built in a Scottish style on an elevation immediately overlooking Lower Lough Erne (Pl. 61) (Johnston 1980; Donnelly 1997). There is a certain amount of English and Scottish planter lake settlement, but much research remains to be done. One interesting feature of planter castles is their occasional continuity with Gaelic Irish crannogs and castles. At Monea Castle, Co. Fermanagh, an early seventeenth-century Scottish-style plantation castle was placed beside a Gaelic Irish crannog in a small drumlin lake. The castle was captured by the Gaelic Irish in the 1641 rebellion and abandoned after 1750. This planter castle was itself, in turn, succeeded by a nineteenth-century landlord demesne house (Evans and Turner 1977, 160). At Ballylough estate, Co. Antrim, the early seventeenth-century estate house of a Scottish tenant was built beside a fifteenth-century tower-house, a motte and a possible crannog (Mallory and McNeill 1991). Thus settlement continuity as well as a profound shift in power and status can be traced in the post-medieval lake settlement landscape.

4. Priorities for archaeological research

Introduction

It has been shown that people have lived by lakeshores in Ireland from the Early Mesolithic to the post-medieval period. Archaeological excavation and survey have investigated the siting and form of crannogs, platforms and palisades, the nature of lithic evidence, metalwork crafts, industry, foraging, fishing and hunting, and the role of lake settlements in local, territorial and regional settlement organisation. Much is known about the archaeology of individual sites, structures, finds and environments. However, future lake settlement research should now move on to a more integrated understanding of the role of lake settlement in the wider social and economic landscapes of the past. This landscape, contextual and social approach should be central to future research and will enable new questions to be asked of a subject that has been part of Irish archaeology since its origins. A lake settlement project should adopt a long-term, regional viewpoint, committed to investigating the full scope of past human activities in Irish lakelands.

Lake settlements are complex, highly rewarding subjects for archaeological research, informing perspectives of time and place in the Irish landscape. These sites can be understood in terms of both the short term (the everyday life of their inhabitants) and the long term (settlement continuities/discontinuities and the processes of site construction, occupation and abandonment). They can be investigated in terms of their profound links with environmental change, such as seasonal and long-term changes in water-levels, ecology and ecosystems. Lake settlements can be classified in terms of settlement size (work-site, hunting camp, homestead and village) and assessed in terms of their settlement duration (permanent, seasonal, periodic or occasional) and social organisation (power, ethnicity, kin-group, rank, prestige, age and gender). Such settlements vary in their economic function (extraction sites, farmsteads, manufacturing and trading centres), in their population (stable to fluctuating, individual, family or community) and in their role in politics, conflict and warfare (defensive refuges, military or offensive sites in rival territories). Sacred and symbolic beliefs also influenced the character and location of some lacustrine settlements (spatial organisation, cult or votive deposition sites, burials, ritual structures or the wider influence of sacred landscapes). Indeed, the term 'settlement' itself is a complex subject, rarely defined or explained. As the landscapes of lake settlements are archaeologically rich and complex, they require ambitious programmes of long-term, multidisciplinary research to realise their full potential. It is proposed in this chapter that three main themes should be explored.

Settling down and moving about

Introduction

An important theme in lake settlement archaeology that has emerged in this study is the constantly changing balance between settling down and moving on, with people living and working for years on permanently occupied settlements or staying for only months, weeks or days on temporary or seasonal camps. This study has shown that lake settlements could have been occupied on a permanent (i.e. all year round), semi-permanent (for most of the year), seasonal (for months), periodic (regular) or occasional (irregular) basis. The duration of occupation was determined by the function of the site. Fishing, fowling, hunting, cattle transhumance, royal tours and the use of temporary defended refuges are all activities that could have led to mobile settlement strategies. It is not always a question of settlement size or culture; some would argue that even the large Early Historic crannogs were only seasonal lodges occupied by the king at certain times of the year. On the other hand, there is strong archaeological evidence that many lake settlements were permanent residences, occupied for long periods, and that they were central to, rather than marginal to, the settlement landscape.

Thus settlement permanence and mobility should be a key theme for investigation in lake settlement archaeology. Indeed, an exploration of the balance between permanent and mobile settlements can usefully inform us about wider aspects of early Irish society. It seems possible that some elements of settlement mobility and even nomadism were a continuous feature of the entire span of human settlement in Ireland, from the Early Mesolithic seasonal extraction camps to any potential sites associated with post-medieval cattle transhumance. Furthermore, if it is important to investigate how long people stayed on a settlement site, it is equally important to understand what they were actually doing there. The various types of house structures, domestic activities and industrial crafts carried out on a site define its function, in essence its sense of home. Finally, if settlement permanence and mobility is being investigated, then we need to look at the means by which people move about in lakelands, exploring the relationship between overland and waterborne travel and communications.

Hearth and home

What did lake settlements actually look like? How were they built? What size were they? What did people do there? These descriptive criteria comprise perhaps the most elementary research theme. Yet there have been few attempts at reconstructing the appearance, size and form of houses, huts, defences and other structures of lake settlements. We know little of how Mesolithic and Neolithic lakeshore occupations were organised in terms of hearths, working floors and house structures. Bronze Age, Early Historic and Viking Age lake settlements must also have been spatially organised in complex ways, in terms of housing, cooking and storage areas and industrial workspaces. Does the organisation of space in settlements change according to their size, status and function? Is it possible to identify such variations in the form and layout of Early Historic and Viking Age crannogs? Given that historic Irish rural settlement was typically dispersed, do Early Historic and medieval crannogs and castles on islands serve as centres for production and regional redistribution? What is the functional relationship between lake settlements and their ancillary structures, such as causeways, stone platforms or fishing/fowling stations? Is it possible to identify the wider landscapes of lake settlements, with the contemporary use of crannogs, stone platforms, enclosures or ringforts, field systems and routeways? What was the nature of the domestic, economic and industrial activities that were practised on lake settlements? Are the Mesolithic and Neolithic lithic scatters evidence for the production of certain types of tools, and why were they located on lakeshores? Were Bronze Age lake settlements the centres for agricultural production or crafts, or were they ritual deposition sites and communal gathering-places? How were crafts organised within crannogs and monastic lake settlements? Were Early Historic and Viking Age crannogs centres for metalworking and glass-working on an industrial scale, for re-circulation by a king to the peoples of wider territories, or were they producing goods only for their inhabitants?

Settlement permanence and mobility

How long did people stay on the lakeshore? What were the patterns of settlement permanence and mobility? How were they related to the seasonal and natural rhythms of lake resources and water-levels? How did these patterns of sedentary living and mobility change through time? Were Mesolithic and Neolithic lakeshore occupation sites temporary or seasonal fishing/fowling and lithic production sites or more permanent habitations? If the former, where are the contemporary base-camps or permanent residences? Were Bronze Age lake settlements also occupied on a periodic or seasonal basis, or were they permanent settlements occupied for several years? Indeed, how would we differentiate between Bronze Age defended refuges/hunting camps and permanent farmsteads, high-status settlements and ritual sites? Did the isolation and insulation of lake settlements lead to their use as temporary refuges in periods of conflict and warfare, or were they actually permanently occupied domestic settlements? The answers probably lie in understanding the role of these sites in the wider landscape. Were Early Historic and Viking Age crannogs only seasonal lodges, served from more permanent settlements on the drylands? Alternatively, is there not also good archaeological evidence for these sites being the permanent residences of small communities, repaired and reconstructed over several generations and serving as industrial and agricultural settlements? Early Historic and Viking Age monastic islands, island cashels and ringforts were probably occupied on a permanent basis, raising the question of how we are biased in our interpretation of wetland sites. Should some Early Historic crannogs and monastic islands be viewed as way-stations or hostels for travellers moving through the lakelands? Other sites were definitely located in isolated lakes away from such potential contacts. It may be interesting to identify the differences in form, siting and date of such lake settlements. Post-medieval crannogs are typically seen as military refuges, occupied only during the wars of the sixteenth and seventeenth centuries. However, it may well be the case that these were full-time residences of lords and their families. Indeed, the historical references seem to indicate that they had a range of functions, such as ammunition stores, gold and silver hoards, hospitals and military strongholds. It would be interesting to explore the role of these settlements in the wider late medieval and post-medieval Gaelic Irish landscape.

Living on the water and moving through the landscape

Life on the water can be investigated in terms of both local and regional communications. It has recently been proposed that pathways through woods and wetlands were important to Mesolithic hunter-gatherers in their perception of the landscape, while places embedded within bounded territories were important to Neolithic farmers. This argument has been extended to the later prehistoric period, so that it is believed that routeways were not as socially important to Bronze Age, Iron Age, Early Historic and medieval farmers, who were supposedly entirely settled within territories. However, lake settlement archaeology argues for the continued importance of seasonality, settlement mobility and movement through the landscape, and these will be useful themes to explore in the future. What was the role of lake settlements in the movement of people, animals and goods through the Irish landscape? Isolation in terms of dryland is not the same as the situation on water, where dugout canoes, coracles or plank-built boats would have provided rapid transport across territories and regions. Indeed, some Irish lakelands could have provided access to the sea and to peoples abroad. Mesolithic and Neolithic lake settlements are frequently situated on islands in vast areas of wetland. Bronze Age lake settlements have produced evidence for dugout boats and boat paddles, while the Iron Age Lough Lene boat-plank is unique evidence for navigation in the period. Several Early Historic crannogs have produced dugout canoes and sloping wooden quays, and monastic islands appear to be situated on routeways. There is also good historical evidence for Viking fleets on several Irish lakes and the use of naval warfare amongst the Gaelic Irish and Anglo-Normans. Medieval ships and boats were probably constantly plying the waters of Ireland's lakes.

What is the archaeology of boats and ships in Irish lakelands? Can we identify nodes and pathways of communications through lakelands, taking into account currents, channels, fords, winds and proximity to settlements? How might such nautical routeways have affected the surrounding social and economic landscape? Is it possible to assess, through experimental archaeology, the speed and range of dugout boats, cots and plank-boats on lakelands, and how might such rates of travel be tested against settlement patterns?

Settlements in their social, economic and sacred landscapes

Introduction

Lake settlements were situated in wider landscapes, their location influenced by physical setting, economic resources, social organisation and ritual beliefs. Although individual lake settlements have been shown to be highly rewarding places for investigation, there has been little attempt to place them in their social, economic and sacred landscapes. By widening the scope of our enquiries to include the wider landscapes of lake settlements, we will be able to ask many more questions of this archaeological record.

Landscapes and society

Settlement archaeology is generally recognised as one of the most important means of tracing past social organisation. However, it should be remembered that society is organised both vertically (in terms of power, prestige, hierarchies and rank) and horizontally (through the ties of family, kin, community, ethnicity, gender and age). Both of these aspects of social organisation should be important themes for lake settlement research. Can we move towards a social interpretation of the activities of Mesolithic forager-fishers in the lakelands? What was the population density, social organisation and territorial control of the Mesolithic hunter-gatherer communities that moved through lakeland landscapes? Are these questions simply not amenable to archaeological enquiry? Can wider emerging social hierarchies be recognised in Neolithic and Bronze Age lake settlement archaeology? Were Bronze Age lake settlements high-status, élite settlements, domestic farmsteads or defended refuges, or were they all of these at the one time? Were all Early Historic, Viking Age and medieval crannogs high-status or royal centres, or is that the case with only a select few? Can historically identified Early Historic and medieval lake settlements and their territories be integrated with this archaeological evidence? Were Bronze Age and Early Historic lake settlements situated at the centre or the margins of political territories? Were they situated adjacent to communication networks or were they in remote, isolated locations? Were the distribution and siting of lake settlements or the organisation of space within individual lake settlements a reflection of stratification within contemporary society? How did crannogs serve as centres of rebellion and resistance in the sixteenth and seventeenth centuries?

Landscapes: economy and production

Lake settlements can also be investigated in terms of their role in the exploitation and management of the economic landscape. These economic resources included the rich harvest of the wetlands, such as fish, fowl and raw materials, and the products of the managed, agricultural landscape. Is it possible to trace changes and shifts in the relative importance of wild and agricultural resources throughout history? Were lake settlements centres for the production and exchange of other goods, such as pottery, worked stone, wooden artefacts, skins and hides, and more exotic, imported goods? It should be recognised that the role of lake settlements in the management of the landscape is open to study in all periods. In the Mesolithic, the open clearings typically found on river and lake margins may have been deliberately kept open by periodic tree clearance and burning of vegetation. On the other hand, does the lack of large browsing animals in post-glacial Ireland make this unlikely? Is there any evidence for contacts between Late Mesolithic forager-fishers and Early Neolithic farmers in lakelands? Bronze Age, Early Historic and Viking Age lake settlements typically produce domesticated faunal assemblages, but relatively few wild animals or fish remains are found, while gathered wild plant foods do not appear to have been very important. Is this true or is it the result of poorly investigated archaeological and palaeobotanical deposits on lake settlement sites? The role of Early Historic and medieval lake settlements in the management of the agricultural landscape is an important area of enquiry. What is the spatial relationship between lake settlements and soil types, geology, aspect, drainage, water-levels and ease of movement, or is it the case that agriculture is actually one of the less important factors in their siting? Were they sited to provide access to good grazing land, arable fields, coppiced woodland and water? How might we identify a typical farm unit? Can agricultural mobility and transhumance be traced in the historical and archaeological record for the Early Historic and late medieval periods?

Industrial production and crafts are another important aspect of the economic landscape in which lake settlements are located. Mesolithic and Neolithic lake settlements may have been lithic production sites, with hunting and fishing going on at the same time. How are these lake settlements sited in terms of proximity to such resources? There is abundant archaeological evidence for bronze-working and crafts on Bronze Age lakeshores. Early Historic and Viking Age crannogs and monastic islands were also centres for bronze-working, the production of glass and iron-working. Some Early Historic lake settlements may have been entirely focused on metalworking. It is also the case that these lake settlements may have served as centres for redistribution and exchange in the surrounding landscape; glass, amber, stone, and Mediteranean pottery have all been found on lake settlements. Viking Age coin hoards, hack silver and ingots have all been found in the midland lakes: are these a result of trade or the aggrandisement of local polities? Is it the case that specialist craftworkers were present on lake settlements, supported by an agricultural surplus and patronised by a secular and ecclesiastical élite?

Landscapes: the sacred and the profane

The traditional emphasis in settlement studies has been on subsistence, economy and production. Recently, archaeologists have been exploring the role of social and ideological beliefs in the organisation of settlement systems. In particular, it is now accepted that religious beliefs and practices and the concept of sacred landscapes need to be integrated with settlement studies. This recognises that people in the past rarely separated the sacred and the profane, that ritual was part of everyday life and that therefore it must be searched for in the settlement record. Sacred sites may be embedded in the settlement landscape, while the siting, form and character of individual settlements may be influenced by their proximity to sacred landscapes. Mesolithic hunter-gatherers may have had highly complex cosmological beliefs and concepts of sacred pathways through lakelands, but these are probably almost impossible to trace in the archaeological record. Neolithic megalithic tombs are known from lakelands, and it may be possible to use these to gain a better understanding of settlement and society in these sacred landscapes. Bronze Age lake settlements are often found in association with, or close to, metalwork tool and ornament hoards or single finds of swords, spearheads and axes placed in watery locations. These patterns may be a useful means of exploring the relationship between the sacred and the profane. Is it possible to trace elements of pagan beliefs and practices on historic period lakeland sites? Early Historic lake settlements could be explored as an integrated pattern of secular or royal crannogs with monastic sites, hermitages, pilgrimage sites and churches. Medieval and late medieval abbeys and monasteries are also frequently sited on lakeshores. What is the relationship between such secular and ecclesiastical settlements in terms of power, politics, society and economy?

Settlement across time, continuity and change

Introduction

The archaeology of lake settlement in Ireland can be traced across vast spans of time, from the Mesolithic to the post-medieval period. Within that archaeological record can be seen striking continuities in the settlement landscape, with the reuse of particular sites over long periods. There are, equally, many examples of complete settlement abandonment and landscape transformation, with sites occupied for only a few years and then totally deserted. These continuities and discontinuities can only be understood by reference to the wider landscape. The archaeology of lake settlement must also be profoundly linked with patterns of environmental change; this too is best understood over long periods of time.

Tracing settlement continuities

How do lake settlements fit in with patterns of continuity and long-term occupation in the Irish landscape? It is a striking feature of the archaeology of lake settlement that many excavated sites have proved to be multiperiod in origin, with some crannogs producing a combination of Mesolithic, Neolithic, Bronze Age, Early Historic and late medieval settlement evidence. What are the reasons for these astonishing long-term settlement continuities? Is it possible that a 'sense of place', conveyed through placenames, folklore, stories and songs, created an ongoing ethnic and community identity whereby particular sites became increasingly important across time, despite the vastness of that time-frame? This could be explored in detail for the medieval and post-medieval periods, where crannogs and island settlements do seem to reflect a sense of personal and community identity with earlier traditions. Ironically, such continuities can also be traced in the forms of Anglo-Norman lake settlements and Scottish and English planter castles on lakeshores, but with a critical difference. These were possibly intended to take over from, and transform, native sites, reflecting profound shifts in power and culture. Indeed, it may have been that particular lakes become more important in the landscape for such social and historical reasons. On the other hand, were lake settlements reoccupied simply for practical reasons, because drier pieces of lakeshore and raised mounds in swampy ground naturally become the focus of settlement activity through time? Do these settlement continuities merely reflect local topographical, social and historical factors, whereby the history of settlement, proximity to good agricultural land and an advantageous situation on routeways mean that sites become reoccupied over long periods? Do these continuities reflect some kind of long-term settlement stability rather than a dynamic reinterpretation of the past by human populations?

Settlement transition and change

How can lake settlement archaeology inform us about critical periods of transition and change in the Irish landscape? The Mesolithic/Neolithic transition, the Late Bronze Age/Iron Age transition, the emergence of Early Historic societies in the fourth and fifth centuries AD, and the clash of, and acculturation between, separate cultural traditions in the medieval and post-medieval periods are all critical to our understanding of the development of Irish society. Are the apparent increased activities on lakeshores in the Late Mesolithic, the Late Bronze Age and the Early Historic period a reflection of wider social and economic developments? Is there really a lack of lake settlement activity in the Neolithic and the Iron Age? Could lake settlement studies produce hitherto unrecognised settlement evidence from these periods? Is the absence of lake settlements in the Iron Age a confirmation of the general absence of Iron Age domestic evidence, or is it due to the failure to recognise Iron Age material in the morass of undated iron objects or undiagnostic material from lake settlements? There are many critical questions relating to settlement transition and change in medieval, late medieval and post-medieval Ireland. How can the reaction of Gaelic Ireland to invasion and gradual subjugation be traced in lake settlement archaeology? Were lake islands and crannogs abandoned as a settlement form or did they actually become more important? Furthermore, many lake settlements were constructed, abandoned and completely forgotten. The processes of settlement abandonment and discontinuities are as important to our understanding of the landscape as continuity.

Settlement and environmental change

The reconstruction of landscape and environment must come to the fore in lake settlement studies. These sites were intimately associated with the natural world, the rhythms of the seasons, the dangers of flooding, storms and wave action, and the use of raw materials of clays, wood, water and stone. In the short term and over generations, people living in lake settlements could have had a great impact on the local and regional environment. Since earliest times, the inhabitants of lakeshores and islands could have cleared or coppiced woodlands for agricultural use, gathered wild foods and plants, grazed cattle on marshes, and tended agricultural fields. There are probably few better places to live when times are good. All of this activity would be recorded in the preserved pollen, diatom, beetle, molluscan and macrofossil evidence from settlements and their watery environs, and should be studied in detail. However, there is also a long-term and global perspective on settlement and environmental change. It is known that climate and environment have changed greatly over thousands of years in Ireland. The archaeology of lake settlement provides us with an opportunity to examine the relationship between social and environmental change at a key location. Dramatic climatic deterioration, increased rainfall, floods, snows, frosts, and periods of cold will be felt all the more harshly on a lake site. Furthermore, as neighbouring uplands are abandoned, communities living in wetlands will find their territories and resources contested by other peoples. In conclusion, tracing the relationship between social and environmental change would be a vital aspect of lake settlement studies.

Conclusions

In conclusion, the many archaeological questions outlined above are clearly wide-ranging and in many ways highly ambitious in terms of their objectives. Nevertheless, these are the questions that spring from the intrinsic nature of the archaeology of lake settlement in Ireland, which itself is rich, complex and arguably largely unresolved. It is argued that future research on lake settlement archaeology should aim to answer at least some of these questions. However, it is also possible to isolate two main questions for a lake settlement project. (i) What are the patterns of change and continuity in lake settlement and environment across time? (ii) What was the role of lake settlements in their wider social and economic landscapes? A project that starts with these elemental questions will be tackling the heart of the subject.

5. THEORETICAL AND METHODOLOGICAL APPROACHES

Introduction

The archaeology of lake settlement is clearly a complex subject. It will require complex, multidisciplinary approaches to bring out its full potential. In this chapter it will be argued that particular theoretical and interpretative approaches will need to be used in future studies, focused on regional landscapes, through various scales of analysis over long time-periods. It is also clear that a wide range of investigative techniques will have to be used, such as geophysics, aerial photography, satellite imagery, underwater archaeology, archaeological survey and excavation, and a range of specialist studies. The importance of multidisciplinary approaches is stressed, as lake settlement archaeology must be studied through the lenses of history, folklore, placename studies, historical geography and palaeoenvironmental studies or we will understand little of it.

Landscape archaeology, an integrated approach to settlement and society

Traditionally, settlement archaeology has primarily been concerned with studying the interaction between past human communities and their environment. Hence many settlement studies have adopted environmental, functionalist and economic perspectives and have concentrated on the structural, spatial and physical organisation of settlement (house, village and town) and the economic exploitation of the natural landscape. However, settlement archaeology has also had a strong tradition of the study of social relationships through archaeological data, whereby the structure and the development of society can be traced through settlement investigations (Trigger 1978, 168–9; 1989, 282–3; Knapp 1997, 4). Recently, it has been recognised that social relationships, production and economy are only part of the human landscape, and that ideological and sacred beliefs were just as important in the patterning of past settlement landscapes. There have been a wide range of theoretical and methodological (e.g. spatial analysis) perspectives in settlement archaeology, reflecting both the importance of the subject and the large amount of scholarship worldwide (Roberts 1996; Knapp 1997). Archaeologists have long had an interest in the settlement landscape, particularly as it refers to the environment, and research projects have typically engaged in integrated multidisciplinary studies employing archaeology, history, geography, placename studies, folklore and palaeoenvironmental studies. Most recently, the emergence of Geographic Information Systems (GIS) has enabled large data-sets to be manipulated in the investigation of settlement patterns (e.g. Gaffney and Stancic 1991).

Recently an innovative theoretical perspective has emerged under the heading of 'landscape archaeology', which is as much a philosophical stance as a series of investigative techniques. There is great potential for settlement studies in adopting the landscape archaeological perspective, which has proven to be diverse, flexible and imaginative in its approach (Bender 1993; 1996; R. Bradley 1993; 1997b; Tilley 1994; Hirsch 1995; Rossignol and Wandsnider 1992; Fleming 1996; Schama 1995; Grogan, forthcoming). It has mostly been used in the study of prehistoric landscapes, but there have been recent attempts to interpret landscapes in the historic period (Austin and Thomas

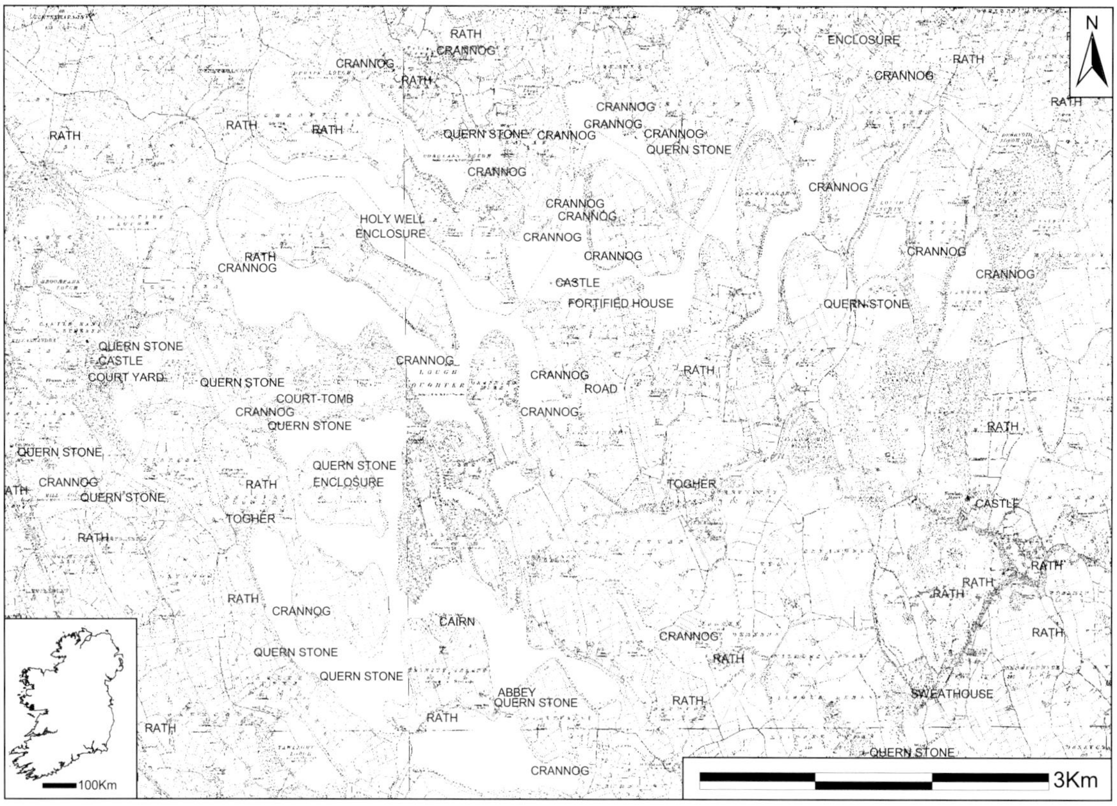

Fig. 35—*Map of Lough Oughter, Co. Cavan. The waterlogged nature of this landscape of river, lake and drumlin hills would have had a profound impact on the settlement patterns of the region (map by Amanda Kelly, based on the records of the National Monuments Service, Dúchas—The Heritage Service).*

1996). Landscape archaeology attempts to integrate the many influences, whether social, ideological, experiential, historical or environmental, on the range of human activities in the landscape. It argues that people live in all the layered landscapes that are formed by these influences, which in turn are interwoven within the complex tapestry of society. The theoretical structure of landscape archaeology has yet to be adequately defined, a reflection of the fact that its origins are eclectic and inspired by developments in the theoretical approaches of both the Processual (e.g. Rossignol and Wandsnider 1992) and Post-Processual schools (Bender 1993; Tilley 1994). It has been described as 'total archaeology' (Fleming 1996), but as writing a total archaeology is impossible, most landscape archaeologists recognise the need to identify and acknowledge 'a point of view'. For example, the 'point of view' in this study is that past societies and their landscapes in Ireland can usefully be explored through an analysis of the archaeology of lake landscapes.

There are many different types of human landscape. There is the *physical landscape,* where the setting of lake settlements is influenced by the character of a lake, by a location's water-depth and shelter from prevailing winds and currents, and by its proximity to river mouths or dryland resources. The nature of the local terrain, in terms of the lakebed sediments (silts, sands or rocks), local vegetation (reed beds, marshes, fens, woodlands) and dryland (soils, drainage and topography), are also aspects of the physical landscape which may have been an influence. The *historic landscape* or the *landscape of the past* may also have been an important factor. There is often considerable continuity in lake settlement archaeology, whereby crannogs produce Mesolithic, Neolithic, Bronze Age and historic period occupations. Landscapes of memory may be responsible for the recreation of these settlements and for the perpetual use of, particular places in the landscape. The *sacred landscape* was also important, whereby religious beliefs about supernatural forces or nature and beliefs about the appropriateness of particular locations for secular activities may have affected lake settlement. The creation and maintenance of sacred landscapes (e.g. megalithic tomb and barrow cemeteries) makes ritual power an important element in the settlement landscape. This phenomenon can also be traced in the historic period, whereby monastic centres, holy wells and burials could have played a part in everyday, and indeed long-term, decisions about settlement siting. It also needs to be recognised that ritual cannot be separated from the secular. People's ritual beliefs and practices were part of their everyday lives. The *social landscape* was a key factor in the structuring and organisation of past settlements. Past societies are often studied in terms of their social hierarchies, rank, authority and power, but it should be remembered that societies are also organised horizontally. The ties of kin, family, age and gender would have influenced past settlement patterns. The internal space of a house could have been organised for such social reasons. People who lived by lakes, or moved through them on the way to other places, would have had wider contacts with communities around them. Proximity to neighbours would have created a dense network of social relations to be observed in the wider landscape. It is possible that several lake settlements were occupied at the same time in one lake, creating in effect a village community linked by water transport. At a regional level, lake-dwellers had contacts through trade, communications and social/political networks with communities living at some distance from the lake. Lake settlements were variously centres for aggression, power and resistance, and their role in social and settlement hierarchies requires research. The *economic landscape* can be studied in terms of foraged resources (plant foods, wild animals and fish), agricultural landscapes (woodland, farmland, arable fields) and industrial resources (wood, clays, metal ores), all of which undoubtedly influenced the siting and distribution of lake settlements. The inhabitants of lake settlements may also have controlled other settlements, field systems and trackways on the neighbouring drylands. In particular, lake settlements may have been sited close to, or far away from, routeways through the landscape (Fig. 35).

Space and place

However, this simple classification of landscapes hides the more complex nature of the theories which underpin landscape archaeology. In particular, many recent works have concentrated on investigating concepts of space and place in the landscape (e.g. Tilley 1994). The concept of 'space' was a product of the New Geography of the 1960s, and was taken up by processual archaeologists who saw space as the abstract backdrop to human behaviour. Spatial analysis was seen as an important means of recognising settlement *patterns* (the spatial distribution of settlements across the landscape) and deriving from them an insight into settlement *systems* (the social and economic relationship between sites in this settlement pattern) (Knapp 1997, 5). Site catchment analysis, nearest-neighbour analysis, Theissen polygons, central place theory and other spatial analytical techniques were used to explore the broad-scale relationship between sites, often against an abstract, undifferentiated space within which there was little room for individual human action. However, there are alternative views of 'space', which are more focused on human experience and the reality of the world around us. Tuan (1977) proposed rather different concepts, focusing on people's experience of the world at different stages of their life and their great need for a sense of belonging and attachment to places. More recently, landscape archaeologists have explored such aspects as Mesolithic hunter-gatherers' and Neolithic farmers' different phenomenological experience of space (Tilley 1994), Neolithic farmers' perception of cosmological space (Darvill 1997), and the interpretation of the use of space in Neolithic megalithic tombs (Thomas 1993) or houses (Grøn *et al.* 1991). We can also trace the emergence of a 'sense of place' in landscape archaeology (Cooney and Grogan 1994). It emerged first

Pl. 62—*Aerial photograph of Lough Derravarragh, Co. Westmeath. There is archaeological evidence for settlement by the shores of this lake since earliest times, from the Mesolithic to the post-medieval period (photo: Aerofilms Ltd).*

amongst some processual archaeologists as a recognition that people use different places in the landscape (many of them off-site or away from settlements) for different reasons (Knapp 1997, 10). However, 'places' are not only mere locations in the physical landscape, but could be important in terms of time (identified in stories with particular people, communities or events), culture or beliefs. An individual's sense of place in the landscape can be based on his or her personal history, social rank, age, gender, etc. There is no 'place' in the landscape which does not require such a human context to explain it. The recently developed concept of 'pathways' can be added to 'places', emphasising the movement of people through the landscape and through time, so that places can be situated both on routeways through the human landscape and on a path of development through time (Tilley 1994; R. Bradley 1997a; 1997b).

Time

The landscapes of settlement develop slowly across potentially vast time-spans, with people and environment, continuity and change, growth and decline the constant themes of the archaeological record. Archaeological methods of studying time include typological studies, radiocarbon dating, dendrochronological dating and comparative archaeology, but these vary in subtlety and resolution. The telescoping of this past time, whereby hundreds of years become the same to us as ten, is one of the problematical features of archaeological research. For example, in prehistory the archaeological record must be synthesised across hundreds or even thousands of years, contrasting with the historic period, when we have the burden of dealing with evidence calibrated in months or years. How can we write archaeology that covers vast time-spans or crosses the artificial prehistoric/historic divide? Recently archaeologists have explored some approaches to time of the French *Annales* school of historical studies, whereby settlement and landscape can be investigated at a number of different time-scales (Bintcliff 1991; 1996; Gosden 1994; R. Bradley 1997b). The *longue durée* provides a long-term, structural perspective on social and environmental change, and could be used to investigate the origins, development and changes in lake settlement from prehistory to post-medieval times. What were the deep, underlying and essential attractions of life on the lakeshore? How was the landscape settled across vast spans of time? Can particular places be picked out as being important at all times, for all people? This approach makes us search for an understanding of the rhythms of life in the landscape as it is lived by an individual person or community, their *modes de vie*, and encourages us to trace people's world-view and perception of the landscape, their *mentalités*. The medium-term perspective, the *moyenne durée,* focuses on *conjunctures* (trends) or developments within shorter periods of time, from hundreds of years to a single person's lifespan, within which the history of communities can be written while change can be more easily explored. The medium-term perspective can be brought to bear on such themes as the Late Mesolithic/Neolithic transition, the agricultural expansion of the Late Bronze Age and the decline of the early Iron Age, and the changing patterns of settlement across the medieval period. Landscape and settlement studies can also focus on the impact of particular historical or political events or the actions of individuals. This is the world of *événements*, whereby we explore the archaeology of settlement at the time-scale of life as it is lived at a particular moment, from day to day or through the year. This approach can also zero in on particular points in time, posing the questions, for example, 'what was it like to live on an Early Historic crannog in the year AD 652, or how was the battle won and lost at this crannog in July 1602?' It should be pointed out that the *Annales* approaches should not be adopted as a theoretical banner or an impressive bibliographical icon, but actually tried out on the Irish archaeological record (Pl. 62).

Regional perspectives

The landscape approach to space, place and time demands that projects investigate settlement and society at a series of different geographical and temporal scales (such as settlement site, locality, micro-region and region). There has also always been a concern in settlement studies to define appropriate scales of analysis. Trigger (1978), for example, proposed that settlement could be viewed as operating within three different levels: (i) building or structure, (ii) communities, and (iii) distribution of communities. Recent studies in landscape archaeology have also been concerned with the definition of appropriate scales of analysis, and it is considered that landscape archaeology is best carried out within a regional context (Crumley and Marquardt 1987; Gaffney and Stancic 1991; Knapp 1997; Grogan *et al.* 1995; 1996; Astill and Davies 1997). The size of this study region is predicated by a number of factors, such as the archaeological questions being asked, the nature of a region's physical terrain, the intensity and quality of its archaeological record, and the staff and resources available to a project. More and more, landscape archaeologists are interested in the micro-region and the locality, which in spatial terms could range from a thousand square kilometres to an area of only some tens of kilometres. However, landscape archaeological projects can also look outside a region, contrasting and comparing its record with another, or with a national picture.

Michael Ryan's (1996, 159) description of the ideal research strategy for an understanding of Early Historic and Viking Age settlement and economy is a useful outline of how regional settlement studies should progress:

> 'Research . . . would begin with the formulation of archaeologically meaningful questions—not often attempted—and it would proceed by means of intensive conventional archaeological survey of a limited area, exhaustive fieldwalking, aerial reconnaissance, application of remote sensing techniques to promising sites and selective excavation to attempt to shed light on clearly-defined problems . . . Such a study should not be period-specific and it should attempt to relate the archaeological evidence for early medieval activity with that of later prehistory and with the Later Medieval period'.

Mallory and McNeill (1991, 335) also recognised the potential usefulness of the regional approach in exploring long-term changes and continuities in society and environment. They emphasise the importance of wetland sites:

> 'These aims of exploring environmental and social links lead towards the intensive study of a particular area. This could be studied either at a certain chosen period, where sites can be identified, such as megaliths, raths or mottes, or else through time. The more we think of such questions, the more we are led to demand that we study sites where organic remains might be preserved in wet conditions. In either case the study would require two things. One is a long-term commitment to it by a team of people with expertise, not just in the field of the archaeology of the period, but also of environmental study and documentary evidence. The second commitment would be that this should be done as a matter of research, as opposed to response to a threat of destruction'.

Indeed, it seems likely that a regional study of settlement around lakes could make a great contribution to Irish archaeology. Lake settlements could be investigated at various scales, national, regional, local and site-based. Lake settlement could be examined on a national basis, through long-term research, survey and excavation. The existing literature could be used as a basis for writing major thematic reviews (e.g. Late Bronze Age lake settlement in Ireland). The regional scale is a more effective approach, using particular study areas (midlands, north-west, Connemara) for a rather more detailed review of the evidence. A regional study would be multiperiod, focusing on key issues depending on the area (i.e. the monastic islands of Lough Ree). Lake settlement research could focus on the local, site and micro-site (house, workspace) scale.

Multidisciplinary approaches

Archaeology alone cannot tell the story of lake settlement. Any future programme of research on the subject will have to adopt multidisciplinary approaches. This should certainly include the work of scholars in early Irish, medieval and early modern history. The settlement of lakelands in the historic period can only be fully understood through the use of their sources, such as the genealogies, annals, hagiographies, law tracts, topographical texts and pseudo-historical literature. This work could best be carried out by a full-time researcher, occasionally meeting the needs of a lake settlement project, but also setting an independent historical research agenda. There is also the topographical evidence of bardic poetry and onomastics, while Early and Middle Irish sagas and mythological tales could provide interesting insights. For example, the late medieval story of the tragic fate of the Children of Lir (*Oidheadh Chlaine Lir*) describes how they reputedly spent seven years in the form of swans on Lough Derravarragh, Co.

Pl. 63—*Medieval woodworking axes from the foreshore of Lough Gara, Co. Sligo (photo: David Jennings, Dept of Archaeology, UCD).*

Westmeath (Ó hÓgáin 1991, 272). The lake is now known to be rich in prehistoric and historic settlement sites. There are also a range of later historical sources to be used, right up to the estate records and cartographic sources of the eighteenth and nineteenth centuries. Placename studies can be used to trace the origins of townland and local names around the lakes and to show how they relate to topography and settlement history. Folklore and ethnological studies would be important in lake settlement studies, tracing local traditions, boat routeways and economies on the lakes. For example, there are a range of types of boats (dugouts, reed-rafts, cots) that were used until recently on Ireland's lakes, now no longer in existence, that probably derive from much earlier craft. Folklife studies would be a means of tracing their appearance. Lakes could also be studied from an anthropological perspective, exploring the impact of the reality of these particular landscapes on local communities.

A range of scientific disciplines will need to be adopted in lake settlement studies, primarily palaeoenvironmental studies and geophysics (outlined in more detail below), but also those of peat and soil scientists, geologists and physical geographers. Lake settlement archaeology can best be investigated using a combination of archaeological, geophysical and palaeoenvironmental techniques, including the use of aerial photographs, archaeological survey and underwater survey, various remote-sensing techniques and coring programmes. A wide range of potential information on Ireland's lakes is held by other institutions, including the records of the Geological Survey of Ireland, the National Parks and Wildlife Service, regional fishery authorities and local authorities. The Ordnance Survey of Ireland are currently publishing maps with detailed information on topography and contours, based on aerial photographs (the 'Discovery Series' 1:10,000 maps). Bathymetric (underwater contour) surveys have have been carried out on some Irish lakes for purposes of boat navigation and fisheries. There have also been many palaeoenvironmental investigations over the years in the Irish midlands, north-west and west. These would certainly provide a good base for further work.

There is much of value in the approaches of ordinary, everyday archaeological fieldwork. It is still possible to discover new archaeological sites in the Irish landscape,

Pl. 64—*Aerial photograph of Lough-na-Cranagh, Fair Head, Co. Antrim (photo: Environment and Heritage Service, DOE(NI)).*

particularly in places where people tend not to have looked in recent years (e.g. lakeshores). It is true that the concept of the archaeological 'site' has come under attack in recent years, as people argue that an overemphasis on particular places of high archaeological visibility, usually permanent settlement or ritual monuments, ignores the full range of people's activity in the landscape. The idea of 'off-site activity' has become increasingly important, based on the idea of perpetual movement through the wider landscape (Knapp 1997, 12). Nevertheless, there is much that remains useful about investing archaeological resources and energy in the examination of particular archaeological sites. For one thing, they still have much to tell us. A lake settlement project could well be both site-oriented and landscape-oriented. The Archaeological Survey of Ireland, through the published SMR and County Inventories, has provided an invaluable database for lake settlement studies. Some of the counties with the most extensive lakelands (Cavan, Monaghan, Galway) have been published, and other surveys are at an advanced stage (Victor Buckley, pers. comm.). Similar data are available for the archaeology of Northern Ireland, where the detailed archaeological survey of County Down has been published and there are extensive files on sites and monuments in other counties.

There is also much potential for traditional artefact studies. The National Museum of Ireland, the Ulster Museum and a range of local museums hold extensive collections of finds from Irish lakelands, islands and shores. A complete list of prehistoric and medieval artefacts from Irish lakeshores, islands and lakebeds could usefully be carried out, although it would take much time and resources. More detailed work within regional areas could produce more complete catalogues, enabling study of both monument and artefact distributions within an integrated landscape study. Detailed analyses of particular categories of artefacts, such as Mesolithic and Neolithic lithic assemblages (stone axes, retouched tools, waste material) or medieval finds, could also be carried out. Large numbers of Early Historic and medieval finds have recently been found by treasure-hunters on crannogs and lake settlements (Eamonn Kelly, pers. comm.). Artefact studies could have a significant impact on our understanding of the function and character of lake settlements and could also contribute to wider issues in Irish archaeology (Pl. 63).

Aerial photography and satellite imagery

Aerial photography would be an important means of archaeological research, analysis and illustration in a lake settlement project (Pl. 64). It has been shown that crannogs, causeways, jetties and other features can be seen from the air in lake shallows, even in high-level vertical photographs (Morrison 1985, 85). Aerial photography has been a major component of the research carried out on the Swiss lake-dwellings (Arnold 1986) and on the Scottish crannogs (Morrison 1985, 85). The North Munster Project's aerial photographic work over the Late Bronze Age lake settlement of Knocknalappa indicated several shallows and shoals in the lakebed adjacent to the site, and underwater surveys confirmed that archaeological features were present (O'Sullivan 1997a). It can produce large amounts of evidence for settlement, agricultural activity and burial sites, and is a useful means of describing topography and drainage. The most commonly used series in Irish archaeology is the Geological Survey of Ireland (GSI) high-level vertical coverage, typically taken at a scale of 1:30,000. GSI low-level vertical coverage (scale 1:5000) and the Air Corps low-level vertical coverage are also available for some regions. More recent series of aerial photographs are also available, many of very high resolution and stored in digital format. There are a range of low-level oblique aerial photographs useful for archaeologists. The Cambridge University Collection of Air Photographs (CUCAP) taken by the English archaeologist J.K.S. St Joseph (Norman and St Joseph 1969) in the 1960s includes photographs of crannogs and island monasteries, as well as general panoramas of lakelands before the era of modern landscape development and arterial drainage. Infrared aerial photography can be used to trace features in otherwise waterlogged environments. However, Irish archaeologists have made little use of satellite imagery and multi-spectral radar imagery. These would be very useful in a lakeland context because they can be used to locate and classify vegetation zones and ecosystems. Lakes, rivers, wetlands, bogs, woodlands, grasslands and ploughsoil can all be identified on satellite imagery. High-resolution imagery could even locate archaeological features. Air photographs and satellite imagery could also be draped over contour models of landscapes for illustration or analytical purposes.

Geophysics

The use of geophysics is now well established in Irish archaeology (e.g. Newman 1997). However, underwater geophysical surveys have barely begun. Yet they offer the ability to search large underwater areas quickly. They are also capable of providing a continuous data-set at sites which contain both dryland and underwater archaeology. There is an increasing range of geophysical remote-sensing equipment which can be used on underwater sites (Dean *et al.* 1992, 135–44). There are several techniques suitable for archaeological prospecting of shallow lakes, rivers or coastal environments. They all require accurate (sub-metre) locational information, which is usually provided by a Differential Global Positioning System (DGPS). This requires a terrestrial GPS base-station and a roving GPS receiver which accompanies the geophysical equipment as it is being towed on a pontoon over the water surface.

The geophysical techniques may be divided into three main categories, depending upon the physical property being sensed: acoustic, sonar and electromagnetic. Acoustic or sonar techniques measure the time it takes for a pressure pulse (sound wave) to travel from a transmitter on the pontoon to a reflector and then back to a receiver on the pontoon. An echo-sounder is the simplest example. The pulse is reflected from an interface (e.g. the lakebed) where there is a contrast in acoustic impedance between the water and the sediments. The depth to the lakebed can be estimated by knowing the velocity of sound in water. There are more sophisticated types of sonar remote-sensing techniques. Electromagnetic techniques are subdivided into two categories: ground-penetrating radar (GPR) and metal-detectors.

Side-scan sonar

Side-scan sonar is the marine equivalent of aerial photography. It can map bathymetry (underwater contours) or detect features projecting above the surface of the sediments, and can resolve even fairly small structures. Vertical posts, substantial timber beams, stone causeways and other structures may provide sufficient acoustic impedance contrasts with lake-bottom sediments to be visible, provided that the lakebed is not too deep. Side-scan sonar cannot image any structures below the surface. While it has most commonly been used in marine conditions (e.g. Grøn *et al.* 1996), European lake settlement projects that have successfully used side-scan sonar include the Scottish crannog surveys (Morrison 1985, 85, pls 18–19), the Swiss Neolithic and Bronze Age lake settlement projects (e.g. Stickel and Garrison 1988), the underwater survey of the late Viking Age lake fortress at Lake Tingstäde, on Gotland, Sweden (Rönnby 1990), and underwater medieval ship surveys in Lake Constance, southern Germany (Mainberger *et al.* 1995).

'Chirp'

'Chirp' is a towed, wide-band sonar technique that produces high-resolution images of sub-bottom sediments. Like side-scan sonar, it measures the time it takes an acoustic pulse to travel from a transmitter on the pontoon to a reflector and then back to a receiver on the pontoon. However, the acoustic pulses sweep over a frequency range which allows the Chirp signal to penetrate below the lake-bottom sediments. Objects or sediment layers as close as 10cm apart can be resolved at depths of several metres below the lakebed. Chirp is one example of a *sub-bottom profiler* which enables the detection of buried archaeological remains. Other sub-bottom profilers (e.g. Pingers, Boomers) work at a lower frequency range which allows the acoustic energy to penetrate tens of metres in sediments. The advantage of good penetration is offset by a decrease in resolution—typically objects with dimensions of 50cm can be imaged. Sub-bottom profilers are generally used for targeted surveys, to obtain detailed information from already identified structures or features.

Ground-probing radar

Ground-probing radar (GPR) is the electromagnetic equivalent of a sonar sub-bottom profiler. It is used to produce an image of variations in lake-bottom sediment electrical conductivity properties, and can be sensitive to both metallic and non-metallic materials. A short-pulse of high-frequency electromagnetic energy is generated on a transmitting antenna placed on the pontoon, and the pulse travels through the water and into the lakebed sediments. Ground-probing radar has been used with some success in wetland investigations, for example on Viking Age bridges (Schou Jørgensen 1991). GPR offers the advantage that it can be deployed in both a terrestrial and a waterborne mode, thus providing a direct link between surveys carried out from land to water.

Metal-detectors

The well-known damage done to many Irish archaeological sites, including lake settlements, by illegal or irresponsible use of metal-detectors in recent times makes metal-detecting a controversial tool. However, metal-detectors have their role within a properly formulated research design. Underwater metal-detectors work on the principle of electromagnetic induction, whereby an electromagnetic signal induces currents in an electrical conductor. These give rise to a magnetic field which can be detected by the receiver. Metal-detectors can detect both ferrous and non-ferrous objects. They can either be towed behind a boat or smaller versions can be held in the hand. They can be used in an archaeological project in three ways: (a) as part of a remote-sensing survey of a general area; (b) as part of a pre-disturbance survey on a specific site to map possible locations of metal objects; and (c) to investigate an archaeological layer or context immediately prior to its excavation. Future lake settlement projects will have to consider the use of some or all of these techniques.

Palaeoenvironmental studies

Pl. 65—*A sharpened ash post from the Late Bronze Age lake settlement of Clonfinlough, Co. Offaly. Palaeoenvironmental studies of wood can include species identification, tree-ring analysis, beetle studies and rot patterns (photo: Irish Archaeological Wetland Unit).*

Prehistoric and historic lake settlements, whether they were located on the edges and margins of lakes, in the shallow waters by lake foreshores or on lake islands, would have been profoundly influenced in their siting, form and use by the local wetland environment. Lake settlements were subject to the forces of the physical environment in ways that dryland settlements were not. Indeed, lake settlements can have a major impact on the local environment too. Neolithic lake villages in the Alpine region were ultimately abandoned after one or two decades, as the timber of the woodlands adjacent to the lakes became exhausted (J.M. Coles and Coles 1996, 38). Furthermore, increased water-levels and flooding are not merely a source of discomfort but have been shown to be a cause of permanent abandonment of medieval lake settlement sites in France (e.g. Collardelle and Verdel 1993), and Irish crannogs and lake settlements were undoubtedly flooded out on occasion. The environmental contexts of lake settlements mean that their study requires much closer integration with palaeoenvironmental investigations, within multidisciplinary approaches at a series of geographical scales (site, locality and region). A strong emphasis on palaeoenvironmental investigations of lake settlement does not have to lead to explanations driven by environmental determinism, functionalism and the reduction of human communities to the role of mere players on an ecological stage. Palaeoenvironmental studies can also be driven by the theoretical and social questions that comprise the landscape archaeological approach (e.g. O'Sullivan 1996b).

Wetland archaeology shows that the physical environment was not a passive backdrop to, but an active player in, the landscapes of early societies. Wetlands cannot be viewed as merely an abstract, undifferentiated space within which human cultural landscapes are constructed. They are too prone to rapid change; instability is actually their normal status. It is common in archaeology to reconstruct past physical landscapes from geology, soils and drainage, but this is not an option in wetland archaeology, where there are a wide range of potential environments represented by buried stratigraphical deposits (peats, clays, silts). For example, there is a world of a difference between the watery closeness of carr woodland and the open expanses of a raised bog, yet both will produce 'peats'. Because of a lack of any tradition of serious multidisciplinary palaeoenvironmental research, Irish archaeology has generally failed to make use of the diverse, complementary techniques that are part of modern palaeoenvironmental investigations. A lake settlement project would need to be profoundly linked to a palaeoenvironmental research programme.

Lake sediments and peats

Lake sediments and peats act as repositories for various types of palaeoenvironmental evidence, such as macrofossils (organisms detectable by the eye) and microfossils (organisms that require the use of a microscope). Macrofossils include plant remains, molluscs, insects, and bird and animal bone. Microfossils include pollen, diatoms, microscopic crustaceans and charred particles (tiny fragments of charcoal) (Bell and Walker 1992, 23–32). Most palaeoenvironmental investigations concentrate on the fossil evidence preserved in peats and clays, but it is also possible to look at the climatic and environmental evidence buried in the sediments themselves. The stratigraphic, physical, chemical and biological properties of sediments hold information on their deposition patterns and how these patterns change across time. Many wetland settlement sites, structures and finds, now found in raised bogs, were formerly in lakes or ponds. The stratigraphy of peats can be an indicator of climatic and palaeohydrological change, and the presence of sand, ash and minerogenic sediments in peats can also be an indirect indicator of agricultural activity on the drylands. Lake sediments can also record inwash from dryland soil erosion, indicating the exposure of soils through the agricultural clearance of woodlands (Bell and Walker 1992, 29–32).

Fruits, seeds, wood and other plant macrofossils

Plant macrofossils include fruits, seeds, wood and other parts of plants (stems, leaves, buds, scales and spines). They tend to be deposited near the location of the original parent vegetation, but can also be brought onto a site by human, animal or natural agency. They can be used to reconstruct on-site, local and regional vegetation patterns and changes in temperature, climate and rainfall. Most importantly, plant macrofossils can be used to reconstruct the nature of prehistoric and historic economies. The gathering and processing of fruits, nuts, grain and other plant foods on settlement sites can be investigated through macrofossil studies, thus giving vital insights into early diet and subsistence. This approach paid great dividends at Oakbank crannog, Scotland (Clapham and Scaife 1988). Wood and charcoal studies can be used to reconstruct the species composition, age and extent of contemporary woodlands, the deliberate management of such woodlands, and the choices of raw materials made by craftworkers and carpenters (Pl. 65) (O'Sullivan 1994a; 1996c; 1998). Tree-ring studies can also be carried out on structural timbers and the trunks of natural submerged forests to provenance imported timbers, to reconstruct climate changes and, through the use of isotope analyses, to study alteration in precipitation patterns (Baillie 1979; 1995a).

Mollusca

Mollusca are preserved in both dryland and freshwater environments, particularly in sediments containing high calcium carbonate concentrations (e.g. in soils or lake sediments over limestone bedrock). Mollusca are generally habitat-specific, so that their presence on archaeological sites provide insights into past vegetation cover, shade and changes in land use and climate. Mollusca have rarely been used in Irish archaeological studies, although they have been used to explore Mesolithic activities in woodlands (Preece *et al.* 1986).

Fossil insects

The study of insects is a growing aspect of palaeoenvironmental macrofossil investigations. In particular, the Coleoptera (beetles) are known to be highly habitat-specific, different types living in only slightly varying environmental niches. Beetles vary according to water, temperature, soils, and seasons. Regional and local habitats can be assessed from the presence of different beetles. Beetles can also be used to reconstruct human and animal activities on a settlement site (the presence of cow-dung, woodpiles, bedding material, etc.) (e.g. Coope 1981) or to reconstruct the natural wetland environment that surrounded wooden structures (Reilly 1996). Beetle studies would be especially important in an excavation context.

Pollen analysis

Microfossil pollen grains from seed-producing plants and trees are spread over the landscape by wind, water, birds and insects, and are typically preserved in the anaerobic conditions of lake sediments, peats and some soils. Pollen analysis is easily the most commonly used technique for reconstructing past environments. It enables reconstruction of the character, species composition and extent of past woodland cover, the periodic clearance of these woodlands by human populations, and the use of arable crops in the landscape (Edwards 1979). Pollen analysis has proved to be of vital importance in understanding the evolution of the woodlands and vegetation cover of the early Irish landscape, and would be central to any palaeoenvironmental studies of lakelands (Mitchell and Ryan 1997; O'Connell 1980; Molloy 1997). Most pollen studies are carried out by sampling a vertical core of peat or clay at 10–15cm intervals, giving an impression of vegetational change across centuries (e.g. Molloy 1997). Recent developments in palynology have included the use of 'fine resolution pollen analysis', whereby pollen samples are taken at intervals of 1–2mm, which has the potential to supply much more detailed imformation about human activities in the landscape on a year-by-year basis (Bell and Walker 1992). It may be possible to study in detail very localised agricultural activities on lakeshores or to trace the impact of the construction and seasonal use of a lake settlement.

Diatoms, Cladocera and ostracods

Pollen analysis is useful for reconstructing local environmental conditions during periods of peat formation. However, when inorganic sedimentation commences,

Pl. 66—*Archaeologists walking the artificially exposed foreshore of Lough Gara, Co. Sligo, in the 1950s found an astonishing range of sites and finds, such as this stone mound with causeway (photo: Dept of Archaeology, UCG).*

Pl. 67—*Divers working on Goose Island, Lough Ennell: the bamboos mark the location of a crannog's palisade posts (photo: Niall Brady, Crannog Archaeological Project).*

pollen cannot give such precise information. The alternative source of information is diatoms—microscopic unicellular algae that live in lakes, ponds, estuaries and the sea. Their distribution is controlled by acidity, salinity, oxygenation, water depth, temperature and vegetation cover. Microfossil diatoms are found in lake muds and can be used to reconstruct changes in water-levels, vegetation, climatic cycles and human activities around lakes. Diatoms have increasingly been used in wetland archaeological investigations (Bell and Walker 1992, 28) and were used with some success at the Mesolithic site of Lough Boora, Co. Offaly (Griffiths 1985). Cladocera and ostracods are microscopic crustaceans that live in lakes, ponds, rivers, estuaries and the sea. Cladocera are most commonly found in lake sediments, while ostracods are found in lakes, estuaries and marine sediments. Both are indictors of temperature, salinity and changes in acidity (eutrophication) of lake waters (Bell and Walker 1992, 28) and could be used in lake settlement studies.

Archaeological investigations

Lake settlement projects should aim to carry out long-term programmes of extensive and intensive archaeological survey. These are, after all, landscapes where little wider archaeological investigation has yet taken place. The majority of known lake settlement sites in Ireland were recovered as a result of the lowering of lake levels during drainage works in the midlands (Pl. 66). This archaeological record is dominated by the study of particular sites, mostly crannogs, as both antiquarians, archaeologists and modern treasure-hunters were concerned with extracting the diagnostic material culture (i.e. the finds) of the period. A lake settlement project should aim to integrate the archaeology of drylands and water, both visible and invisible. On a lake, a large proportion of the archaeological record will be on the lakebed and may often be inaccessible to conventional archaeological survey. However, while this is seemingly a disadvantage, it is in fact possible to view a far greater amount of this archaeology (wooden structures, hearths, substructures) than would be the case on a dryland site. It is exposed already, and awaiting recording and sampling.

Underwater archaeological survey

Morrison (1985) has suggested that lake settlement surveys can aim to achieve a 'total cull' of the surviving archaeological remains, because lakes will have retained 'most or even all of their original complement of crannog sites'. The underwater archaeologist can therefore aim to map the distribution of lake settlements with a greater degree of confidence. Most underwater archaeological sites will be situated in the shallows, or at least at shallow depths (3–5m). This means that extended periods of work can be carried out, restricted only by cold and visibility. There are no problems of decompression or nitrogen narcosis, as less compressed air is consumed at shallow depths. Although water temperatures can be low in many lakes, the use of dry-suits can enable longer working hours. Visibility can occasionally be a problem. The growth of weeds around lake margins and the suspension of sediments in still lake waters can make some work difficult. Indeed, underwater survey is typically best carried out in the winter and early spring. There are a range of advantages for a lake settlement project if it chooses to engage in underwater investigations. Such permanent waterlogging on a settlement site produces much more for the archaeologist to recover. Indeed, it has been pointed out that

> 'the study of crannogs is severely hampered if one does not dive. Exposed portions of sites are generally less informative than submerged parts, where timbers and middens are protected from weathering and vandalism. Little is achieved by peering through a glass-bottomed bucket' (Morrison 1985, 81).

There are various means of carrying out extensive underwater survey (Pl. 67). In its most basic form, a team of three archaeologists in a rigid inflatable boat could engage in brief swim-searches in particular study areas, using both snorkel and SCUBA gear. It may also be possible to use remotely operated vessels to carry out remote surveys from a boat stationed over a site. These surveys would aim to characterise the visibility, sediment composition, currents, depths and likelihood of archaeological remains. A second stage of survey would aim to be more comprehensive and systematic and would use various forms of line-search. A grid (conceptual or actual) of lanes and cross-lanes is laid on the lakeshore and systematically searched. A third stage of survey, more intrusive and aimed at gathering material, may be undertaken as part of an artefact collection strategy or to prepare for an underwater excavation.

Site survey

The Discovery Programme has already developed highly efficient methods of site survey, enabling complex modelling and the production of a range of types of site drawings. The instrument survey of individual sites for analysis and illustration can increasingly be carried out with both speed and accuracy. It is likely that Total Station survey technology would be the dominant survey method, utilising a localised control system based on the National Grid and established using GPS (Global Positioning Systems). This approach would be useful in cases where the inaccessibility of the lakeland environment makes traditional survey techniques difficult. Hand-held GPS could also be used during rapid boat surveys to locate sites quickly in the field. These data could be transferred directly to GIS for mapping purposes. It is not true that underwater site survey is costly and time-consuming. The Scottish crannog surveys pioneered the use of EDM (Electronic Distance Measurement) technology and three-man teams to survey individual crannogs (Morrison 1985; Dixon 1982b). The Lough Kinale surveys indicate that a fairly large, complex crannog in difficult conditions can be surveyed in a week using a team of ten (Farrell 1989). More recently, it has been pointed out that the use of EDM technology linked with data-loggers means that

Pl. 68—*Excavation of an Early Historic lake settlement at Crannog 124, Tivannagh, Co. Roscommon (photo: Dept of Archaeology, UCG).*

individual sites can be closely surveyed in under three days. The result is a comprehensive digital model, capable of providing complex volumetric data and any number of cross-sections, profiles and detailed survey of individual features (Henderson and Burgess 1996). It is also possible to consider underwater photogrammetric survey, and the use of video-recording. For example, Digital Video Mosaicking can be used on an underwater archaeological site, whereby video imagery of an excavation level can be successfully processed through computerised technology to provide an accurate, planimetric mosaic of excavated features (Howland 1997).

Site excavation

Introduction

Lake settlements occur in various locations and vary in size, form and degree of preservation. Archaeological excavation will often be required to establish an individual site's chronology, occupation history and function. Wetland excavations have proven to be amongst the most productive and revealing investigations carried out by archaeologists (Pl. 68), typically because organic material, such as wooden structures and artefacts, leather, vegetal materials, seeds, insects, etc., are all preserved to a high degree on wetland sites. Excavations of wetland sites need to be multidisciplinary to extract the maximum information from a site. Because there are more data, there is more information to enable interpretations. However, the excavation of such material brings its own problems of sampling strategies, on-site conservation and lengthy post-excavation programmes.

Chronological and palaeoenvironmental sampling

The least destructive form of excavation on a lake settlement site will be sampling for radiocarbon and dendrochronological dating and for palaeoenvironmental studies. The former will often only require snapping off a piece of roundwood or sawing across a palisade post. It needs to be clearly understood that such samples could relate to many phases of activity on a site, such as the primary construction phase, an intermediate occupation phase or a time subsequent to the settlement's abandonment. Therefore this type of uncontexted or unstratified sample can only identify human 'activity' on a site, with little sense of the place of that activity in the site's history. But the approach still has its uses. The Historic Scotland crannog surveys sampled extensively for such purposes with highly successful results, ultimately indicating that Scottish lake settlements were being used in the Neolithic, Bronze Age, Iron Age, Dark Ages, medieval and post-medieval periods. It was then possible to choose a site for more detailed excavation (Barber and Crone 1993). The dendrochronological sampling programme carried out by Queen's University, Belfast, has also had a major impact on Irish crannog studies (Baillie 1995a).

A long-term dating programme would be a vital part of any lake settlement project in Ireland. Dendrochronology has only begun to tap the potential of lake settlements, and has concentrated on the Early Historic and Viking Age types. The use of radiocarbon dating has also been infrequent. Artefactual and typological studies dominate the dating of most sites. Indeed, the typological dating of Lagore, Ballinderry 1 and Ballinderry 2 continues to be the subject of constant reinterpretation. After a programme of underwater archaeological survey and sampling, it may be possible to date large numbers of sites. A lake settlement project should aim to be ambitious in its use of radiocarbon and dendrochronological dating, which should be linked to the palaeoenvironmental investigations. Stratigraphical coring of a wetland site to establish its spread and preservation is also a form of minimally intrusive excavation. In a complex wetland environment, coring in the vicinity of a site may also enable the reconstruction of a settlement's original environmental context and economic activities (Clapham and Scaife 1988).

Small-scale excavation

Test-excavation, the use of sampling trenches or the brief investigation of smaller features could all be described as small-scale excavations. There are a number of situations in which small-scale excavation could produce a significant range of information. Mesolithic or Neolithic lithic scatters on lakeshores could be investigated by means of small, spaced trenches, separated at regular intervals to enable recovery of a sample of their assemblages and to investigate their spatial variation. This could be targeted to produce statistically valid samples. Other lake settlements, burnt mounds, jetty structures, slipways, fisheries, etc., could also be sampled to quickly establish their date and function.

Large-scale excavation

Recent large-scale wetland excavations of lake settlement sites include the Buiston crannog excavations in Scotland (Barber and Crone 1993) and the Moynagh Lough excavations in Ireland (J. Bradley 1991). These major wetland excavations will have provided national archaeological resources for wide-ranging interpretation of the archaeology of their periods. The benefits are there to be seen—well-preserved structures and finds and high-quality palaeobotanical deposits—and these more than outweigh the extra financial costs. Barber and Crone (1993) have also indicated that settlements in drained land will typically have lost much of their organic material. Underwater excavation has the advantage in that it allows 'the selection of a site on academic grounds, free from the exigencies of casual drainage' (Morrison 1985, 93). Underwater excavators can remain suspended above the structures and finds, and waterlogged material stays wet throughout the excavation. Underwater excavation does bring its own logistical problems, but the benefits probably outweigh the drawbacks. The most recent underwater excavation of crannogs includes the Oakbank excavations (Dixon 1984) and the Llangorse crannog excavations (Redknap and Lane 1994), while underwater archaeological excavation is now established in Ireland (Boland and O'Sullivan 1997).

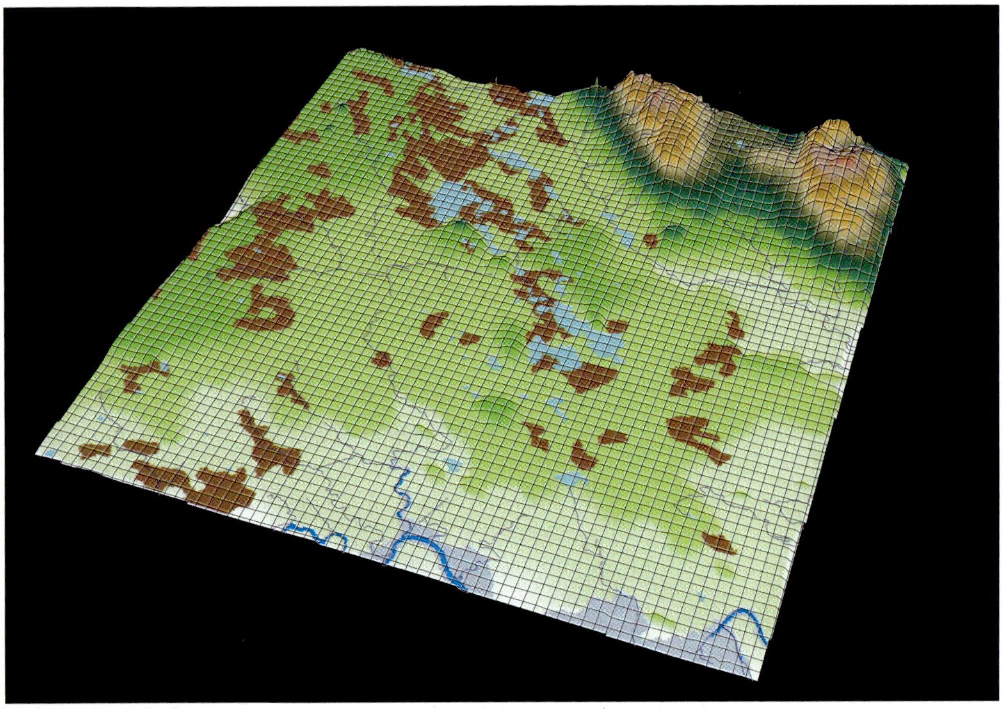

Fig. 36—*The lakes and landscape of south-east Clare: a 3-D model prepared in GIS (by Barry Masterson; reproduced with the permission of the North Munster Project).*

Conservation

The excavation of a waterlogged settlement site will typically produce well-preserved wooden structures and artefacts, palaeobotanical and macrofossil material, mammal, fish and bird bone, and leather and vegetal artefacts. While this ensures a much higher return in terms of data retrieval, potential interpretation and publication, it also raises areas of concern with regard to site preservation, artefact curation and conservation. In particular, conservation work arising from an excavated wetland settlement could be costly, time-consuming and occasionally problematic. Any lake settlement research programme will have to be funded to a sufficient level to manage its conservation needs. However, many archaeological projects in Ireland have coped with these issues already, so conservation should not be seen as an objection to ambitious programmes of research. Medieval urban excavation projects (roughly comparable to a wetland settlement project) typically employ full-time conservators and commonly export finds for conservation. Fortunately, there are now also a growing number of fully qualified archaeological conservators in Irish archaeology, and large-scale conservation facilities are being developed. In terms of costs, conservation is not ruinously expensive. Medieval urban excavations usually make allowances for conservation costs at about 15–20% of the total excavation budget. Indeed, a lake settlement project could be in the forefront of promoting (and publishing) conservation techniques and innovations. The short-term curation of environmental and organic material during post-excavation work would also need to be addressed by the provision of suitable storage facilities. In conclusion, it should be pointed out that while conservation is a serious issue, it is not an insurmountable problem. The benefits in terms of high-quality archaeological data are more than worth the costs.

Reconstructing and modelling past landscapes using Geographical Information Systems

Future lake settlement studies should aim to integrate all the results of archaeological, historical and palaeoenvironmental investigations in Geographical Information Systems. The exciting potential of this computerised technology for archaeological investigation has been outlined in various publications and will not be detailed here. It has typically been used in spatial analysis, in the management of regional databases and in predictive modelling (Allen *et al.* 1990; Gaffney and Stancic 1991; Lock and Stancic 1995; Synnott 1996). It should be possible to integrate the diverse results of a lake settlement project's palaeoenvironmental and archaeological investigations with a region's topography, geology, soils, vegetation, hydrology, rainfall and temperature, as well as the bathymetric contours of the lakebeds (Fig. 36). It should also be possible to download directly the results of geophysical surveys, aerial photography and satellite imagery into GIS databases. The resulting integration of archaeological and palaeoenvironmental investigations in the GIS could be used to trace how local and regional settlement patterns evolved across time and how they might have been affected by environmental changes. Lakes, river valleys and wetlands could be simulated for different time-periods against natural routeways and topography, enabling predictive models for the location of lake settlement archaeology. At an economic level, the optimum location for catching salmon and eels could be modelled in a reconstructed early prehistoric landscape, which could then be compared with archaeological data (i.e. Mesolithic lithic scatters). These site predictions could then be tested by field-walking. The social and economic landscapes of Early Historic crannogs and medieval castles could be statistically modelled, exploring how they were sited in terms of site visibility, routeways, territorial boundaries, settlement continuity and other secular and ecclesiastical settlements. Obviously these are only basic examples, because research would not only aim to reconstruct the character of the physical landscape but would explore the complex relationships between settlement, society and environment in a lakeland setting.

6. Conclusion

This monograph has reviewed the archaeology of lake settlement in Ireland and on that basis has recommended the directions which future studies should take. It has shown how the history of lake settlement studies on this island has greatly influenced the approaches of archaeologists to the subject. It describes in detail the archaeology of lake settlement, presenting the results of many archaeological surveys and excavations. Clearly this is a rich archaeological resource built up over many years of research, a resource that is surprisingly wide-ranging in terms of its chronology and social and cultural contexts. There is good evidence for the lakeshore occupation sites of Mesolithic and Neolithic communities, but the author believes that this particular archaeological evidence has been barely explored. The archaeology of Bronze Age lake settlement has, in contrast, received much more attention, but much still remains to be investigated and understood. The archaeology of Early Historic and Viking Age crannogs, lakeshore settlements and monastic islands is also explored. It could be pointed out that very few crannogs have been excavated to modern standards, and all of these at locations outside the main distribution of these sites. We know relatively little about the chronology, function and history of the vast majority of them. The historical, artefactual and structural evidence for medieval and post-medieval settlement on crannogs and lakeshore earthwork and masonry castles is also described, and clearly much remains to be done. Despite the chronological diversity of the subject, it is apparent that most archaeological research has been focused entirely on Early Historic crannogs. Even then it has been focused particularly on the structures and artefacts found on those few crannogs that seem to be of 'royal' origin. It is undoubtedly true that these high-status sites have greatly skewed the archaeological record, whereas we know little about 'ordinary' lake settlements. Indeed, archaeologists generally have only paid attention to individual settlement 'sites', making little attempt to understand the use of the spaces between 'sites', the landscapes in which people live most of their lives.

The priorities for archaeological research are outlined, focusing on questions within the following broad themes: tracing settlement permanence and mobility; exploring the role of lake settlements in the wider landscape; understanding the patterns of continuity and change in lake settlement and environment across time. It is now apparent that what we need are multidisciplinary, regional, landscape studies to investigate the phenomenon of lake settlement from prehistory to the early modern period. The theoretical and methodological approaches which would be needed are briefly outlined. The projects should integrate the results of prehistoric and historic period archaeology with early Irish, medieval and early modern history, historical geography, literary studies, placename studies and folklife evidence. This should be closely linked with a programme of palaeoenvironmental research and new archaeological fieldwork, the latter comprising both extensive and intensive underwater survey, field-walking and targeted archaeological excavation. What are likely to be the main future challenges to this ambitious programme of research? What is it that we are likely to find out? A few broad comments along these lines will be made here.

The archaeology of lake settlement stretches from the Mesolithic to the post-medieval period (and beyond). The author believes that the multiperiod character of the subject is one of its strengths, providing us with the chance to look at settlement in the Irish landscape across a vast span of time and thereby to examine the processes of social and environmental continuity and change across thousands of years. It is, of course, an intimidating challenge and much energy and many resources will be required, but the benefits will be worth it. We can, in essence, write biographies of important parts of the Irish landscape and gain insights into the nature of life as it was lived there by people of widely differing societies and mentalities. It is worth saying that 'continuity' not only embraces such previously explored concepts as the 'timelessness' of the Irish landscape, but more complex topics such as a community's use and renewal of tradition, and their reinterpretation of the monuments of the past. Change, whether social or environmental, is equally important in the archaeology of lake settlement. Particular periods of sudden change or gradual transition can be seen in the archaeology of lake settlement, often coinciding with the same phases of transition which are among the most puzzling periods in the Irish archaeological record. Lake settlement studies may provide us with some unexpected insights. We also need to think about temporal rhythms within shorter periods of time, such as years, seasons and months. It is also true that the excellent preservation of evidence, unique to wetland archaeological sites, will provide us with clues both to catastrophic events and to the daily lives of ordinary people. A sunken dugout boat, the toolmarks on a hewn wooden post, and the evidence of nuts, berries and animal bone within a house-space all bring us closer to the moments of an individual life.

Lake settlements should not be seen as exotic, slightly isolated places to live, with little attempt made to understand their role in wider social, economic and ideological landscapes. People who lived, hunted, trapped, farmed, worked and moved around lakes would have been well aware of the social and economic networks of family, neighbours and community that stretched away across the water. It will be important, then, to study the archaeology of lake settlement at various different geographical scales—from the local to the regional and on to the national picture. In terms of regional perspectives, it is obvious that lake settlement studies can only be carried out in those parts of the island where lakes are an important topographical feature. In other words, in a country like Ireland, with such diverse landscapes of uplands, coasts and rolling dryland plains, the archaeology of lake settlement cannot answer all the questions. But it is doubtful whether any place can do that. In any case, it is also true that the archaeology of lake settlement in Ireland is a fascinating subject in itself. This is a rainy country, with sluggish drainage and an abundance of lakes, fens and marshes. It is a fact that, over most of this island, to dwell means choosing to dwell beside, or near, wetlands. Irish archaeologists have only recently come to terms with this. Life on a lake settlement was a life led on water, and it is that watery perspective that we need to take to this archaeology. Lake settlement studies will also need to be closely linked to palaeoenvironmental investigations. However, this should not be seen as a means of simply reconstructing the physical backdrop of woodlands and water-levels against which people lived their daily lives. Palaeoenvironmental studies will need to proceed at various levels of enquiry and detail, from the immediate site habitat to the impact that people had on the local landscape, to the role of global climatic and environmental change in the decisions made about settlement in the past. Patterns in the construction, use and abandonment of lake settlements may enable us to tease out the relationships between social and environmental change in early Ireland.

There is much behind us, years of research, discovery and excavation carried out by many, many different scholars. This Discovery Programme monograph has gone some way towards pulling this information together and suggesting the way forward. In front of us now is the dark and peaty gloom of Ireland's lakes, from which will undoubtedly emerge many exciting discoveries over the years ahead. The challenge to us as archaeologists, working with our colleagues in other disciplines, is to understand these as yet undiscovered sites, structures and finds, in terms of their place in the long story that can be told by the archaeology of lake settlement in Ireland.

References

Aalen, F.H.A. 1978 *Man and the landscape in Ireland*. London.

Addyman, P.V. 1965 Coney Island, Lough Neagh: prehistoric settlement, Anglo-Norman castle and Elizabethan native fortress. *Ulster Journal of Archaeology* **28**, 78–101.

Allen, M.S., Green, S.W. and Zubrow, E.B.W. 1990 *Interpreting space: GIS and archaeology*. London.

Andersen, N.H. 1997 *The Sarup enclosures*. Jysk Arkaeologisk Selskab. Moesgaard.

Anderson, E. 1993 The Mesolithic: fishing for answers. In E.S. Twohig and M. Ronayne (eds), *Past perceptions. The prehistoric archaeology of south-west Ireland*, 16–24. Cork.

Anderson, E. and Johnson, G. 1995 Irish Later Mesolithic flint technology: further developments. In E. Grogan and C. Mount (eds), *Annus archaeologiae: proceedings of the OIA winter conference 1993*, 7–21. Dublin.

Andrews, J.H. 1997 *Shapes of Ireland: maps and their makers 1564–1839*. Dublin.

Andrian, B. 1995 Scottish crannog centre—opening soon! *NewsWARP* **18**, 3–6.

Anon. 1952 Crannog finds at Lough Gara. *Journal of the Royal Society of Antiquaries of Ireland* **82**, 182–3.

ApSimon, A.M. 1969 An Early Neolithic house in Co. Tyrone. *Journal of the Royal Society of Antiquaries of Ireland* **99**, 165–8.

Armit, I. 1986 *Excavations at Loch Olabhat, North Uist 1986: first interim report*. Department of Archaeology, University of Edinburgh, Project Paper 5. Edinburgh.

Armit, I. 1987 *Excavation of a Neolithic island settlement in Loch Olabhat, North Uist 1987: second interim report*. Department of Archaeology, University of Edinburgh, Project Paper 8. Edinburgh.

Armit, I. 1988 *Excavations at Loch Olabhat, North Uist 1988: third interim report*. Department of Archaeology, University of Edinburgh, Project Paper 10. Edinburgh.

Armit, A. 1989 *The Loch Olabhat project, North Uist 1989: fourth interim report*. Department of Archaeology, University of Edinburgh, Project Paper 12. Edinburgh.

Arnold, B. 1982 The architectural woodwork of the Late Bronze Age village Auvernier-Nord. In S. MacGrail (ed.), *Woodworking techniques before A.D. 1500*, 111–28. British Archaeological Reports, International Series 129. Oxford.

Arnold, B. 1986 *Cortaillod-Est, un village du Bronze final. Fouille subaquatique et photographie aérienne*. Archéologie Neuchâteloise 1. Saint-Blaise.

Arnold, B. 1990 *Cortaillod-Est et les villages du lac de Neuchâtel au Bronze final. Structure de l'habitat et proto-urbanisme*. Archéologie Neuchâteloise 6. Saint-Blaise.

Ashmore, P.J. 1996 *Neolithic and Bronze Age Scotland*. London.

Astill, G. and Davies, W. 1997 *A Breton landscape*. London.

Austin, D. and Thomas, J. 1996 The 'proper' study of medieval archaeology: a case study. In D. Austin and L. Alcock (eds), *From the Baltic to the Black Sea: studies in medieval archaeology*, 43–78. London.

Baillie, M.G.L. 1979 An interim statement on dendrochronology at Belfast. *Ulster Journal of Archaeology* **42**, 72–84.

Baillie, M.G.L. 1982 *Tree ring dating and archaeology*. London.

Baillie, M.G.L. 1985 Irish dendrochronology and radiocarbon calibration. *Ulster Journal of Archaeology* **48**, 11–23.

Baillie, M.G.L. 1995a *A slice through time: dendrochronology and precision dating*. London.

Baillie, M.G.L. 1995b Patrick, comets and Christianity. *Emania* **13**, 69–78.

Barber, J.W. 1981 Excavations on Iona 1979. *Proceedings of the Society of Antiquaries of Scotland* **111**, 282–380.

Barber, J.W. and Crone, B.A. 1993 Crannogs; a diminishing resource? A survey of the crannogs of south-west Scotland and excavations at Buiston crannog. *Antiquity* **67**, 520–3.

Bardan, P. 1898a Lough-a-trim crannoge, Co. Westmeath. *Journal of the Royal Society of Antiquaries of Ireland* **27**, 276.

Bardan, P. 1898b White Lough crannoge, Co. Westmeath. *Journal of the Royal Society of Antiquaries of Ireland* **27**, 275–6.

Barrett, G.F. and Graham, B.J. 1975 Some considerations concerning the dating and distribution of ring-forts in Ireland. *Ulster Journal of Archaeology* **38**, 33–45.

Barry, T.B. 1977 *Medieval moated sites of south-east Ireland.* British Archaeological Reports, British Series 35. Oxford.

Barry, T.B. 1981 Archaeological excavations at Dunbeg promontory fort, Co. Kerry. *Proceedings of the Royal Irish Academy* **81C**, 295–329.

Barry, T.B. 1987 *The archaeology of medieval Ireland.* London and New York.

Barry, T.B. 1992 Dispersed rural settlement in Ireland in the later Middle Ages. In *Medieval Europe 1992: Rural Settlement. Pre-printed papers. Volume 8,* 175–80. York.

Barry, T.B. 1993 Late medieval Ireland: the debate on the social and economic transformation, 1350–1550. In B.J. Graham and L.J. Proudfoot (eds), *A historical geography of Ireland*, 99–122. London.

Barry, T.B. 1997 Recent research in medieval rural nucleated settlement in Ireland. In G. De Boe and F. Verhaeghe (eds), *Rural settlement in medieval Europe—papers of the 'Medieval Europe Brugge 1997' conference,* vol. 6, 87–92. Zellik.

Bell, M. 1993 Intertidal archaeology at Goldcliff in the Severn Estuary. In J.M. Coles, V. Renwick and G. Hutchinson (eds), *A spirit of enquiry: essays for Ted Wright,* 9–13. Exeter.

Bell, M. and Walker, M.J.C. 1992 *Late Quaternary environmental change: physical and human perspectives.* Harlow.

Bender, B. (ed.) 1993 *Landscape, politics and perspectives.* Oxford.

Bender, B. 1996 Landscape and anthropology. In F.H.A. Aalen (ed.), *Landscape study and management*, 93–102. Dublin.

Bengsston, H. and Bergh, S. 1984 The hut sites on Knocknarea Mountain. In G. Burenhult, *The archaeology of Carrowmore: environmental archaeology and the megalithic tradition at Carrowmore, Co. Sligo, Ireland,* 216–318. Stockholm.

Benkert, A. 1993 *Hauterive-Champréveyres, 8. Les structures de l'habitat au Bronze final, zone A.* Archéologie Neuchâteloise 16. Saint-Blaise.

Bermingham, N. 1996 Ardrea Lough, Co. Sligo. *The Corran Herald* **29**, 31–3.

Berry, R.G. 1906 Crannoge at Loughgall, County of Armagh. *Ulster Journal of Archaeology* (2nd ser.) **12**, 16.

Bersu, G. 1947 The rath in townland Lissue, Co. Antrim. Report on the excavations in 1946. *Ulster Journal of Archaeology* **10**, 35–8.

Bhreathnach, E. 1998 Topographical note: Moynagh Lough, Nobber, Co. Meath. *Ríocht na Mídhe* **9** (4), 16–19.

Bintcliff, J. 1991 The contribution of an Annaliste/structural history approach to archaeology. In J. Bintcliff (ed.), *The Annales school and archaeology*, 1–33. London and New York.

Bintcliff, J. 1996 Interactions of theory, methodology and practice. *Archaeological Dialogues* **3** (2), 248–55.

Bitel, L. 1990 *Isle of the saints. Monastic settlement and Christian community in early Ireland.* Cork.

Blot, J.-Y. 1996 *Underwater archaeology.* London.

Bocquet, A. 1987 Le village Néolithique des Baigneurs à Charavines, Isere, France. *NewsWARP* **2**, 4–5.

Bocquet, A., Brochier, J.L., Emery-Barbier, A., Lundstrom-Baudais, K., Orcel, C. and Vin, F. 1986 A submerged Neolithic village: Charavines 'Les Baigneurs' in Lake Paladru, France. In J.M. Coles and A.J. Lawson (eds), *European wetlands in prehistory*, 33–54. Oxford.

Boland, D. 1990 River Suck project 1989. *Subsea* **59**, 32–3.

Boland, D. and O'Sullivan, A. 1997 An early medieval wooden bridge at Clonmacnoise, Co. Offaly. In F.J.G. Mitchell and C. Delaney (eds), *The Quaternary of the Irish midlands,* 55–63. Irish Association for Quaternary Studies Field Guide No. 21. Dublin.

Bourke, C. 1986 Newtownlow. In C. Cotter (ed.), *Excavations 1985*, 40. Dublin.

Bourke, C. 1987 Newtownlow. In C. Cotter (ed.), *Excavations 1986*, 37. Dublin.

Bourke, C. 1988 A ringed pin from Lough Ravel crannog, County Antrim. *Ulster Journal of Archaeology* **51**, 55–60.

Bourke, C. (forthcoming) Excavations at Newtownlow, Co. Westmeath. In V. Buckley (ed.), *Irish crannogs: proceedings of the W.G. Wood-Martin conference.*

Bourke, E. 1994 Glass vessels of the first nine centuries AD in Ireland. *Journal of the Royal Society of Antiquaries of Ireland* **124**, 163–209.

Bradley, J. 1982 A separate-bladed shovel from Moynagh Lough, County Meath. *Journal of the Royal Society of Antiquaries of Ireland* **112**, 117–22.

Bradley, J. 1982–3 Excavations at Moynagh Lough, Co. Meath 1980–81: interim report. *Ríocht na Mídhe* **7** (2), 12–32.

Bradley, J. 1984 Excavations at Moynagh Lough, Co. Meath 1982–83: interim report. *Ríocht na Mídhe* **7** (3), 86–93.

Bradley, J. 1985–6 Excavations at Moynagh Lough, Co. Meath 1984: a summary report. *Ríocht na Mídhe* **7** (4), 79–82.

Bradley, J. 1987 Conference: Irish crannogs 1986. *NewsWARP* **2**, 23–4.

Bradley, J. 1988 The interpretation of Scandinavian settlement in Ireland. In J. Bradley (ed.), *Settlement and society in medieval Ireland: studies presented to F.X. Martin, o.s.a.,* 49–78. Kilkenny.

Bradley, J. 1990–1 Excavations at Moynagh Lough, Co. Meath, 1985 and 1987. *Ríocht na Mídhe* **8** (3), 21–35.

Bradley, J. 1991 Excavations at Moynagh Lough, Co. Meath. *Journal of the Royal Society of Antiquaries of Ireland* **111**, 5–26.

Bradley, J. 1993 Moynagh Lough: an insular workshop of the second quarter of the 8th century. In R.M. Spearman and J. Higgitt (eds), *The age of migrating ideas,* 74–81. Edinburgh.

Bradley, J. 1994–5 Excavations at Moynagh Lough, Co. Meath. *Ríocht na Mídhe* **9** (1), 158–69.

Bradley, J. 1996 Living at the water's edge. *Archaeology Ireland* **35**, 24–6.

Bradley, J. 1997 Archaeological excavations at Moynagh Lough, Co. Meath 1995–96. *Ríocht na Mídhe* **9** (3), 50–61.

Bradley, J. (forthcoming) Moynagh Lough, Co. Meath. In I. Bennett (ed.), *Excavations 1997*. Bray.

Bradley, J. and Dunne, N. 1988 *Urban Archaeological Survey—County Roscommon.* Limited distribution report. Office of Public Works, Dublin.

Bradley, R. 1990 *The passage of arms: an archaeological analysis of prehistoric hoards and votive deposits.* Cambridge.

Bradley, R. 1993 *Altering the earth.* Edinburgh.

Bradley, R. 1997a *Rock art and the prehistory of Atlantic Europe.* London.

Bradley, R. 1997b *The significance of monuments: on the shaping of human experience in Neolithic and Bronze Age Europe.* London.

Brady, C. and Gillespie, R. (eds) 1986 *Natives and newcomers: essays on the making of Irish colonial society 1534–1641.* Dublin.

Brady, N. 1994a Labor and agriculture in early medieval Ireland: evidence from the sources. In A.J. Frantzen and D. Moffat (eds), *The work of work: servitude, slavery and labor in medieval England,* 126–45. Glasgow.

Brady, N. 1994b Report on the excavation of a stone platform in Robinstown, Co. Westmeath. Unpublished manuscript, National Monuments Service.

Brindley, A. 1986 *Archaeological Inventory of County Monaghan.* Dublin.

Brindley, A. and Lanting, J.N. 1990 A Roman boat in Ireland. *Archaeology Ireland* **4** (3), 10–11.

Brindley, A.L. and Lanting, J.N. 1991 A boat of the Mediterranean tradition in Ireland: preliminary note. *International Journal of Nautical Archaeology and Underwater Exploration* **20**, 69–70.

Brindley, A.L., Lanting, J.N. and Mook, W.G. 1989–90 Radiocarbon dates from Irish fulachta fiadha and other burnt mounds. *Journal of Irish Archaeology* **5**, 25–33.

Brunning, R. 1997 Two Bronze Age wooden structures in the Somerset Moors. *NewsWARP* **22**, 24–8.

Buckley, V.M. (ed.) 1990 *Burnt offerings: international contributions to burnt mound archaeology.* Dublin.

Buckley, V.M. 1996 The National Archive as a research tool. *IAPA Newsletter* **23**, 8.

Buckley, V.M. and Sweetman, P.D. 1991 *Archaeological Survey of County Louth.* Dublin.

Buick, G.R. 1893 The crannog of Moylarg. *Journal of the Royal Society of Antiquaries of Ireland* **23**, 27–43.

Buick, G.R. 1894 The crannog of Moylarg. *Journal of the Royal Society of Antiquaries of Ireland* **24**, 316–31.

Bulleid, A. and Gray, H. St G. 1911 *The Glastonbury lake village,* vol. 1. Glastonbury.

Bulleid, A. and Gray, H. St G. 1917 *The Glastonbury lake village,* vol. 2. Glastonbury.

Burenhult, G. 1980 *The Carrowmore excavations. Excavation season 1980.* Stockholm Archaeological Reports 7. Stockholm.

Burgess, C.B. and Gerloff, S. 1981 *The dirks and rapiers of Great Britain and Ireland.* Prähistorische Bronzefunde 4 (7). Munich.

Byrne, F.J. 1973 *Irish kings and high-kings.* London.

Cairns, C.T. 1987 *Irish towerhouses, a Co. Tipperary case study.* Athlone.

Campbell, E. and Lane, A. 1989 Llangorse: a tenth century royal crannog in Wales. *Antiquity* **63**, 675–81.

Canny, N. 1987 *From Reformation to Restoration: Ireland 1534–1660.* Dublin.

Caulfield, Dr 1870 Assault on a crannog. *Journal of the Royal Society of Antiquaries of Ireland* (4th ser.) **1**, 14–25.

Caulfield, S. 1978 Neolithic fields: the Irish evidence. In H.C. Bowen and P.J. Fowler (eds), *Early land allotment,* 137–44. British Archaeological Reports, British Series 48. Oxford.

Caulfield, S. 1981 Some Celtic problems in the Irish Iron Age. In D. Ó Corráin (ed.), *Irish antiquity,* 205–15. Cork.

Caulfield, S. 1983 The Neolithic settlement of north Connaught. In T. Reeves-Smyth and F. Hamond (eds), *Landscape archaeology in Ireland,* 195–215. British Archaeological Reports, British Series 116. Oxford.

Caulfield, S. 1988 *Céide Fields and Belderrig guide.* Killala.

Clapham, A.J. and Scaife, R.G. 1988 A pollen and plant macrofossil investigation of Oakbank Crannog, Loch Tay, Scotland. In P. Murphy and C. French (eds), *The exploitation of wetlands,* 293–326. British Archaeological Reports, British Series 186. Oxford.

Clark, J.G.D. 1954 *Excavations at Star Carr.* Cambridge.

Clarke, D.L. 1976 Mesolithic Europe: the economic basis. In G. de G. Sieveking, I.H. Longworth and K.E. Wilson (eds), *Problems in economic and social archaeology,* 449–81. London.

Cleary, R.M. 1995 Later Bronze Age settlement and prehistoric burials, Lough Gur, Co. Limerick. *Proceedings of the Royal Irish Academy* **95C**, 1–92.

Coffey, G. 1906 Craigywarren crannog. *Proceedings of the Royal Irish Academy* **26C**, 109–18.

Coles, B.J. 1990 Anthropomorphic wooden figures from Britain and Ireland. *Proceedings of the Prehistoric Society* **56**, 315–33.

Coles, B.J. (ed.) 1992 *The wetlands revolution in prehistory*. WARP Occasional Paper 6. Exeter.

Coles, B.J. and Coles, J.M. 1989 *People of the wetlands. Bogs, bodies and lake-dwellings*. London.

Coles, J.M. 1984 *The archaeology of wetlands*. Edinburgh.

Coles, J.M. 1991 *From the waters of oblivion*. Reuvens-Lezing 2. Assen.

Coles, J.M. 1995 Araisi, Latvia. Excavation and reconstruction of a ninth century AD settlement. *NewsWARP* **18**, 12–13.

Coles, J.M. and Coles, B.J. 1996 *Enlarging the past. The contribution of wetland archaeology*. Society of Antiquaries of Scotland Monograph Series 11/WARP Occasional Paper 10. Exeter.

Coles, J.M. and Lawson, A. 1987 *European wetlands in prehistory*. Oxford.

Coles, J.M. and Minnitt, S. 1995 *Industrious and fairly civilised: the Glastonbury lake village*. Exeter.

Coles, J.M., Goodhall, A. and Minnitt, S. 1992 *Arthur Bulleid and the Glastonbury lake village 1892–1992*. Exeter.

Collardelle, M. and Verdel, E. 1993 *Chevaliers-Paysans de L'An Mil au Lac de Paladru*. Paris.

Collins, A.E.P. 1955 Excavations at Lough Faughan crannog, Co. Down, 1950–51. *Ulster Journal of Archaeology* **18**, 45–82.

Collins, A.E.P. and Proudfoot, B. 1959 A trial excavation at Clea Lakes crannog, Co. Down. *Ulster Journal of Archaeology* **22**, 92–101.

Collins, A.E.P. and Seaby, W.A. 1960 Structures and small finds discovered at Lough Eskragh, Co. Tyrone. *Ulster Journal of Archaeology* **23**, 25–37.

Condit, T. 1993 Ritual enclosures near Boyle, Co. Roscommon. *Archaeology Ireland* **7** (1), 14–16.

Condit, T. 1997 *Ireland's archaeology from the air*. Dublin.

Condit, T. and Buckley, V.M. 1989 The 'Doon' of Drumsna—gateway to Connacht. *Emania* **6**, 12–14.

Condit, T. and Gibbons, M. 1989 An introduction to County Leitrim. *Archaeology Ireland* **3** (1), 6–9.

Condit, T., Gibbons, M. and Timoney, M. 1991 Hillforts in Sligo and Leitrim. *Emania* **9**, 59–62.

Cooney, G. 1979 Some aspects of the siting of megalithic tombs in County Leitrim. *Journal of the Royal Society of Antiquaries of Ireland* **109**, 74–91.

Cooney, G. 1983 Megalithic tombs in their environmental setting, a settlement perspective. In T. Reeves-Smyth and F. Hamond (eds), *Landscape archaeology in Ireland*, 179–94. British Archaeological Reports, British Series 116. Oxford.

Cooney, G. 1987 North Leinster in the earlier prehistoric period. Unpublished Ph.D. thesis, University College Dublin.

Cooney, G. 1989 Stone axes of North Leinster. *Oxford Journal of Archaeology* **8**, 145–57.

Cooney, G. 1995 Theory and practice in Irish archaeology. In P.J. Ucko (ed.), *Theory in archaeology: a world perspective,* 263–77. London.

Cooney, G. 1997 Images of settlement and the landscape in the Neolithic. In P. Topping (ed.), *Neolithic landscapes,* 23–31. Oxbow Monograph 86. Oxford.

Cooney, G. (forthcoming) Reading a landscape manuscript: a review of progress in prehistoric settlement studies in Ireland. In T. Barry (ed.), *A history of settlement in Ireland*. London.

Cooney, G. and Grogan, E. 1991 An archaeological solution to the 'Irish' problem? *Emania* **9**, 33–43.

Cooney, G. and Grogan, E. 1994 *Irish prehistory, a social perspective*. Dublin.

Cooney, G. and Mandal, S. 1998 *The Irish stone axe project: monograph 1*. Dublin.

Coope, G.R. 1981 Report on the Coleoptera from an eleventh-century house at Christ

Church Place, Dublin. In H. Bekker-Nielsen, P. Foote and O. Olsen (eds), *Proceedings of the Eighth Viking Congress,* 51–6. Odense.

Corlett, C. 1997 A fulacht fiadh at Moynagh Lough, County Meath *Ríocht na Mídhe* **9** (3), 46–9.

Corlett, C. and Shanahan, B. 1998 Evidence for a horizontal mill on the River Dee, near Nobber, County Meath. *Ríocht na Mídhe* **9** (4), 20–7.

Cotter, C. (ed.) 1986 *Excavations 1985.* Dublin.

Cotter, C. 1996 Western stone fort project. *Discovery Programme Reports* **4**, 1–14.

Crone, B.A. 1993 Crannogs and chronologies. *Proceedings of the Society of Antiquaries of Scotland* **123**, 245–54.

Cross, R.E. 1953 Lough Gara: a preliminary survey. *Journal of the Royal Society of Antiquaries of Ireland* **83**, 93–6.

Cross, S. 1996 Identifying complexity in the record: a case study of the Irish and British Mesolithic. In D.A. Meyer, P.C. Dawson and D.T. Hanna (eds), *Debating complexity. Proceedings of the twenty-sixth annual Chacamool conference,* 254–62. Calgary.

Crowes, J. O'B. 1869 Etymology of 'crannog'. *The Irish Builder* **2**, 201.

Crumley, C.L. and Marquardt, W.H. 1987 *Regional dynamics: Burgundian landscapes in historical perspective.* New York.

Cullen, L.M. 1981 *The emergence of Modern Ireland, 1600–1900.* London.

D'Arcy, S.A. 1897 A crannog near Clones. *Journal of the Royal Society of Antiquaries of Ireland* **27**, 205–20, 389–403.

D'Arcy, S.A. 1900 An account of the examination of two lake-dwellings in the neighbourhood of Clones. *Journal of the Royal Society of Antiquaries of Ireland* **30**, 204–44.

Darvill, T. 1997 Neolithic landscapes: identity and definition. In P. Topping (ed.), *Neolithic landscapes,* 1–13. Oxbow Monograph 86. Oxford.

Davies, O. 1938 Davy's Island Church, Lower Lough Erne. *Ulster Journal of Archaeology* **1**, 222–6.

Davies, O. 1940 Excavations on Round Island. *Ulster Journal of Archaeology* **3**, 1–4, 122–6.

Davies, O. 1941 Trial excavations on Lough Enagh, Co. Londonderry. *Ulster Journal of Archaeology* **4**, 88–101.

Davies, O. 1942 Contributions to the study of crannogs in south Ulster. *Ulster Journal of Archaeology* **5**, 14–30.

Davies, O. 1946a Excavation of a crannog at Deredis Upper in Lough Inchin, Co. Cavan. *Journal of the Royal Society of Antiquaries of Ireland* **76**, 19–34.

Davies, O. 1946b Excavations around Lough Eske, Co. Donegal. *Ulster Journal of Archaeology* **9**, 91–100.

Davies, O. 1950 *Excavations at Island MacHugh.* Supplement to the *Proceedings of the Belfast Natural History and Philosophical Society.* Belfast.

Dean, M., Ferrari, B., Oxley, I., Redknap, M. and Watson, K. (eds) 1992 *Archaeology underwater: the NAS guide to principles and practice.* Dorchester.

Deevy, M. 1995 Medieval ring brooches in Ireland; jewellery, art and symbolism. Unpublished M.A. thesis, University College Dublin.

Deevy, M.B. 1998 *Medieval ring brooches in Ireland: a study of jewellery, dress and society.* Dublin.

De hÓir, S. 1990 A letter from W.F. Wakeman to James Graves in 1882. *Journal of the Royal Society of Antiquaries of Ireland* **120**, 112–19.

De Paor, L. 1962 Antiquities of the Viking period from Inchbofin, Co. Westmeath. *Journal of the Royal Society of Antiquaries of Ireland* **92**, 187–91.

De Paor, L. 1972 Inishcaltra. *Excavations 1971,* 8–9.

De Paor, L. 1974 Inishcaltra. *Excavations 1973,* 5–6.

De Paor, L. 1975 Inish Cealtra. *Excavations 1974,* 10–11.

De Paor, M. and de Paor, L. 1960 *Early Christian Ireland.* London.

Dixon, T.N. 1981 Preliminary excavation of Oakbank crannog, Loch Tay: interim report. *International Journal of Nautical Archaeology and Underwater Exploration* **10** (1), 15–21.

Dixon, T.N. 1982a Excavation of Oakbank crannog, Loch Tay. Interim report. *International Journal of Nautical Archaeology and Underwater Exploration* **11** (2), 125–32.

Dixon, T.N. 1982b A survey of crannogs in Loch Tay. *Proceedings of the Society of Antiquaries of Scotland* **112**, 17–38.

Dixon, T.N. 1984 Oakbank Crannog. *Current Archaeology* **90**, 217–20.

Dixon, T.N. 1991 The history of crannog survey and excavation in Scotland. *International Journal of Nautical Archaeology and Underwater Exploration* **20** (1), 1–8.

Donnelly, C.J. 1997 *Living places: archaeology, continuity and change at historic monuments in Northern Ireland*. Belfast.

Doody, M. 1995 The Ballyhoura Hills project. *Discovery Programme Reports* **2**, 12–44.

Doody, M. 1997 Bronze Age settlements in Co. Tipperary: fifteen years of research. *Tipperary Historical Journal* (1997), 94–106.

Dunne, General 1868–9 Proceedings and papers; notices of a cranog in Lough Annagh, King's County. *Journal of the Royal Society of Antiquaries of Ireland* **10**, 154–7.

Earwood, C. 1991–2 Turned wooden vessels of the early historic period from Ireland and western Scotland. *Ulster Journal of Archaeology* **54–5**, 154–9.

Earwood, C. 1993 *Domestic wooden artefacts in Britain and Ireland from Neolithic to Viking times*. Exeter.

Edwards, K.J. 1979 Palynological and temporal inference in the context of prehistory, with special reference to the evidence from lake and peat deposits. *Journal of Archaeological Science* **6**, 255–70.

Edwards, K.J. and Hirons, K.R. 1984 Cereal pollen grains in pre-elm decline deposits: implications for the earliest agriculture in Britain and Ireland. *Journal of Archaeological Science* **11**, 71–80.

Edwards, N. 1990 *The archaeology of early medieval Ireland*. London.

Eogan, G. 1957 Recent crannog discoveries in County Meath. *Ríocht na Mídhe* **1** (3), 50–4.

Eogan, G. 1965 *Catalogue of Irish bronze swords*. Dublin.

Eogan, G. 1966 A bronze double-edged knife-dagger with openwork handle and ring terminal from Lagore, Co. Meath, and its affinities. *Journal of the Royal Society of Antiquaries of Ireland* **96**, 147–56.

Eogan, G. 1983 *Hoards of the Irish Later Bronze Age*. Dublin.

Eogan, G. 1984 *Excavations at Knowth 1*. Dublin.

Eogan, G. 1990 Ballynee souterrains, County Meath. *Journal of the Royal Society of Antiquaries of Ireland* **120**, 41–64.

Eogan, G. 1993 The Late Bronze Age: customs, crafts and cults. In E.S. Twohig and M. Ronayne (eds), *Past perceptions. The prehistoric archaeology of south-west Ireland*, 121–33. Cork.

Evans, E.E. 1966 *Prehistoric and Early Christian Ireland*. London.

Evans, E.E. and Turner, B.S. 1977 *Ireland's Eye: the photographs of Robert John Welch*. Belfast.

Falkiner, W. 1898–1900 Notice of a crannog at Loughatrim, Killucan, county of Westmeath. *Proceedings of the Royal Irish Academy* **21**, 216–17.

Fanning, T. 1983 Ballaghkeeran Little, Athlone. *Medieval Archaeology* **27**, 221.

Farrell, R. 1989 The crannog archaeological project (CAP), Republic of Ireland II: Lough Lene—offshore island survey. *International Journal of Nautical Archaeology and Underwater Exploration* **18** (3), 221–8.

Farrell, R. 1990a The crannog survey project: the lakes of the west midlands. *Archaeology Ireland* **4** (1), 27–9.

Farrell, R. 1990b Crannog archaeology project. In I. Bennett (ed.), *Excavations 1989*,

56. Dublin.
Farrell, R. 1991 The crannog archaeological project (CAP). Archaeological field research in the lakes of the west midlands of Ireland. In C. Karkov and R. Farrell (eds), *Studies in Insular art and archaeology*, 99–110. American Early Medieval Studies 1. Cornell.
Farrell, R. and Buckley, V. 1984 Preliminary examination of the potential of offshore and underwater sites in Loughs Ennell and Analla, Co. Westmeath, Ireland. *International Journal of Nautical Archaeology and Underwater Exploration* **13** (4), 281–5.
Farrell, R., Kelly, E.P. and Gowen, M. 1989 The crannog archaeological project (CAP), Republic of Ireland I: a pre-preliminary report. *International Journal of Nautical Archaeology and Underwater Exploration* **18** (2), 123–36.
Feehan, J. and O'Donovan, G. 1996 *The bogs of Ireland: an introduction to the natural, cultural and industrial heritage of Irish peatlands*. Dublin.
Fennell, W.J. 1904 Church Island or Inismore, Lough Gill. *Ulster Journal of Archaeology* **10**, 166–9.
Ffrench, J.F.M. 1902 Notes on three bone pins found at the bottom of the Ballinderry lake in the county Westmeath. *Journal of the Royal Society of Antiquaries of Ireland* **32**, 153–7.
Flanagan, L.N.W. 1988 Irish annals as a source for maritime history, 1400–1600 A.D. In G. Mac Niocaill and P.F. Wallace (eds), *Keimelia: studies in medieval archaeology and history in honour of Tom Delaney*, 500–3. Galway.
Flanagan, L.N.W. 1992 *A dictionary of Irish archaeology*. Dublin.
Fleming, A. 1996 Total landscape archaeology: dream or necessity? In F.H.A. Aalen (ed.), *Landscape study and management*, 81–91. Dublin.
Frame, R. 1981 *Colonial Ireland, 1169–1369*. London.
Fredengren, C. 1998a Lough Gara through time. *Archaeology Ireland* **12** (1), 31–3.
Fredengren, C. 1998b Islands as crannogs. *Aktuell Arkeologi* **6**, 125–42. Stockholm.
Gaffney, V.L. and Stancic, Z. 1991 *Approaches to regional analysis: a case study of the island of Hvar*. Ljubljana.
Gibbons, M. and Condit, T. 1991 Lake promontory forts in Co. Mayo. *North Mayo; IQUA Field Guide* **14**, 39–40.
Gibbons, M., Alcock, O., Condit, T. and Tunney, M. 1991 Some observations on the sites and monuments record of County Mayo. *Cathair na Mart* **2** (1), 1–19.
Gillespie, R. 1993 Explorers, exploiters and entrepreneurs: Early Modern Ireland and its context, 1500–1700. In B.J. Graham and L.J. Proudfoot (eds), *A historical geography of Ireland*, 123–57. London.
Glasscock, R.E. 1975 Mottes in Ireland. *Château Gaillard* **7**, 95–110.
Glasscock, R.E. 1993 Land and people *c*. 1300. In A. Cosgrove (ed.), *A New History of Ireland II: Medieval Ireland 1169–1534*, 205–39. Oxford.
Gosden, C. 1994 *Social being and time*. Oxford and Cambridge.
Gosling, P. 1993 *Archaeological Inventory of County Galway: Volume 1—West Galway*. Dublin.
Gowen, M. 1988 *Three Irish gas pipelines: new archaeological evidence from Munster*. Dublin.
Gowen, M. 1997 Palaeoenvironment and archaeology—excavations at Derryville bog. *Archaeology Ireland* **11** (4), 27–9.
Gowen, M. and Halpin, E. 1992 A Neolithic house at Newtown. *Archaeology Ireland* **6** (2), 25–7.
Graham, B.J. 1980 The mottes of the Norman liberty of Meath. In H. Murtagh (ed.), *Irish midland studies: essays in commemoration of N.W. English*, 39–56. Athlone.
Graham, B.J. 1985 *Anglo-Norman settlement in Ireland*. Athlone.
Graham, B.J. 1988 Medieval settlement in County Roscommon. *Proceedings of the Royal Irish Academy* **88C**, 19–38.
Graham, B.J. 1993 Early medieval Ireland; settlement as an indicator of social and

economic transformation, *c.* 500–1100. In B.J. Graham and L.J. Proudfoot (eds), *A historical geography of Ireland*, 19–57. London.

Graham-Campbell, J. 1974 A Viking-age gold hoard from Ireland. *Antiquaries Journal* **54**, 269–72.

Gramsch, B. 1992 Friesack Mesolithic wetlands. In B.J. Coles (ed.), *The wetland revolution in prehistory*, 65–72. Exeter.

Graves, J. 1883–4 Stone and bone antiquities, some with oghamic inscriptions, found at a crannog in Ballinderry Lough. *Journal of the Royal Society of Antiquaries of Ireland* **16** (6), 196–202.

Gray, W. 1883–4a The crannogs of Lough Mourne. *Journal of the Royal Society of Antiquaries of Ireland* **16** (6), 177.

Gray, W. 1883–4b A crannoge canoe from Lough Mourne, county of Antrim. *Journal of the Royal Society of Antiquaries of Ireland* **16** (6), 371–2.

Grazawski, K. and Niegowski, J. 1998 Research on palafittes in Skarlin lake, Brodnica, North Poland. *NewsWARP* **23**, 19–20.

Green, S.W. and Zvelebil, M. 1990 The Mesolithic colonization and agricultural transition of south-east Ireland. *Proceedings of the Prehistoric Society* **56**, 57–88.

Griffiths, H.I. 1985 The application of freshwater ostracods to the study of Late Quaternary palaeoenvironments in north-western Europe. Unpublished Ph.D. thesis, University of Wales.

Grigor, J. 1863 Notice of the remains of two ancient lake-dwellings in the Loch of the Clans. *Proceedings of the Society of Antiquaries of Scotland* **5**, 116–18.

Grogan, E. 1989 The early prehistory of the Lough Gur region: Neolithic and Bronze Age settlement patterns in north Munster south of the River Shannon. Unpublished Ph.D. thesis, National University of Ireland.

Grogan, E. 1996a Neolithic houses in Ireland. In T. Darvill and J. Thomas (eds), *Neolithic houses in northwest Europe and beyond*, 41–60. Oxbow Monograph 57. Oxford.

Grogan, E. 1996b Excavations at Mooghaun South, 1994. Interim report. *Discovery Programme Reports* **4**, 47–57.

Grogan, E. (forthcoming) Landscape archaeology in Ireland and the prehistory of north Munster. *Discovery Programme Reports* **5**.

Grogan, E. and Condit, T. 1994a The later prehistoric landscape of south-east Clare. *The Other Clare* **18**, 8–12.

Grogan, E. and Condit, T. 1994b New hillfort gives clue to Late Bronze Age. *Archaeology Ireland* **8** (2), 7.

Grogan, E. and Donaghy, C. 1997 Navel-gazing at Uisneach, Co. Westmeath. *Archaeology Ireland* **11** (4), 24–6.

Grogan, E. and Eogan, G. 1987 Lough Gur excavations by Seán P. Ó Ríordáin: further Neolithic and Beaker habitations on Knockadoon. *Proceedings of the Royal Irish Academy* **87C**, 299–506.

Grogan, E., Condit, T., O'Carroll, F., O'Sullivan, A. and Daly, A. 1995 Preliminary assessment of the prehistoric landscape of the Mooghaun study area. *Discovery Programme Reports* **2**, 47–56.

Grogan, E., Condit, T., O'Carroll, F., O'Sullivan, A. and Daly, A. 1996 Tracing the later prehistoric landscape in north Munster. *Discovery Programme Reports* **4**, 26–46.

Grøn, O., Christoffersen, H. and Jolly, J.B. 1996 Side-scan sonar. *Maritime Newsletter from Roskilde, Denmark* **6**, 14–16.

Grøn, O., Engelstad, E. and Lindlom, I. (eds) 1991 *Social space: human spatial behaviour in dwellings and settlements*. Odense.

Hall, T. 1907 Crannoge near Belturbet. *Journal of the Royal Society of Antiquaries of Ireland* **37**, 240–1.

Hall, T. 1910 Barnagrow Lake and crannogs, County Cavan. *Journal of the Royal Society of Antiquaries of Ireland* **40**, 361–2.

Hamlin, A. 1988 Why dig at a site in state care? In A. Hamlin and C. Lynn (eds), *Pieces*

of the past, 52–4. Belfast.
Harbison, P. 1969a *The axes of the Early Bronze Age in Ireland.* Prähistorische Bronzefunde 9 (1). Munich.
Harbison, P. 1969b *The daggers and halberds of the Early Bronze Age in Ireland.* Prähistorische Bronzefunde 6 (1). Munich.
Harbison, P. 1988 *Pre-Christian Ireland.* London.
Harbison, P. 1991 *Pilgrimage in Ireland: the monuments and the people.* London.
Harding, A.F. 1980 *The lake-dwellings of Switzerland; retrospect and prospect.* Department of Archaeology, University of Edinburgh, Occasional Paper 5. Edinburgh.
Harkness, R. 1863 On a crannoge found in Drumkeery Lough, near Bailieborough, Co. Cavan, Ireland. *Archaeologia* **39**, 483–90.
Hayes-McCoy, G.A. 1964 *Ulster and other Irish maps,* c. *1600.* Dublin.
Hencken, H. 1936 Ballinderry crannog no. 1. *Proceedings of the Royal Irish Academy* **43C**, 103–239.
Hencken, H. 1942 Ballinderry crannog no. 2. *Proceedings of the Royal Irish Academy* **47C**, 1–76.
Hencken, H. 1950 Lagore crannog: an Irish royal residence of the seventh to tenth century A.D. *Proceedings of the Royal Irish Academy* **53C**, 1–248.
Henderson, J.C. (forthcoming a) Islets through time: the definition, dating and distribution of Scottish crannogs. *Oxford Journal of Archaeology* **17** (2).
Henderson, J.C. (forthcoming b) A survey of crannogs in the Lake of Menteith, Stirlingshire, Scotland. *Proceedings of the Society of Antiquaries of Scotland* **127**.
Henderson, J.C. and Burgess, C. 1996 Close contour survey of submerged sites using datalogging software with particular reference to Scottish crannogs. *International Journal of Nautical Archaeology and Underwater Exploration* **25** (3–4), 250–6.
Henry, F. and Marsh-Micheli, G. 1993 Manuscripts and illuminations, 1169–1603. In A. Cosgrove (ed.), *A New History of Ireland II: Medieval Ireland 1169–1534,* 780–815. Oxford.
Herity, M. and Eogan, G. 1977 *Ireland in prehistory.* London.
Hillam, J. 1976 The dating of Cullyhanna hunting lodge. *Irish Archaeological Research Forum* **3** (1), 17–20.
Hirsch, E. (ed.) 1995 *The anthropology of landscape: perspectives on space and place.* Oxford.
Hodder, I. 1982 *The present past.* London.
Hodges, H.W.M. 1958 A hunting camp at Cullyhanna Lough near Newtown Hamilton, Co. Armagh. *Ulster Journal of Archaeology* **21**, 7–13.
Howland, J. 1997 Video mosaic. In J.P. Delgado (ed.), *Encyclopedia of underwater and maritime archaeology*, 458–9. London.
Hughes, W. 1886 The habitations of the ancient Irish. *The Irish Builder* **26**, 253–5.
Hurl, D. 1995 Killymoon—new light on the Late Bronze Age. *Archaeology Ireland* **34**, 24–7.
Ireland, A. (forthcoming) Colonel W.G. Wood-Martin: the antiquary—the man. In V. Buckley (ed.), *Irish crannogs: proceedings of the W.G. Wood-Martin conference.*
Ivens, R.J. 1988 Notes on medieval coarseware pottery in the Ulster Museum. *Ulster Journal of Archaeology* **51**, 127–31.
Ivens, R.J. and Simpson, D.D.A. (forthcoming) Island MacHugh, Co. Tyrone. In V. Buckley (ed.), *Irish crannogs: proceedings of the W.G. Wood-Martin conference.*
Ivens, R.J., Simpson, D.D.A. and Brown, D. 1986 Excavations at Island MacHugh 1985—interim report. *Ulster Journal of Archaeology* **49**, 99–103.
Johnson, R. 1997 An archaeological and art historical investigation into the supposed hiatus in Irish art during the tenth century AD: with particular reference to excavations carried out in Dublin city (1962–81) and Ballinderry crannog no. 1 (1936). Unpublished Ph.D. thesis, Trinity College Dublin.
Johnston, J.D. 1980 Settlement and architecture in County Fermanagh, 1610–1641. *Ulster Journal of Archaeology* **43**, 79–89.

Jope, E.M. 1953 Three Late Bronze Age swords from Ballycroghan, near Bangor, Co. Down. *Ulster Journal of Archaeology* **16**, 37–40.

Jope, E.M. 1966 *An archaeological survey of County Down*. Belfast.

Karkov, C. and Ruffing, J. 1990–1 The crannogs of Lough Ennell: a computer survey. *Ríocht na Mídhe* **8** (3), 105–13.

Karkov, C. and Ruffing, J. 1992–3 The settlement patterns of Lough Ennell: the 1992 survey. *Ríocht na Mídhe* **8** (4), 54–61.

Karkov, C. and Ruffing, J. 1997 The southern Uí Néill and the political landscape of Lough Ennell. *Peritia* **11**, 336–58.

Keane, M. 1995 Lough More, Co. Mayo: the crannog. *Irish Archaeological Wetland Unit Transactions* **4**, 167–82.

Keller, F. 1866 *The lake-dwellings of Switzerland and other parts of Europe*. London.

Keller, F. 1878 *The lake-dwellings of Switzerland and other parts of Europe* (2nd edn). London.

Kelly, D.H. 1850 On certain antiquities recently discovered in the lake of Cloonfree, Co. Roscommon. *Proceedings of the Royal Irish Academy* **5**, 208–14.

Kelly, E.P. 1974 Aughinish Island. *Excavations 1974*, 20–1.

Kelly, E.P. 1991a Observations on Irish lake-dwellings. In C. Karkov and R. Farrell (eds), *Studies in Insular art and archaeology*, 81–98. American Early Medieval Studies 1. Cornell.

Kelly, E.P. 1991b Crannogs. In M. Ryan (ed.), *The illustrated archaeology of Ireland*, 120–3. Dublin.

Kelly, E.P. 1993a Treasure-hunting in Ireland—its rise and fall. *Antiquity* **67**, 378–81.

Kelly, E.P. 1993b The Lough Kinale book-shrine. In R.M. Spearman and J. Higgitt (eds), *The age of migrating ideas: early medieval art in northern Britain and Ireland*, 168–74. Edinburgh.

Kelly, E.P. 1993c Investigation of ancient fords on the River Suck. *Inland Waterways* **20** (1), 4–5.

Kelly, E.P. 1994 Protecting Ireland's archaeological heritage. *International Journal of Cultural Property* **2** (3), 213–25.

Kelly, E.P. 1995 The role of the National Museum of Ireland in underwater archaeology. In F. Williams (ed.), *The future of underwater archaeology in Ireland*, 44–9. Limited circulation report. Belfast.

Kelly, F. 1988 *A guide to early Irish law*. Early Irish Law Series III. Dublin.

Kelly, F. 1997 *Early Irish farming*. Early Irish Law Series IV. Dublin.

Kenny, M. 1984 A find of Anglo-Saxon pennies from Newtownlow, Co. Westmeath. *Ríocht na Mídhe* **7** (3), 37–43.

Kenny, M. 1987 The geographical distribution of Irish Viking-Age coin hoards. *Proceedings of the Royal Irish Academy* **87C**, 507–25.

Kilbride, W. 1869 Etymology of 'crannog'. *The Irish Builder* **2**, 192–3.

Kinahan, G.H. 1861–4 On crannoges in Lough Rea. *Proceedings of the Royal Irish Academy* **8**, 412–27.

Kinahan, G.H. 1864–6 Notes on crannoges in Ballin Lough. *Proceedings of the Royal Irish Academy* **9**, 172–6.

Kinahan, G.H. 1866–9 Notes on a crannoge in Lough Naneevin. *Proceedings of the Royal Irish Academy* **10**, 31–3.

Kinahan, G.H. 1870–1 Proceedings: Observations on the exploration of crannogs—Iron tools and a canoe discovered at the crannog of Cornagall, Co. Cavan. *Journal of the Royal Society of Antiquaries of Ireland* **11**, 459–61.

Kinahan, G.H. 1886a On Loch Betha, Co. Donegal. *Proceedings of the Royal Irish Academy* **16**, 472–4.

Kinahan, G.H. 1886b Castlebar Lake, Co. Mayo. *Proceedings of the Royal Irish Academy* **16**, 474.

Kinahan, G.H. 1886c Columbkille Lake, Co. Donegal. *Proceedings of the Royal Irish Academy* **16**, 474.

Kinahan, G.H. 1897 Stone crannoge in Lough Bola. *Journal of the Royal Society of Antiquaries of Ireland* **27**, 438.

Knapp, A.B. 1997 *The archaeology of Late Bronze Age Cypriot society: the study of settlement, survey and landscape*. Glasgow.

Knowles, W.J. 1897 Portion of a harp and other objects found in the crannoge of Carncoagh, Co. Antrim. *Journal of the Royal Society of Antiquaries of Ireland* **27**, 114–15.

Knowles, W.J. 1903 Crannogs or artificial islands in the counties of Antrim and Derry. *Ulster Journal of Archaeology* **9**, 168–76.

Knowles, W.J. 1904 Crannogs or artificial islands in the counties of Antrim and Derry. *Ulster Journal of Archaeology* **10**, 26–32, 49–56.

Knowles, W.J. 1912 Prehistoric stone implements from the River Bann and Lough Neagh. *Proceedings of the Royal Irish Academy* **30**, 195–222.

Knox, H.T. 1902 Crannogs in Lough Carra, County Mayo. *Journal of the Royal Society of Antiquaries of Ireland* **32**, 407.

Knox, H.T. 1908 Carved stone found in a crannog. *Journal of the Royal Society of Antiquaries of Ireland* **38**, 280–1.

Lacy, B. 1983 *Archaeological Survey of County Donegal*. Lifford.

Lanting, J. and Brindley, A. 1996 Irish log-boats and their European context. *Journal of Irish Archaeology* **7**, 85–95.

Lavelle, D. 1992 The Lough Carra causeway, Ireland. *NewsWARP* **11**, 13–15.

Lavelle, D. 1994 *An archaeological survey of Ballinrobe and district including Lough Mask and Lough Carra*. Castlebar.

Lawless, C. 1992 Lough More, Bofeenaun, Co. Mayo: crannog, fulachta fiadh, deer traps and associated archaeological sites. *Cathair Na Mart* **12** (1), 13–31.

Lawless, C. 1993 Carrowmacloughin ancient settlement, Turlough, Co. Mayo, cashel, ringfort and hut sites. *Cathair Na Mart* **13**, 53–71.

Lawless, C., Ó Floinn, R., Baillie, M. and Brown, D. 1989 Levallinree crannog: an early seventh century lake-dwelling in Co. Mayo. *Cathair na Mart* **9** (1), 21–5.

Layard, E.L. 1897 Fortified stone lake-dwellings on islands in Lough Skannive, Connemara. *Journal of the Royal Society of Antiquaries of Ireland* **27**, 373–8.

Layard, E.L. 1899 On a fortified stone lake-dwelling on an island in Lough Cullen, County Mayo. *Journal of the Royal Society of Antiquaries of Ireland* **29**, 32–4.

Leask, H.G. 1941 *Irish castles and castellated houses* (1st edn). Dundalk.

Lett, H.W. 1905 The island in Lough Bricklan (Loughbrickland, County Down). *Journal of the Royal Society of Antiquaries of Ireland* **35**, 249–54.

Lewis, S.A. 1837 *A topographical dictionary of Ireland* (2 vols). London.

Limbert, D. 1996 Irish ringforts: a review of their origins. *Archaeological Journal* **153**, 243–89.

Liversage, G.D. 1958 An island site at Lough Gur. *Journal of the Royal Society of Antiquaries of Ireland* **88**, 67–8.

Liversage, G.D. 1968 Excavations at Dalkey Island, Co. Dublin, 1956–1959. *Proceedings of the Royal Irish Academy* **66C**, 53–233.

Lock, G. and Stancic, Z. 1995 *Archaeology and Geographical Information Systems: a European perspective*. London.

Lockwood, W.J. 1883–4 The examination of crannogs in Lough Mourn, near Carrickfergus. *Journal of the Royal Society of Antiquaries of Ireland* **16**, 194–5.

Loeber, R. 1991 *The geography and practice of English colonisation in Ireland from 1534 to 1609*. Athlone.

Lowry-Corry, D. 1933 The stones carved with human effigies on Boa Island and on Lustymore Island, in Lower Lough Erne. *Proceedings of the Royal Irish Academy* **41C**, 200–4.

Lowry-Corry, D. 1959 A newly discovered statue at the church on White Island, County Fermanagh. *Ulster Journal of Archaeology* **22**, 60–6.

Lucas, A.T. 1968 National Museum of Ireland: archaeological acquisitions in the year

1965. *Journal of the Royal Society of Antiquaries of Ireland* **98**, 93–154.

Lucas, A.T. 1989 *Cattle in ancient Ireland*. Kilkenny.

Lydon, J.F.M. 1987 A land of war. In A. Cosgrave (ed.), *A New History of Ireland II: Medieval Ireland 1169–1534*, 240–302. Oxford.

Lynch, A. 1981 *Man and environment in south-west Ireland, 4000 BC–AD 800*. British Archaeological Reports, British Series 85. Oxford.

Lynn, C.J. 1975 The medieval ringfort—an archaeological chimera? *Irish Archaeological Research Forum* **2**, 29–36.

Lynn, C.J. 1983 Some 'early' ring-forts and crannogs. *Journal of Irish Archaeology* **1**, 47–58.

Lynn, C.J. 1985–6 Lagore, County Meath, and Ballinderry No. I, County Westmeath, crannogs: some possible structural reinterpretations. *Journal of Irish Archaeology* **3**, 69–73.

Lynn, C.J. 1989 An interpretation of 'the Dorsey'. *Emania* **6**, 5–10.

Lynn, C.J. 1994 Houses in rural Ireland, A.D. 500–1000. *Ulster Journal of Archaeology* **57**, 81–94.

Lyttleton, J. 1997 Reassessment of the excavation of Loughpairc crannog, near Tuam, Co. Galway. Unpublished M.A. thesis, University College Dublin.

Lyttleton, J. 1998 Loughpark 'crannog' re-visited. *Journal of the Galway Archaeological and Historical Society* **50**, 151–83.

Macalister, R.A.S. 1928 *The archaeology of Ireland*. London.

Macalister, R.A.S. 1938 On an excavation conducted at Cro-Inis, Loch Ennell. *Proceedings of the Royal Irish Academy* **44C**, 248–51.

Macalister, R.A.S., Armstrong, E.C.R. and Praeger, R.L. 1914 The excavation of LochPairc crannog near Tuam. *Proceedings of the Royal Irish Academy* **32C**, 147–51.

McCormick, F. 1983 Dairying and beef production in Early Christian Ireland: the faunal evidence. In T. Reeves-Smyth and F. Hamond (eds), *Landscape archaeology in Ireland*, 253–67. British Archaeological Reports, British Series 116. Oxford.

McCormick, F. 1985–6 Interim report on the animal bones from Moynagh Lough. *Ríocht na Mídhe* **7** (4), 86–90.

McCormick, F. 1995 Cows, ringforts and the origins of Early Christian Ireland. *Emania* **13**, 33–7.

McCurtain, M. 1972 *Tudor and Stuart Ireland*. Dublin.

MacDermott, M. 1949 Lough Gur excavations. Two barrows at Ballingoola. *Journal of the Royal Society of Antiquaries of Ireland* **79**, 139–45.

M'Henry, A. 1886 Crannog of Lough na Cranagh, Fair Head, Co. Antrim. *Proceedings of the Royal Irish Academy* **16**, 462.

MacNamara, G.U. 1901 Inchiquin, County Clare. *Journal of the Royal Society of Antiquaries of Ireland* **31**, 341–64.

MacNeill, E. 1923 Ancient Irish law: the law of status or franchise. *Proceedings of the Royal Irish Academy* **36C**, 265–316.

McNeill, T. 1980 *Anglo-Norman Ulster*. Edinburgh.

McNeill, T. 1997 *Castles in Ireland: feudal power in a Gaelic world*. London and New York.

Mainberger, M., Mueller, A. and Schlichterle, H. 1995 Schiffswracks im Bodesee. In *Archäologische Ausgrabungen in Baden-Württemberg 1994*, 325–30. Stuttgart.

Mallory, J.P. 1995 Haughey's Fort and the Navan complex in the Late Bronze Age. In J. Waddell and E.S. Twohig (eds), *Ireland in the Bronze Age. Proceedings of the Dublin conference, April 1995*, 73–86. Dublin.

Mallory, J.P. and Hartwell, B.N. 1997 Down in prehistory. In L. Proudfoot and W. Nolan (eds), *Down: history and society*, 1–32. Dublin.

Mallory, J. and McNeill, T. 1991 *The archaeology of Ulster: from colonisation to plantation*. Belfast.

Malmer, M.P. 1991 Social space in Alvastra and other pile dwellings. In O. Grøn, E. Engelstad and I. Lindlom (eds), *Social space: human spatial behaviour in dwellings and settlements*, 118–22. Odense.

Manning, C. 1989–90 Clough Oughter castle, Cavan. *Breifne* **7**, 575–8.

Manning, C. 1995 *Early Irish monasteries*. Dublin.

Meyer, K. 1911 *Betha Colmáin maic Lúachain: Life of Colmán son of Lúachan*. Todd Lecture Series 17. Dublin.

Miklyaev, A.M. 1990 Underwater researches in Lake Sennica, USSR. *NewsWARP* **8**, 10–13.

Milligan, S.F. 1885 Crannogs or lake-dwellings in the County Cavan. *The Irish Builder* **27**, 229.

Milligan, S.F. 1885–6 On crannogs in County Cavan. *Journal of the Royal Society of Antiquaries of Ireland* **17**, 148–52.

Mitchell, G.F. 1955 The Mesolithic site at Toome Bay, Co. Londonderry. *Ulster Journal of Archaeology* **18**, 1–16.

Mitchell, G.F. 1970 Some chronological implications of the Irish Mesolithic. *Ulster Journal of Archaeology* **33**, 3–14.

Mitchell, G.F. 1972 Some ultimate Larnian sites at Lake Derravarragh, Co. Westmeath. *Journal of the Royal Society of Antiquaries of Ireland* **102**, 160–73.

Mitchell, G.F. 1987 *Reading the Irish landscape*. Dublin.

Mitchell, G.F. 1989 *Man and environment in Valencia Island*. Dublin.

Mitchell, G.F. 1990 *The way that I followed*. Dublin.

Mitchell, G.F. and Ó Ríordáin, S.P. 1942 Early Bronze Age pottery from Rockbarton Bog, Co. Limerick. *Proceedings of the Royal Irish Academy* **48C**, 23–272.

Mitchell, G.F. and Ryan, M. 1997 *Reading the Irish landscape*. Dublin.

Molloy, K. 1997 Prehistoric farming at Mooghaun—a new pollen diagram from Mooghaun Lough. *Archaeology Ireland* **11** (3), 22–6.

Molloy, K. and O'Connell, M. 1988 Neolithic agriculture—fresh evidence from Cleggan, Connemara. *Archaeology Ireland* **2** (2), 67–70.

Moloney, A., Jennings, D., Keane, M. and MacDermott, C. 1993 *Excavations at Clonfinlough, Co. Offaly*. Irish Archaeological Wetland Unit Transactions 2. Dublin.

Monk, M. 1993 People and environment. In search of the farmers. In E.S. Twohig and M. Ronayne (eds), *Past perceptions. The prehistoric archaeology of south-west Ireland*, 35–52. Cork.

Moody, T.W., Martin, F.X. and Byrne, F.J. (eds) 1976 *A New History of Ireland III: Early Modern Ireland*. Oxford.

Moore, M. 1987 *Archaeological Inventory of County Meath*. Dublin.

Morant, G. 1868–9 Remains of an ancient oak structure found beneath a peat bog at Cargaghoge near Carrickmacross. *Journal of the Royal Society of Antiquaries of Ireland* **10**, 269–70.

Mordant, C. and Mordant, D. 1992 Noyen-sur-Seine: a Mesolithic waterside settlement. In B.J. Coles (ed.), *The wetland revolution in prehistory*, 55–64. Exeter.

Morrison, I. 1981 The extension of the chronology of the crannogs of Scotland. *International Journal of Nautical Archaeology and Underwater Exploration* **10** (4), 344–6.

Morrison, I. 1985 *Landscape with lake-dwellings: the crannogs of Scotland*. Edinburgh.

Morrison, I. 1996 Evaluation of crannogs—a landscape approach based on Scottish experience. *IAPA Newsletter* **22**, 8–9.

Moryson, F. 1908 *An itinerary...* (rev. edn), vol. III. Glasgow. (First published in 1617.)

Mulvany, W.T. 1850–3 Collection of antiquities presented to the Royal Irish Academy. *Proceedings of the Royal Irish Academy* **5**, Appendix xxxi–xliii.

Munro, R. 1882 *Ancient Scottish lake-dwellings or crannogs*. Edinburgh.

Munro, R. 1894 The structural features of lake-dwellings. *Journal of the Royal Society of Antiquaries of Ireland* **24**, 105–14, 210–21.

Munro, R. 1885–6 Notes of lake-dwellings in Lough Mourn, Co. Antrim, Ireland. *Proceedings of the Society of Antiquaries of Scotland* **8**, 321–30.

Mytum, H.C. 1992 *The origins of Early Christian Ireland.* London.

Nayling, N. and Caseldine, A. 1997 *Excavations at Caldicot, Gwent: Bronze Age palaeochannels in the lower Nedern valley.* CBA Research Report 108. York.

Newman, C. 1986 The archaeology of Ballinderry Lough. Unpublished M.A. thesis, National University of Ireland.

Newman, C. 1995 Raffin Fort, Co. Meath: Neolithic and Bronze Age activity. In E. Grogan and C. Mount (eds), *Annus archaeologiae: proceedings of the OIA winter conference 1993*, 55–66. Dublin.

Newman, C. 1997 *Tara: an archaeological survey.* Discovery Programme Monograph 2. Dublin.

Newman, C. (forthcoming) Ballinderry crannog no. 2, Co. Offaly: the Later Bronze Age. In C. Newman and E. Grogan (eds), *Bronze Age settlement in Ireland.* Dublin.

Nicholls, K. 1972 *Gaelic and Gaelicised Ireland in the Middle Ages.* Dublin.

Nicholls, K. 1993 Gaelic society and economy. In A. Cosgrove (ed.), *A New History of Ireland II: Medieval Ireland 1169–1534*, 397–438. Oxford.

Niewiarowski, W., Noryskiewicz, B., Piotrowski, W. and Zajaczkowski, W. 1992 Biskupin fortified settlement and its environment in the light of new environmental and archaeological studies. In B.J. Coles (ed.), *The wetland revolution in prehistory,* 81–92. Exeter.

Norman, E.R. and St Joseph, J.K.S. 1969 *The early development of Irish society: the evidence of aerial photography.* Cambridge.

O'Brien, B. 1995 Ross Island and the origins of Irish-British metallurgy. In J. Waddell and E.S. Twohig (eds), *Ireland in the Bronze Age. Proceedings of the Dublin conference, April 1995*, 38–48. Dublin.

O'Brien, C. and Sweetman, P.D. 1997 *Archaeological Inventory of County Offaly.* Dublin.

O'Connell, M. 1980 Pollen analysis of fen peat from a Mesolithic site at Lough Boora, County Offaly, Ireland. *Journal of Life Sciences of the Royal Dublin Society* **2**, 45–9.

O'Connell, M. 1987 Early cereal-type pollen records from Connemara, western Ireland, and their possible significance. *Pollen et Spores* **29**, 207–24.

O'Connor, N. 1989 Underwater archaeology. *Archaeology Ireland* **3** (1), 26–9.

O'Conor, K. 1993 The earthwork castles of medieval Leinster. Unpublished Ph.D. thesis, University of Wales.

O'Conor, K. 1998 *Medieval rural settlement in Ireland.* Discovery Programme Monograph 3. Dublin.

O'Conor, K. (forthcoming) The moated site in Inishtirra Island, Drumharlow Lough, Co. Roscommon. *Discovery Programme Reports* **5**.

Ó Corráin, D. 1972 *Ireland before the Normans.* Dublin.

Ó Cróinín, D. 1995 *Early medieval Ireland, 400–1200.* Harlow.

O'Dowd, M. 1986 Gaelic economy and society. In C. Brady and R. Gillespie (eds), *Natives and newcomers: essays on the making of Irish colonial society 1534–1641*, 120–47. Dublin.

O'Donovan, P. 1995 *Archaeological Inventory of County Cavan.* Dublin.

Ó Floinn, R. 1988 Handmade medieval pottery in S.E. Ireland—'Leinster' cooking ware. In G. Mac Niocaill and P.F. Wallace (eds), *Keimelia: studies in medieval archaeology and history in honour of Tom Delaney,* 325–48. Galway.

Ó Floinn, R. 1995 Recent research into Irish bog bodies. In R.C. Turner and R.G. Scaife (eds), *Bog bodies: new discoveries and new perspectives,* 137–45. London.

Ó Floinn, R. (forthcoming) From Fictile ware to Everted-rim ware. A re-assessment of crannog ware and related pottery. In V. Buckley (ed.), *Irish crannogs: proceedings of the W.G. Wood-Martin conference.*

Ó hEailidhe, P. 1992 'The Monk's boat'—a Roman period relic from Lough Lene, Co. Westmeath, Eire. *International Journal of Nautical Archaeology and Underwater Exploration* **21** (3), 185–90.

Ó hÓgáin, D. 1991 *Myth, legend and romance: an encyclopedia of Irish folk tradition.* New York.

O'Keefe, T. 1987 Rathnageeragh and Ballyloo: a study of stone castles of probable fourteenth century date in County Carlow. *Journal of the Royal Society of Antiquaries of Ireland* **114**, 48–56.

O'Kelly, M.J. 1951 An Early Bronze Age ring-fort at Carrigillihy, Co. Cork. *Journal of the Cork Historical and Archaeological Society* **56**, 69–86.

O'Kelly, M.J. 1962 Two ringforts at Garryduff, Co. Cork. *Proceedings of the Royal Irish Academy* **45C**, 83–181.

O'Kelly, M.J. 1970 Problems of Irish ringforts. In D. Moore (ed.), *The Irish Sea province in archaeology and history,* 50–4. Cardiff.

O'Kelly, M.J. 1983 The excavation. In M.J. O'Kelly, R.M. Cleary and D. Lehane, *Newgrange, Co. Meath, Ireland: the Late Neolithic/Beaker period settlement,* 1–57. British Archaeological Reports, International Series 190. Oxford.

O'Kelly, M.J. 1989 *Early Ireland, an introduction.* Cambridge.

O'Meara, J. 1982 *Giraldus Cambrensis: The history and topography of Ireland.* Mountrath.

Ó Nualláin, S. 1972 A Neolithic house in Ballyglass near Ballycastle, Co. Mayo. *Journal of the Royal Society of Antiquaries of Ireland* **102**, 49–57.

Ó Ríordáin, B. and Waddell, J. 1993 *The funerary bowls and vases of the Irish Bronze Age.* Galway.

Ó Ríordáin, S.P. 1940 Excavations at Cush, Co. Limerick. *Proceedings of the Royal Irish Academy* **45C**, 83–181.

Ó Ríordáin, S.P. 1942a *Antiquities of the Irish countryside.* Cork.

Ó Ríordáin, S.P. 1942b The excavation of a large earthen ringfort at Garranes, Co. Cork. *Proceedings of the Royal Irish Academy* **47C**, 77–150.

Ó Ríordáin, S.P. 1948 Further barrows at Rathjordan, Co. Limerick. *Journal of the Cork Historical and Archaeological Society* **53**, 19–31.

Ó Ríordáin, S.P. 1949 Lough Gur excavations. Three marshland habitation sites. *Journal of the Royal Society of Antiquaries of Ireland* **79**, 126–39.

Ó Ríordáin, S.P. 1954 Lough Gur excavations: Neolithic and Bronze Age houses on Knockadoon. *Proceedings of the Royal Irish Academy* **56C**, 297–459.

Ó Ríordáin, S.P. and Lucas, A.T. 1946–7 Excavation of a small crannog at Rathjordan, Co. Limerick. *North Munster Antiquarian Journal* **5**, 68–77.

O'Sullivan, A. 1993–4 An Early Historic period fishweir on the upper Fergus Estuary, Co. Clare. *North Munster Antiquarian Journal* **35**, 52–61.

O'Sullivan, A. 1994a The use of trees and woodland in early medieval Ireland. *Botanical Journal of Scotland* **46** (4), 674–81.

O'Sullivan, A. 1994b Harvesting the waters. *Archaeology Ireland* **27**, 10–12.

O'Sullivan, A. 1995a Marshlanders. *Archaeology Ireland* **31**, 8–11.

O'Sullivan, A. 1995b Medieval fishweirs on the Deel estuary, Co. Limerick. *Archaeology Ireland* **32**, 15–17.

O'Sullivan, A. 1996a Later Bronze Age discoveries on north Munster estuaries. *Discovery Programme Reports* **4**, 63–72.

O'Sullivan, A. 1996b Exploring ancient woodlands. *Archaeology Ireland* **36**, 14–15.

O'Sullivan, A. 1996c Neolithic, Bronze Age and Iron Age woodworking techniques. In B. Raftery, *Trackway excavations in the Mount Dillon bogs, Co. Longford 1985–1991,* 291–342. Irish Archaeological Wetland Unit Transactions 3. Dublin.

O'Sullivan, A. 1997a Knocknalappa: Bronze Age lake settlements. In I. Bennett (ed.), *Excavations 1996*, 8. Bray.

O'Sullivan, A. 1997b Last foragers or first farmers? *Archaeology Ireland* **40**, 16–18.

O'Sullivan, A. 1997c Medieval fishtraps at Bunratty, Co. Clare. *The Other Clare* **21**, 40–2.

O'Sullivan, A. 1998 Woodmanship and the supply of timber and underwood to Anglo-Norman Dublin. In C. Manning (ed.), *Dublin and beyond the Pale: essays in honour of Patrick Healey*, 63–73. Dublin.

O'Sullivan, A. and Condit, T. 1995 Bronze Age settlement and agriculture by the marshlands of the upper Fergus estuary. *The Other Clare* **19**, 5–9.

O'Sullivan, A. and Sheehan, J. 1997 *The Iveragh peninsula. An archaeological survey of south Kerry.* Cork.

Parkinson, D. 1905 Some notes on the Clare crannogs of Drumcliff and Clareen. *Journal of the Royal Society of Antiquaries of Ireland* **35**, 391–401.

Patterson, N. 1994 *Cattle lords and clansmen: the social structure of early Ireland.* London.

Perini, R. 1984 *Scavi archeologici nella zona palafitticola di Fiavè-Carera. Part I. Campagne 1969–76. Situazione dei depositi e dei resti strutturali.* Servizio Beni Culturali della Provincia Autonoma di Trento.

Petrequin, P. 1989 *Les sites littoraux Néolithiques de Clairvaux-les-lacs (Jura). II. Le Néolithique moyen.* Paris.

Petrequin, P. 1997a *Les sites littoraux Néolithiques de Clairvaux-les-lacs et de Chalain (Jura). III. Chalain station 3, 3200–2900 av. J.-C. Volume 1.* Paris.

Petrequin, P. 1997b *Les sites littoraux Néolithiques de Clairvaux-les-lacs et de Chalain (Jura). III. Chalain station 3, 3200–2900 av. J.-C. Volume 2.* Paris.

Petrie, G. 1850–3 On crannoge islands. *Proceedings of the Royal Irish Academy* **16**, 214–15.

Piggott, S. 1953 Three metal-work hoards of the Roman period from southern Scotland. *Proceedings of the Society of Antiquaries of Scotland* **87**, 1–50.

Piotrowski, W. and Zajaczkowski, W. 1993 Protecting Biskupin by an artificial barrier. *NewsWARP* **14**, 7–11.

Pollack, A.J. and Waterman, D.M. 1964 A Bronze Age habitation site at Downpatrick. *Ulster Journal of Archaeology* **27**, 31–58.

Preece, R.C., Coxon, P. and Robinson, J.E. 1986 New biostratigraphic evidence of the post-glacial colonisation of Ireland and for Mesolithic forest disturbance. *Journal of Biogeography* **13**, 487–509.

Price, L. 1950 The history of Lagore, from the annals and other sources. In H. Hencken, 'Lagore crannog: an Irish royal residence of the seventh to tenth century A.D.', 18–35. *Proceedings of the Royal Irish Academy* **53C**, 1–248.

Proudfoot, V.B. 1961 The economy of the Irish rath. *Medieval Archaeology* **5**, 94–122.

Proudfoot, V.B. 1970 Irish raths and cashels: some notes on origin, chronology and survivals. *Ulster Journal of Archaeology* **33**, 37–48.

Pryor, F. 1991 *Flag Fen: prehistoric fenland centre.* London.

Raftery, B. 1972 Irish hill-forts. In C. Thomas (ed.), *The Iron Age in the Irish Sea province*, 37–58. London.

Raftery, B. 1976 Rathgall and Irish hillfort problems. In D.W. Harding (ed.), *Hillforts—later prehistoric earthworks in Britain and Ireland*, 339–57. London.

Raftery, B. 1983 *A catalogue of Irish Iron Age antiquities.* Veroffentlichung des Vorgeschichtlichen Seminars Marburg, Sonderbund 1. Marburg.

Raftery, B. 1984 *La Tène in Ireland: problems of origins and chronology.* Veroffentlichung des Vorgeschichtlichen Seminars Marburg, Sonderbund 2. Marburg.

Raftery, B. 1994 *Pagan Celtic Ireland.* London.

Raftery, B. 1996 *Trackway excavations in the Mount Dillon bogs, Co. Longford 1985–1991.* Irish Archaeological Wetland Unit Transactions 3. Dublin.

Raftery, J. 1942 Knocknalappa crannog, Co. Clare. *North Munster Antiquarian Journal* **3**, 53–72.

Raftery, J. 1957 Lake-dwellings in Ireland. *Scientific Service* **4** (3), 5–15.

Raftery, J. 1966 Drainage and the past. *Oibre* **4**, 11–13.

Raftery, J. 1972 National Museum of Ireland: archaeological acquisitions in the year 1969. *Journal of the Royal Society of Antiquaries of Ireland* **102**, 181–223.

Raftery, J. 1973 National Museum of Ireland: archaeological acquisitions in the year 1970. *Journal of the Royal Society of Antiquaries of Ireland* **103**, 17–213.

Raftery, J. 1981 Concerning chronology. In D. Ó Corráin (ed.), *Irish antiquity*, 173–204. Cork.

Raftery, J. 1988 A backward look. *Archaeology Ireland* **2** (1), 22–4.

Raftery, J. (forthcoming a) Lough Gara and the Irish 'crannog' question. In V. Buckley

(ed.), *Irish crannogs: proceedings of the W.G. Wood-Martin conference.*
Raftery, J. (forthcoming b) *Excavations at Crannog 61, Rathtinaun, Lough Gara, Co. Sligo.*
Rajewski, Z. 1980 *Biskupin: a fortified settlement dating from 500 BC.* Poznan.
Ralegh Radford, C.A. 1970 Devenish. *Ulster Journal of Archaeology* **33**, 55–62.
Redknap. M. 1991 Crossing the divide: investigating crannogs. In J.M. Coles and D.M. Goodburn (eds), *Wet site excavation and survey*, 16–22. WARP Occasional Paper 5. Exeter.
Redknap, M. and Lane, A. 1994 The early medieval crannog at Llangorse, Powys: an interim statement on the 1989–1993 seasons. *International Journal of Nautical Archaeology and Underwater Exploration* **23** (3), 189–205.
Reeves, W. 1857–61a On certain crannoges in Ulster. *Proceedings of the Royal Irish Academy* **7**, 153–9.
Reeves, W. 1857–61b An account of the crannoge of Inishrush, and its ancient occupants. *Proceedings of the Royal Irish Academy* **7**, 163–215.
Reeves-Smyth, T. 1995 *Irish castles.* Belfast.
Reilly, E. 1996 The insect fauna (Coleoptera) from the Neolithic trackways Corlea 9 and 10: the environmental implications. In B. Raftery, *Trackway excavations in the Mount Dillon bogs, Co. Longford 1985–1991*, 403–10. Irish Archaeological Wetland Unit Transactions 3. Dublin.
Reilly, G.E. 1902 The crannoges of Lough Mourn, Co. Antrim. *Ulster Journal of Archaeology* **8**, 1–4.
Richter, M. 1988 *Medieval Ireland: the enduring tradition.* Dublin.
Roberts, B.K. 1996 *Landscapes of settlement: prehistory to the present.* London and New York.
Robinson, M., Shimwell, D. and Cribbin, G. 1996 Boating in the Bronze Age—two logboats from Co. Mayo. *Archaeology Ireland* **10** (1), 12–13.
Robinson, T. 1997 Connemara, Co. Galway. In F.H.A. Aalen, K. Whelan and M. Stout (eds), *Atlas of the Irish rural landscape*, 329–44. Cork.
Rönnby, J. 1990 New research at Bulverket Lake building, Gotland, Sweden. *International Journal of Nautical Archaeology and Underwater Exploration* **19** (3), 233–7.
Rossignol, J. and Wandsnider, L. (eds) 1992 *Space, time and archaeological landscapes.* New York.
Ryan, M. 1973 Native pottery in Early Historic Ireland. *Proceedings of the Royal Irish Academy* **73C**, 619–45.
Ryan, M. 1978 Lough Boora excavations. *An Taisce Journal* **2**, 13–14.
Ryan, M. 1980 An early Mesolithic site in the Irish midlands. *Antiquity* **80**, 46–7.
Ryan, M. 1984 Archaeological excavations at Lough Boora, Broughal townland, Co. Offaly (1977). *Proceedings of the Seventh International Peat Congress, Dublin, 18–23 June 1984*, 407–13. Dublin.
Ryan, M. 1988 Fine metalworking and early monasteries: the archaeological evidence. In J. Bradley (ed.), *Settlement and society in medieval Ireland: studies presented to F.X. Martin, o.s.a.*, 32–48. Kilkenny.
Ryan, M. 1996 Archaeology. In K. McCone and K. Simms (eds), *Progress in medieval Irish studies*, 155–64. Maynooth.
Ryan, M. 1997 Irish ringforts: Matthew Stout. *History Ireland* **5** (4), 54–5.
Ryan, M., Ó Floinn, R., Lowick, N., Kenny, M. and Cazalet, P. 1984 Six silver finds of the Viking period from the vicinity of Lough Ennell, Co. Westmeath. *Peritia* **3**, 334–81.
Rynne, E. and Mac Eoin, G. 1978 The Craggaunowen crannog: gangway and gatetower. *North Munster Antiquarian Journal* **20**, 47–56.
Schadla-Hall, R.T. 1989 The Vale of Pickering in the Early Mesolithic in context. In C. Bonsall (ed.), *The Mesolithic in Europe*, 218–24. Edinburgh.
Schama, S. 1995 *Landscapes and memory.* London.
Schlichterle, H. (ed.) 1997 *Pfahlbauten rund um die Alpen.* Stuttgart.

Schou Jørgensen, M. 1991 Looking into the wetland—using a new ground-penetrating radar system. *NewsWARP* **10**, 2–5.

Scott, B.G. 1978 Iron 'slave-collars' from Lagore crannog, Co. Meath. *Proceedings of the Royal Irish Academy* **78C**, 213–30.

Scott, G. 1905–8 Some unrecorded finds of gold ornaments, from the counties of Limerick, Clare and Tipperary. *Journal of the Limerick Field Club* **3** (10), 27–37.

Scott, J.G. 1960 Loch Glashan. *Discovery and excavation in Scotland,* 8–9.

Selirand, J. 1988 Archaeological discoveries in Lake Valgjärv of Koorküla, Estonian S.S.R. *NewsWARP* **4**, 23–5.

Sheehan, J. 1989–90 A Viking-Age silver arm-ring from Portumna, Co. Galway. *Journal of the Galway Archaeological and Historical Society* **42**, 125–30.

Shirley, E.P.S. 1846 On crannogs, and remains discovered in them. *Archaeological Journal* **3**, 44–9.

Simms, A. 1983 Rural settlement in medieval Ireland: the example of the royal manors of Newcastle Lyons and Esker in south County Dublin. In B.K. Roberts and R.E. Glasscock (eds), *Villages, fields and frontiers,* 133–52. British Archaeological Reports, International Series 185. Oxford.

Simms, K. 1977 The medieval kingdom of Lough Erne. *Clogher Record* **9**, 139–40.

Simms, K. 1986 Nomadry in medieval Ireland. *Peritia* **5**, 379–91.

Simpson, D.D.A. 1986 A Late Bronze Age sword from Island MacHugh, Co. Tyrone. *Ulster Journal of Archaeology* **49**, 103–4.

Simpson, D.D.A. 1990 The stone battle axes of Ireland. *Journal of the Royal Society of Antiquaries of Ireland* **120**, 5–40.

Simpson, D.D.A. 1995 The Neolithic settlement site at Ballygalley, Co. Antrim. In E. Grogan and C. Mount (eds), *Annus archaeologiae: Proceedings of the OIA winter conference 1993,* 37–44. Dublin.

Smith, S.J., Wolfe-Murphy, S.A., Enlander, I. and Gibson, C.E. 1991 *The lakes of Northern Ireland: an annotated inventory*. Belfast.

Smyth, A.P. 1979 *Scandinavian York and Dublin, 2*. Dublin.

Smyth, J. 1953–6 Crannogs in north Monaghan. *Clogher Record* **1** (2), 1–7.

Somerville, O. 1993 Kite-shaped brooches. *Journal of the Royal Society of Antiquaries of Ireland* **123**, 59–101.

Stanley, T. 1868–9 Notice of the cranoge in Lough Annagh. *Journal of the Royal Society of Antiquaries of Ireland* (3rd ser.) **1**, 156–7.

Stickel, E.G. and Garrison, E.G. 1988 New applications of remote sensing: geophysical prospection for underwater archaeological sites in Switzerland. In B. Purdey (ed.), *Wet site archaeology,* 69–87. New Jersey.

Stout, G. and Stout, M. 1997 Early landscapes: from prehistory to plantation. In F.H.A. Aalen, K. Whelan and M. Stout (eds), *Atlas of the Irish rural landscape,* 31–63. Cork.

Stout, M. 1991 Ringforts in the south-west midlands of Ireland. *Proceedings of the Royal Irish Academy* **91C**, 201–43.

Stout, M. 1997 *The Irish ringfort.* Dublin.

Stuart, J. 1864–6 Notices of a group of artificial islands in the Loch of Dowalton, Wigtonshire, and of other artificial islands or 'crannogs' throughout Scotland. *Proceedings of the Society of Antiquaries of Scotland* **6**, 114–78.

Swan, L. 1988 The Early Christian ecclesiastical sites of County Westmeath. In J. Bradley (ed.), *Settlement and society in medieval Ireland: studies presented to F.X. Martin, o.s.a.,* 3–32. Kilkenny.

Sweetman, P.D. 1995 *Irish castles and fortified houses*. Dublin.

Synnott, P. 1996 Geographical Information Systems—an archaeological application. *Discovery Programme Reports* **4**, 73–84.

Talbot, J. 1849 Memoir on some ancient arms and implements found at Lagore, near Dunshaughlin, county of Meath; with a few remarks on the classification of northern antiquities. *Archaeological Journal* **6**, 101–9.

Therkorn, L.L., Brandt, R.W., Pals, J.P. and Taylor, M. 1984 An early Iron Age farmstead: Site Q of the Assendelver Polders project. *Proceedings of the Prehistoric Society* **50**, 351–73.

Thomas, J. 1991 *Rethinking the Neolithic*. Cambridge.

Thomas, J. 1993 The hermeneutics of megalithic space. In C. Tilley (ed.), *Interpretative archaeology*, 73–98. Oxford.

Tilley, C. 1994 *A phenomenonology of landscape: places, paths and monuments*. Oxford.

Trench, H.B. and Kinahan, G.H. 1864–6 Notes on a crannog in Lough Nahinch. *Proceedings of the Royal Irish Academy* **9**, 176–9.

Trigger, B. 1978 *Time and traditions: essays in archaeological interpretation*. New York.

Trigger, B. 1989 *A history of archaeological thought*. Cambridge.

Tuan, Y.F. 1977 *Space and place*. Minneapolis.

Ussher, R.J. 1903 The crannog at Ardmore, County Waterford. *Journal of the Royal Society of Antiquaries of Ireland* **33**, 387–8.

Ussher, R.J. and Kinahan, G.H. 1879 On a submarine crannog discovered by R.J. Ussher at Ardmore, Co. Waterford. *Proceedings of the Royal Irish Academy* **16**, 61–5.

Van Wijngaarden-Bakker, L.H. 1989 Faunal remains and the Irish Mesolithic. In C. Bonsall (ed.), *The Mesolithic in Europe: papers presented at the third international symposium*, 125–33. Edinburgh.

Waddell, J. 1983 Rathcroghan—a royal site in Connacht. *Journal of Irish Archaeology* **1**, 21–46.

Waddell, J. 1990 *The Bronze Age burials of Ireland*. Galway.

Waddell, J. 1995 Celts, Celticisation and the Irish Bronze Age. In J. Waddell and E.S. Shee-Twohig (eds), *Ireland in the Bronze Age. Proceedings of the Dublin conference, April 1995*, 158–9. Dublin.

Wailes, B. 1990 Dun Ailinne: a summary excavation report. *Emania* **7**, 10–21.

Wakeman, W.F. 1861 The lake homes of the Irish. *Duffy's Hibernian Magazine* **13**, 10–15.

Wakeman, W.F. 1870 Crannogs in Drumgay Lake, near Enniskillen. *The Irish Builder* **12**, 250.

Wakeman, W.F. 1870–1a Remarks upon three hitherto unnoticed crannogs in Drumgay Lake, near Enniskillen. *Journal of the Royal Society of Antiquaries of Ireland* **11**, 232–5.

Wakeman, W.F. 1870–1b On the crannog at Ballydoolough, Co. Fermanagh. *Journal of the Royal Society of Antiquaries of Ireland* **11**, 360–71.

Wakeman, W.F. 1870–1c On some iron tools discovered in the crannog of Cornagall, Co. Cavan. *Journal of the Royal Society of Antiquaries of Ireland* **11**, 461–5.

Wakeman, W.F. 1870–1d The crannogs in Lough Eyes, Co. Fermanagh. *Journal of the Royal Society of Antiquaries of Ireland* **11**, 553–64.

Wakeman, W.F. 1872 Observations on the principal crannogs of Fermanagh. *Journal of the Royal Society of Antiquaries of Ireland* (4th ser.) **2**, 216.

Wakeman, W.F. 1879 White Island, Lough Erne. *Journal of the Royal Society of Antiquaries of Ireland* **15**, 66–9.

Wakeman, W.F. 1879–82a Proceedings; Bronze pin and a carved wooden vessel, Co. Fermanagh. *Journal of the Royal Society of Antiquaries of Ireland* **15**, 97–9.

Wakeman, W.F. 1879–82b On certain recent discoveries of ancient crannog structures, chiefly in the County of Fermanagh. *Journal of the Royal Society of Antiquaries of Ireland* **15**, 324–39.

Wakeman, W.F. 1883–4 Trouvaille of the Bronze and Iron Age finds from the crannog at Lisnacroghera, Co. Antrim. *Journal of the Royal Society of Antiquaries of Ireland* **16**, 375–408.

Wakeman, W.F. 1885–6 The crannogs of Drumdarragh, otherwise Trillick, and Lankhill, Co. Fermanagh. *Journal of the Royal Society of Antiquaries of Ireland* **17**, 372–89.

Wakeman, W.F. 1889 On the crannog and antiquities of Lisnacroghera, near

Broughshane, Co. Antrim. *Journal of the Royal Society of Antiquaries of Ireland* **19**, 96–106.

Wakeman, W.F. 1890–1 On the crannog and antiquities of Lisnacroghera, near Broughshane, Co. Antrim. *Journal of the Royal Society of Antiquaries of Ireland* **21**, 673–5.

Walsh, A. 1987 Excavating the Black Pig's Dyke. *Emania* **3**, 5–11.

Walsh, G. 1995 Iron Age settlement in Mayo. *Archaeology Ireland* **32**, 7–8.

Warner, R.B. 1983 Ireland, Ulster and Scotland in the earlier Iron Age. In A. O'Connor and D. Clark (eds), *From the Stone Age to the 'Forty-five*, 161–87. Edinburgh.

Warner, R.B. 1985–6 The date of the start of Lagore. *Journal of Irish Archaeology* **3**, 75–7.

Warner, R.B. 1988 The archaeology of Early Historic Irish kingship. In S.T. Driscoll and M.R. Nieke (eds), *Power and politics in early medieval Britain and Ireland*, 47–68. Edinburgh.

Warner, R.B. 1993 Tree-rings, catastrophes and culture in early Ireland: some comments. *Emania* **11**, 13–19.

Warner, R.B. 1994 On crannogs and kings (part 1). *Ulster Journal of Archaeology* **57**, 61–9.

Waterman, D. 1971 A marshland habitation site near Larne, Co. Antrim. *Ulster Journal of Archaeology* **34**, 65–76.

Waterman, D.M. 1979 St Mary's Priory, Devenish: excavations of the east range, 1972–74. *Ulster Journal of Archaeology* **42**, 34–50.

Waterman, D.M. 1997 *Excavations at Navan Fort 1961–71*. Northern Ireland Archaeological Monographs No. 3. Belfast.

Wazny, T. 1993 Dendrochronological dating of the Lusatian culture settlement at Biskupin, Poland—first results. *NewsWARP* **14**, 3–5.

Weir, D. 1993 A palynological study in County Louth. Interim report. *Discovery Programme Reports* **1**, 104–9.

Weir, D. 1995 A palynological study of landscape and agricultural development in County Louth from the second millennium BC to the first millennium AD. *Discovery Programme Reports* **2**, 77–126.

Westropp, T.J. 1895 A find at Coolnasluasty Lough, Co. Clare. *Journal of the Royal Society of Antiquaries of Ireland* **25**, 179.

Westropp, T.J. 1901 Crannoge at Mountcashel, County Clare. *Journal of the Royal Society of Antiquaries of Ireland* **31**, 433–4.

Whittle, A. 1996 *Europe in the Neolithic: the creation of new worlds*. Cambridge.

Wilde, W.R. 1840 Antiquities recently discovered at Dunshaughlin. *Proceedings of the Royal Irish Academy* **1**, 420–6.

Wilde, W.R. 1857 *A descriptive catalogue of the antiquities of stone, earthen and vegetable materials in the museum of the Royal Irish Academy*. Dublin.

Wilde, W.R. 1857–61 Account of three crannoges. *Proceedings of the Royal Irish Academy* **7**, 147–53.

Wilde, W.R. 1861–4 On a crannoge in the county of Cavan. *Proceedings of the Royal Irish Academy* **8**, 274–8.

Williams, B.B. 1978 Excavations at Lough Eskragh, Co. Tyrone. *Ulster Journal of Archaeology* **41**, 37–48.

Williams, B.B. 1984 Excavations at Ballyutoag, Co. Antrim. *Ulster Journal of Archaeology* **47**, 37–49.

Williams, B.B. 1988 Archaeology almost under water: Lough Eskragh, Co. Tyrone. In A. Hamlin and C. Lynn (eds), *Pieces of the past*, 17–19. Belfast.

Williams, J. 1971 A crannog at Loch Arthur, New Abbey. *Transactions of the Galloway Natural History and Antiquarian Society* **48**, 121–4.

Woodman, P.C. 1977 Recent excavations at Newferry, Co. Antrim. *Proceedings of the Prehistoric Society* **43**, 155–200.

Woodman, P.C. 1978 *The Mesolithic in Ireland: hunter-gatherers in an insular environment*. British Archaeological Reports, International Series 58. Oxford.

Woodman, P.C. 1985 *Excavations at Mount Sandel 1973–77*. Northern Ireland Archaeological Monographs No. 2. Belfast.

Woodman, P.C. 1986 Problems in the colonisation of Ireland. *Ulster Journal of Archaeology* **49**, 7–17.

Woodman, P.C. and Anderson, E. 1990 The Irish Later Mesolithic: a partial picture. In P.M. Vermeersch and P. Van Peer (eds), *Contributions to the Mesolithic in Europe*, 377–87. Leuven.

Woodman, P.C. and Johnson, G. 1991–2 A petrological examination of some Mesolithic stone artefacts. *Ulster Journal of Archaeology* **54–5**, 134–7.

Woodman, P.C. and Johnson, G. 1996 Excavations at Bay Farm 1, Carnlough, Co. Antrim, and the study of the Larnian technology. *Proceedings of the Royal Irish Academy* **96C**, 137–235.

Woodman, P.C. and O'Brien, M. 1993 Excavations at Ferriter's Cove. In E.S. Twohig and M. Ronayne (eds), *Past perceptions. The prehistoric archaeology of south-west Ireland*, 25–34. Cork.

Wood-Martin, W.G. 1886a *The lake-dwellings of Ireland or ancient lacustrine habitations of Erin commonly called crannogs*. Dublin.

Wood-Martin, W.G. 1886b Description of a crannog site in the County Meath. *Proceedings of the Royal Irish Academy* **16**, 480–4.

Wood-Martin, W.G. 1902 *Traces of the elder faiths of Ireland*. London.

Youngs, S.M. (ed.) 1989 *'The Work of Angels'. Masterpieces of Celtic metalwork, 6th–9th centuries AD*. London.

Zvelebil, M., Macklin, M.G., Passmore, D.G. and Ramsden, P. 1996 Alluvial archaeology in the Barrow valley, southeast Ireland: the Riverford Culture revisited. *Journal of Irish Archaeology* **7**, 13–40.

Appendix I.
Discovery Programme project proposals

Introduction

Lake settlement archaeology in Ireland is a potentially rich and rewarding field of enquiry, one that will undoubtedly repay investment by the Discovery Programme. This study has identified many subjects and topics that urgently require investigation. It has been argued that archaeological research should focus on two primary questions.

(1) What are the patterns of long-term change and continuity in lake settlement and environment across time?
(2) What were the diverse roles of lake settlements in their wider social and economic landscapes?

If these questions are to be answered, then any future lake settlement project should adopt a multiperiod, landscape archaeological approach, integrating a diverse range of prehistoric and medieval archaeological, historical and palaeoenvironmental data. The project should aim to investigate settlement and environment in lakelands since earliest times, from the Mesolithic to the post-medieval period (7000 BC–AD 1650), exploiting the rich archaeological resource of lake settlement to inform our understanding of the settlement of the early Irish landscape.

It is clear that there is a rich and unexplored archaeological and historical resource in the hunting camps and structures of Mesolithic forager-fishers and the various habitations and defended enclosures of Neolithic and Bronze Age farmers. There is intriguing evidence for Iron Age ritual deposition sites against an apparent hiatus in actual lake settlement. In particular, there is abundant archaeological evidence for complex Early Historic social and settlement landscapes on lakes, including crannogs, ringforts, promontory forts and monastic islands, all of which should be examined together. This review has also shown that there is a range of hitherto overlooked medieval evidence for the construction and occupation of lake settlements by the Gaelic Irish and the Anglo-Normans, and that there is firm historical, archaeological and cartographic evidence for post-medieval occupation and military activities on lake settlements.

It could be argued that this vast time-span is too much for us to grasp, that there are too many questions to be answered by research. It might also be argued that it would be better just to concentrate on one period or type of site. However, to cast away the long-term approach and to retreat to the narrow focus on a cultural period or site type would actually be to lose the vital element of this rich archaeological record, which is to explore the way people interacted with each other and the natural environment and how this changes across time in Ireland. The solution to the practical and logistical problems of studying settlement over such a large time-span is to focus on the regional and local scale—to study a particular place across time and to thereby inform and interrogate the wider archaeological evidence for lake settlement in Ireland.

In this section, a number of proposals are made as to how the Discovery Programme should proceed in the investigation of lake settlement in Ireland. It should be remembered that the Discovery Programme has established itself as a major European archaeological research institute, admired by many archaeologists at home and abroad for its vision, ambition and capabilities. Perhaps it is one of the few archaeological institutions that is capable of the long-term, multidisciplinary 'pure' research programme that is required in the study of lake settlement archaeology. A range of long-term, medium-term and short-term projects, varying in objectives, scale, funding and staff resources, are proposed here. The common thread in these proposals is that a multi-period, landscape archaeological view should be applied to lake settlement archaeology, exploring long-term change and continuity in settlement, society and environment.

Long-term project

Lake settlement archaeology in Ireland

The Discovery Programme could aim through a long-term project to provide a substantive and ambitious investigation of the subject of lake settlement archaeology in Ireland. A long-term project could firstly integrate the existing data on site and monument distributions and artefact collections to establish the baseline archive. This archive could be opened to other researchers and institutions, encouraging the development of additional research topics. The project could then pursue a long-term research programme on lake settlement archaeology in Ireland, to be carried out on an island-wide basis, concentrating on a series of themes, with regional study areas to provide wider settlement and social contexts.

Geophysical and underwater diving surveys could be carried out to extend the known distribution, character and dating of lake settlements. The Discovery Programme could also establish a long-term dendrochronological and radiocarbon-dating programme to transform our knowledge of the chronology of these sites. It could then aim, through targeted archaeological survey and landscape studies in three chosen lakeland regions, to pose particular questions about this archaeological resource. The lakeland regions would be carefully chosen after an initial period of cartographic, archival and artefactual study. They should be diverse in topography and size to provide comparisons and insights into different landscapes. They could include regional studies of the midland lakes (e.g. the Lough Derravarragh–Lough Ennell region), the northern drumlin belt (Cavan–Fermanagh lakelands), the great western lakes (e.g. Lough Conn) or the Connemara lakelands. The study areas could also include areas of dryland and upland, to provide a broad landscape context. The aim would be to compare and contrast prehistoric and medieval settlement of the Irish midlands, west and north-west.

An important aspect of the Discovery Programme's study of lake settlement in Ireland would be an increased level of cooperation and integration with the Environment and Heritage Service, Northern Ireland, and the National Monuments Section, Heritage Service, as well as with the National Museum of Ireland and the Ulster Museum. It is worth pointing out that it is likely that the Heritage Service will in the next few years begin work on an SMR of lake archaeology. It is also possible that this task will be contracted out to an archaeological company or university department. The Discovery Programme could obtain such a contract and funding. It could also work in partnership with other European archaeological institutions and archaeological groups to widen interest in Irish lake settlement archaeology, often recognised abroad as a major aspect of Ireland's archaeological heritage.

In terms of contributing to a programme of management and conservation of lake settlement archaeology, the Discovery Programme could help in identifying the threats to and condition of a representative sample of Irish crannogs and lake settlements, assessing the impacts of drainage, desiccation, pollution and treasure-hunting on previously identified archaeological sites. The Discovery Programme could establish itself as a European centre of excellence for underwater archaeology. It could cooperate with various university departments (e.g. archaeology, geography, history and botany) to establish scholarships, promote Ph.D. researchers in many aspects of lake settlement, and enhance its funding base by EU funding applications and cooperation with other institutions.

In terms of staff and financial resources, a long-term project would require a full-time team consisting of a director, archaeologists and a palaeoenvironmentalist, supported by short-term or seasonally employed archaeological assistants, divers and specialists. It should run for a minimum period of ten to fifteen years' fieldwork, with ongoing publication and post-excavation programmes. The annual budget for such a project should not be less than £200,000. If the Discovery Programme was to operate this project, in conjunction with other institutions and EU environmental programmes, it is possible to see how financial resources could be extended. In many ways this type of project, while greatly needed in Irish archaeology, is not typical of the research agendas hitherto pursued by the Discovery Programme. However, it is important to remember that a long-term project is a real option, which would probably be highly successful and should certainly be considered.

Medium-term project

A regional landscape study

Introduction

The Discovery Programme could establish a medium-term lake settlement research project to explore the patterns in long-term prehistoric and historic settlement and environmental change in a particular lake region. The chosen region should be topographically varied, with lakes featuring as an important element of the landscape. Ideally, there should also be areas of former lake (i.e. bog or marsh) which would provide insights into environmental change. A medium-term research project could usefully be carried out in such lakelands with rich archaeological and palaeoenvironmental potential as the midland lakes of the River Inny and River Brosna drainage (Lough Sheelin, Lough Derravarragh, Lough Ennell), the extensive drumlin lakelands centring on Lough Oughter or Upper Lough Erne, the lakes of north Roscommon or Lough Gara, or perhaps a single large lake (e.g. Lough Ree, Lough Conn).

Research design

The region should be selected for the quality of its archaeological potential from the Mesolithic, Neolithic, Bronze Age, Iron Age, Early Historic and post-medieval periods. It should not be chosen until after a research design period, involving rapid archival and museum research and exploratory fieldwork in three or four regions. The research design phase could be carried out over a six-month period, with one or two archaeological assistants, and would aim to produce a desk-top study and preliminary archive of the 'candidate regions'. The final choice of the project study region would thereafter be influenced by the potential of each region, modified by the restrictions posed by a relatively limited budget and time-frame. It is obvious that some regions would be richer in some types of archaeological information than others, indicating the usefulness of examining different regions for different topics. The solution to this problem is to establish a medium-term regional lake settlement project concentrating on a core area but also carrying out annual targeted short-term investigations in other small study areas or themes (see below).

Archaeological and historical research

The selected lakeland region could then be subjected to the first phase of intensive archaeological and historical research, which could be carried out in the first year of the project, concentrating on amassing all available archaeological, historical and environmental knowledge of the region. This could include extensive bibliographical research, mapping of site and monument distributions, a preliminary catalogue of artefacts, a compilation of the results of previous palaeoenvironmental studies, a complete cartographic library, and an archive of all available aerial and site photographs. There would also be a rapid review of the historical sources, with the production of a report. The project would also aim to quickly acquire computerised digital information on satellite imagery, geology, soils and topography from various sources for ultimate use in the Discovery Programme's GIS. This initial phase would also incorporate archaeological fieldwork in the form of exploratory site visits and boat-based lake surveys to acquire a 'feel' for the region. This would establish the vital baseline of knowledge, with the preliminary mapping of known archaeological evidence. The aim of this initial research phase would be to build a comprehensive archive of the information that the project would work from in the following years.

Archaeological survey

The second phase could be one of large-scale fieldwork, including both intensive and extensive archaeological survey linked to a dendrochronological and radiocarbon sampling and dating programme. This could be carried out primarily in the second year. It may be necessary to break the region down into a series of 'localities', comprising topographical or cultural study areas, which would be the focus for the most intensive research. The archaeological survey phase could include aerial photography, the instrument survey of selected lake and dryland sites, underwater prospection and survey, fieldwalking and lake foreshore survey in sample areas. Underwater archaeological investigations would be a major part of the programme, with necessary funding for equipment and dive facilities. A geophysical survey, using mostly side-scan sonar followed up by intensive sub-bottom profiling on identified anomalies, would also be aimed at particular sites or locations, to identify sites and structures and to provide bathymetric maps of the lakebed.

An integrated programme of palaeoenvironmental research, driven by archaeological questions, could include sampling for pollen, micro-organisms (diatoms), macrofossils, molluscs, dendrochronology and wood studies, with palaeostratigraphical transect coring investigations at several (rather than one) key locations. This programme would aim to model past landscapes and calibrate environmental change in local and regional terms. The palaeoenvironmental programme would be coordinated by a specialist (preferably an individual with both archaeological and palaeoenvironmental experience) inside the project. Both the archaeological and the palaeoenvironmental data could be used within the Discovery Programme's Geographical Information System (GIS) to enable the reconstruction of past lake levels and surrounding landscape, to study the siting of lake settlements, and to carry out various forms of spatial analysis (e.g. site catchment analysis, nearest-neighbour analysis, site clustering and dispersal).

Archaeological excavation

The third phase of the project would include archaeological excavation, aimed at answering specific questions formulated during the research and survey phases. While testing and dendrochronological sampling would already be up and running, it is envisaged that excavations would mostly be carried out in the third, fourth and fifth years of the project. The Discovery Programme could potentially carry out detailed chronological and palaeoenvironmental studies, small-scale and large-scale excavations of Mesolithic occupations, Bronze

Age lake settlements, Early Historic crannogs and medieval lake settlements. It is important to emphasise that 'archaeological excavation' as a term can cover a range of options, not all involving large-scale investment of time and resources. These excavations could include a range of investigative techniques, from test-trenching of flint scatters using a sampling grid to open-area excavations of wetland occupation horizons. The excavations should aim to adopt the full battery of multidisciplinary techniques employed on modern wetland excavations, so as to extract the full range of social and economic evidence. A vital aspect of the project would be an emphasis on the themes of settlement continuities, occupation history, landscape exploitation, environmental change and social organisation.

Post-excavation and publication

The final phase of the project would be post-excavation studies and publication. Such research often throws up new themes and areas of enquiry and should therefore not be seen as an end but as a vitally important area of research in its own right. It may be possible in this phase to return to sites to obtain further samples for dating or other studies, or to review ideas that emerge in the post-excavation work (e.g. the organisation of the agricultural landscape, evidence for dire environmental conditions, emerging hints of Iron Age settlement). It should be accepted that archaeological research is potentially open-ended and an open mind must be kept as regards the impact of discoveries on any research design. For example, if the lake settlement project were to discover an intact Iron Age lake settlement complex, then the Discovery Programme might consider a substantial wetland excavation.

In terms of staff and financial resources, a medium-term project would have a team of director, two archaeologists and one palaeoenvironmentalist, supported by short-term or seasonally employed archaeological assistants, divers and specialists. It should run for a minimum period of five years' research, survey and excavation, followed by a two-year post-excavation programme and a concluding year for final publication. The annual budget for such a project should not be less than £180,000, rising to over £240,000 for a period during excavation and post-excavation research, The project would aim to run a single thematic study each year to widen its enquiries and to inform the main project (see short-term studies below). The project would be supported by the Discovery Programme's surveyors and GIS staff. The Discovery Programme would also appoint a research fellow to carry out historical research on Early Historic and medieval lake settlement in the region.

Short-term projects

Thematic and 'cameo' studies

Introduction

Lake settlement archaeology is a broad subject, with interesting questions and issues that can hardly be contained within a single region. The Discovery Programme should aim to run a number of small-scale thematic studies, each one year in length, designed to answer focused questions on particular problems. It should be emphasised that this author's review of lake settlement archaeology in Ireland has confirmed that such single-site or single-period studies are limited in scope and potential, but against the background of the larger projects described above they would make a useful contribution to Irish archaeology.

These studies should operate within, rather than outside, the long-term or medium-term projects described above. The project director and staff would have the required experience (and would be acquiring more) of carrying out such lake settlement research. Depending on the topic, an individual project staff member could be designated as 'thematic study supervisor' or some other term which would recognise their responsibility. On other occasions it may be necessary to employ an artefact specialist, archaeologist or historian on contract for various tasks. The main aim of each thematic study would be a significant academic paper or short monograph.

The short-term studies would operate much like the Shannon estuary survey successfully operated within the broader North Munster Project, contributing to the aims of that project as well as feeding off the experience and resources of the larger study. An independent, short-term project with its own agenda and time-frame is unlikely to contribute as much or to be as integrated with ongoing research, and would lead to a replication of staff and equipment and extra costs. The short-term studies would be funded to a level of about £25,000. The costs would be substantially less if existing medium-term project staff carried out the research. The short-term studies could investigate one or two of the following each year.

Mesolithic and Neolithic flint and chert scatters on lakeshores

A short-term thematic study could include the investigation of the wider cultural and technological contexts of the Mesolithic lakeshore lithic scatters at Lough Kinale, Lough Iron, Lough Derravarragh and Lough Gara. This would be primarily accomplished by the detailed functional analysis of the lithic assemblages by an experienced specialist. The study might also investigate whether there is any evidence for Neolithic activity on these sites.

Bronze Age landscapes and lake settlements

A short-term thematic study could aim to investigate the wider social and settlement landscapes of an individual Bronze Age lake settlement (e.g. Ballinderry, Clonfinlough) or other Bronze Age lake structure (e.g. the Lough Carra post alignment). This would be accomplished by archival, artefact and monuments research, supported by targeted fieldwork. The aim would be to reassess a well-known site in terms of its wider settlement landscape. It would also provide additional insights for the main regional study.

Iron Age artefact findspots in lakes

There is little or no evidence for Iron Age lake settlement in Ireland. The few finds from lakeshores and islands could be investigated through archival research and the locations subjected to rapid underwater surveys. The benefits of locating an Iron Age wetland settlement in Ireland would be worth the relatively limited work required. The Discovery Programme might also consider cooperating with the Environment and Heritage Service and leading a geophysical survey and prospection of Lisnacrogher.

Iron Age stone-built crannogs and promontory forts of the west?

A short-term thematic study could be carried out on a number of the crannogs and lake promontory forts of the west. It is possible that these sites date to the Late Bronze Age or Iron Age. The identification of an Iron Age lake settlement fortification would in itself be a major contribution to Irish archaeology. Underwater survey, dendrochronological and radiocarbon dating could be carried out over a few weeks on a number of these sites to test this possibility.

The Vikings on Lough Ree

A short-term thematic study could re-examine the historical and archaeological evidence for Viking naval fleets and longphorts on Lough Ree (or Lough Erne, Lough Derg or Lough Neagh). This would be a multidisciplinary study, requiring detailed historical research, some archaeological fieldwork and artefact research on the Viking Age metalwork findspots. Short-term underwater diving and geophysical surveys would be carried out at optimal locations. The fieldwork would be carried out over one or two months. The identification of a potential Viking longphort or settlement or other nautical evidence would in itself be a major contribution to Irish archaeology.

Early Historic and Viking Age lake settlement complex

A short-term thematic study could aim to investigate the wider social and settlement landscapes of a particular complex of Early Historic and Viking Age crannogs, ringforts and monastic islands. This landscape could be centred on a well-known site or lake settlement complex, such as Ardakillen, Lagore or Ballinderry. This study would involve archival, artefact and monument research, supported by limited fieldwork. Artefactual research could concentrate on studying and publishing an assemblage of finds from an unpublished antiquarian excavation of an Early Historic crannog. The aim would be to reassess a well-known site in terms of its wider settlement landscape. It would also provide additional insights for the main regional study.

Medieval lake settlements, culture and society

A short-term thematic study could be carried out on artefacts of medieval date from Irish crannogs or other island settlements. This study would be primarily artefactual, the aim being to identify, compare and contrast Gaelic Irish and Anglo-Norman pottery, weaponry, glass, coins or dress accessories in excavated assemblages. The study would be integrated with historical research and possibly with a limited programme of dendrochronological dating to open up the question of medieval activity on crannogs and lake settlements. The work could be carried out in conjunction with the Medieval Rural Settlement project, sharing costs and results.

Post-medieval occupation and attacks on crannogs

A short-term thematic study could explore and publish further historical evidence for post-medieval (in particular sixteenth- and seventeenth-century) activities on crannogs. This would include a review of various contemporary accounts and could also consider post-medieval finds from crannogs. Fieldwork and site visits might be warranted in south Ulster and the north midlands to examine the scene of such events and to explore the relationship between the crannogs and any other evidence for post-medieval settlement.

Final recommendations

It is clear that lake settlement archaeology is an exciting field. There are many options for future research; this study has identified the topics that most require investigation. Which project should be chosen? It is recommended that the Discovery Programme should opt for a medium-term landscape research project to be established in a carefully chosen study area. It is felt that the Discovery Programme is primarily skilled at such regional studies, where its resources can be focused on obtaining best results in the shortest time. This project should run as described above.

The project should have a team of director, archaeologists, a historian and a palaeoenvironmentalist. It should run for at least five years of research, survey and excavation, and for a subsequent three years of post-excavation and publication. Archaeologists, divers and specialists should be employed as necessary at crucial stages of the investigations. The project should be funded at an annual budget of between £180,000 and £240,000, depending on the stage of research, and would also have the brief to carry out one or two short-term studies every year in other regions, each designed to widen our knowledge of particular topics. If the Discovery Programme's funding is enhanced and the ongoing project is successful, then the Discovery Programme may opt to extend its research to a number of regions, such as those examined but not adopted during the research design phase.